ENTREPRENEURSHIP

ENTREPRENEURSHIP

Fourth Edition

PEGGY A. LAMBING
University of Missouri–St. Louis

CHARLES R. KUEHL
University of Missouri–St. Louis

PEARSON
Prentice
Hall

Upper Saddle River, New Jersey 07458

Library of Congress Cataloging-in-Publication Data
Lambing, Peggy A.
    Entrepreneurship/Peggy A. Lambing, Charles R. Kuehl.-4th ed.
      p. cm.
    Includes bibliographical references and index.
    ISBN 0-13-228174-0
    1. Entrepreneurship.   2. Entrepreneurship—United States.   I. Kuehl, Charles R.
    II. Title.
HB615.1265 2007
658.4′21—dc22   2005055467

Director of Production and Manufacturing: Bruce Johnson
Senior Acquisitions Editor: Gary Bauer
Editorial Assistant: Jacqueline Knapke
Development Editor: Deborah Hoffman
Marketing Manager: Leigh Ann Sims
Marketing Coordinator: Alicia Dysert
Managing Editor—Production: Mary Carnis
Manufacturing Buyer: Ilene Sanford
Production Liaison: Denise Brown
Full-Service Production/Composition: Lindsey Hancock/Carlisle Publishing Services
Manager of Media Production: Amy Peltier
Media Production Project Manager: Lisa Rinaldi
Senior Design Coordinator: Christopher Weigand
Cover Design: Eva Ruutopold
Printer/Binder: Hamilton Printing
Cover Printer: Phoenix Color

Pearson Education Ltd.
Pearson Education Australia PTY, Limited
Pearson Education Singapore, Pte. Ltd.
Pearson Education North Asia Ltd.
Pearson Education Canada, Ltd.
Pearson Education de Mexico, S. A. de C. V.
Pearson Education-Japan
Pearson Education Malaysia, Pte. Ltd.

10 9 8 7 6 5 4 3 2

ISBN 0-13-228174-0

CONTENTS

11   GLOBAL BUSINESS   125

Part II: The Business Plan

THE BUSINESS PLAN   142

Part III: Case Studies in Entrepreneurship

CASE STUDIES   255

APPENDIX: SUMMARY OF BUSINESS PLAN CHECKLISTS   293

PREFACE

THE GROWING NEED FOR ENTREPRENEURS

Life as an entrepreneur is a challenging but rewarding career choice. Within recent years, changes in the marketplace have created both displacement and opportunities. The "downsizing" of many corporations has caused massive layoffs at the same time that changes in technology and consumer behavior have generated new business opportunities. Many former corporate executives have chosen to start a business, not because it guarantees them financial success but because it has given them more control over their careers. In addition, a few executives who survived the initial cutbacks chose to leave on their own terms before they were targeted in the next round of layoffs.

Rapid improvements in technology have also helped fuel the increase in small business. Technological changes have made it much easier to start a home-based business. This appeals to many people who are trying to balance family and business concerns. Many entrepreneurial couples have emerged, their marriages and careers intertwined.

Finally, the increasing demand for services, including day care, home renovation, and computer repair, has created a market for entrepreneurs who can meet these needs. Services cannot be mass-produced. Entrepreneurs have established businesses to serve the customer on an individual basis.

LEARNING HOW TO BE A SUCCESSFUL ENTREPRENEUR

The decision to start a business has a substantial impact on both the life and family of the entrepreneur. This book is systematically divided into two major parts that work together in teaching basic entrepreneurial concepts and developing a business plan.

Part I contains chapters 1–11 and provides background information on topics such as the role of small businesses as an economic force, family-owned businesses, and the effect of the company's growth on the entrepreneur's satisfaction. Separate chapters cover starting a business, buying a business, and franchising.

Part II uses the concepts taught in chapters 1–11 in providing a detailed approach to writing a business plan. Each section of the business plan is carefully explained to lead the entrepreneur through the planning process. At the end of the text, the appendix provides a step-by-step approach to writing a business plan.

Also included are authentic cases that provide examples of situations entrepreneurs have faced. Real experiences and decisions are excellent learning tools for those who are just beginning the entrepreneurial process. Finally, the book includes three very different business plans—one for a music promoter, another for a shoe store, and one for a vodka bar. Readers are encouraged to review the plans and identify strengths and weaknesses.

IMPROVEMENTS AND CHANGES IN THE FOURTH EDITION

The fourth edition contains many changes, additions, and updated information. The new material includes:

— a revised text organization that reflects market feedback. Starting a new business, buying an existing business, and franchising and other alternatives are now covered within the first five chapters.

— more case options. The 12 case studies include three business plans.

— a new section at the end of each chapter that ties chapter material to the business plan.

— recent research concerning the decision to become an entrepreneur.

— expanded information on the advantages and disadvantages of home-based businesses.

— information on new wage laws concerning overtime pay.

— an updated chapter reflecting the changes in women-owned and minority-owned businesses.

— new terms now defined in the margins.

SUPPLEMENTARY MATERIAL

A full set of instructor's material and a Web site is also available at http://www.prenhall.com/lambing.

The CD that accompanies this text is designed to give a step-by-step approach to writing a business plan. Many business plan software packages exist, but often they seem to emphasize financial statements more than strategy. Unless a good strategy for the company is crafted, the projected financial numbers will be an exercise in wishful thinking.

If the questions on this CD are answered completely, it will result in a thorough business plan that can be used to obtain financing. It should also help the entrepreneur think about all of the issues that need to be addressed when starting a business.

ACKNOWLEDGMENTS

Special thanks to the reviewers of this text:

Samira Hussein, Johnson County Community College, Overland Park, KS
Timothy R. Mittan, Southeast Community College, Lincoln, NE
Laura Portolese Dias, Shoreline Community College, Seattle, WA

ABOUT THE AUTHORS

Peggy Lambing has experienced entrepreneurship from several perspectives—as a business owner, as a small business consultant, and as an educator. She and her husband owned a tool and equipment distributorship during the 1980s that was sold at a profit after five years. She has provided small business consulting services for 18 years, specializing in helping entrepreneurs obtain financing. In addition, she has taught entrepreneurship and small business management classes at the University of Missouri–St. Louis since 1980 and has served as the director of the university's Small Business Institute program. She received her bachelor of science in business administration degree and a master's degree in business from the University of Missouri–St. Louis.

Charles R. Kuehl is a member of the management faculty at the University of Missouri–St. Louis. He has published in various scholarly journals and is coauthor of *Small Business: Planning and Management*, third edition. He received his baccalaureate, master's, and doctoral degrees from the University of Iowa. His teaching and research areas include entrepreneurship, strategic management, international business, and organizational behavior.

Entrepreneurship Today

Chapter 1

LEARNING OBJECTIVES

$ To become aware of the way in which entrepreneurship emerged as a leading economic force during the 1980s and 1990s.

$ To appreciate the nature of the U.S. economy undergoing important changes early in this new century.

$ To see that countries around the world have discovered entrepreneurship as a source of economic vitality.

$ To comprehend that a small business has what it takes to compete successfully with much larger organizations.

During the 1980s and the 1990s, we saw historic changes in the world economy. These changes were part of what is called the *new world order*. At its heart have been transformations in the way in which business is conducted. Technology is assuming an increasingly important role; service industries are steadily growing; world competition is more open and spirited than ever; and outsourcing—once an obscure staffing strategy—has become a household word as thousands of jobs have been eliminated in industry after industry. Another of these landmark changes is the unparalleled rise in entrepreneurship, which has become a major source of vitality in today's world economy.

In this text, we provide an introduction to entrepreneurship. We explore the issue of **who** is an entrepreneur, considering personality traits of the individual as we examine the question "What is an entrepreneur?" We then explore the issue of **how**, as we describe the three primary routes into independent business ownership.

Also addressed are the unique problems and opportunities entrepreneurship poses for women and minority members. Next we describe the growing importance of home-based businesses, new product development as a basis for establishing new ventures, and the opportunities and problems presented by international markets.

Before we deal with any of those topics, however, we describe the spread of entrepreneurship. As you will see, while it has had a surprisingly strong impact on economies around the globe, entrepreneurship is most robust and pervasive here in the United States. We explain why so much interest in entrepreneurship has developed in recent years and why that level of interest is likely to continue. Our early focus is on the United States, after which we broaden our view, looking at the diversified textures and shapes of entrepreneurship around the world.

ENTREPRENEURSHIP IN THE UNITED STATES

Entrepreneurship is flourishing in many places around the world; here in the United States, new venture creation has been the chief source of economic vigor for the last several years. We have benefited from the emergence of a new spirit of entrepreneurship, the reasons for which we will explore in this section. This exploration should be placed in the context of how our economy has evolved during the past 40 to 50 years.

Industry Structure

Fortune 500 – a listing of the 500 largest firms in the country.

The year was 1955. World War II had ended 10 years before and the country had experienced a decade of rapid economic growth. **Fortune** had established its list of the country's 500 largest firms and much interest centered on who topped the list. (It was General Motors, with nearly $10 billion in sales and 575,000 employees.)[1] The interest in our industrial giants continued, with most observers concluding that size meant strength, and through strength these giants had established positions that were unassailable.

In contrast to the excitement surrounding big business, the attitude toward entrepreneurship seemed to be indifference. Very few universities offered studies in this area, and few books were written on the topic. In 1955 there were approximately 4.5 million small businesses in the United States.[2] The country's population was 165 million, which meant that there was one small business for every 38 people.[3] It was about that time that an interesting trend started, and since then small business has become an increasingly important part of our lives.

By 1965 the population had increased to 194 million, but the number of small businesses had increased at an even faster rate to 6.7 million, or one for every 29 people.[4] By 1975 it was one for every 26. In 2000, the U.S. population was approximately 280 million; the number of small businesses was estimated by the SBA's Office of Advocacy at about 22 million.[5] Using these figures, the ratio had fallen to one small business for every 12.7 people, approximately one-third of what it had been in 1955.

The steady decline in the number of people per small business—or conversely, the increase in the number of small businesses serving the population—emphasizes the growing significance of small business in our nation's economy. This trend is perhaps impossible to explain completely because it reflects so many societal trends or conditions, but two factors deserve special mention because of their impact on our economy.

First, competition from foreign companies became significant during the 1960s, and by the end of that decade, the United States was importing nearly as much as it exported. Change was rapid for many of our large markets by the end of the 1970s. In automobiles, electronics, industrial equipment, clothing, and construction and agricultural machinery, the changes were particularly unsettling for our domestic producers. They were losing market share to competitors who operated differently from "old-line" members. This industry shake-up meant problems for traditional competitors, but it brought opportunities for its smaller, more agile members.

Second, the late 1970s marked another watershed in the country's economic history: the start of deregulation. It drastically changed many areas, such as trucking, airlines, and the communications and financial industries. Outstanding among deregulation's many profound changes was the entry of many small firms into industries that for years had been dominated by giant companies.

Both factors—foreign competition and deregulation—were disruptive; they changed the structure of much of American industry and in the process provided many entrepreneurs with the opportunity they needed. These opportunities continue and entrepreneurship continues to flourish. In 1996 our economy set a record of nearly 850,000 new business incorporations; 1997 was even better with 884,000. Since those banner years the figure has dropped to a still robust level of approximately 600,000.[6]

Just how big a role entrepreneurship plays in our economy, as suggested in the number of start-ups, seems to be a matter of opinion and the method of counting used. The estimates vary widely. Dun & Bradstreet, using an extremely conservative approach to counting, includes businesses only as they begin to compete actively in the marketplace; the estimate for 2000 was about 130,000 start-ups. The U.S. Small Business Administration, using census data, pegs its estimate at nearly 600,000, as mentioned previously. Finally, an Omaha company, New Business USA, gathers data on new business permits, new incorporations, and so on. Its figures for 2000 show more than 900,000 home-based and 600,000 commercial-site businesses, totaling more than 1,500,000 start-ups.

Two other gradual, but potentially profound, changes have contributed to the wave of entrepreneurship. One is organizational in nature, the other is broader.

Organizational strategies and the practice of downsizing Since the start of the Industrial Revolution, large organizations have been the most important source of economic stability for the nation and have provided boundless opportunities for individuals. Managers, unskilled workers, professionals, and highly trained technicians have all experienced the comfort of knowing that hard work and loyalty to the employer would bring bright career prospects and a secure retirement.

Employees were rewarded with improved earnings and benefits linked to the success of the organization. Employees thought, "If I work hard for the company, the company will take good care of me." For countless people, that was the American Dream, and for years it was real.

As our country's economic landscape has changed, so have the assumptions underlying the relationship between the organization and the individual. Many people who used to believe that their ability and dedication to their employer protected them from job loss have learned they were wrong. Massive layoffs, or downsizing programs, have become commonplace, even in good times. As Table 1–1 indicates, despite the robust performance of the economy during the first quarter of 1998, some prominent firms announced staff reductions. The period covered in the table was selected not because it was unusually active in job losses, but because it was a typical slice of business life in the late 1990s. For any other week the results would likely be much the same.

A sampling from a time of economic slowdown (August 2001) not too surprisingly shows even greater job losses. See Table 1–2. It seems that in good times and in times of uncertainty, layoffs continue. Why is this pattern of job reduction so pervasive and persistent? Two types of answers are frequently given.

The first explanation is that organizational survival is at stake. In order to compete in today's market, firms must cut costs to the lowest level possible, and this means that staffing is kept at an absolute minimum. Any company that has more people than it needs is headed for trouble. Support for this explanation can be found in changes in markets as they become more open to international competition and subject to the constant pressure from producers in third-world countries. Every organization with costs beyond those of its competition faces serious disadvantages and an uncertain future. Procter & Gamble chairman Edwin L. Artzt, commenting on his firm's reduction from 106,000 to 93,000 employees, said, "We must slim down to stay competitive. The consumer wants better value. Our competitors are getting leaner and quicker, and we are simply going to have to run faster to stay ahead."[7]

The second explanation is that it is less a matter of need than one of greed on the part of top managers. Those holding this view cite the fact that the bonus plans of many executives are typically based on cost improvements, which are generally achievable only through massive reductions in payroll expenditures.

Downsizing – the practice of firms by which they systematically and substantially reduce the number of people they employ to achieve a reduction in costs.

TABLE 1–1 Workforce reduction announcements during the first week of June 1998

DATE	COMPANY	NUMBER
June 2	Data General, Westboro,	400 worldwide
	MS Kemet, Greenville, SC	540 United States
		900 Mexico
June 3	American Standard, Piscataway, NJ	Texas plant closed
		Operations sent to Mexico
June 4	Handleman, Troy, MI	900–1,000—10% of workforce
June 5	Motorola, Chicago	15,000 worldwide
June 6	Diebold, North Canton, OH	600 worldwide—9% of workforce

Source: The New York Times, "Company News," section C, dates given.

TABLE 1–2   Workforce reduction announcements during the last week of August 2001

DATE	COMPANY	NUMBER
August 28	Deere & Company, Moline, IL	2,000
August 28	Toshiba, Tokyo	19,000—10% of workforce
August 29	Gateway, San Diego	5,000—25% of workforce
August 29	Honeywell, Minneapolis	700
August 29	Otis Elevator, Farmington, CT	500–600
August 30	Corning, Corning, NY	1,000
August 31	Hitachi, Tokyo	14,700—5% of workforce
August 31	Charles Schwab, San Francisco	2,400

Source: The New York Times, "Business Day" section, dates given.

They point to the fact that some of the biggest layoffs occur in firms that report healthy financial results.

Important support for this view can be found in a report issued by DRI/McGraw-Hill, an economic consulting firm.[8] A study done by the company found that corporate profits rose 11 percent in 1994, after increasing 13 percent in 1993. During 1994, however, corporate America cut 516,069 jobs. This was nearly as many as were laid off in 1991, which marked the deepest point of the most recent previous recession.

Societal change   The end of jobs? Some writers claim that our economy has developed to the point where the job is no longer the best way to accomplish the things that need to be done. They contend that jobs were a societal invention that provided the needed human resource element to allow the Industrial Revolution to proceed. Up to that point in history, people didn't have, or need, jobs as we define them today. What the Industrial Revolution made necessary, the post-industrial society does not need. We now have the technology to run large production facilities—the kind that used to employ thousands of workers—with a skeleton crew. This is what one observer had in mind when he said, "The plant of the future will have only two employees: a man and a dog. The man will be there to feed the dog and the dog will be there to see that the man doesn't touch the equipment."

Whatever the plant of the future may look like, today's large organizations do not hesitate in eliminating jobs, and they are slow in establishing new ones, frequently choosing to have current employees work overtime instead. As a result, large firms no longer generate jobs as they once did. For example, between 1979 and 1993, total employment in Fortune 500 manufacturing firms dropped from 16.2 million to 11.5 million, a decrease of nearly one-third. This pattern of job loss in big companies has meant that any expansion in the number of jobs in our economy has been in the small business arena. Indeed, most analysis of job generation indicate that in recent years, the source of job creation is much more likely to have been a small firm rather than a large one.

> **Post-industrial society –** a country where large-scale businesses are declining in importance.

Consequences for the Individual

Regardless of which explanation for corporate job loss is most accurate, the fact is working for a large organization no longer seems to provide the kind of security and career opportunities it once did. Consequently, it should come as no surprise that many people are looking for a new route to take in the world of work. For growing numbers of people, that new route is entrepreneurship, and today that route has greater accessibility than ever. Just as the restructuring described earlier resulted in massive job losses—and continues to do so—the changes have led to unprecedented opportunities for small business.

> **Underemployed** – being in a job that requires skill and knowledge below your capabilities.

The new economic face of America includes large numbers of capable unemployed, or underemployed, managers for whom the chances of regaining a comparable position in a large organization are slim. For many of these people, the appeal of making it on their own is easy to understand. They have talent, experience, drive, and contacts but nonetheless find themselves without a job. The need for productive channels for these managers to be able to make their contribution is clear; entrepreneurship is that channel for many.

Even for people who have not been directly touched by layoffs or by the uncertainties and pressures associated with corporate downsizing, the lure of the independence of entrepreneurship is strong. According to *Inc.* magazine, the number of universities and colleges offering courses or programs in entrepreneurship has increased to its current level of well beyond 1,000 from about 150 in 1979. Beyond the dramatic increase in the numbers of programs and courses, entrepreneurship education has grown in the ways in which it is offered. As Illustration Capsule 1-1 shows, some of the nation's leading entrepreneurship programs, as ranked in a 2004 survey conducted by *Forbes* magazine and *The Princeton Review*, go to great lengths to provide experiences, incentives, and opportunities to help start an entrepreneurial career.

ILLUSTRATION CAPSULE 1-1

TOMORROW ENTREPRENEURS

While some communities and regions—Seattle, Austin, Boston, Silicon Valley—are seen as hotbeds for business start-ups, many other locations around the country have vibrant programs for developing and encouraging young people interested in starting a business. Listed here are the to ten top-ranked university programs in entrepreneurship in a 2004 survey conducted by *Forbes* magazine and *The Princeton Review*. Notice the diverse and creative features of the programs and the way in which they prepare students to launch a business.

#1 – University of North Carolina — Chapel Hill
Programs include the Carolina Entrepreneurial Initiative, the Carolina Entrepreneurship Club, Students in Free Enterprise, and the Carolina Launch Program.

#2 – University of Notre Dame
Students may work the IrishAngels, a network of university alums from around the world, representing a variety of industries and markets.

#3 – Louisiana State University and A&M College
Independent studies, geared toward exploring a business idea or developing a feasibility study, are offered.

#4 – Northeastern University
Through its Entrepreneurship Center the university provides a business plan competition and co-op program opportunities.

#5 – Indiana University — Bloomington
The Young Entrepreneurs Association sponsors projects and internships; the university provides experiential learning through the Start-up Training Assistance Research Center.

#6 – Carnegie Mellon University
Students participate in activities offered by the Undergraduate Entrepreneurship Association, Students in Free Enterprise, Innovation Works, Pittsburgh Life Science Greenhouse, and Pittsburgh Digital Greenhouse.

#7 – Syracuse University
The university's Orange Hatchery is a student incubator, accommodating eight student ventures. In addition, the school sponsors the Syracuse Business Plan, which awards $40,000 to student-initiated ventures.

#8 – University of Arizona
Students work in teams with large and small corporations to identify new markets and opportunities for existing technologies and products, then develop business plans for commercialization.

#9 – University of Iowa
The school's entrepreneurial center provides coordination of a mentor program and runs the Wellmark Venture Capital Fund, which serves students, faculty, and area entrepreneurs.

#10 – University of New Hampshire
Entrepreneurship students are given the chance to operate the campus's convenience store, and can participate in the High Tech internship program.

Source: 2004 Survey of University Entrepreneurship Programs; *Forbes* magazine and *The Princeton Review.*

THE GLOBAL SCENE

While it may be true that by almost any measure the United States has the most vibrant entrepreneurship of any of the world's economies, by no means does it have a monopoly. The advantages of widespread entrepreneurial activity have not gone unnoticed by economic planners in countries around the globe, and recent years have seen the initiation of many programs to encourage small business formation. China was a traditional opponent of any economic ideas that even hinted of capitalism, and yet it, like many countries with socialist traditions, has seen entrepreneurship emerge as a major force in its economy. See Illustration Capsule 1-2.

ILLUSTRATION CAPSULE 1-2

ROADS TO ENTREPRENEURSHIP IN CHINA

Some historic movements start in barely noticeable ways. Years ago, the village elders of Xiangyang, an obscure town in the southwestern part of China, decided to remove a sign that designated the town as a "people's commune." The move came as a result of a 1978 decision by the country's leaders to allow communities to change from communes to "townships." Although the elders took more than a year to respond to the opportunity, Xiangyang was the first community to do so and thereby set in motion some profound changes. In the years following World War II, the Communist government had banned private commerce, so the move toward establishing free markets required considerable political courage. The first Xiangyang businesses to be involved in the transformation were in agriculture; the success there led to changes in other industries, particularly in the emergence of individual private enterprise. By the 1980s entrepreneurship was changing the country. In 1984 an authority on modern China, Orville Schell, wrote the book *To Get Rich Is Glorious: China in the Eighties.* Not everyone has been able to get rich, of course, but the possibility of doing so has energized, and continues to energize, enough people to have made a significant difference in the nation's economic fortunes.

In recent years China's ability to compete internationally has created considerable unrest in overseas markets. For example, *BusinessWeek,* in its December 6, 2004, cover story, identified the "three scariest words" in U.S. industry as "the China price." Manufacturing companies are told that their price is too high. To keep selling to an aggressive retailer, which insists on lowest prices from its suppliers, U.S. manufacturers often turn away from domestic plants and to offshore outsourcing. China's industrial might, based on many profound cost advantages and threatening to transform international business, prompted *The New York Times Magazine* to speculate that we have entered the "The China Century."

Often overlooked in the analysis of China's ability to compete is a strong entrepreneurial urge in many of its people. *Inc.* magazine gives as an example of this urge the case of a woman from the Zhejiang province, Hong Dongyang. She started as a school teacher but began making socks in the 1970s. She did well and therefore decided to open a roadside stand, calling her modest enterprise, "Zhejiang Stocking Company." Her success did not go unnoticed and her efforts were copied by others in the province. Many others—today 8,000 companies—in the province produce 8 billion pairs of socks, or one-third of the world's supply.

Sources: Tony Walker, "Communing with the Future," *Financial Times Weekend,* May 30/May 31, 1998, I; Orville Schell, *To Get Rich Is Glorious: China in the Eighties* (New York: Pantheon Books, 1984); Ted C. Fishman, "How China Will Change Your Business," *Inc.,* March 2005; Ted C. Fishman, "The China Bind," *The New York Times Magazine,* July 4, 2004.

The wave of interest in entrepreneurship has also made its way around the world. This interest has been particularly strong in organizations whose objective is to improve the economic life of underdeveloped nations. The World Bank has had a role in each of the following projects:

$ In Rio de Janeiro, 36,000 students are being given training to enhance their computer and literacy skills, with the objective of developing entrepreneurs capable of starting small information technology businesses.

$ In the African country of Niger, marketing and entrepreneurial skills are taught to farmers to bolster their independence.

$ Various forms and applications of information technology are being used in Bangladesh to develop entrepreneurship. Cellular telephones, for example, are provided to individuals who in turn sell calls and services in rural areas that do not have a traditional communications infrastructure.

$ The government of Peru and the World Bank are engaged in a program to develop "entrepreneurial capacity" in indigenous and Afro-Peruvian peoples.

$ In Guatamala, a program called MicroNet, sponsored by the government, Microsoft, and the World Bank, is helping people develop entrepreneurial skills to allow them to start their own businesses. The goal is 25,000 starts annually.

$ The Enterprise Incubator Project in Armenia provides assistance to emerging businesses, particularly those in information technology. Furthermore, entrepreneur grants cover initial business investment costs.

$ The Malawi Entrepreneurship Program was established to aid in food distribution in response to the country's severe drought problems.

Of all the institutional efforts to nurture small business, none has had more dramatic results than that of an economist from Bangladesh. His idea was simple: provide financing to the poor so that they can become self-sufficient entrepreneurs. Muhammad Yunus founded the Grameen Bank, because, as he says, "Capital does not need to be the handmaiden only of the rich." See Illustration Capsule 1-3 for a description of the bank and its remarkable accomplishments.

ILLUSTRATION CAPSULE 1-3

ENTREPRENEURSHIP IN A CHANGING ENVIRONMENT

Muhammed Yunus's idea for Grameen Bank came 20 years ago when he visited one of Bangladesh's desperately poor villages. It was obvious to him that the village's people, especially the women, needed loans to let them start their own businesses, and it was just as obvious that they were not going to get them from conventional banking circles. The warnings Mr. Yunus had heard from traditional bankers that the Grameen poor people would not repay their loans did not trouble him, so he started a "micro-credit for micro-enterprises" program at his Grameen Bank.

The program has grown impressively. Small loans have been made to 2 million families in 35,000 villages in Bangladesh, incredible numbers by any standard. Not only is there impressive volume in terms of customers, but the repayment record is outstanding, with a rate of over 90 percent.

The success of the program has led to an extension to the beggars of Bangladesh, and they too have vindicated Mr. Yunus's belief in them. Like the village women, they have improved their lives and have repaid their loans faithfully.

More recently microenterprise programs have been established in Haiti and Bolivia. Both show the same kinds of remarkable results, most notably repayment rates of 97 percent. The Haiti program, established in 1997, has grown at an annual rate of 73 percent and has women as 68 percent of its borrowers. The Bolivian program has 60 percent women in its borrower ranks and attracts primarily marginalized low-income members of the population.

Continued

Continued

Mr. Yunus's faith in the creditworthiness of the poor people of the world was well founded, and as a result, countless numbers of poor people, primarily women, from around the world have achieved a level of financial and personal success they would otherwise have not experienced.

Sources: Patrick E. Tyler, "Banker Is Star at Parley on Women," *The New York Times,* September 14, 1995, A7; David Bornstein, "The Barefoot Bank with Cheek," *Atlantic Monthly,* December 1995, 40–47.

ENTREPRENEURSHIP IN A CHANGING ENVIRONMENT

Perhaps the most powerful element of today's environment is change. Although it is more dramatic in some sectors of our economy than in others, none is immune to its threat. Change is everywhere, and according to most observers, it will continue to accelerate. It has important implications for entrepreneurs, and we will examine two of its aspects: changes in markets and the emergence of new markets.

Changes in Markets

A tactic commonly used when a company's management feels the pressure of competitors using aggressive pricing is to reduce costs to the lowest possible levels. As we noted in discussing downsizing, the target of these cost reduction efforts is frequently the workforce. Fewer people on the payroll obviously means lower costs, but the need to produce the product or provide the service remains. Many firms have handled this dilemma by having an outside supplier perform the tasks. They are engaging in outsourcing.

> **Outsourcing** – the practice of using outside firms to perform tasks that could be performed internally.

Outsourcing has become an increasingly common practice, an opportunity for small firms. The tasks performed by the victims of downsizing usually have to be taken care of, and small companies are typically used to do so. Consequently, as big firms experience threats, small firms are given opportunities.

In addition to receiving such outsourcing requests, small businesses can also compete in markets where size and scope are required to compete effectively, by themselves contracting with outsiders to provide services. Using this method in the extreme, an individual can enter into alliances with a variety of suppliers to design a product, produce it, and even market it. The relationship, or alliance, between the company and supplier continues until the contract requirements are met, after which the relationship ceases to exist. Should a new opportunity emerge, a new set of alliances is formed. By creating such relationships to cover all the tasks needed to bring the product to market, the entrepreneur can enter markets that otherwise would have been out of reach. The term for a business that operates this way is *virtual organization*, a firm that operates as though it has all of the customary parts of an ongoing business, when in fact it may consist of only the entrepreneur and a file of contacts for establishing relationships.

> **Virtual organization** – a company that does not have the internal resources needed to compete, choosing rather to form alliances with other firms to perform the necessary tasks.

Another change taking place in markets is one of continued fragmentation, or the development of niches. The population of the United States is so large that for almost any product, the overall size of the market would preclude small businesses from competing effectively. Within markets, however, are small groups of customers looking for a unique set of attributes in a product; these groups constitute a niche. Many niches are too small to interest large firms and therefore provide small firms with opportunities. Benefiting from these opportunities requires focusing on a clearly defined niche in the market, understanding exactly the expectations of the customer in that niche, and filling those expectations.

> **Fragmentation of market –** when markets become divided into unique and distinctive parts.

New Markets

For the past 20 years or so, many firms have tried to take advantage of the opportunities provided by a heightened concern for our environment. Wide arrays of goods and services, marketed under the "green" label and ranging from recycled paper goods to environmentally friendly lawn care products, now compete for our dollars. The green market provides opportunities that small firms may be particularly well suited to address.

> **Green markets –** those that develop in response to our society's concerns for our physical environment.

They typically bring to the market a fresher image and a more convincing case than do many of the old-line firms whose reputations have been tarnished in this area. See Illustration Capsule 1-4.

ILLUSTRATION CAPSULE 1-4

THE GREENING OF ENTREPRENEURSHIP

While big business seems anxious to promote its efforts to save the planet, many ambitious plans remain just that: plans. Companies learn that the market isn't large enough, or that entering it may require turning its back on its old customers, or that more study is needed, and so on. These obstacles seem to be less formidable to small business. Here are two examples of entrepreneurs who have established companies that are making money while making a difference.

In the town of Sebastopol, California, entrepreneur Gary Starr is determined to use his product, the electric bicycle, to accomplish something that the big automobile manufacturers do not seem willing to tackle. Mr. Starr would like to reduce our nation's dependence on the internal-combustion engine. He has developed the ZAP bike, which provides supplemental power to help the rider negotiate hills and to provide a higher cruising speed. He hopes that after a period of using the ZAP, the owner will be ready to move up to an electric car, and when that happens, his company will sell that vehicle as well.

In the early 1980s John Schaeffer founded his "hippie hardware store," Real Goods, in Willetts, California. The firm's early years were, at best, modestly successful. In 1986, however, Mr. Schaeffer started a mail-order operation with hopes of increasing sales from $18,000 to $1 million by 2000. His projection was not very accurate: the firm sold $18.3 million in 1996. The firm sells environmentally friendly goods, including energy-efficient and renewable items and some rather unusual items such as ultrasonic toothbrushes and Zen alarm clocks. The company catalog has established itself as a premier purveyor of environmentally friendly items not only with consumers—7 million copies were printed last year—but with the sources of the items as well. Now inventors and developers of new "green" items seek out Mr. Schaeffer for inclusion in the catalog.

Source: Marc Reisner, "Green Expectations," *The Amicus Journal,* Summer 1998, 19–23.

Marketplace – a physical location where buyers and sellers meet.

Market space – the techniques, machines, and processes that allow buyers and sellers to transact business electronically.

As the World Wide Web develops, we will see a change in the way commerce is conducted. This change has been called the transformation from "marketplace" (meaning physical business activities) to "market space" (business done electronically). Predictions of how this new technology-driven process will develop are always hazardous, but it seems likely that some of the major players will be companies we have not heard of, and many of them will be companies that have not even been started. Among the ingredients for success in this kind of embryonic industry are insights as to what it takes to serve customers who have not yet been identified, and the inspiration to follow through on those insights. Someone with those characteristics will move us in the direction toward market space from marketplace, and that someone is likely to be an entrepreneur rather than a manager with a large company.

The Competitive Advantages of Small Business

Competitive advantage – a characteristic of a business that allows it to compete successfully.

Regardless of whether it is an upheaval in existing markets or the emergence of a new one, small businesses have important advantages that allow them to succeed. One is their responsiveness to conditions and trends in the market, which comes from a close relationship with customers and therefore a thorough understanding of their needs. For many entrepreneurs the relationship with the customer is a personal one, and that means being the first to learn of changes in preferences that will affect the market. Not only does such a relationship give the entrepreneur the chance to learn from the customer, but it also gives the entrepreneur the chance to reverse the communication process: to give the customer the message that he or she matters to the business. Large companies spend considerable amounts of money and energy to learn from the customer and to send messages of concern; for small firms, both learning and showing concern are natural parts of the process of doing business. Successful small businesses never lose sight of that.

Another factor that distinguishes the successful small business from the typical large company is its ability to innovate. The independence of an entrepreneurial company allows it to move quickly when something changes or a new opportunity arises. While many large firms recognize the need to change directions quickly, most seem to be burdened with procedures and administrative controls that slow things down, no matter what the sense of urgency might be. This ability of small businesses to innovate can take on many forms, including product innovation (new features, improvements), process innovation (improvements to how production is carried out), and service innovation (offering something new to serve the market). Regardless of its form, innovation enables small business to compete successfully.

Closely related to innovation is flexibility. For many successful small businesses, a change requested (or even hinted at) by the customer or a new product feature developed by a competitor typically becomes a call for action that leads to new ways of doing things or modifications to the product line. The reasons for this flexibility are both attitudinal and practical. Entrepreneurs know that responding to the customer is important enough to deal with the disruption brought on by change; it "goes with the territory." As a practical matter, small companies tend to invest less than many big firms in expensive, single-purpose machines, large inventory levels, and rigid production tools and techniques. As a result, they can change what they do, or the way they do it, with far less difficulty.

Taken together, these characteristics—responsiveness, the ability to innovate, and flexibility—provide a small business with what it takes to compete in a rapidly changing environment. But clearly the entrepreneur, the individual, is at the core of any success achieved by the small company. Chapter 2 describes that individual.

SMALL BUSINESS AND THE BUSINESS PLAN

One of the most important documents needed by entrepreneurs is a business plan. In this text we discuss the topics important to small business owners and then address each of these topics in the business plan section in the second half of the text. The topics mentioned—competitive advantage, innovative ideas, and markets to be served—must be described in detail in the business plan. This helps the entrepreneur to develop the business concept and shows bankers and investors that the entrepreneur has carefully thought through the business idea.

SUMMARY

Here in the United States entrepreneurship has had profound effects on our economy since the years after World War II. During the 1990s and the first years of the new century, we have witnessed a continuation in the number of independent small businesses relative to our population. Some reasons for this increasing popularity of small business include the manner in which large firms have dealt with their economic imperatives, competition from overseas companies, and the spread of many forms of technology that make it possible for small firms to compete effectively with large ones. Recent years have brought the recognition that entrepreneurship can be an important source of vitality in countries whose economies are still developing.

DISCUSSION QUESTIONS

1. What are the major reasons for entrepreneurship becoming so important in our economy?
2. What are the two leading explanations for the massive job losses that have characterized the nation's largest firms in recent years?
3. Will the concept of a job become obsolete?
4. Give some examples of the sources of strength of the entrepreneurial movement in different countries.
5. What is outsourcing, and how has it given a boost to entrepreneurship?
6. Define market space and explain how it represents an opportunity for entrepreneurs.

ENDNOTES

1. "The Fortune Directory," *Fortune,* July 1955, 2.

2. *2004–2005 Statistical Abstract of the United States* (Washington, DC: U.S. Department of Commerce, Bureau of the Census), 734.

3. Ibid.

4. *1970 Statistical Abstract of the United States* (Washington, DC: U.S. Department of Commerce, Bureau of the Census), 468.

5. *2004–2005 Statistical Abstract of the United States* (Washington, DC: U.S. Department of Commerce, Bureau of the Census), 716.

6. "TAPEWATCH," *The Wall Street Journal,* May 4, 1995, 1.

7. Ibid.

8. Jennifer Click, "Downsizing Continues As Profits Climb," *HRMagazine,* July 1995, 14.

The Entrepreneur

Chapter 2

LEARNING OBJECTIVES

$ To realize that there is no consensus concerning the definition of *entrepreneur*.

$ To understand that the decision to become an entrepreneur is influenced by many factors.

$ To comprehend the advantages and disadvantages of entrepreneurship.

WHAT IS ENTREPRENEURSHIP?

Peter Drucker, an authority on management theory, noted that although the term *entrepreneur* has been used for over 200 years, "there has been total confusion over the definition."[1] Substantial disagreement concerns the concept of entrepreneurship and the individual who is called an entrepreneur.

In an article published in the *Advanced Management Journal,* Michael Morris states that early definitions of entrepreneurs were developed by economists. These definitions emphasized factors such as risk and financial capital.[2] Thus, one of the earliest references to the term *entrepreneurship* has been traced to Richard Cantillon's work in the field of economics in 1734. To Cantillon, entrepreneurship was self-employment with an uncertain return.[3] By the early 1900s, Joseph A. Schumpter had described an entrepreneur as "a person who carries out new combinations, which may take the form of new products, processes, markets, organizational forms, or sources of supply."[4] Schumpter is known for his concept of "creative destruction," which states that entrepreneurs are a force for change and make existing products obsolete. This definition and others during this time period emphasized innovation.[5] Research in the later 1990s often focused on personality traits of entrepreneurs, trying to determine if entrepreneurs had different personality traits than people who chose to work in corporations.

Michael Morris and his coauthors have tried to combine many of these varying concepts of entrepreneurship by developing the following definition:

> Entrepreneurship is a process activity. It generally involves the following inputs: an opportunity; one or more proactive individuals; an organizational context; risk; innovation; and resources. It can produce the following outcomes: a new venture or enterprise; value; new products or processes; profit or personal benefit; and growth.[6]

> **Entrepreneur** – person who tries out new combinations of products, processes, markets, organizational forms, and supplies.

> **Entrepreneurship** – involves an opportunity, an individual, an organizational context, risk, and resources.

THE ENTREPRENEURIAL PROCESS

The entrepreneurial process is common in the United States, where each year about 4 percent of the adult population (1 person in every 25) is actively involved in trying to start a new business. Most have full- or part-time jobs, or they are already running another business and do not devote themselves full time to the new venture until it is a going concern.[7] Evidence suggests that one out of every two adults in this country has tried to start a new business at some time in his or her life.[8] The general public often believes that entrepreneurs always have a "flash of genius" that results in the new business. In fact, "flashes of genius" are rare.[9] It is also true that some of the companies we consider great today did not start out with a compelling idea for a product or service. For example, in 1945, Masaru Ibuka and seven employees started a company in a bombed-out department store in Tokyo. However, they did not have an idea of what the business would do. For weeks, they tried to figure out what business the company could enter. Today, that company is known as Sony Corporation.[10]

Similarly, when Bill Hewlett and Dave Packard founded Hewlett-Packard, they had no specific idea to pursue. Although the business was vaguely defined as electronic engineering, the owners did not have any formative plans. Hewlett explains, "We did anything that would bring in a nickel. . . . Here we were with about $500 in capital trying whatever someone thought we might be able to do."[11]

James Collins, a columnist for *Inc.,* explains "you don't have to have a great idea if you execute it better than anyone else." In fact, Collins states that identifying with a specific idea may actually be detrimental, because if you equate the success of your company with the success of a specific idea, then you're more likely to give up if that idea fails. If instead you consider the business the ultimate product, it is more likely to survive if the first product concept fails. Thus, for the person who has thought of being an entrepreneur but has not had a flash of inspiration or a unique idea, business ownership is still quite possible.[12]

There are many types of entrepreneurial activities, however, and not everyone would classify the individual involved in each case as an entrepreneur. Consider the following possibilities:

$ *New concept/new business.* The classic entrepreneur develops a new product or a new idea and builds a business around the new concept. This requires a substantial amount of creativity and an ability to see patterns and trends before they are evident to the general public. The business concept may be so new and revolutionary that it may create an entirely new industry. Examples of creative entrepreneurs include Steven Jobs, one of the founders of Apple Computer and NEXT, and Bill Gates, founder of Microsoft. Most people would agree that these innovative businesspeople are true entrepreneurs.

$ *Existing concept/new business.* Some individuals start new businesses based on old concepts. For example, if someone opens a convenience food store, the idea is not new and the founder may not be described as innovative, but the business still represents a financial risk to the owner, and the person is developing something where nothing previously existed. Most people would consider this person an entrepreneur, although others may disagree because of the lack of creativity and innovation involved. It should be pointed out, however, that individuals who engage in this type of activity seldom do so without introducing some change. The likelihood of a business succeeding if it is patterned exactly after one that already exists is remote. Therefore, most entrepreneurs who start a business to compete with those that already exist do so in the hope that theirs will offer something new or better. The additional something is born of creativity.

$ *Existing concept/existing business.* Even less innovative is the person who buys an existing business without many plans to change the company operations. There is little need for creativity or innovation, but the individual is still taking a personal and financial risk. Therefore, many people describe this person as an entrepreneur.

FACTORS OF ENTREPRENEURSHIP

The information just discussed shows that more than one factor must be considered when studying entrepreneurs. There is still no agreement as to why some people choose self-employment and others choose to work for someone else. One recent study has identified four spheres of influence in determining entrepreneurial behavior: the individual, the ethnocultural environment, the circumstances in society, and a combination of these.[13] These factors are discussed next.

The Individual

Despite the fact that personality traits have not been found to be reliable predictors of future behavior,[14] many studies still focus on the entrepreneur's personality.

Some people, such as Peter Drucker, do not believe that traits are a deciding factor and believe that anyone can be taught to be an entrepreneur. One professor of entrepreneurship agrees:

> For every risk seeker, I'll show you someone who's risk averse. For every first-born child who is a successful entrepreneur, there's a successful last-born or only child. For every entrepreneur who grew up listening to tales of entrepreneurial success at the dinner table [had entrepreneurial parents] there are those whose parents were military or corporate or absent.[15]

There is also concern as to cause and effect. Since many studies of entrepreneurs are completed once the person is a successful business owner, it is possible that the experience of entrepreneurship affects the individual's personality. Michael Morris points out that the psychology and behavior of the entrepreneur may change as the business evolves.[16]

However, many believe that entrepreneurs have a special personality and that these traits cannot be taught. One writer for *BusinessWeek* who disagrees with Peter Drucker states, "While [Drucker's] probably right that the nuts and bolts of entrepreneurship can be studied and learned, the soul of an entrepreneur is something else altogether. An entrepreneur can be a professional manager, but not every manager can be an entrepreneur."[17] One entrepreneur explains,

> You cannot teach drive or initiative or ingenuity or individuality. You cannot teach a mind-set or a personality. You cannot teach in the classroom the lessons learned by starting a company with nothing more than hope and the ability to talk a bank officer into giving you a loan.[18]

Another expert states, "Good ideas are common; the people who can implement them are rare."[19]

As Stan Cromie noted in his article on entrepreneurship, many vocational counselors consider personality in helping people decide on a career choice. Factors that may be considered include basic values and beliefs, personality traits, personal needs, and the person's self-concept. It is often argued that people choose jobs that fill their needs and are consistent with their self-image.[20]

One recent study found that "personality is a core antecedent of entrepreneurship." This study looked at how views on self-employment are related to personality. The study explored the "Big Five" personality characteristics and the impact of these on views of entrepreneurship. The Big Five characteristics include extraversion, conscientiousness, agreeableness, openness, and neuroticism. The study found that the characteristic of openness is an important factor for entrepreneurship. This is the "part of personality that fosters creativity, originality, and receptiveness to new experience."[21]

Whether entrepreneurial tendencies exist at birth or are developed as a person matures, certain traits are usually evident in those who enjoy success. Many of these traits have been found in successful managers as well as entrepreneurs. Let's examine some of these traits.

Passion for the business James Salter, cofounder of Gen-X Sports, Inc., says, "Burning passion? Absolutely!"[22] The entrepreneur must have more than a casual interest in the business because he or she must overcome many hurdles and obstacles. If there is no passion or consuming interest, the business will not succeed.

"Big Five" personality traits – extraversion, conscientiousness, agreeableness, openness, and neuroticism.

This personal or emotional commitment was described by someone saying, "I couldn't live without giving this a full try."[23]

Tenacity despite failure Because of the hurdles and obstacles that must be overcome, the entrepreneur must be consistently persistent. Many successful entrepreneurs succeeded only after they had failed several times. It has been stated that "Successful entrepreneurs don't have failures. They have learning experiences."[24] They know that "difficulties are merely opportunities in work clothes."[25] Paul Goldin, CEO of Score Board Inc., says, "You can't be afraid of failing. You may have to try seven or eight times."[26]

Walt Disney went bankrupt three times before he made his first successful film.[27] Henry Ford failed twice. They would never have been successful if they had given up easily. Joe Namath, the successful football quarterback, best described the positive attitude toward failure by saying, "I've never lost a ball game, but I have run out of time on a few occasions."[28]

Confidence Entrepreneurs are confident in their abilities and the business concept. They believe they have the ability to accomplish whatever they set out to do.[29] This confidence is not unfounded, however. Often they have an in-depth knowledge of the market and the industry, and they have conducted months (and sometimes years) of investigation.[30] It is common for entrepreneurs to learn an industry while working for someone else. This allows them to gain knowledge and make mistakes before striking out on their own. One successful entrepreneur described this advantage by saying, "I'd rather learn how to ride a bike on somebody else's bicycle than on my own."[31]

Self-determination Nearly every authority on entrepreneurship recognizes the importance of self-motivation and self-determination for entrepreneurial success.[32] Jon P. Goodman, director of the University of Southern California Entrepreneur Program, states that self-determination is a crucial sign of a successful entrepreneur because successful entrepreneurs act out of choice; they are never victims of fate.[33] Entrepreneurs believe that their success or failure depends on their own actions. This quality is known as an **internal locus of control**.[34] A person who believes that fate, the economy, or other outside factors determine success has an external locus of control and is not likely to succeed as an entrepreneur.

> **Internal locus of control** – belief that one controls one's own success.

Management of risk A partner at a London-based accounting firm states, "Risk is at the very heart of running your own business, and the ability to manage risk is one of the qualities of any successful entrepreneur."[35] The general public often believes that entrepreneurs take high risks; however, that is usually not true. First, more than two-thirds of those trying to get a business started have a full- or part-time job or they are running another business. They do not put all of their resources and time into the venture until it appears to be viable.[36] Entrepreneurs often define the risks early in the process and minimize them to the extent possible.[37]

Entrepreneurs also see risk differently from others, although this is often because of their knowledge of the industry. One writer for *BusinessWeek* uses the example of Chuck Yeager, the test pilot, and Scott Schmidt, founder of "extreme skiing," to illustrate this point. Yeager's years of experience in the cockpit and his uncanny talent for flying airplanes made his perception of risk different from that of others when it came to testing new designs.

Scott Schmidt skis off 60-foot cliffs, sponsored by ski-equipment companies. Videos of his extraordinary jumps convince the general public that he is a reckless maniac. For every jump, however, he has carefully calculated the takeoff and landing spots. Therefore, Schmidt doesn't consider himself a maniac but rather a very good skier.[38]

Lane Nemeth, founder of Discovery Toys, stated that entrepreneurs see risk differently. When she began the company with $50,000, she looked at the money and asked herself, "What if I fail?" But, she stated, that was the last time she thought of failing.[39]

Seeing changes as opportunities To the general public, change is often frightening and is something to be avoided. Entrepreneurs, however, see change as normal and necessary. They search for change, respond to it, and exploit it as an opportunity, which is the basis of innovation.[40]

Tolerance for ambiguity The life of an entrepreneur is unstructured. No one is setting schedules or step-by-step processes for the entrepreneur to follow. There is no guarantee of success. Uncontrollable factors such as the economy, the weather, and changes in consumer tastes often have a dramatic effect on a business. An entrepreneur's life has been described as a professional life riddled by ambiguity—a consistent lack of clarity. The successful entrepreneur feels comfortable with this uncertainty.[41]

Initiative and a need for achievement Almost everyone agrees that successful entrepreneurs take the initiative in situations where others may not. Their willingness to act on their ideas often distinguishes them from those who are not entrepreneurs. Many people have good ideas, but these ideas are not converted into action.

Entrepreneurs act on their ideas because they have a high need for achievement, shown in many studies to be higher than that of the general population. That achievement motive is converted into drive and initiative that results in accomplishments.

Detail orientation and perfectionism Entrepreneurs are often perfectionists, and striving for excellence, or "perfection," helps make the business successful. Attention to detail and the need for perfection result in a quality product or service. However, this often becomes a source of frustration for employees, who may not be perfectionists themselves. Because of this, the employees may perceive the entrepreneur as a difficult employer.

Perception of passing time Entrepreneurs are aware that time is passing quickly, and they therefore often appear to be impatient. Because of this time orientation, nothing is ever done soon enough and everything is a crisis.[42] As with the tendency for perfectionism, this hurry-up attitude may irritate employees who do not see the same urgency in all situations.

Creativity One of the reasons entrepreneurs are successful is that they have imagination and can envision alternative scenarios.[43] They have the ability to recognize opportunities that other people do not see. Nolan Bushnell, who created the first home video game and the Chuck E. Cheese character, believes the act of creation is nothing more than taking something standard in one business and applying it to another. For example, Bushnell had worked in amusement parks while in college and was able to combine his knowledge of amusement with video technology to create a home video game. He believes that entrepreneurs must know what the customers want—sometimes a little before they know they want it and before they know it's possible.[44]

> **Tolerance for ambiguity –** comfortable with uncertainty.

Ability to see the big picture Entrepreneurs often see things in a holistic sense; they can see the "big picture" when others see only the parts.[45] One study found that successful owners of manufacturing firms gathered more information about the business environment, and more often, than those who were less successful. This process, known as **scanning the environment,** allows the entrepreneur to see the entire business environment and the industry and helps to formulate the larger picture of the business activity. This is an important step in determining how the company will compete.[46]

Motivating factors Although many people believe that entrepreneurs are motivated by money, other factors are actually more important. The need for achievement, mentioned earlier, and a desire for independence are more important than money. Entrepreneurs often decide to start their own businesses in order to avoid having a boss. Many are self-employed for less pay than they would receive if they worked for someone else.

One study of approximately 3,000 entrepreneurs identified the following factors as "very important" reasons for being self-employed:

> To use personal skills and abilities
>
> To gain control over his or her life
>
> To build something for the family
>
> Because he or she liked the challenge
>
> To live how and where he or she chooses[47]

Other studies have identified other motivating factors, such as the need for recognition, a need for tangible and meaningful rewards, and a need to satisfy expectations.[48]

Self-efficacy A recent study has suggested that the concept of self-efficacy influences a person's entrepreneurial intentions.[49] Self-efficacy has been defined as a person's belief in his or her capability to perform a task. One study found that a sense of personal efficacy that is both accurate and strong is essential to the initiation and persistence of performance in all aspects of human development.[50] Therefore, a person who believes he or she would be successful as an entrepreneur is more likely to pursue it as a career option.

A separate study looked at the concept of **thought self-leadership** (TSL) and self-efficacy. TSL states that people develop functional and dysfunctional habits in the ways they think. This in turn influences their "perceptions, the way they process information, and the choices they make." Thus, entrepreneurs may develop a habit of "opportunity thinking," a functional habit that focuses on opportunities and positive ways of handling challenging situations. The dysfunctional way of thinking, known as "obstacle thinking," focuses on negative aspects of a problem and would most likely result in giving up. These thought patterns affect self-efficacy since an entrepreneur who engages in functional, opportunity thinking is likely to see an increase in self-efficacy.[51] Thus, a habit of opportunity thinking may make a person more likely to pursue entrepreneurship.

Cultural Factors

A common finding is that ethnic enterprise is often overrepresented in the small business sector; that is, members of some ethnocultural groups typically have a higher rate of business formation and ownership than do others. However, the effect of culture on entrepreneurial tendencies is not completely clear, because

Scanning the environment – a process of gathering information about trends such as social and economic trends.

Self-efficacy – a person's belief in his or her ability to perform a task.

Thought self-leadership – the concept that people develop functional and dysfunctional habits in thinking.

Opportunity thinking – focuses on opportunities and positive ways of thinking.

Obstacle thinking – focuses on negative aspects of a problem.

individuals from different cultural groups do not all become entrepreneurs for the same reason.[52]

The effect of culture and traits may be intertwined, since some studies have shown that different cultures have varying values and beliefs. For example, the Japanese have been known to have an achievement-oriented culture that helps entrepreneurs persist until they succeed. Another potentially important factor is whether a culture generally has an internal locus of control. For example, U.S. culture tends to support an internal locus of control, whereas the Russian culture does not. Individuals from a culture with an internal locus of control may be more predisposed to believe they have a chance of succeeding as entrepreneurs.[53]

Cultures also affect the image or status of entrepreneurs. One study of immigrant entrepreneurs in Canada found that those from India saw entrepreneurship as something positive while the Haitian respondents tended to view entrepreneurship as an occupation of low self-esteem. Cultural expectations were also an obstacle for one Puerto Rican woman in Washington, D.C. While she was thinking of starting a business, her brother was reminding her that she should be married.[54]

Circumstances in Society

In all societies, there are those who had not planned to be entrepreneurs but who find at some point that they are pushed toward self-employment. Workers in the United States who have been downsized might be included in this group. The decision to become an entrepreneur was precipitated by the changes in the marketplace. Immigrants in many countries follow this route if they find that their language and job skills do not meet the needs of employers. This is considered an **adaptive-response behavior**. One study of ethnocultural factors found that although some people do not come from an ethnocultural group that values entrepreneurship, they chose entrepreneurship as an adaptive response to marginality and a means to social integration.[55]

> **Adaptive-response behavior** – an individual's behavior helps him or her adjust to a new situation.

A Combination of Factors

Whether a person becomes an entrepreneur or decides to be an employee is therefore the result of many factors, including the three we have just discussed.[56]

Because such tendencies might be enhanced under the right set of circumstances, some people suggest that we should concentrate on nurturing the entrepreneurial spirit in young children. One study of kindergarten children indicated that one of every four children showed entrepreneurial tendencies. By high school age, however, only 3 percent of students still retained that spark. The current educational system does not encourage entrepreneurship and, in fact, teaches conformity rather than individuality. The creative abilities of young children are discouraged, although creativity is necessary for most entrepreneurs.[57]

Wilson Harrell, a business consultant, recommends that parents stop giving allowances and start "joint ventures" with their children instead. For example, at age six, Harrell had a lemonade stand in which his father supplied all lemons, sugar, and so on, and Harrell supplied the labor. At the end of each month, all profits were then split between the two of them. He believes the joint venture approach teaches children responsibility and also shows them that fairness builds a business. Thus, the child learns that integrity is not a legal document but a way of life.[58]

ADVANTAGES AND DISADVANTAGES OF ENTREPRENEURSHIP

There are many advantages and disadvantages to self-employment (see Figure 2–1), and the entrepreneur must be aware of both before starting a business.

Advantages

Autonomy The need for independence and the freedom to make decisions is one of the major advantages. The feeling of being your own boss is very satisfying for many entrepreneurs.

Challenge of a start-up/feeling of achievement For many entrepreneurs, the challenge of a start-up is exhilarating. The opportunity to develop a concept into a profitable business provides a significant feeling of achievement, and the entrepreneur knows that he or she is solely responsible for the success of the idea.

Financial control Because it is often stated that entrepreneurs have financial independence, one might get the impression that they are wealthy. Many are not necessarily seeking great wealth, but they do want more control over their financial situation. They do not want a boss who can unexpectedly announce a layoff after they have dedicated years of work to a company.

Disadvantages

If self-employment were easy, the number of self-employed people would be much higher. In fact, it is one of the most difficult careers one can choose. A few of the disadvantages are described next.

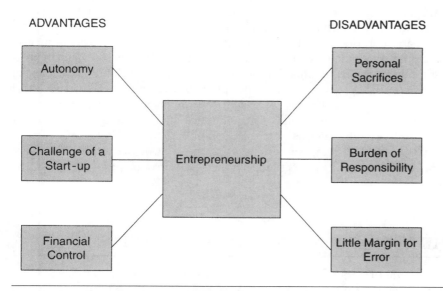

FIGURE 2–1   Advantages and disadvantages of entrepreneurship.

Personal sacrifices Especially in the early years of a business, the entrepreneur often works extremely long hours, possibly six or seven days each week. This leaves almost no time for recreation, family life, or personal reflection. The business consumes the entrepreneur's life. This often results in a strain on family relationships and a high level of stress. The entrepreneur must ask how much he or she is willing to sacrifice to make the business successful. Remi Toh, a successful entrepreneur who immigrated to the United States from Africa, found that his friends became jealous of his success. In addition, Remi and his wife separated because they could not agree on the business venture. Remi, though, was willing to pay this price of success. He stated, "I promised myself I would become somebody even if I had to kill myself trying."[59]

Burden of responsibility/jack-of-all-trades The entrepreneur has a burden of responsibility unlike that of corporate workers. In corporations, employees are usually surrounded by other people at the same level with the same concerns. It is possible to share information at lunch or after work, to have a sense of camaraderie. The entrepreneur, however, knows that it is lonely at the top. No one else in the company has invested his or her life savings; no one else must ensure that enough money is available to meet the payroll on Friday. One entrepreneur described this feeling of loneliness by saying, "I feel like I'm on an island yelling for help and no one can hear me."

The entrepreneur must also be a jack-of-all-trades. While corporate workers usually specialize in specific areas such as marketing, finance, or personnel, entrepreneurs must manage all of these functions until the business is profitable enough to hire employees with necessary expertise. The need to be an expert in many areas is an enormous burden.

Little margin for error Large corporations often make decisions that prove to be unprofitable. They introduce products that are not well accepted and they open stores in unprofitable locations. Consider, for example, EuroDisney, the theme park opened by the Walt Disney Company in France. During its first few years, it incurred enormous losses, although it had been projected to be profitable. Large corporations, such as the Disney Corporation, will usually survive because they have adequate financial resources to pay for the losses. Small businesses, however, operate on a thin financial cushion because the only financial resources available are those of the entrepreneur. Even after years of successful operation, one wrong decision or weakness in management can result in the end of the business. One small construction firm had operated successfully for seven years, reaching sales of more than $5 million, only to fail because of poor internal controls. A company is only as strong as its weakest area. Excellent performance in five areas does not compensate for poor performance in the sixth.

THE ENTREPRENEUR AND THE BUSINESS PLAN

It is important for the entrepreneur to convince bankers and investors that he or she is the right person to own and manage a business. While education and work experience are important (and will be discussed on the management section of the business plan), it is also a good idea to identify personality characteristics and other factors that indicate you will be a good entrepreneur. Therefore, a paragraph should be included in the management section of the business plan that addresses these issues.

SUMMARY

There is no consensus concerning the definition of *entrepreneur,* but most descriptions include a willingness to take risks in the pursuit of an opportunity. Paths to entrepreneurship are varied, including starting a business based on a new concept, starting a business based on an existing concept, or buying an existing business. Many forces interact to determine whether a person chooses to be self-employed or to work for someone else. These forces include the individual's traits, the culture, the circumstances in society, or a combination of these factors. There are many advantages and disadvantages of being an entrepreneur, and the life of an entrepreneur is one of challenge, personal satisfaction, personal sacrifices, and stress. Anyone considering self-employment should consider these factors carefully before making a personal and financial commitment.

DISCUSSION QUESTIONS

1. Why is there no easy way to define *entrepreneur*?
2. Do you believe that entrepreneurs are born with special characteristics, or is it possible to teach someone to be an entrepreneur?
3. Do you have any of the common characteristics of successful entrepreneurs? Which do you not have?
4. Identify some of the advantages and disadvantages of being an entrepreneur. Which advantage would be most important to you? Which disadvantage do you feel is the greatest obstacle?
5. What factors play a role in the decision to become an entrepreneur?

ENDNOTES

1. Peter F. Drucker, *Innovation and Entrepreneurship* (New York: Harper & Row, 1985), 21.

2. Michael Morris, Pamela S. Lewis, and Donald L. Sexton, "Reconceptualizing Entrepreneurship: An Input-Output Perspective," *Advanced Management Journal*, Winter 1994, 21.

3. Pramodita Sharma and James J. Chisman, "Toward a Reconciliation of the Definitional Issues in the Field of Entrepreneurship," *Entrepreneurship Theory and Practice,* Spring 1999, 11–27.

4. Ibid.

5. Morris, 21.

6. Morris, 21.

7. Paul Reynolds, "What We Don't Know May Hurt Us," *Inc.,* September 1994, 25.

8. George Gendron, "Start-up Fact and Fiction," *Inc.,* October 1994, 11.

9. Joseph A. Yarzebinski, "Understanding and Encouraging the Entrepreneur," *Economic Development Review,* Winter 1992, 32.

10. James C. Collins, "Sometimes a Great Notion," *Inc.,* July 1993, 90.

11. Ibid.

12. Ibid.

13. Leo-Paul Dana, "The Origins of Self-Employment in Ethnocultural Communities: Distinguishing Between Orthodox Entrepreneurship and Reactionary

Enterprise," *Canadian Journal of Administration Sciences,* March 1997, 52–68.

14. Nancy G. Boyd and George S. Vozikis, "The Influence of Self-Efficacy on the Development of the Entrepreneur," *Entrepreneurship Theory and Practice,* Summer 1994, 63.

15. Jon P. Goodman, "What Makes an Entrepreneur," *Inc.,* October 1994, 29.

16. Michael Morris, "From the Editor: Revisiting Who Is the Entrepreneur." *Journal of Development Entrepreneurship*, April 2002, V.

17. Michael Oneal, "Just What Is an Entrepreneur?" *Business Week/Enterprise,* 1993, 105.

18. Jeffrey P. Sudikoff, "Street Smarts," *Inc.,* March 1994, 23.

19. Goodman, 29.

20. Stan Cromie, "Entrepreneurship: The Role of the Individual in Small Business," *IBAR*, 1994, 62.

21. Gangaram Singh and Alex DeNoble, "Views on Self-Employment and Personality: An Exploratory Study," *Journal of Development Entrepreneurship*, December 2003, 265.

22. Phillip Quinn, "Living the Dream 24 Hours," *National Post Canada*, September 17, 2002, SRI.

23. Donald J. McNerney, "Truths and Falsehoods about Entrepreneurs," *HRFOCUS,* August 1994, 7.

24. Goodman, 29.

25. Leon Richardson, "The Successful Entrepreneur," *Asian Business,* July 1994, 71.

26. Lori Bongiorno, "Hot Growth Company CEOs," *BusinessWeek/Enterprise,* 1993, 133.

27. Richardson, 71.

28. Michael Warshaw, "The Entrepreneurial Mind," *Success,* April 1994, 51.

29. Yarzebinski, 32.

30. Goodman, 29.

31. Oneal, 25.

32. McNerney, 7.

33. Goodman, 29.

34. McNerney, 7.

35. Kristy Dorsey, "Entrepreneurs Who Can't Stop Taking Risks May Lose the Plot," *The Herald*, Glasgow, January 27, 2003, 19.

36. Reynolds, 25.

37. Yarzebinski, 32.

38. Oneal, 25.

39. "*Entrepreneurs,*" a film produced by Nathan Tyler Productions, 1985, aired on PBS TV.

40. Yarzebinski, 32.

41. Oneal, 25.

42. Yarzebinski, 32.

43. Goodman, 29.

44. Paul Chu, "Nolan Bushnell Brainstorms," *Success,* October 1993, 30.

45. Yarzebinski, 32.

46. Thomas M. Box, Margaret A. White, and Steve H. Barr, "A Contingency Model of New Manufacturing Firm Performance," *Entrepreneurship Theory and Practice*, Winter 1993, 31.

47. Oneal, 25.

48. Yarzebinski, 32.

49. Boyd and Vozikis, 63.

50. R.W. Lent and G. Hackett, "Career Self-Efficacy: Empirical Status and Future Directions," *Journal of Vocational Behavior,* No. 30, 347–382.

51. Christopher Neck, Heidi Neck, Charles Manz, and Jeffrey Goodwin, "I Think I Can, I Think I Can: A Self Leadership Perspective Toward Enhancing Entrepreneur Thought Patterns, Self-Efficiency, and Performance," *Journal of Managerial Psychology*, 1999, 477.

52. Dana, 52–68.

53. Ibid.

54. "Women & Minority Entrepreneurs," http://www.intuit.com/quickbooks/feature_articles/fa10007-3.html.

55. Dana, 52–68.

56. Ibid.

57. Toddi Gutner, "Junior Entrepreneurs," *Forbes*, May 9, 1994, 188.

58. Wilson L. Harrell, "Make Your Kid an Entrepreneur," *Success*, September, 1994, 80.

59. Tracy Dahlby, "The New Americans," *The Inc. Life*, a supplement to the May issue of *Inc.*, Spring 1990, 42.

Starting a New Business

LEARNING OBJECTIVES

$ To understand that the idea for a new business can come from anywhere, but the most common source is the work experience of the entrepreneur.

$ To see that the advisability of entering an industry depends on how well the customers are being served by the companies already in the industry.

$ To comprehend that the basic strategies that may be adopted by new firms are low cost, differentiation, and focus.

$ To be aware of the fact that the great majority of businesses in the United States are operated by one person, rather than some kind of partnership, despite some important advantages of multiple-person management.

Each year nearly a million people go into business for themselves. They do so in one of three ways: by buying an existing business, by becoming a franchisee, or by starting an independent business. In this chapter, we describe the process by which new businesses are established.

Have you ever wondered how businesses come into existence? On one level this question is easily answered: Someone has an idea and starts a business to exploit the opportunity that the idea represents. This, of course, is the essence of entrepreneurship and we can see it happening all around us. New businesses pop up as regularly as individuals have ideas and act on them.

When explored on a different level, however, the question of how businesses get established becomes much more complex, and a variety of issues emerge. In this chapter, we describe the process of starting a new business by exploring four sets of questions. The first concerns what the business will be—that is, what product or service will it provide, and for whom? After the issue of what has been examined, we turn our attention to why. Why do it? Why will our prospective customers buy from us? What are we going to give them that is not already available? How is the competition not serving the market? What advantage will we have over the competition? The third set of questions deals with how. Even with a well-conceived idea for which a favorable market exists, a new firm needs careful planning if it is to survive. Do we have the needed resources? Is our technical knowledge sound? Will we get orders, and will they come soon enough? Finally, we consider the issue of who. Specifically, we examine the question of whether to involve a partner.

INNOVATION AND ENTREPRENEURSHIP

One of the characteristics many people associate with entrepreneurship is innovation. People find a better way or a better mousetrap and use innovation as the basis for a new business. This is the classic pattern of entrepreneurship, and we have seen countless examples of it in our economy. Until Frederick Smith developed the hub-and-spoke system, no company could provide nationwide overnight package delivery.[1] Smith's firm, Federal Express, showed that his system worked far better than any other, and, as a result, the term *Fed Ex* has since come to be a synonym for overnight delivery.

This kind of success story supports the view that entrepreneurship and innovation go hand in hand. However, for every case of a creative idea leading to success there are many instances of innovations that did not make it. Federal Express can again be used as an example. In 1984, the company introduced ZapMail, as a supplement to its overnight letter delivery service.[2] The market rejected the service; ZapMail was discontinued in 1986 after the company had lost $340 million on the project. Federal Express's failure was by no means a first failure involving fax technology; the numerous unsuccessful attempts to commercialize the technology (patented in 1843) date back to the 1860s. As the author of an article in the publication *Business & Economic History* puts it, "Failure, the lack of technical and commercial success for a product in the marketplace, is endemic to innovative technology."[3]

Each attempt at capitalizing on innovation has its own set of problems that can keep it from succeeding. But each of the early moves toward using facsimile technology had two things in common with the others: They were based on innovative ideas, and they failed. From these examples we can conclude that innovation does not ensure survival of the enterprise; successful entrepreneurship takes more. Entrepreneurship and innovation are not one and the same.

Another reason to doubt the link between entrepreneurship and innovation is that most new businesses are very similar to many that already exist. The entrepreneur who opens a Chinese restaurant, for example, may be serving a new market, may be providing wonderful food and service, and may offer an excellent menu—a combination of factors allowing him to succeed. Whether any of these elements constitute innovation, however, is doubtful. Many similar examples of businesses starting and succeeding despite doing something that has been done many times before can be found.

In summary, while innovation is held by many people to be an essential ingredient of entrepreneurship, it is neither sufficient nor necessary for entrepreneurial success.

SOURCES OF IDEAS

Where does the idea for a new business originate? Research into this question identifies a number of sources. We examine some of the more common ones, basing our description on a survey of some of the country's fastest-growing private companies, as reported in *Inc.*[4]

Nearly half (43 percent) of the people responding to the survey reported that they got the idea for their business from the experience they gained while working in the same industry or profession. For these entrepreneurs, the move into their own business was not complicated by the task of getting to know who's who and what's what in the industry. They knew how things operate, and they typically had a network of contacts—so important in the start of a new business. The years of being in the industry gave them insights into unfilled needs and how those needs translated into opportunities for new businesses.

The importance of industry experience as a source of ideas for new businesses leads to the conclusion that the most promising preparation for an entrepreneur may be a conventional job. In addition to providing the means to discover opportunities upon which to start a business, this approach has the advantage of being much more forgiving of mistakes arising from inexperience. Mistakes are never welcome, even in a well-established business; but they are far more serious for a new business and can threaten its very existence. Not surprisingly then, many of our most successful small businesses were founded by individuals who learned what it takes to succeed while working for somebody else.

The idea second most frequently mentioned was "I saw someone else trying it, and figured I could do better." This response was given by 15 percent of the respondents. This finding is in keeping with the confidence level enjoyed by many entrepreneurs; they feel that their abilities and perseverance will give them the edge to succeed at something in which others are already engaged. This inspiration to enter into business often starts with dissatisfaction with something that is currently on the market. For example, the owner of a liquid plant-food manufacturing company found that the equipment for filling bottles was much too slow for his plant's needs.[5] He felt his company should be able to produce an improved line. The entrepreneur's confidence was warranted; his firm now sells $11 million worth of filling equipment annually.

About 11 percent of the entrepreneurs surveyed said that an "unfilled niche in the consumer marketplace" gave them the idea to start their business. This is a variation of the idea source just described. In this instance, however, the entrepreneur sees an overlooked market niche rather than one that is being ineffectively served. The wife of a Presbyterian pastor found it difficult to arrange for volunteers to provide support for the elderly and infirm members of her husband's church, but found that they were willing to pay for the help.[6] She then began to hire students to do the work, and the business quickly grew into a multistate operation with $10 million in annual revenue.

While many of us may think of the founders of successful enterprises as people who engage in careful planning, only 7 percent of the responses to the survey cited the idea for the business as having resulted from a "systematic search for business opportunities." Nearly as many (5 percent) said their business was based on an idea that resulted from a "brainstorm; can't really explain it."

The smallest category of ideas mentioned by the entrepreneurs was that of "hobby or avocational interest." Only 3 percent of the respondents mentioned hobbies.

In order to assess the importance of the *Inc.* survey results, keep two things in mind. First, the companies included in the study were members of the Inc. 500, an elite group of extraordinarily successful businesses. If the survey had included a cross section of small businesses, would the results have been the same? Probably not, we can only speculate about what differences we would have seen. (Incidentally, the problem of deciding whom to include in the study is one social scientists encounter regularly in survey research.)

The second limitation has to do with possible differences between the group of entrepreneurs who returned the data collection forms used in the study and those who did not. The issue here is whether the entrepreneurs who shared their stories have different idea sources than those who declined to participate.

These limitations notwithstanding, the *Inc.* study provides useful insights into the sources of entrepreneurial ideas and allows us to draw some general conclusions. First, the results clearly indicate the role of experience as a source of ideas. To the largest category, "working in the same industry or profession," we can add that of "hobby or avocational interest," giving us a total of 46 percent, indicating the significance of both types of experience. Nearly half of the firms were based on something the founder knew before starting the enterprise.

The Inside-Out Approach

It is useful to distinguish between two basic approaches people use as they search for opportunities for entry into business. Some entrepreneurs approach the task by looking at their own skills, abilities, background, and so on to determine what kind of business they should start. This is the inside-out approach, which is based on the notion that the key determinant of business success is, after all, the entrepreneur himself or herself. This method of entry into business is sometimes referred to as **idea generation.**

At its most basic level, this approach involves identifying your most promising skills and generating ideas as to how these skills might be shaped into the foundation of a business. Some skills have a great deal of economic potential; others do not. If you are an expert in reaching markets in third-world countries, for example, you will likely find a favorable response from many firms that are seeking to develop trade with those nations. Similarly, if you've developed a system by

Idea generation – an "inside-out" process to starting a business that starts with the entrepreneur exploring his/her skills, abilities, and interests as a means of identifying the kind of business to enter.

which organizations can reduce their energy costs, you have a promising basis for a successful new business. On the other hand, being a world-class movie trivia expert, although impressive, is not a promising base on which to found a business.

The inside-out approach is reflected in that famous piece of advice for prospective entrepreneurs, "If you build a better mousetrap, the world will beat a path to your door." The idea that your capabilities determine the right business has a sound basis. By providing something that sets you apart, you have established a possible basis for a successful business.

If we follow this approach, then, our first concern is to identify the product or service that can make our business unique. The best advice may be to be creative; consider everything that is possible. Idea generation should identify possibilities, with the evaluation of those possibilities to be made later. The logic here is first to define just what our business can do, or what it will be capable of, with the issue of whether the world needs and/or wants it to be examined later.

The Outside-In Approach

While many prospective entrepreneurs follow the inside-out approach, some turn this process around, looking first for existing opportunities. The outside-in approach, also called **opportunity recognition,** has as its basis the idea that a business can succeed only if it responds to, or creates, a need in the market.

The process is largely one of translation from general conditions or trends to specific opportunities. Many of our nation's most spectacularly successful businesses resulted from the recognition by their founders of the significance of two or more societal or economic conditions. The home shopping networks, for example, require some degree of dissatisfaction with traditional in-store shopping and widespread access to cable television. The displacement of full-service gas stations by self-serve gasoline outlets and the increasing costs of automobiles combined to create a need for facilities to provide lubrication and related services.

> **Opportunity recognition** – an approach to starting a business that begins with the question of what the world, region, or community needs and moves to design of an effective response to that need. It is an outside-in process.

Hindsight allows us to identify the trends and understand their significance; the task of the entrepreneur, however, is much more difficult, for it requires spotting the trend before others have exploited it as an economic opportunity. One requirement, then, of opportunity recognition is environmental scanning. This means deliberately searching for developments that can be translated into economic opportunity. News of these opportunities can come from a variety of sources including:

$ Newspapers allow the entrepreneur to stay abreast of emerging trends in society, fashion, technology, and home and work life as they may affect the public.

$ Business periodicals provide coverage of changes in the economy.

$ Trade journals and trade shows describe the events affecting a particular industry.

$ Government publications cover a wide range of topics. Examples include publications that give information on new patents from the Patent Office and reports on foreign markets that are published by the Department of Commerce.

$ Product licensing information is provided by independent brokers, universities, and corporations.

Although these are some of the more commonly used sources, they are by no means the only ones. Entrepreneurs are always looking for news of economic developments that will provide an opportunity for a new business.

Serendipity

Finally, it should be acknowledged that many businesses are established as the result of something other than a deliberate plan or search on the part of the founder. The name given to these starts is serendipity. Serendipity is defined as "the faculty of making happy chance finds." A serendipitous start, then, is one in which the right factors come together in such a way to allow it to happen. Examples of such starts include a manager taking over a division of a company that is about to be liquidated. The result of the takeover is that the division is reborn as an independent business. Cases such as these, in which the manager responded to the liquidation decision and as a consequence finds himself or herself thrust into the role of entrepreneur, are examples of serendipity. Other examples can be seen in cases of individuals whose jobs are eliminated but whose work remains critical. In instances such as these, the individual often provides his former employer with his or her services on a contractual basis. As an example, in 1994, an employee of a large aerospace company lost his job as a graphics designer. The company, despite its decision to lay off the designer as part of a general reduction in its workforce, realized it needed his services in graphic design and therefore hired him immediately as an outside contractor. What started as a one-customer business quickly expanded, and the designer-turned-entrepreneur now has a stable base consisting of several corporate clients.

To summarize, the genesis of business ideas has many forms, ranging from self-appraisal in the hope of finding something upon which to base a business, to a systematic search of the environment for opportunities, to simply being in the right place at the right time. Getting the idea of what the business is to be is the first step; the next step examines why. Put differently, our concern here is whether the idea makes sense. Will the business succeed? The following section describes two important determinants of small business success.

THE RATIONALE: WHY THE NEW BUSINESS IS NEEDED

Very few new businesses create new markets; for the vast majority of new businesses, the task is one of taking customers away from firms currently serving those customers. With this in mind, we see that the why issue concerns primarily the advantage the new firm will bring to the market. This advantage can be defined by customer needs and competitor capabilities.

No business, regardless of size, can serve every market. Mass marketing has given way to market segmentation. Markets may be segmented in several ways. Among the more commonly used methods of segmentation are demographic, benefit, geographic, and socioeconomic. Regardless of the basis of segmentation, the idea is to group individuals by a characteristic that has relevance to their buying decisions. For example, among the large number of breakfast cereals are many that are intended for children—an example of demographic segmentation. Some cereals are produced and marketed for people who are concerned about having a nutritious breakfast; these manufacturers are using benefit segmentation. Some firms have cereals sold only in a certain part of the country—geographic segmentation. As a final example, one of socioeconomic segmentation, consider the case of the lowest-priced cereal on the shelf. It is intended for consumers for whom price plays the most significant role in the purchasing decision.

How the members of the cereal industry compete with one another is determined to a considerable extent by how they segment the market. One of the first decisions, then, for any firm considering entry into the cereal market is who the target customer will be. And so it is with almost any industry; our products will have more appeal for certain kinds of consumers than for others. Finding out who these individuals are, how they are similar to one another, and how they differ from other members of the market is necessary for effective segmentation.

Recognizing that the market consists not of one homogeneous group of prospective buyers but rather of segments leads to the issue of benefits expected from the product. No one buys something simply to be buying it; we buy products from which we expect to receive certain benefits. We do not buy soap to own soap; we buy soap because we are convinced it will make us clean, or it will make us smell better, or it will soften our skin. We buy things because of what we feel they do for us. It is our definition, as the consumer, of a product's benefits, then, that matters most, rather than the product's attributes themselves.

We may have been able to build into our product some extremely impressive technical features only to find that consumers have no interest in them. For example, in the mid-1960s, American Motors Company had, as the mainstay of its automobile line, the Rambler. Most experts rated the car positively for its sound engineering, dependability, simplicity, and low cost. Unfortunately for AMC, these were not the kind of things being sought by many car buyers in those days, so the firm was never able to capture more than about 6 percent of the market. As sensible and straightforward as the strategy of providing the car-buying public with a low-cost, dependable automobile may have been, it didn't work. Because of what many people would describe as "irrational" motives, people chose other cars. For many people—perhaps the great majority—buying a car involves far more than getting a means of transportation. What "benefits" do you want from a car? Are dependability and low cost enough, or do you also want excitement?

Although the answer to the question of what the critical expectations of benefits of car ownership are varies with each individual, automobile firms have learned that they can get reasonably solid answers by breaking down the overall market into groups of individuals that share certain things with one another. They know, for example, that safety features are much more important to the over-50 segment than to buyers in their 20s. Does the single, white male in his early 30s have different ideas about what makes a vehicle desirable than those of his female counterpart? What if he is married, or African American? Is he a likely Rambler buyer? Probably not.

While the automobile industry provides a rich example of segmentation and how it can affect purchasing decisions, every entrepreneur must understand that markets must be broken down into distinct segments. The breakdown is the first step in identifying our company's target customers.

After identification, we must analyze the needs of the group. Who will buy from us and why will they do so? Is it because it costs them less? In some markets, this is indeed the critical element in the purchasing decision, so any firm not offering the low price is at a serious disadvantage. Most motorists, for example, will compare prices carefully when it is time to replace their tires. In other settings, quality may be the overriding consideration. If you have as your target market the drag-racing community, the key to sales is not price but performance. Providing a tire that gives those buyers even a modest improvement in acceleration will open up many prospects. Service is yet another possible reason for buying from a particular supplier. Cross-country truck drivers need to keep their rigs moving, so prompt, readily available service figures prominently in their tire buying.

After we have established a profile of who we hope will be buying from us, and for what reason, we must identify and analyze the customers' alternatives. Among these alternatives is the choice of not buying at all. If you plan to start a car-wash facility, for example, you will be providing something that customers obviously can defer, or can do on their own. Consequently, being the best and cheapest car wash in town is no guarantee of success.

Another alternative is to satisfy the need through a different means, involving a different route entirely. It wasn't until Alfred Sloan, the head of General Motors for many years, redefined the competition for Cadillacs as not Lincolns and Chryslers, but ocean cruises and expensive fur coats, that the car was effectively marketed. General Motors' task was to position the Cadillac as a status symbol rather than simply an excellent automobile. In a similar vein, the dollars spent on a European tour could have been used instead for an in-ground pool. While the travel agency and the pool seller would not identify one another as competitors, they are nonetheless competing for recreational dollars held by people who are prospective customers for both.

The most obvious, and most important, alternative to buying from our firm is buying from a competitor. This is a particularly troublesome problem as new firms enter a market. They can survive only by taking customers away from companies already established. Taking customers from another member of the industry is always difficult; for some new companies that have entered highly competitive markets, it can be nearly impossible.

THE OBSTACLES: BARRIERS TO ENTERING AN INDUSTRY

Among the barriers to entry that firms new to an industry face are customer attitudes and habits, practical concerns such as switching costs, and factors such as the likely response of established industry players.

$ *Customer attitudes and habits.* A great deal of the resistance to trying the product of a new supplier may be irrational in nature. This resistance can have as its source blind loyalty to suppliers who have served the company for years or the lethargy that develops over the years and causes people to choose the easiest way (in this case, keeping the same supplier). In both instances, the attitudes and habits of the customer create a difficult obstacle for the new firm to overcome; getting the first order can be a formidable task. Attitudes and habits typically change slowly, so the new competitor often faces a long struggle.

At issue is what it will take to get the customer to buy from the new firm. Sometimes a lower price will do it; other times it is better or faster service, or perhaps some combination of these and other factors. Beyond these considerations, the entrepreneur often must put himself or herself in the shoes of the prospective customer to be able to offer a deal that will be accepted. Although such conditions can give rise to difficult demands from the customer, the start-up business usually has the flexibility to respond in ways that most established companies cannot or will not.

$ *Switching costs.* These can be incurred when going from one supplier to the next. The costs include those of retraining workers. If the new supplier's product differs from the old one, some period of adjustment will be necessary. Another switching cost is the one encountered in modifying fixtures, tools, and so on when switching to the new system. Finally, there are the costs of checking the new supplier and phasing out the old.

$ *Response of existing competitors.* The entry of a new business into a mature or declining market is anything but a welcome development for those already there. Consequently, many companies will respond aggressively, with vigorous efforts to maintain their market shares. This is done in the hope of driving the new firm back out of the industry. The likelihood of this response is great when the market offers little or no growth or is declining, when there are exit barriers that make it costly to leave the industry, and when the industry is the only or main source of revenue for most of the industry members.

In this section, we've described how the question of why the new business is needed might be explored. The answer to the question involves two issues: the needs of consumers and the extent to which they are being satisfied by the current members of the industry. If no gap exists between what consumers want and what they are being provided, in terms of quality, price, service, selection, and product features, there is no reason to go on.

If there is a gap, however, we should explore how we can exploit the opportunity it represents. That is the issue of how, and it is the topic of our next section.

THE METHOD: HOW THE NEW BUSINESS WILL BE ESTABLISHED

Two basic routes exist for a start-up: The new firm can introduce a product that is not available to consumers, or it can add its product to those already being marketed. Each of these routes presents its own opportunities and difficulties.

The new product option is regarded by many as the purest type of entrepreneurship because it has innovation as its source. The innovative response to a need, or the creation of a need, can provide splendid opportunities for the start-up business. Introduction of a product needed by large numbers of consumers, but previously unavailable, occasionally leads to the stories of spectacular results we read of in newspapers and magazines prompting us to wonder why we didn't think of that.

The difficulties with this as a route into business include the uncertainty of consumer response to the product. Some of this uncertainty can be reduced through careful market research, as anything less than careful research can lead to disastrous results. Sound, objective analysis of the market has proven difficult for countless entrepreneurs who find it impossible to imagine that there are many people who would not buy their products. The founder of the firm is often "in love with the product" and, as a result, exaggerates the interest consumers have in his or her product. This groundless optimism, often buoyed by supportive friends, leads to reassuring, but worthless, conclusions such as "If only 2 percent of the potential market buys from us, we'll break even and we'll surely get more than that."

Even carefully conducted, unbiased market research can be hazardous as a source of data for use in financial planning. The primary problem with new product research concerns the difference between the expression of interest and actual behavior. Getting supportive answers in market research interviews is a lot easier than getting orders.

One of the major vehicles by which today's innovations are tested is provided by the cable television's home shopping channels. The first of these channels, the Home Shopping Network, was itself a service that previously had not been available.[7] The service, started in 1984, successfully challenged the conventional means of product distribution and, as the first such service, was able to establish an early dominant presence in the industry. Today many innovators compete with one another for the opportunity to showcase their products, because appearance on one of the channels brings great exposure and, with it, sales beyond that which the firm could achieve any other way. For these firms, market research was based on actual buying behavior of consumers and not just responses to survey questions.

Another shopping channel, QVC, founded in 1986, has established an important forum for introducing new products. It was through an appearance on the channel that inventor Bob Albertson was able to crack the barriers surrounding Target and Wal-Mart. As Albertson explains, "My product had been field-tested."[8] The network holds periodic open houses to determine who will be given the chance for mass market success. Think of the networks as an "Amercan Idol" for entrepreneurs.

In addition to the difficulties attendant to conventional market research, new products frequently require sizable financial commitments. The commitments, called front-end because they are encountered early in the process, include patent fees, costs of promotion and advertising, and manufacturing expenses.

For most start-ups, the situation is the opposite of that just described, that is, while a market obviously exists, so does the competition. A newcomer to a market must attract customers away from firms already in the industry. The difficulty of this task depends on a number of factors, including the intensity of competition, how well customers are being served, and the degree to which the new firm's product is differentiated from those already available.

In most industries, customers are given a great deal of attention. Buyers typically have a choice of sellers, with no need to tolerate dissatisfaction for long. If a firm does not meet the expectations of its customers, the chances are great that many of them will find another supplier. Given these circumstances, most firms try hard to please their customers. The consequences of bad service are clear: Customers will take their business elsewhere.

The importance of customer expectations is obvious, so the question of how to meet them demands careful analysis and planning. Three basic options are available. The start-up can develop a low-cost strategy, a differentiated product, or a focus on a segment of the market.[9]

In situations in which a large number of sellers are competing for buyers, competition is likely to be intense. Under these conditions, failure to meet a customer's needs will have unfortunate consequences for the seller—it will lose the customer. Buyers are seldom unaware of the bargaining power they enjoy in the buyer–seller relationship. Not only is it clear that expectations must be met; the set of expectations often becomes increasingly demanding. This escalating set of demands frequently focuses on price. When the pressure for lower price is heavy, many sellers submit to it rather than lose customers.

Occasionally new firms have the advantage of lower production costs. As examples, consider some of the airlines formed in the wake of industry deregulation in 1979. Although the market was being served by many capable airlines, the new entrants (among them Southwest, People Express, and AirWest) had the important advantage of lower labor costs because they were nonunion firms.

> **Low-cost strategy** – when a firm offers its product or service for less than its competitors.

These lower costs allowed the new firms to capture significant market shares in a highly competitive market.

Most start-up firms entering established markets, however, have costs beyond those of the established competitors. This cost disadvantage means that a low-cost strategy is not available for a start-up to enter a market; hence, the entrepreneur must develop a strategy of product differentiation or one of focus. Differentiation can be based on any feature or characteristic of the product. For example, a firm may choose to differentiate its product by providing outstanding quality. Such a strategy can succeed only if the quality advantage of the firm's products are recognized and valued by customers. Making the world's best wooden pencil will not create one additional sale if no one notices or cares. On the other hand, there may be pencil buyers who want only the best and are willing to pay for it. In this set of circumstances, a differentiation strategy based on product quality may be appropriate.

> **Differentiation strategy** – entering a market with an offering discernibly different from the competition.

Quality is only one of the possible bases upon which to build a differentiation strategy. Other possibilities include styling, service, and availability. Whatever the basis, product differentiation can be a powerful device by which a start-up can gain entry into a market.

A final strategy to consider for use in market entry is that of focus. This strategy is customer-oriented in that its basis is to understand and respond to the needs of a segment of the market in the most complete way possible. A supplier of office products, for example, may find that its real strength is its ability to anticipate and serve the needs of the educational market. Such a focus may allow the firm to establish itself as the segment leader and thereby protect itself—at least to a degree—from the difficulties of competing strictly on price.

> **Focus strategy** – based on a superior understanding of needs of customers and using that understanding to serve the market.

THE PEOPLE: WHO WILL BE INVOLVED?

Most new businesses are started by one person. That's the way entrepreneurs are and that's the way they do things. In this section, we discuss whether this solo approach makes sense.

First, let's look at the numbers. During 2001, the latest year for which nationwide totals are available, there were approximately 18.3 million sole proprietorships and 2.1 million partnerships in existence.[10] That, as you can see, is approximately a 9-to-1 ratio; small businesses are overwhelmingly a one-person undertaking. The image of the entrepreneur as the "rugged individual" is supported by the data.

Among the probable reasons that people choose to go it alone is the appeal of uncontested control of the enterprise. Things are decided by the entrepreneur in the way he or she sees fit; there is no need to clear decisions with anyone and this makes life simpler. Coordination is less complicated, and information has to be shared only to the extent that the task requires it. For the person with a firm grasp of what needs to be done to succeed and a high degree of confidence in his or her abilities to accomplish these things, the sole proprietorship is more appealing than going into partnership. Add to these attractions the fact that the profits will go to the founder only, and the 9-to-1 ratio becomes less surprising.

While the motivation is easily understood, the choice deserves careful consideration. There are some compelling reasons to enlist another person as the business is started. First is the old, and scientifically sound, adage that two heads are better than one. Having a partner may be regarded as a measure toward mistake prevention. A good partner will ask the kinds of questions and provide the kind of input that will lead to the exposure of flaws in the plans or strategy of the firm.

Another advantage of taking on a partner is that more can be accomplished by the team than by the individual. Entrepreneurs have a great deal of drive and frequently work extremely long hours, yet there obviously are limits to what they can get done. Having a partner increases the pool of time and energy available to the start-up.

Finally, a partner can provide the skills that the entrepreneur lacks but the business needs if it is to succeed. Many entrepreneurs are technically talented but have poorly developed people skills. Some are terrific salespeople but need the kind of discipline provided by an accountant.

Research into the question of the chances of success faced by the sole proprietor versus those of partners seems to be on the side of partnerships but not overwhelmingly so. For certain kinds of ventures—particularly those that are high-tech—having a partner or partners provides a clear advantage. Other important factors noted in the research are the entrepreneur (does he or she have broad experience and a balance of skills, or are there significant voids?) and the partner (what can the partner contribute?).

The demands of starting a business are such that regardless of how talented and energetic the founder of the start-up may be, help is often needed. Taking on a partner is one way to deal with this; however, a number of other means to fill the void can be identified. One route is to hire the people with the skills needed. While the hiring decision should not be taken lightly, taking on an employee is a much less momentous move than taking on a partner. Another option is to use outsiders. The outsider can be a consultant, advisor, or vendor whose role is to provide a service to the firm. This route can bring the start-up exactly what it needs while having the advantage of no expectations beyond those specified in the contract. While these services are often too costly for a new business, occasionally advisors provide free service. Some entrepreneurs have been able to make good use of boards of advisors that consist of suppliers, bankers, accountants, university professors, and others who volunteer their assistance.

THE NEW BUSINESS AND THE BUSINESS PLAN

When starting a business, there are many issues that the entrepreneur must consider. The business plan helps the entrepreneur to fully consider all of the topics that must be addressed in order for the business to be successful. It is especially helpful to develop the plan and give it to others for feedback. Often, the entrepreneur is so optimistic that the flaws in the proposed business are not evident. Giving the plan to others who are objective may provide insight on how potential customers will see the business and may prevent costly mistakes.

SUMMARY

Starting a business is a difficult undertaking that requires painstaking analysis and planning. The idea for the business can originate from a variety of sources and in a variety of ways. A new business entering an established market faces the task of taking customers from firms that have been serving those customers; the entrepreneur must examine the question of how the new firm will land those customers. A firm introducing a new product, while not faced with direct competition, has the task of winning customers nonetheless. In either case the entrepreneur must ask exactly what the new business will do for the people it hopes to have as customers. One important issue the entrepreneur must deal with is whether to start the firm alone or have a partner. Although many individuals insist on complete independence as a condition of starting a business, partnerships have important advantages that should be acknowledged.

DISCUSSION QUESTIONS

1. What role does past experience play in business start-ups? What advantages does it provide?
2. Describe the inside-out, outside-in, and serendipity processes as they relate to establishing a new business.
3. What are the primary bases for market segmentation?
4. Distinguish between differentiation and focus strategies.
5. What are the advantages of having a partnership as opposed to a sole proprietorship management structure?
6. What are the biggest difficulties faced by firms as they enter new markets?

ENDNOTES

1. "A New Kind of Flight Plan for Small Freight," *BusinessWeek*, November 3, 1973, 66–68.

2. Barton Crockett, "Federal Express Net Supports Global Cause," *Network World*, March 6, 1989, 19–20.

3. Jonathon Coopersmith, "The Failure of Fax: When a Vision Is Not Enough," *Business & Economic History*, Fall 1994, 272–282.

4. John Case, "The Origins of Entrepreneurship," *Inc.*, June 1989, 51–62.

5. Ibid.

6. Ibid.

7. "Home Shopping Readies for Second Season," *Chain Store Age Executive*, July 1988, 30–34.

8. Sasha Issenberg, "Getting Ready for Prime Time," *Inc.*, November 2003, 17–19.

9. Michael E. Porter, *Competitive Strategy* (New York: Free Press, 1980), 34–46.

10. *2004–2005 Statistical Abstract of the United States* (Washington, DC: U.S. Department of Commerce, Bureau of the Census), 718.

Chapter 4

Buying an Existing Business

For someone who is seeking the independence of small business ownership but who is not interested in undergoing the trials so frequently encountered in starting a new business, the purchase option should be explored. While both routes—starting a new business and buying an existing one—have as their goal ownership of a business, the routes themselves differ considerably. In the previous chapter, we examined the challenge of starting a business. In this chapter, we explore the process leading to the purchase of a business.

We first compare the purchase and start-up options. The process for finding a business to buy is then discussed, followed by a description of the processes used to determine the value of a business. Our last topic is negotiating; we describe it as a process and identify the sources of power held by participants.

ADVANTAGES OF BUYING A BUSINESS

A number of reasons for buying an existing business, rather than starting a new one, can be identified. There is less risk, it is easier, and there is a chance to buy the business at a bargain price.

Less Risk

Regardless of how much pre-entry planning has been done, there is always the chance that a critical factor has been overlooked, that our investigation missed some fatal flaw. If such misfortune awaits the entrepreneur, it will not matter that all other elements are as good as hoped. For example, imagine you spotted the opportunity to open a bookstore to serve students at your school. The university-run facility looks successful to you despite what seems to be a less-than-total dedication to customer satisfaction. There is a large facility across the street from campus that would be suitable in terms of both size and costs. The school has about 14,000 students, each of whom buys four to five books per semester. You figure that you should easily capture 10 percent of the market, and, with book prices and profit margins being what they are, you'll make handsome profits even during the first semester. Everything points to go, until you discover that professors' book selection information goes only to the bookstore. The information is not available to anyone else until it is too late to order from the publishers. How viable does your new business idea look now?

While more exhaustive investigation into how bookstores do business could have uncovered the problem, the point of the illustration is that every business has a number of elements that must mesh if the enterprise is to accomplish its goals. When we start a business from scratch, we occasionally do not know what these elements are. By buying a business we are able to side-step that problem, thereby reducing the level of risk we face.

Less Time and Effort Required

A moment's reflection tells us that any firm needs enough customers to generate the sales volume it must have to meet its expenses. Seldom do start-ups achieve this base until they have been in business for a while; often they need a year or more. The early days of many businesses are in large part devoted to intensive efforts to expand the customer base.

Furthermore, the operations of any business require more than customers. Employees must be hired, suppliers must be located, and service providers must be lined up. Each of these contacts takes time; arrangements must be made, details must be worked out and costs negotiated. Every entrepreneur has a number of groups or individuals with whom to deal as the business gets off the ground.

Beyond these dealings, many details require careful planning before the business can open. Inventory, furniture, layout, and physical facilities must be given attention—in some cases, painstaking attention. Items like these can require analysis, decision making, and planning. There is no escaping these requirements for the start-up entrepreneur, but the buyer of an ongoing business is spared such demands.

The Possibility of Buying at a Bargain Price

Sometimes businesses are sold for less than they are worth. This possibility gives us the last advantage of buying, instead of starting, a business. Obviously, not all businesses are underpriced; many are overpriced, and some are correctly priced. The chance of a business being priced too low seems to be largely dependent on three factors: the owner's reasons for selling, the owner's financial sophistication, and the way in which the sale is handled.

The owner's reasons for selling the business frequently have an important influence on the price demanded for the business. For example, an owner who is involved in the operation of the firm, who enjoys good health, and who has no plans other than to "maybe try something else" is not likely to accept one cent less than what he or she feels is fair. On the other hand, someone who is no longer involved in managing the business, has health worries, and has concrete plans to move on to the next phase of his or her life may want to reach a prompt conclusion by offering an attractive price.

Determining the real reason, or set of reasons, may be as simple as asking the owner. Some important parts of the story may get left out of the response, however, so the best advice here is to probe a little and investigate a lot. While most owners are forthright and honest in what they tell a prospective buyer, to assume that you will be told everything that has a bearing on their reasons for getting out is naive. It is the buyer's responsibility to talk with customers, suppliers, employees, and even competitors, where possible. In addition, company records must be closely scrutinized and information about the industry gathered and analyzed. Nowhere in this information will the list of the owner's "real" reasons for selling be found, of course, but the prospective buyer will understand the situation far more thoroughly and be much more likely to make accurate assessments about the owner's attitude toward selling.

Some owners do a better job of building their business than they themselves realize. In these situations, basic financial and competitive analysis will quickly show that a difference between the owner's evaluation and an objective appraisal exists. That difference can be the result of the owner not recognizing the strengths of his or her business and/or using poorly conceived methods of evaluation. Three inadequate methods of evaluation are described here: the "I know what it cost me" approach, the "I know what I have to take out of here" approach, and an approach based on the price commanded by similar firms.

In the "I know what it cost me" approach, the owner reflects back on all he or she has put into the business. The hard work, the risks, the personal sacrifices, and so on all go into the computations. Do these things tell us how much the business is worth? Of course not. The value of a business is independent of what was put into it—but try telling the owner to ignore these investments. Many owners, perhaps the great majority of them, will let this reasoning lead them to an inflated estimate of the business's value. For some, however, the inputs are less dearly valued, and in these circumstances the possibility of discovering a bargain exists.

The second nonanalytical approach is based on what the owner needs to gain from the sale of the business. Some owners have goals for not only their own financial security but that of their offspring as well. These, obviously, can be formidably large amounts and, indeed, are often far beyond what any objective appraisal would show as the value of the business. But once again, the possibility of an owner's aspirations being below the actual value of the business does exist. Some entrepreneurs have lived simply and have saved lavishly; to such owners, the proceeds from the sale are little more than frosting on their financial cake.

Another of these nonanalytical methods involves basing the selling price on what a similar business has been able to fetch. This approach has its roots in real estate selling, where the sale of one four-bedroom house in a neighborhood has an important bearing on the value of another. While this is a useful source of information in the housing market, it provides little guidance in determining the value of a business. Where it is used, the possibility of a firm being underpriced is created.

A final influence that may give rise to a bargain price concerns the way in which the sale is made. First, there is the matter of the conditions leading to the firm being put on the market. Was it planned, with ample opportunity to find out what the market was like? Under such conditions, the seller was probably trying to time the sales with the economy being robust, with the industry enjoying good times and the firm experiencing a profitable period. This rare combination is a seller's delight and puts strong upward pressure on the asking price.

Businesses put up for sale without the benefit of any of these conditions are subjected to considerable skepticism and pessimism. The resulting downward pressure on the selling price can be strong enough to lower it substantially. If the seller does not have the option to ride out the bad times, a bargain may be available.

In addition to the kinds of conditions just described, the person doing the selling can affect the sales price. The seller may choose to handle the sale himself or herself. This common choice, while it fits with the entrepreneur's image of self-reliance, may be a mistake. Buying a business from its founder can be a difficult experience. Most people who start and develop a business have a sizable emotional investment in it. Through the years, the business has often had a negative impact on family relations, leisure pursuits, and personal health. For them, selling is a major step, perhaps the biggest single move of a lifetime. The chances of a buyer getting a bargain are not good, but they can be improved if the owner sees in the prospective buyer qualities the business needs.

In contrast, the family of a deceased company founder may be very cooperative and willing to negotiate. Often the family's chief concern is to sell the business while it remains a viable, ongoing concern. Obviously this set of circumstances works to the advantage of the prospective buyer.

Selling a business is a time-consuming and demanding task, one that requires skills and background beyond that of most entrepreneurs. The complexity of the

Business brokers – agents who are contracted by the owner of a business to arrange its sale.

task of selling being what it is, owners typically get help to do it. Intermediaries, also called *brokers* are agents who arrange the sale. Although the owner can do it alone, intermediaries are frequently employed because they provide some important advantages, including experience, objectivity, negotiation skills, knowledge of buyers, and maintenance of confidentiality.

In summary, the independence of spirit and action, so characteristic of many entrepreneurs, can betray the entrepreneur when it comes time to sell the business. The prospective buyer should take this into account as he or she proceeds in the search for the right business.

DISADVANTAGES OF BUYING A BUSINESS

As you can see, there are many good reasons for buying, rather than starting, a business, but some problems or disadvantages should be acknowledged. Put differently, although an ongoing business does not require the entrepreneur to look after the many details and problems of a start-up, it does provide certain limitations. Before an entrepreneur decides on the buy option, he or she should understand the kinds of inherent limitations that may be encountered in the purchase of an existing business. These limitations, or disadvantages, can be categorized as external (environmental), internal, and the impact of the owner's departure.

The Environment

One reason for selling a business is inadequate sales volume. If sales levels are low, even an extremely well-run operation can fall short of the profit level needed to support the owner. Firms with low sales either face too much competition or are in a market that is too small. For example, a bakery in a community of 100,000 may face such difficult competition that it will be stuck with marginal sales volume until it finds a more effective way to compete. That same bakery in a community of 2,500 may have no competition but nonetheless face the same inadequate sales problem. The problem looks the same, but in the first instance, it is caused by tough competition, something the store can respond to; in the second case, the market is simply too small. There are not enough customers in a town of 2,500 to support the store, and no amount of hard work or clever promotion is going to change that. See Table 4-1 for a list of estimates of population bases needed to support different kinds of businesses.

Both problems—the competition and the size of the market—are environmental, meaning they are outside the firm. But they have an important impact on profitability and, therefore, on the attractiveness of the business as a possible purchase. In addition to identifying the competitors, the prospective buyer must analyze how the competition is carried out. Do the members of the industry compete on price? On quality? On service? What are the market segments? How aggressive are the competitors? Is there a dominant industry leader?

Other questions are relevant to the market as a whole. What is its size? Is it growing? At what rate? Are changes in technology about to affect the industry? Every business must cope with its environment; some environments are friendly, some are hostile. Knowing what kind of environment the prospective purchase is in is an important part of the background for the interested buyer.

TABLE 4–1   Estimated population needed to support business ventures

TYPE OF BUSINESS	NUMBER OF INHABITANTS NEEDED PER STORE	TYPE OF BUSINESS	NUMBER OF INHABITANTS NEEDED PER STORE
Food Stores		Building Material, Hardware, and Farm Equipment Dealers	
Grocery stores	1,534		
Meat andΩ seafood markets	17,876	Lumber and other building materials	
Candy, nut, and confectionery stores	31,409	dealers	8,124
Retail bakeries	12,563	Paint, glass, and wallpaper stores	22,454
Dairy product stores	41,587	Hardware stores	10,206
Eating, Drinking Places		Farm equipment dealers	14,793
Restaurants, lunchrooms, caterers	1,583	Automotive Dealers	
Cafeterias	19,341	Motor vehicle dealers—new and	
Refreshment places	3,622	used cars	6,000
Drinking places (alcoholic beverages)	2,414	Motor vehicle dealers—used	
General Merchandise		cars only	17,160
Variety stores	10,373	Tire, battery, and accessory dealers	8,864
General merchandise stores	9,837	Boat Dealers	61,526
Apparel and Accessory Stores		Household Trailer Dealers	44,746
Women's ready-to-wear stores	7,102	Gasoline Service Stations	1,195
Women's accessory and specialty stores	25,824	Miscellaneous	
Men's and boys' clothing and furnishing		Antique and secondhand stores	17,169
stores	11,832	Book and stationery stores	28,584
Family clothing stores	16,890	Drugstores	4,268
Shoe stores	9,350	Florists	13,531
Furniture, Home Furnishings, and		Fuel oil dealers	25,425
Equipment Stores		Garden supply stores	65,118
Furniture stores	7,210	Gift, novelty, and souvenir shops	26,313
Floor covering stores	29,543	Hay, grain, and feed stores	16,978
Drapery, curtain, and upholstery stores	62,460	Hobby, toy, and game shops	61,430
Household appliance stores	12,585	Jewelry stores	13,495
Radio and television stores	20,346	Liquified petroleum gas (bottled gas)	
Record shops	112,144	dealers	32,803
Musical instrument stores	46,332	Liquor stores	6,359
		Mail-order houses	44,554
		Merchandising machine operators	44,067
		Optical goods stores	62,878
		Sporting goods stores	27,063

Source: Starting and Managing a Small Business of Your Own (Washington, DC: Small Business Administration, 1973).

Internal Problems

These are problems unique to the business. Perhaps the most vexing of these problems is one of poor corporate image or reputation. We have all seen signs telling us a business is "under new management." The real message is "We know you have not been happy with the company. Please give us another try." It is impossible to say how effective the appeal is in winning back customers, but it seems clear that there would be no such announcement if there weren't some concern about image or reputation.

Another difficult type of problem occasionally faced by buyers is provided by employees. A history of employee–management conflict will not be erased by a change in ownership. The employees, or their union representatives, may use the opportunity to improve relations, or they may dump on the new owner a number of unsettled grievances. The nature of their reception of the new boss is obviously crucial and must be carefully assessed. Even a friendly reception, however, can be accompanied by some powerful union restrictions on any personnel changes, no matter how reasonable and badly needed they may be.

Another example of an internal problem is something as basic as location. This factor is particularly important, of course, in retailing. If the business is in a mall or shopping district that has developed a bad reputation, the business will surely suffer. If the business depends on automobile traffic, any future or even potential rerouting of highways could have devastating effects.

Departure of the Current Owner

Many businesses are "one-person shows." Any firm in which the owner is the only employee is probably linked inextricably to that individual. Taking over the business may mean having to operate in the shadow of the founder for a long time. This kind of situation is particularly troublesome when the company's business involves providing close service to clients. One-person firms in public relations, advertising, and accounting are examples of such businesses. The level of trust and confidence that the founder has worked for years to establish cannot be automatically transferred to the new owner.

FINDING THE BUSINESS

Once you have decided to go into business by buying one that is up and running, the next step is to find it. In doing so, you'll probably have to consider a number of them before you get to the one that fills the bill for you. Locating these candidates is a daunting prospect, but consider the fact that there are 22 million businesses in existence.[1] Granted, some of them are extremely large and therefore beyond the price range of individuals, some are unacceptable because of the kind of industry in which they operate, and some are owned by people who would sooner sell their souls than their businesses. But if these and other factors result in the pool of candidates being reduced by 99 of every 100 possibilities, there are still more than 200,000 remaining—a vast pool of prospects. Your tasks are to cut that figure down to a manageable number— that is, one for which careful research can be conducted—and then find the best of those remaining businesses to determine how much it is worth and to negotiate the right deal for it. We cover those topics in the rest of this chapter.

Businesses on the Market

These businesses are often listed in the classified ads of newspapers in much the same way that houses and cars are listed. Sometimes, the owner is doing the selling, just as is the case with houses. For many businesses, however, a broker has been enlisted to make the sale. Although brokers have a number of channels for telling prospective buyers what is available, they use the classified ads, as do private sellers. Local businesses can be found in the local newspapers; *The Wall Street Journal* features businesses from around the country and the world in its classified section. In addition to the candidates appearing in the newspaper ads, business brokers can be used. Not all brokers use the ads, and, for those that do, not all of their listings are put in newspaper ads. Consequently, discussions with the brokers of a community should be an early part of any search.

Finding businesses for sale is not a problem; finding a good one may be. Think for a minute of the things that may prompt the owner to decide to sell the business. There are many reasons for selling out, but one that may be more common than any other is that the business is struggling; it is not giving the owner the kind of return to make it all worthwhile. Is that the business you want? It may be if you can bring to it important improvements, the kind of improvements in operations or strategy that will lead to better returns. Those improvements should be clearly developed ideas that you know can be put into place, rather than an optimistic, but vague, notion that under your management, the place will surely run better than it does now.

If slumping sales seem to be the cause of the problem of a business you are investigating, it is essential that you have a firm plan for remedying the problem before you proceed far toward purchase. Is the entire industry experiencing the same kind of turndown? Is it a cyclical movement or is long-term demand decreasing? The need for an exhaustive search for information about the company and the industry is clear. Only with a thorough understanding of the company's strengths and weaknesses will you be able to determine the nature of the problem and what it means for the long-term prospects of the business.

Businesses Not on the Market

Not all businesses on the market have serious problems, of course, but enough of them do to make us broaden the search and look for candidates for purchasing that are not on the market. Why would we be able to buy a business that has not been listed in the newspaper ads or been put in the hands of a broker? The answer is that for most businesses, we can't. They will remain in the hands of their current owners because these people have no interest in selling.

For some owners, however, the thought of selling has been with them for a while. Many business owners will tell you that anybody who owns a business and tells you he or she has never thought of selling it is lying. For most, the feeling passes quickly, and they get on with running their company. For some, however, the feeling never leaves completely even as they attend to the demands of their firm. This press of business, procrastination, inertia, and uncertainty may keep the owner from taking the first steps toward putting the company on the market.

How can you find these businesses? Two approaches are available. The first is to contact people who are likely to have contact with this group of prospects. Some people you might contact are bankers, lawyers, and accountants. Notice that the list does not contain brokers; we are looking for possibilities that are not listed anywhere. Our dealings with these contact people are simple and direct; we ask them if they know of any business that might be available for sale. We do not ask for names; that would be suggesting that they betray the confidence of their clients. We are hoping that the individual passes along the news of our interest to anyone he or she knows, or suspects, would be interested. This is the indirect approach.

The direct approach puts us into contact with the prospect without the use of an intermediary. We call, or visit, the owners of businesses that we have identified as suitable. Rather than risk offending them or looking presumptuous, we ask if the owner knows of any similar businesses that may be for sale. There are three possible answers: (1) no, (2) yes, I think there is one across town, and (3) yes, as a matter of fact, I've been thinking a bit about that possibility myself.

The process we have just described is straightforward, but a word of warning should be given: It takes a great deal of homework to make yourself a creditable prospective buyer. If the owner views you as doing nothing more than fishing around, he or she is not going to treat you seriously. The same holds true for the indirect approach, incidentally.

Now that a prospect has been located, we must determine what price we should pay for the firm and we must prepare for negotiation of the transfer.

DETERMINING THE PRICE OF A BUSINESS

Price – the amount for which the owner of a business is willing to sell that business.

Value – the worth of a business as determined by the market, that is, the level at which the buyer and seller agree.

Book value – the value of a firm's assets, as reported on its financial statements.

Replacement value – the cost of purchasing an asset.

Liquidation value – the price an asset would bring if it were offered for sale.

Appraised value – an asset's value as determined by an independent industry expert.

Before any bid on the business is made, the prospective buyer will have to determine the value of the enterprise. Notice we used the word *value*. Value is defined by Webster as "the monetary worth of something: marketable price."[2] It is the price for which the business can be purchased; consequently, it is the figure we are given when we ask how much the owner wants for the business. The owner can put the business on the market for any price he or she chooses. The response of prospective buyers determines whether the price exceeds the value they ascribe to the business. We have more to say about the difference between price and value in the next section. For now let's just say the seller has to set the price of the business, while the market will determine its value—and that happens when a buyer agrees that it is worth the amount the owner is asking. While coming up with a figure is an inexact process that takes on many forms, two basic considerations should be included: the value of the business's assets and its future earnings.

When a business is purchased, the new owner gets the assets. There are four ways to figure the value of these assets. First, we can simply look up the values in the firm's books; this figure is called, not too surprisingly, the *book value*. The figure reflects the original cost of the assets minus the depreciation that has occurred. The *replacement value* is also a straightforward figure but not as readily available as book value. To get this figure, we have to check the market for each of the firm's assets to determine what it would cost to purchase them. Another way to view the value of assets is by what they would bring if we were to sell them; this is their *liquidation value*. Finally, there is the assets' *appraised value*, or the value of an asset as determined by an independent industry expert. This figure should reflect the appraiser's knowledge of the market for the asset, and it should take into account both the supply of and demand for the item. These four different views of value usually lead to four different results; we use an example to illustrate why this is so.

Suppose you are interested in buying a certain restaurant. You have a copy of the company's books and you have inspected the facility closely, making notes of all of the assets as you did. Among the company's many assets is a large, stainless steel sink-counter combination. The original cost of the unit was $8,000. It has been depreciated at the rate of $800 per year for five years, leaving a book value of $4,000. You contact the local institutional kitchen supplier and are told that to replace the combination would take $10,000; this is, of course, the replacement value. Very few kitchens will be able to use the sink-counter, so selling it is going to be quite difficult. Let's say the liquidation value is $500. This range of "values" is so wide that it is hard to have confidence in any of them, so you decide to hire an appraiser, and she says it is worth $1,500.

These figures are so widely ranging that you're not sure what to do, but you do want to know which of these figures is best because you must come up with an offer. Your first instinct is to be cautious, but if you are too conservative and use liquidation value for all of the restaurant's assets, you will likely settle on a figure so low that your bid is certain to be rejected. Yet one of the concerns you have is how much would it cost you if you were to fail in this undertaking. The liquidation figure provides protection because among the things you would have to cushion your losses are the proceedings from the sale of the assets. How much is the five-year-old large, stainless steel sink-counter combination worth? Very little, as we have said. The liquidation value, then, is the "best" only if the buyer's concern about possible financial loss is so strong that even a little risk is unacceptable.

If, on the other hand, you want very badly to buy the business because you are so sure it's right for you, you may decide to go with the replacement cost figure. If you do, you will likely be bidding far more for the business than necessary to reach agreement with the owner.

Is the book value the "right" amount? It is not likely to be, because it is only a bookkeeping entry. Had the restaurant's accountant decided the unit had an 8-year life instead of 10, the more rapid depreciation rate would have dropped the book value to $3,000 instead of its current $4,000. Book value seldom matches actual value.

This leaves us with the appraised value. It is the most useful of figures and is, therefore, the basis for seller–buyer negotiations. Knowing the other methods of evaluation, however, will deepen your understanding of the value of the business and allow you to judge whether the appraised-value figure is accurate.

As you scan the financial records of the restaurant, you notice that in addition to items such as the sink-counter, ovens, tables, chairs—the firm's tangible assets—there is something labeled goodwill. This is one of the company's assets, albeit an intangible asset. Any company that has been in business for a number of years and has established a reputation for being reasonable or better in terms of price, quality, and service is worth more than the sum of individual items it owns. Is it worth something to a company to have people know that it can serve them? Of course it is, and that is why goodwill is listed as an asset on financial records. The definition of goodwill is the value of a firm that can be traced to its reputation in the marketplace. Other intangible assets include such things as proprietary processes, established distribution systems, customer databases, and custom-designed software.

It is easy to see that these kinds of assets are of value, for without them the company would be worth less—in some cases, much less. It is not easy, however, to determine *how much* they are worth. For the most common of these kinds of assets, goodwill, a number of factors are taken into account: the age of the business, its record of profitability, and its share of the market among them. The tendency for sellers is to exaggerate the importance of these items, but buyers will often counter by downplaying their significance. The buyer must recognize the

> **Tangible assets** – a firm's material possessions.

> **Intangible assets** – elements of the value of a business, including goodwill, established processes, and customer relationships.

TABLE 4–2   Present value of future earnings of $10,000

YEAR PAYMENT IS RECEIVED	3%	6%	9%	12%
		INTEREST RATE		
1	$9,709	$9,434	$9,174	$8,929
5	8,626	7,473	6,499	5,674
10	7,441	5,584	4,224	3,220
15	6,419	4,173	2,745	1,827
20	5,537	3,118	1,784	1,037

legitimacy of goodwill and other intangible assets, but must be alert to sellers who have an inflated assessment of their value.

In addition to the assets—tangible and intangible—the buyer gets upon acquiring the business, he or she gets the liabilities. These are the legal obligations of the firm to its creditors. When we buy the business, as a business, we get both sides of the balance sheet—the assets and the liabilities. There are two basic ways we handle liabilities: We can ask that the obligations be met by the owner, thereby removing them from the balance sheet; or we can adjust our offer by deducting the amount owed from the figure we got for the company assets.

After we have determined the value of all of the business's assets and deducted the amount it owes to creditors, we have completed one method of evaluation. This method, however, is regarded by many as inadequate, because a business is more than a collection of assets. A business is a means of generating future financial returns, or profits. These expected future earnings provide the basis for the other method of evaluation. If we expect that a business will be around for the next 10 years and that it will earn $50,000 per year during the period, we can calculate just how much the business is worth as an income producer. The simple answer is that it is worth $500,000. Unfortunately, this answer is too simple because it does not reflect the time value of money. That is, the $50,000 we will earn in year 10 is worth considerably less than the $50,000 we earn in year 1. The reason for this is that we can accumulate approximately $50,000 in 10 years if we invest $25,000 now and let it accumulate interest at 7 percent. That is the magic of compounded interest. But we will not be receiving this sum for several years, and so today, future money is worth less than the same sum in hand today. The method by which these differences in time value are determined is called *discounting future cash flows*. The process uses a formula or table to bring to the present the value of the money we will be earning. As another example of the difference resulting from the use of this discounting, consider the fact that $0.62 invested at 10 percent will be worth $1 in five years, so $50,000 in year 5 is actually worth $31,000 today. Table 4-2 provides examples of the future value of $10,000 at various interest rates.

If we knew for certain what the business's future earnings would be, the process would simply be one of computation. The process is by no means that simple, unfortunately, because we do not know what the earnings stream will be. We know what the past earnings record has been, of course, and that gives

Compounded interest – the amount earned on interest accumulated during past periods.

Discounting future cash flows – a process by which the present value of money to be earned (or owed) in the future is determined.

TABLE 4–3   Determining the price of a business

The value of a business can be determined many different ways. The following method uses three factors to determine a company's value: the adjusted net worth, past earnings, and future earnings.

Step 1:   Determine the company's net worth.

Tangible net worth = market value − liabilities + goodwill

Example:

Tangible net worth = $120,000 − $40,000 + $20,000
Tangible net worth = $100,000

Step 2:   Incorporate past earnings. A company with a history of making money will usually continue to make money. Using that assumption, we capitalize a company's annual earnings by multiplying by a factor usually ranging from 5 to 10. The number we use depends on our judgment of how good the business is, using elements such as growth rate, market share, company reputation, quality of the product line, and so on. We will say the firm earned $20,000 last year and that it has little competition, loyal customers, and an excellent growth record, so we will use 9 as our multiplier.

Capitalized earnings = $20,000 × 9
Capitalized earnings = $180,000

Step 3:   Discount future earnings. The closest thing to the true value of a business is its future stream of earnings. Let's assume here that the business will stay at its current earnings level of $20,000. As stated in the text, we must consider the discount rate. If we use a discount rate of 10%, and if we assume that the annual earnings will continue forever, the discounted future earning will be:

Discounted future earnings $20,000/.10 = $200,000

Step 4:   Compute market value. We just used three approaches to determine the value of the business; because each of the approaches has strengths and weaknesses, the last step is to combine them to arrive at a price. To do so, we will use a method of weighted average. This method requires judgment and insight into the business. For example, the price of a business with large holdings in physical assets, operating in an industry where the market is shrinking, would perhaps best be computed using a 50 percent weight for the Step 1 figure, and 25 percent for each of the earnings amounts. Using these weights, the price would then be computed as follows: ($100,000 × .5) + ($180,000 × .25) + ($200,000 × .25) = $50,000 + $45,000 + $50,000 = $145,000.

Source: Adapted from Thomas W. Goldberg, R.L. Hulett & Company, St. Louis, MO.

---

us a basis for making a projection, but change is a rule of life, and each change can affect earnings. Consequently, determination of value based on future profits requires more than computation. Judgment must be used, assumptions need to be made, and the results of the process must be held up for close scrutiny.

As an example of a method that blends the methods described here, see Table 4-3.

THE NEGOTIATING PROCESS

Suppose you decided to sell something—a bike, we'll say. You set the price at $100. You thought about this figure for a while, and you checked with some friends, so you feel pretty comfortable with it. The first person that responds to your ad asks you how much you want for the bike, and you tell him $100. He responds instantly that he'll take it. How do you feel now? A little empty, maybe, like you should have asked for more, is our guess. What if he had said, "I'll give you $90," you had said "Make it $95," and he then accepted? Would you feel better then, even though the final price is $5 less than in the first case? If you are like most people, you would. Price is important, of course, but so is the process by which we arrived at it.

The same thing is true on the buying side. If you were the buyer of the bike and your counterproposal of $90 had been immediately accepted, you might feel that you should have tried $75. Here, too, the final price is not the only thing; the process is important as well.

Price Versus Value

Ask a business owner what the business is really worth and you will likely get the response that he or she does not know. This would be the case with many owners, and yet when it comes time to sell the business, a price must be set. So there is the seller's dilemma: He or she does not know the value but must nonetheless set the price. Setting a price obviously does not make the business worth that amount, so price and value are two different things.

While there are computational methods for arriving at a figure that a business is worth, its value is set only in the marketplace. The value of a business is what someone is willing to pay for it. As was mentioned earlier, the price may be set by the seller, but the value is determined by buyers. When one agrees that the business is worth as much or more than the price being asked, the sale gets made.

Another factor that can keep price from matching value is seen when the owner does not realize the potential of the business. As examples, we describe a dry-cleaning business under several conditions. First, consider a facility that is located adjacent to a station on a newly completed mass transit system. If the owner evaluates the business on the basis of profitability during recent years, he or she may be guilty of serious undervaluation. A more accurate evaluation might be reached by regarding the facility as a possible site for an entirely new business. Such an evaluation might be significantly higher than one that focuses on the business as it currently exists. If the store were in a less desirable location, however, the owner's use of the financial statements of the last few years might lead to an overestimate of the value of the business because it does not take into account such factors as the emergence of the new competitors and changes in traffic patterns.

In some cases the owner may realize the value of the business but choose to set the price elsewhere. For example, it may be important to the owner that the business be operated in the manner that she finds reasonable and in keeping with the tradition she has established. With these concerns in mind, the owner may be inclined to sell to "the right person" at a price that is a bit more attractive than the maximum she could get for it.

Finally, we should keep in mind that price is only one of the factors making up the sales package. The terms of the deal, the rate of payment, and various nonfinancial arrangements are examples of such factors. One owner may respond favorably to office space and other support of his interests, another may enjoy serving as a company director, and yet another may want to continue to deal with her longtime customers. Such arrangements may fit nicely into the seller's plans while costing the buyer little or nothing and even being beneficial on occasion.

Sources of Power in Negotiations

From time to time during the negotiations between the two parties, differences in power become obvious. In order to negotiate effectively, it is important to understand how each side obtains power.

Perhaps the most important source of power during negotiations of any kind is information. The value of the firm is influenced by a number of factors, including the market, the competition, and societal and environmental trends. Unless the buyer has full and reliable information, he or she is at a serious disadvantage. Information is vital to a strong bargaining position, and that information should come from a number of sources. The worst mistake a buyer can make in this regard is to rely completely on the seller for information. Under such an arrangement, the seller decides what to let you have access to, and this, of course, means anything that sheds a bad light on the company may be withheld. The best advice for the buyer, then, is to be as self-reliant as possible. Do your homework thoroughly; trusting the seller is commendable, but relying on him or her as your only source of information is not wise.

In addition to information, negotiating power is affected by pressure from others. If a firm has several owners and two of them are more eager to sell than the others, the person representing the company will be in an uncomfortable position. Part of the group is interested in a quick sale; another part will want to maximize the final settlement; and others may want certain stipulations included in the contract. The distractions that these demands create for the selling side can work to the buyer's advantage.

Negotiations are also affected by timing. If, for example, the seller has already purchased another business and must make the first payment on that purchase before long, the prospective buyer finds his or her situation quite desirable. This is particularly true if the buyer is the only or leading candidate to purchase the firm. If the shoe is on the other foot, however, and the buyer has been given a deadline by his or her backers to make the deal or go without them, the buyer will find that time is his or her enemy. The best situation is to have more time than the other side.

Power in negotiations is also influenced by the alternatives held by each side. Someone who is selling a business because it is the only way to clear up a difficult problem is likely to be much more agreeable than someone for whom selling is only one of a number of possibilities. For the buyer, the same is true. If you have already identified three or four businesses that you feel are attractive possibilities, going into discussions to investigate another is an entirely different matter than if you saw this as your last resort. Another alternative that the typical buyer has is conventional employment. It may not appeal to you if you have made up your mind to go out on your own, but having a job offer in hand can nevertheless change the way in which the negotiations proceed. The counterpart option for the seller is to have the business run by a professional manager. It may not be the owner's first choice, but it may be better than selling for too low a price.

BUYING A BUSINESS AND THE BUSINESS PLAN

When buying a business, many people may think a business plan is not necessary since the business already exists. However, the entrepreneur must still complete a business plan because many things will change when the new owner assumes control. In order to make sure that the business has been fully researched and that no surprises occur, it is best to complete a business plan detailing how the business will operate. Projected financial statements are essential since the expenses may increase if the buyer borrows money for the purchase price. Conversely, some expenses of the previous owner may be eliminated if they are not essential. Legal issues must also be addressed, such as whether or not the former owner has signed a non-compete clause, preventing him from opening a similar business nearby. For this reason, a detailed business plan is just as important when buying a business as when starting a new one.

SUMMARY

Buying an existing business can provide an entrepreneur with an expeditious route into small business. The processes of locating, selecting, and negotiating for the enterprise require careful preparation. The process of locating a business to buy should include businesses that are on the market as well as those that are not. In the search for a candidate for purchase that is not on the market, the prospective entrepreneur would likely ask a large circle of people whether they knew of any businesses that might be for sale, but have not yet been put on the market. After identifying the target for purchase, the entrepreneur must research the possibility to determine the current value of the firm and its future prospects. This information will give the entrepreneur a basis to negotiate effectively. Without solid information, the odds of striking a favorable deal diminish considerably.

DISCUSSION QUESTIONS

1. Why is buying a business a less risky proposition than starting one?
2. How could you go about finding a business to buy if you didn't see anything in the classified ads that you liked?
3. Why is the negotiating process so important in the purchase of a business?
4. What are the two major determinants of the value of a business? Explain each of them.
5. Distinguish between price and value. What does it mean to say that the owner sets the price of a business, but the buyer sets its value?
6. Explain the sources of power for the parties in negotiations.

ENDNOTES

1. *2004–2005 Statistical Abstract of the United States* (Washington, DC: U.S. Department of Commerce, Bureau of the Census), 544.

2. *Webster's Ninth New Collegiate Dictionary* (Springfield, MO: Merriam-Webster, Inc., 1983), 1303.

Chapter 5

Franchising and Other Alternatives

LEARNING OBJECTIVES

$ To know why franchising has become an extremely popular way of going into business.

$ To understand the many significant advantages to an entrepreneur being a part of a franchise chain.

$ To know the franchisees' legal protection from being rushed into a premature decision by the franchisor.

$ To be aware that despite government regulations, many individuals are cheated by unscrupulous sellers of franchises and business opportunities.

$ To understand what the failure rate of franchises really is and what it means.

We have just examined two ways for an entrepreneur to go into business: by starting one or by buying one. In this chapter, we describe a third option—becoming franchised. We first define it as a concept; we next consider some of the reasons for its popularity, and we identify and explain some of the problems associated with the practice. Finally, we discuss the growing use of "business opportunities" as a means of entry into small business.

One of the more remarkable economic developments in the 20th century was been the growth in franchising as a way to do business. Much of the early activity in franchising was of a type known as *product franchising*.[1]

Under this arrangement, dealers were given the right to distribute goods for a manufacturer. For this right, the dealer (the franchisee) paid a fee for the right to sell the trademarked goods of the producer (the franchisor).

Perhaps the first important use of product franchising can be seen in the efforts of the Singer Corporation during the 1800s to distribute its sewing machines.[2] This practice then became common in the petroleum and automobile industries early in the 20th century.

Manufacturing franchising is commonly used in the soft-drink industry. Using this kind of franchising, the franchisor gives the dealer (bottler) the exclusive right to produce and distribute the product in a particular area.

The last type of franchising, business-format franchising, is what most people today mean when they use the term *franchising*. It is the most popular form, accounting for nearly 75 percent of all franchised outlets in the United States.[3] Business-format franchising is an arrangement under which the franchisor offers a wide range of services to the franchisee, including marketing, advertising, strategic planning, training, production of operations manuals and standards, and quality-control guidance. Because of the wide and growing popularity of this type of franchising, we focus on it in this chapter.

> **Franchising** – a legal arrangement by which one company allow its products, services, or business format to be used by others for a fee.

> **Franchisee** – a company or individual who pays for the legal right to use the product, service, or format of another.

> **Franchisor** – the party that grants to a company or individual the legal right to use the franchisor's products, services, or format.

THE POPULARITY OF FRANCHISING

Franchising has made its mark not only in the United States but throughout the world. The logos of many retailing giants are seen in shopping centers around the globe, as are the logos of many small and moderate-sized establishments. This has not been the result of franchising practices exclusively, but clearly they have played a major role in the globalization of products.

Much of the vitality of franchising has come from U.S. firms looking for new markets and finding them on all the continents. But while the United States may still have the dominant role in the spread of franchising, the rest of the world is becoming increasingly active. There remains, however, great potential for expansion in franchising in the international arena; in the European economy, for example, to reach the same level of penetration as achieved by U.S. franchisers would require doubling the existing number of franchised outlets.

In the United States, the influence of franchising can be clearly seen in the results of a recent study, which found that franchised businesses accounted for more than $1 trillion in sales during 2000.[4] The same study showed that franchised outlets account for 40 percent of all retail sales.[5] To these impressive indicators of growth can be added important considerations concerning employment and job creation. More than 8 million people are employed by franchised establishments, and more than 170,000 new jobs are created each year by franchised businesses.[6] In summary, it is clear that franchising is an increasingly significant component in the U.S. economy. We now discuss some of the reasons why franchising has grown as it has.

ADVANTAGES FOR THE FRANCHISEE

Firms that use franchising as a means to expand do so because they believe the franchisor-franchisee relationship is a symbiotic one. That is, each party provides the other something beneficial it would not have been able to provide for itself. Both gain from the relationship and both must contribute. The two parties are interdependent. The franchisor's interests are best served by having each of its outlets succeed, and because this is so, the franchising firm provides a number of advantages to its franchisees.

Start-up Assistance

The franchisor will typically provide services intended to make the task of getting started easier. Among these services are site selection advice, facilities layout analysis, financial assistance (sometimes directly, but more often indirectly, by making it a bit easier to get other sources of capital due to the presence of the franchisor), management training, employee selection, and training assistance.

Basis for Judging Prospect of Success

In addition to these services, the franchising option provides a ready-made basis for assessing the possibilities for making money. The process by which future profitability of a new business is determined is always an uncertain one. Whenever a new undertaking is launched, no one can predict exactly how things will turn out. With the purchase of a franchise, however, making a projection of profit level becomes an easier task. A "Burger Heaven" in Peoria will probably do about as well as the one in Portland. The two towns are not the same, of course, so if you are interested in buying a franchise you will want to check the results of sister outlets in other cities as well. These stores provide as good a comparison as you will be able to find and they should be accessible and cooperative to you as a prospective franchise owner.

Instant Recognition

Well-established franchise chains bring with them the important advantage of recognition. Many new businesses experience lean months, or years, after start-up. Obviously, the longer the period the firm must endure this, the greater the chances of failure. With the right franchise this period of agony may last only weeks, or perhaps just days.

Purchasing Power

Being part of a large organization means paying less for a variety of things such as supplies, equipment, inventory, services, and insurance. It also can mean getting better service from suppliers because of the importance of the national account of which you are part.

Advertising Scope and Sophistication

Franchise companies are often national in scope, and because they are, they do national advertising. This advertising is not only less expensive on the basis of cost per contact than most locally produced and distributed material, it is usually far better. To pay for this, most franchisors levy a certain amount on each franchisee. This contribution brings quality and coverage beyond what that amount would pay for if it were used on its own.

Operational Improvements

In many industries, competition is so tough that the difference between success and failure can be the result of minor efficiency improvements. Because of the importance of the success of each franchised outlet to the franchisor, the organization will concentrate a great deal of its time and other resources on making methods more efficient. Once again, centralization of effort can lead to improvements that the individual units would not be able to accomplish. The improvements are made available as systemwide consulting services and are targeted toward areas such as financial and inventory control, use of custom-designed information systems, and maintenance and repair guidelines.

DISADVANTAGES FOR THE FRANCHISEE

Although there are some significant advantages to having a franchise as one starts into business, some disadvantages should also be acknowledged.

Restrictions

Many entrepreneurs start their own business because they believe there is a better way to operate and they have discovered it, or will soon do so. This kind of creative urge has no place in most franchised outlets. The interest in efficiency runs high in many franchisor headquarters. This efficiency and uniformity of operation mean that the individual operator faces numerous restrictions on how to go about managing the business. One classic example of regimentation in franchising can be found in the McDonald's restaurant organization. A McDonald's franchisee is given very little operational latitude; indeed, the operations manual attends to such minor details as when to oil the bearings on the potato slicer. The purpose of these regulations is not to frustrate the franchisee but to ensure that each outlet is run in a uniform, correct manner.

Restrictions are also found on the owner's decisions regarding the product line. It may be in the best interest of one particular PoFolks restaurant to add chocolate truffles to its product line, but the franchisor, who may be skeptical, has the last say and will make the determination on the basis of what is good for all the restaurants in the chain.

Costs

The costs associated with being a franchise member are an additional consideration. These costs include the original outlay to get the franchise, the share of profits that must go to the franchisor, and fees for advertising and other services.

Termination

Another disadvantage facing franchisees is the threat of termination of the franchise. Although some states have laws restricting franchisor actions that result in the loss of the franchise, many franchisees are vulnerable to this development.

Unrealistic Expectations

For years, we have heard claims that buying a franchise was far safer than trying to start a business. The industry's top group, the International Franchise Association (IFA), reports that 97 percent of all franchise units opened nationwide during the last five years are still in operation.[7] This figure is consistent with the 95 percent survival rate cited by the IFA and other industry observers in the past. The conclusion is obvious: Buying a franchise is not risky, and, compared to the hazards of opening your own business, it is clearly the better way to go.

What makes these figures believable is the logic behind the process: An idea that is a proven winner in one location is transplanted to another and then another. At each new place all of the old ideas, with refinements, that worked so well elsewhere are put to use. Add to this compelling idea all those important advantages mentioned earlier and you have the formula for success. The difference between the security offered by franchising and the risks of starting a new business is substantial, perhaps even dramatic when the commonly held, but mistaken, perception of small business mortality rates (that one-third fail the first year and that by year 5 the figure climbs to near 80 percent) is factored into the comparison.

With the available "information," it is no surprise that many people held the opinion that franchises were safe and start-ups were risky. Recent studies have cast a different light on the topic, however. One of the problems with information provided by industry groups like the IFA is the manner by which the data are collected. The 97 percent survival rate is based on a survey of franchisors only, to which less than 20 percent responded. If we assume that the most successful franchisees are the ones most likely to want to talk about their experience, the survival rate looks considerably different. Indeed, the bias is strong enough to make the results suspect, perhaps even meaningless. See Illustration Capsule 5-1 for a description of the disappointment encountered by a

---

ILLUSTRATION CAPSULE 5-1

EXPECTATIONS NOT FULFILLED

The prospect of running his own business appealed to Gene Swanzy of Arlington, Maryland, so, at age 58, he bought two Mail Boxes Etc. franchises. He had just retired from a long career as a broadcasting executive and with $300,000 in savings, he and his wife, Mary Anna Severson, made the plunge. He regrets the move greatly. "It's been a horrendous experience, I blew my retirement money and now I'm trapped," he says. To add to his woes, he is in debt $250,000.

The couple and 29 other franchisees are suing the San Diego-based franchisor for fraud and misrepresentation. The company denies the charges and has filed a cross-complaint.

Source: Earl C. Gottschalk, Jr., "Tax Shop? Gym? Finding a Franchise without Losing Your Shirt," *The New York Times*, March 26, 1995, section F, 12.

franchisee who had high hopes for what franchising would mean for him upon his retirement.

A more recent survey was conducted among franchisees. The results are important because they differ so greatly from those of the IFA. The study, conducted by Timothy Bates of Wayne State University, found that of the people who had purchased their franchises in 1987, only 54 percent were still running the business in 1991, 8 percent had sold it, and 38 percent had lost their franchise.[8] This figure is substantially larger than anything we were given in the past. Moreover, the fate of independent entrepreneurs was better: 62 percent were still in business, 6 percent had sold, and 32 percent had lost their businesses.[9]

Do these new results mean that franchising is no longer a desirable way to go into small business? Certainly not; it is a proven concept. What they do mean, however, is that the security that some people associate with franchising is an illusion. Hard work, realistic expectations, and careful investigation are required if becoming a franchisee is to be a successful, satisfying experience. Our next section describes the process of evaluation.

EVALUATING THE FRANCHISE OPTION

The choice between buying a franchise and starting a business can be a difficult decision. It involves looking at yourself as a prospective franchisee, including reflection on such personal concerns as your interests, personality, and background. Then conduct a careful investigation and analysis of the franchisor. The process is frequently long and demanding, but the costs associated with a bad decision can be devastating.

You as a Franchisee

What are the requirements to be successful as a franchisee? A U.S. Department of Commerce publication, the *Franchise Opportunities Handbook*, cautions that anyone going into franchising must be willing to work long hours, engage in hard work, and face personal sacrifices.[10] Furthermore, the individual must enjoy working with others, be a good supervisor, and be an organized person. To this list could be added the ability to accept orders and policy as handed down by the franchisor and the willingness to be a team player.

Considering the entire list of "requirements" leads one to the conclusion that the ideal franchisee might be a blend of the entrepreneur and the corporate manager. This may, in fact, be a reasonable way to characterize the job of the franchisee. Much of what happens in the conduct of the franchised outlet's business is carefully programmed and therefore within the area covered by corporate policy. This activity, then, is similar to that engaged in by many managers in large companies. Life in a franchised business is by no means completely predictable, however, and the franchisee soon learns that he or she is on the firing line much the same as he or she would be if the business were independent.

A study reported in the April 1995 issue of the *Journal of Small Business Management* examined the determinants of franchisee satisfaction of 127 franchisee owner-managers in Australia.[11] The author provides the following observation: ". . . the finding that most franchisee characteristics were unrelated to their postpurchase satisfaction is a significant step towards differentiating the personal characteristics of franchisees from those of independent entrepreneurs." In other words, the results found in this study were contrary to those describing "conventional" entrepreneurs. This difference in personality underscores the significance of franchising as a route into business distinct from the independent start-up.

Beyond their psychological makeup, prospective franchisees are evaluated by franchisors as to their background. Knowing about the business can have a powerful influence on whether the undertaking succeeds. Although many franchisors provide operating directions that are carefully and precisely written, having actual experience is seen as an important advantage. A high school history teacher who hopes to operate an automobile paint and repair franchise may find the franchisor manual helpful but not enough to allow him to deal with all of the technical problems encountered in the shop. For this individual to prosper, or perhaps just survive, would require some rather dramatic changes. The best advice may be to build on the skills you already have, rather than try to develop a whole new set.

A final area of concern is whether you would enjoy the business you are thinking about entering. Suppose your investigation pointed to the muffler repair business as one that met all of your growth and profitability criteria nicely. Does this mean you should buy a franchise to get you into this line of work? No, not unless you know what it is like to inspect and replace mufflers. Try it, see if you like it by actually spending some time under the car, working with rusted nuts and bolts and occasionally coming into contact with a very hot muffler or exhaust pipe. It will be worth your time to invest a week or two getting this kind of introduction to the work, even if it means working for free at the kind of shop you are thinking about getting into.

The Industry

An important element in any prospective franchise agreement that you may enter into is the industry in which your business will compete. An exploration of the industry requires library research and data gathering with the goal of deepening your understanding of how the industry operates. Among the questions that should be addressed are the following:

- ❑ What are the industry's dominant economic characteristics? How big is it? What is its growth rate? How many competitors are there? How easy is it to enter or exit the industry?
- ❑ What is the competition like? Who are the major forces in the industry? Who buys the product? How much emphasis is there on price? Are new entrants likely?
- ❑ What changes are on the horizon? Are substitute products being marketed? Are there any big organizations that may enter? Are foreign competitors likely to emerge?
- ❑ What are the key factors for competitive success? Are they technological in nature? Marketing-related? Distribution-related? Manufacturing-related?

The concern here is to see how good the market or industry is and what it takes to compete successfully in it. The research will probably involve a great deal of time in the library, conversations with people who have experience in the industry, examination of company-provided materials, trade shows visits, and use of government information.

The Franchisor

Clearly, the most important single element for the prospective franchisee to investigate is his or her business partner, the franchisor. Whether the franchisor is fraudulent or just inept, making the wrong choice here can be catastrophic. Another reason for learning as much as possible about the company is that there are so many from which to choose.

The point is, you do not have to settle for any company that has the least question associated with it. If you have decided to explore the opportunities provided by franchising, many possibilities await. Let's look at http://www. franchise.org/, which provides a wide range of information. For those who are seeking a franchise, information is easily accessed. Let's use as an example here, the first category listed, "Accounting/Tax Services." In addition to the category we are asked to specify our investment range. For the lowest range, under $10,000, only one franchisor is given—ExpressTax. When we increase our range to $10,000 to $25,000 we get no hits; at $25,000 to $50,000, however, five appear. The only one above this investment is United Check Cashing in the $100,000 to $250,000 investment range. To illustrate the kinds of information available at the site, we have provided three company listings, from three different industries, each requiring an investment in the $25,000 to $50,000 range. They are listed as Options 1–3 in Figure 5-1. These are only three of many; go to the site, or the one that follows, and do your own investigation.

Another such Web site is http://opportunities.franchise.org/Public/Index. aspx, which lists 27 "industries" from Advertising to Wholesale/Distribution. Within each of the industries are "Industry Sectors." Within the industry "Home/Mobile Services" list are 28 industry sectors, including businesses such as Debt Consolidation, Air Purification, and Decoration/Remodeling. Finally within each sector are franchise listings; Air Purification yields 4 prospects, another "sector," Residential Cleaning has 11.

Another promising source of franchise prospect information is *The Wall Street Journal*. The Thursday edition of each week includes advertisements from companies looking for new franchisees. Local newspapers also carry ads for franchisors, as do many magazines.

By now it should be clear that there is no shortage of franchise opportunities. Selecting the one that is right for you will be considerably more demanding. After selecting the industry that looks most promising, the next step is to get in touch with its members who are franchising. A telephone call or letter will do it; chances are all of the firms you contact will provide everything you need to make some early cuts. Assemble the company materials so you can make a side-by-side comparison of what each offers and how much it costs. To help in this round of screening, use the checklist in Figure 5-2.

Read the material provided by each franchisor carefully and compare the details. Who seems to have the best training program? If that is of no concern to you because of your experience in the business, the amount of financial assistance may be. How much is the franchise fee? What kind of ongoing financial obligations are there? Is it a percentage of profit? Of sales? How much? Will you be assessed a fee for advertising and support services that you do not even want?

One piece of information that you probably will not be given is an estimate of what you can expect to earn with the franchise. Any franchisor making claims about sales or profitability is required by the federal government to provide substantiation for those claims. Review any claims carefully. Are they based on

OPTION 1   EXAMPLES OF FRANCHISE OPPORTUNITIES

Tedeschi Food Shops, Inc.
Company details
Description: We are a turnkey franchise convenience food store company operating in urban and suburban locations offering "fast and friendly" service. Provide groceries, beverages, general merchandise, dairy products, lottery. Deli and gasoline available in some locations.
Business established: 1962
Franchised since: 1972
# of franchised units: 87
Company owned: 114

Contact info.
Address: 14 Howard Street, Rockland, MA
ZIP code: 02370
Country: USA
No-800: (800)833-3724
Phone1: (781)878-8210
Fax: (781)878-0476
Primary contact name & title: Mike Ota - Director of franchising, Ext.2
Secondary contact name & title: –
Email: mota@tedeschifoodshops.com
Web site: http://www.tedeschifoodshops.com

Financial info.
Start-up cash required: $20,000 - $60,000
Investment required: $45,000 - $137,000
Financial comment: Financial assistance is available.

Training
Extensive 3 weeks in-store training. In-depth instructional seminars offered in accounting, merchandising, P&L reviews, sales. Field personnel counsel weekly to advise on operations and financial issues. Annual companywide trade show.

Qualifications
Commitment to excel, dedicated team player, positive personality, sales driven and motivated, financially stable. Experience is helpful but not required.

OPTION 2

Aire Serv Heating and Air Conditioning, Inc.
Company details
Description: Aire Serv is a residentail and commercial provider of heating, cooling and air quality related services and systems.
Business established: 1993
Franchised since: 1993
# of franchised units: 85
Company owned: 0

FIGURE 5–1   Examples of franchise opportunities.

Contact info.
Address: 1020 N. University Parks Drive, Waco, TX
ZIP code: 76707
Country: USA
No-800: (800)583-2662
Fax: (254)745-7546
Primary contact name & title: Doyle James - President
Secondary contact name & title: Tracy Brackeen - Executive Assistant
Email: djames@dwyergroup.com
Web site: http://www.aireserv.com

Financial info.
Start-up cash required: $31,595 - $119,500
Investment required: $31,595 - $119,500
Financial comment: Partial financing available to those who qualify.

Training
Training is provided for operations management, sales and administration functions of the business.

Qualifications
People with a strong desire to follow a proven system, with a previous background in business.

OPTION 3

Reality Sports Entertainment, Inc.
Company details
Description: Reality Sports Entertainment, creators of World Championship Armwrestling (WCA), established the sport of arm wrestling as a pervasive, professional and profitable entity.
Business established: 2002
Franchised since: 2003
# of franchised units: 1
Company owned: 2

Contact info.
Address: 303 Sondrol, P.O. Box 882, Ames, IA
ZIP code: 50010
Country: USA
No-800: (866)232-5023
Fax: (515)232-5036
Primary contact name & title: Donald W. Myers - Operations Manager
Secondary contact name & title: Jack Barringer - CEO
Email:
Web site: --NA--

Financial info.
Start-up cash required: $3,000 - $6,000
Investment required: $35,000 - $50,000
Financial comment: Third-party financing available.

FIGURE 5–1   Examples of franchise opportunities (*continued*).

Training
Franchisees receive an extensive three-day training program at national headquarters. After the initial three-day period, RSE will assist in conducting the first tournament, booking events, and sponsor relations.

Qualifications
Entrepreneurial spirit, sports minded, outgoing personality, sales background preferred. RSE interviews each franchisee extensively.

FIGURE 5–1   Examples of franchise opportunities (*continued*).

EVALUATING THE FRANCHISE OPTION

How many franchised units exist? How many company-owned stores?

When was the franchise founded?

What products and services are provided by the franchised outlets?

How much money is needed to start a franchise?

How much is the franchise fee?

How much is the monthly royalty fee?

Is there an advertising co-op fee?

Does the franchisor offer any financing for franchisees?

What type of ongoing assistance does the franchisor provide to the franchisees?

What type of training does the franchisor provide?

FIGURE 5–2   Checklist for evaluating the franchise option.

actual or projected results? Are they average figures for all franchisees or for a selected few? What assumptions were used in making any projections? Do the claims hold for first-year franchises or only for those that have been in existence for some time?

One last piece of advice: Prepare to be confused. Each company will be putting the best possible light on whatever package it offers, but beneath it all may be some unpleasant facts. It is your job to find out what they are and how bad they are.

Beyond the printed materials of the company and conversations with corporate officials, an important source of information is the franchisee group. Talk with both successful and marginal owner-managers. How satisfied are they? Has the company delivered on its promises? Is it continuing to push for market penetration, or is a sense of complacency setting in? If your contacts are not willing to share their views with you openly, be suspicious. People with success stories usually enjoy telling others about them. See Figure 5–3.

The efforts we have just recommended are intended to help you to protect yourself against making a bad decision. Some people in the franchising field have

The Franchise

1. Did your lawyer approve the franchise contract you are considering after he or she studied it paragraph by paragraph?
2. Does the franchise call on you to take any steps that are, according to your lawyer, unwise or illegal in your state, county, or city?
3. Does the franchise give you an exclusive territory for the length of the franchise, or can the franchisor sell a second or third franchise in your territory?
4. Is the franchisor connected in any way with any other franchise company handling similar merchandise or service?
5. If the answer to the last question is yes, what is your protection against this second franchisor organization?
6. Under what circumstances can you terminate the franchise contract and at what cost to you, if you decide for any reason at all that you wish to cancel it?
7. If you sell your franchise, will you be compensated for your goodwill or will the goodwill you have built into the business be lost by you?

The Franchisor

8. How many years has the firm offering you a franchise been in operation?
9. Has it a reputation for honesty and fair dealing among the local firms holding its franchise?
10. Has the franchisor shown you any certified figures indicating exact net profits of one or more going firms that you personally checked yourself with the franchisee?
11. Will the firm assist you with
    a. A management training program?
    b. An employee training program?
    c. A public relations program?
    d. Capital?
    e. Credit?
    f. Merchandising ideas?
12. Will the firm help you find a good location for your new business?
13. Is the franchising firm adequately financed so that it can carry out its stated plan of financial assistance and expansion?
14. Is the franchisor a one-person company or a corporation with an experienced management trained in depth (so that there would always be an experienced person at its head)?
15. Exactly what can the franchisor do for you that you cannot do for yourself?
16. Has the franchisor investigated you carefully enough to assure itself that you can successfully operate one of its franchises at a profit both to itself and to you?
17. Does your state have a law regulating the sale of franchises, and has the franchisor complied with that law?

FIGURE 5–3   Checklist for evaluating a franchise *(continued).*

You—The Franchisee

18. How much equity capital will you have to have to purchase the franchise and operate it until your income equals your expenses? Where are you going to get it?
19. Are you prepared to give up some independence of action to secure the advantages offered by the franchise?
20. Do you really believe you have the innate ability, training, and experience to work smoothly and profitably with the franchisor, your employees, and your customers?
21. Are you ready to spend much or all of the remainder of your business life with this franchisor, offering its product or service to your public?

Your Market

22. Have you made any study to determine whether the product or service that you propose to sell under franchise has a market in your territory at the prices you will have to charge?
23. Will the population in the territory given to you increase, remain static, or decrease over the next five years?
24. Will the product or service you are considering be in greater demand, about the same, or less demand five years from now than today?
25. What competition exists in your territory already for the product or service you contemplate selling?
    a. Nonfranchise firms?
    b. Franchise firms?

Source: *Franchise Opportunities Handbook* (Washington, DC: U.S. Government Printing Office, 1988).

FIGURE 5–3   Checklist for evaluating a franchise (*continued*).

---

observed that many buyers investigate what make of car to get more thoroughly than they investigate the franchise purchase. Do not make that mistake; you are your own first-line and best defense against the wrong kind of franchisor. Some protection is provided by others, however; the federal government and many states have taken measures to limit corrupt practices by franchisors. These limits take the form of causing unscrupulous companies to stop doing business, but the people who were victimized are seldom made whole. Our next section discusses franchising law.

FRANCHISING AND THE LAW

Any activity in which so many people are involved with the exchange of so much money has great potential for abuse. Some franchisors are greedy and willing to mislead prospective franchisees; others will use the agreement as it fits their needs, often in clear violation of what it specifies. Because unfair tactics have so frequently found their way into franchisor-franchisee relations, many regulations have been put into place at both federal and state levels. We will discuss the more important means of protection provided by these regulations.

Because of the aggressiveness of some franchisors, the regulations provide protection starting with the first contact made by the company. If you are intrigued by what you have read or heard about a franchisor and decide to contact it, what happens next? Typically the response will be in the form of promotional material— lots of glossy promotional material. It is, of course, intended to entice you into thinking about what all those benefits of franchise ownership would mean to you. There will also likely be a follow-up of some kind, possibly by phone, and then there will be a letter, accompanied by an application blank. If you complete and return the application, expect some pressure from the sales group in the franchisor home office. Don't worry about the pressure you may get to make a quick decision. You are protected; the law precludes the franchisor from selling you anything or taking any money until 10 days after you have received two things: a copy of the franchise agreement and a copy of the disclosure statement.

The franchise agreement is the contract between franchisor and franchisee. It gives the vital details about the relationship between franchisees and the company. It is precise; unfortunately, it is also hard to read and is therefore probably best put in the hands of a lawyer. The items in the agreement include such important items as costs, terms, obligations of both parties, conditions governing termination of the franchise, and limitations of the franchisee. Remember that it is the franchisor's document; it was written by the franchisor and says what the company wants it to say. Read it very carefully and compare it to others.

The other important document that the regulations state you must be given is the disclosure statement, or, as it is officially called, the uniform franchise offering circular or prospectus. If there is a single most important source of information, this is it. The franchisor must provide information on the 23 topics in Figure 5-4.

The topics covered in the disclosure statement are intended to allow the prospective franchisee to determine whether the company is trustworthy and therefore someone with whom he or she wants to do business. A cautionary note should be added: The information given in the statement is vital, but bear in mind that it is information provided by the franchisor and not subject to independent verification. Furthermore, the Federal Trade Commission (FTC), the agency requiring this statement, makes no claim as to its authenticity. What if the company lies to you? It has broken the law and so is subject to penalties, but that may not help you if you have already given it your money. Typically, the FTC tries to have money returned to those who were victimized by fraudulent claims, but they often are not able to do so, and when they do, it is usually only a partial settlement.

> **Uniform franchise offering circular** – a document, required of franchisors by federal law, that makes available to prospective franchisees information on a wide range of important topics.

Honesty questions aside, the information in the disclosure statement should provide the basis for judging the costs and benefits of franchise ownership. The chances of a comparison of these statements from several franchises leading to a clear winner are slim. That is, the very good franchises, those with excellent reputations and an impressive list of services for franchisees, are usually very expensive. If you want to spend less, you will probably have to settle for less.

In summary, the major thrust of the law is to prevent abuses by franchisors. The prospective franchisee has the legally protected right not to be rushed into doing something he or she otherwise would not have done. The franchisee also has the right to be given information that allows for an informed decision.

The relationship between the franchisor and the franchisee is specified in the franchise agreement. In it, the two parties agree to certain arrangements regarding such things as how the business is to be run, purchase of supplies, royalty levels, charges for management, and advertising and other corporate services.

Important variations exist in franchise agreements; it is a contract between the franchisee and the company and, as such, can be shaped to suit the needs of

1. Information identifying the franchisor and its affiliates and describing their business experience.
2. Information identifying and describing the business experience of each of the franchisor's officers, directors, and management personnel responsible for franchise services, training, and other aspects of the franchise program.
3. A description of the lawsuits in which the franchisor and its officers, directors, and management personnel have been involved.
4. Information about any previous bankruptcies in which the franchisor and its officers, directors, and management personnel have been involved.
5. Information about the initial franchise fee and other initial payments that are required to obtain the franchise.
6. A description of the continuing payments franchisees are required to make after the franchise opens.
7. Information about any restrictions on the quality of goods and services used in the franchise and where they may be purchased, including restrictions requiring purchases from the franchisor or its affiliates.
8. A description of any assistance available from the franchisor or its affiliates in financing the purchase of the franchise.
9. A description of restrictions on the goods or services that franchisees are permitted to sell.
10. A description of any restrictions on the customers with whom franchisees may deal.
11. A description of any territorial protection that will be granted to the franchisee.
12. A description of the conditions under which the franchise may be repurchased or refused renewal by the franchisor, transferred to a third party by the franchisee, and terminated or modified by either party.
13. A description of the training programs provided to franchisees.
14. A description of the involvement of any celebrities or public figures in the franchise.
15. A description of any assistance given by the franchisor in selecting a site for the franchise.
16. Statistical information about the present number of franchises, the number of franchises projected for the future, the number of franchises terminated, the number the franchisor has decided not to renew, and the number repurchased in the past.
17. The financial statements of the franchisor.
18. A description of the extent to which franchisees must personally participate in the operation of the franchise.
19. A complete statement of the basis for any earnings claims made to the franchisee, including the percentage of existing franchises that have actually achieved the results that are claimed.
20. A list of the names and addresses of other franchisees.
21. Copies of the franchisor's financial statements, which are audited and provided to give the prospective franchisee a view of the financial condition of the company.
22. Copies of the contracts the franchisee will be required to sign upon purchase of the franchise.
23. A receipt for the franchisee to sign and return as evidence of receipt of the UFOC.

FIGURE 5–4   Required information in uniform franchise offering circular.

both parties. The prospective franchisee can agree to it or try to negotiate a better deal. Anything unacceptable, or undesirable, should be regarded as something that would be reviewed for change. A large, powerful chain will seldom agree to such requests, but since the agreement specifies the conditions of the relationship, it is important to attempt to shape the document in the interests of the franchisee to the extent possible.

Among the most critical factors in the relationship are those having to do with termination of the contract. It is around this issue that the imbalance of bargaining power is most apparent. The franchisor can refuse to renew the contract, terminate it, or refuse to agree to a sale transferring it to a new owner. Any of these moves will simply mean one less outlet for the franchisor. For the franchisee, however, the decision has far greater significance: It can bring grievous financial loss and the loss of livelihood. Consequently, any prospective franchisee should examine carefully the franchisor's policy on termination of franchise, in light of both state and federal law.

OTHER ENTREPRENEURIAL OPTIONS

Business Opportunities

We have all seen the ads and wondered what they were all about: "Make Big Money"; "Get Rich in Your Spare Time"; "Be Your Own Boss"; and so on. These are doubtful claims, perhaps, but attractive to many people with entrepreneurial tendencies and interests but without sufficient capital, experience, and time for a long-term commitment. These people are turning to yet another route into small business: the business opportunity. While there is no formal definition of the term, it can be described as the sale of a product or service that the seller promises the buyer will provide a profit on the buyer's original investment.

The concept of franchising is based in large part on the trust and confidence that develop in the relationship between franchisee and franchisor. The two parties are interdependent in such a way that the success of one depends on, and fuels, the success of the other. This kind of relationship usually takes time to build. The business opportunity format has a "quickie" quality to it. Even in cases where both of the parties make money on the transaction, they may never see each other again. The short-term nature of the relationship between buyer and seller in a business opportunity is one of the things that distinguish it from franchising.

Another critical difference between the two is that of requirements or restrictions. The buyer is not required to pay fees and is not faced with operating restrictions of the kind usually imposed on franchisees. The flexibility given the buyer has its counterpart in the lack of service from the seller. Although many ads say there will be marketing materials, sales leads, exclusive territories, and the like, not all sellers deliver on these promises, and getting them to do so can be a discouraging undertaking.

To our knowledge, no scientific study of the safety of business opportunities has been conducted, but the anecdotal evidence points to the need for caution. While the business opportunity seller faces the same FTC restrictions that apply to franchisors, enforcement is difficult and spotty. Among the reasons for this ineffective protection is that only about one-half of the states have any regulation of sellers of business opportunities. In addition, there are the skill, methods, and determination of some of the sellers. Consider, for example, the case of a vending machine scam investigated for two years by the FTC. It involved 31 companies run by 16 individuals, including a man who had six aliases. In another incident, six people running 18 Florida-based companies were charged with deceptive business practices.[12]

With a web of businesses, fake identities, and multiple locations, some of the most aggressive and unscrupulous of these operators will be selling business opportunities for a long time to come. Can buyers protect themselves? Yes, at least partially, if they investigate thoroughly, are extremely skeptical, and do not believe any ads that offer anything that seems too good to be true. Even then, unpleasant surprises can occur. When a Seattle woman investigated a Denver company's offer of an exclusive territory (which it wasn't—there were 10 other dealers), she was given the name of a Kansas woman purported to be a satisfied dealer. The woman wasn't a dealer; she was paid to lie to prospects.[13]

Manufacturer's Representative

Another entrepreneurial option is to become a manufacturer's representative. In this arrangement, the entrepreneur represents a manufacturer or other supplier in dealings with customers. Typically, the representative is compensated only on the basis of actual sales on behalf of the company. Consequently, the entrepreneur takes on the expenses of the job with the prospect of a payoff, but only if a sale is made. This relationship is like that between a company and a salesperson who is paid on a commission-only basis, except that the salesperson is an employee and therefore eligible for benefits, possible promotion, reimbursement for travel, and so on. The manufacturer's representative relies on his or her sales ability to generate enough income to at least cover these kinds of items. In some "big-ticket" industries, such as expensive equipment and medical fixtures, an occasional sale is often enough to do just that. While the level of remuneration varies from one situation to another, the standard arrangement is for the manufacturer's representative to receive 10 percent of the sale.

> **Manufacturer's representative** – a firm or individual who represents a manufacturer or supplier in dealings with customers.

Entrepreneurs who operate as manufacturer's representatives have a great deal of autonomy. They can set their own schedule, develop their own prospects, and decide which manufacturers to represent. This is considerably more freedom than the typical franchisee, but, like a franchisee, the manufacturer's representative must depend on the "parent" organization for support and the ability to serve customers effectively.

FRANCHISES AND THE BUSINESS PLAN

If the entrepreneur's business will be a franchise, it is important to include information on the franchise in the business plan. The history and financial stability of the franchisor are critical factors in assessing the viability of the new francise outlet. It is also important to include the amount and type of training that the franchisor will provide and if ongoing advice is available if the franchisee has problems. Because the franchise is often dependent on the franchisor, bankers and investors will be as concerned about the franchisor's information as the franchisee's. Any problems at the parent corporation are likely to impact all businesses in the system. Therefore, the questions listed in "Evaluating the Franchise Option" should be included in the business plan.

SUMMARY

For many people, the dreams of self-employment and financial independence have been realized through the purchase of a franchise. For many others, however, the purchase has brought grief and financial ruin. Buying a franchise is a move that must be painstakingly investigated. While legal protection is available, the best strategy for problem prevention is exhaustive information gathering. As alternatives to starting or buying a business or buying a franchise, business opportunities and manufacturers' representatives should be mentioned. Great caution should be used in responding to "business opportunities." This route to independent business affords far less legal protection than that of franchising and has been the source of many scams through the years. The role of manufacturer's representative is that of an independent salesperson who must make a living—and pay expenses—through commissions on sales.

DISCUSSION QUESTIONS

1. Why has franchising become so popular in recent years?
2. Describe the advantages franchising offers for an entrepreneur.
3. What is the level of risk of failure faced by the buyer of a franchise? How does it compare to the risk faced by entrepreneurs who start businesses?
4. What is the purpose of the franchise agreement?
5. What kind of protection is given by the disclosure statement?
6. Compare and contrast franchises and business opportunities.
7. Why is the regulation of the sellers of business opportunities so difficult?

ENDNOTES

1. Thomas S. Dicke, *Franchising in America* (Chapel Hill, NC: University of North Carolina Press, 1992), 3.

2. Gordon Storholm and Eberhard E. Scheuing, "Ethical Implications of Business Format Franchising," *Journal of Business Ethics*, March 1994, 181–188.

3. Andrew Kostecka, *Franchising in the Economy, 1986–1988* (Washington, DC: U.S. Government Printing Office), 4.

4. IFA Resource Center, "What Is Franchising?" http://www.franchise.org/resourcectr/faq/1.asp.

5. Ibid.

6. Ibid.

7. Arthur Andersen and Co., *Franchising in the Economy: 1989–1992* (Washington, DC: International Franchise Association, 1992).

8. Timothy Bates, "Look Before You Leap," *Inc.*, July 1995, 23–24.

9. Ibid.

10. *Franchise Opportunities Handbook* (Washington, DC: U.S. Department of Commerce, 1994), ix–xii.

11. Nerilee Hing, "Franchisee Satisfaction: Contributors and Consequences," *Journal of Small Business Management*, April 1995, 12–25.

12. Sana Siwolop, "Have I Got a Business Opportunity for You," *The New York Times*, August 27, 1995, section 3, 1, 8.

13. Ibid.

Chapter 6

Women-Owned and Minority-Owned Businesses

FEMALE ENTREPRENEURS

The growth of women-owned businesses over the past few decades has been phenomenal. Within a 16-year period, the number of businesses owned by women grew from 4.4 million to 9.1 million.[1] Women-owned businesses now account for 35 percent of all businesses, generate $2.3 trillion in sales, and employ 19.1 million people in the United States.[2] A study by the Center for Women's Business Research found that during a five-year period, growth in employment in women-owned firms was twice the rate of growth for all firms. By 2004, women-owned businesses were spending $492 billion on salaries and wages.[3] Figure 6-1 shows the percentage change in self-employment for men and women from 1983 to 2005.

The businesses also contribute a substantial amount to the economy by buying goods and services. The Center for Women's Business Research estimated that spending in four areas—information technology, telecommunications, human resource services, and shipping—totaled more than $100 billion annually.[4]

Motivation for Becoming an Entrepreneur

There is no single reason for the dramatic increase in women-owned businesses. Some of the most common reasons include dissatisfaction with corporate life, a desire for balance in work and home life, and desire for challenge.

Dissatisfaction with corporate life Dissatisfaction with corporate life occurs for many reasons, including layoffs, the glass ceiling, and conflict between family and work responsibilities.

By the 1980s, many women had entered the workforce and had advanced educational backgrounds. They became part of middle management in corporations several years before the corporations began massive layoffs. Many who saw their corporate jobs eliminated chose to become their own bosses. But even those who were not laid off often found that corporate life did not always deliver

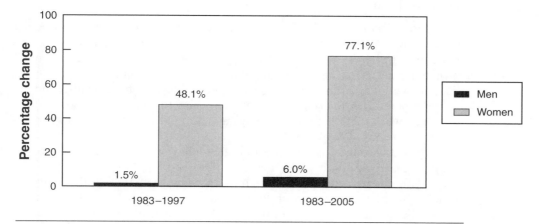

FIGURE 6–1   Percentage change in self-employment for men and women, 1983–2005.

Source: Adapted from "Women in Business," http://www.sba.gov/advo.

meaningful work opportunities. Although women have made incredible progress in the corporate world, it often does not provide the environment women are seeking. A study of women entrepreneurs by Dorothy Moore and E. Holly Buttner stated that "part of the challenge for the woman manager in organizations is to maintain her identity and sense of what is important in environments shaped and largely determined by men."[5]

Desire for balance between work and home An article in *BusinessWeek* stated, "Hundreds of thousands of women have bailed out on Corporate America to start their own companies in the hope of striking a better work-life balance." However, this article also referred to this hope as the "big illusion," noting that the women "are quickly finding out how easy it is to feel overwhelmed by two all-consuming responsibilities: a young company and young children." When a business is very new, it is often easier to get away when necessary. If the business begins to grow quickly, though, flexibility often disappears.[6] For that reason, women may choose to keep the company small until the responsibilities of child rearing have subsided.

Desire for a challenge As with male entrepreneurs, many women start a business because they have a good business idea. In the study cited previously, 44 percent of the female entrepreneurs stated that they started a business in order to implement a winning business idea or because they realized they could do for themselves what they were doing for an employer. Debra Esparza, director of the Business Expansion Network at the University of Southern California, states, "Entrepreneurship is about finding a market and filling it. That's true whether the business owner is male or female."[7]

Company Size

In recent years, comparisons have been made of women-owned businesses and those owned by men. Generally, women-owned businesses have been smaller in size.

Why are women-owned businesses smaller? There are several possible reasons, including differences in motivation between men and women, the age of the business, the industry chosen, and possible obstacles.

Motivational differences There is disagreement among analysts as to whether women-owned businesses are small by choice or because of other factors. Flexibility in work hours is often a motivating factor, and those who believe women-owned businesses are small by choice point out that flexibility is more important than money. One article in *Inc.* magazine stated, "These women are just trying to support themselves, to bring balance and flexibility to their lives in ways that the corporate world can't. And won't. They are out to redefine work, not to restructure the economy."[8]

One study found that women and men define success differently. Women define it as having control over their own destinies, building ongoing relationships with clients, and doing something fulfilling.[9] Another study showed a relationship between motivation for starting a business and the measurements of success. Women who were frustrated by the lack of challenge in a prior position might measure success internally in terms of personal growth. Women who experienced work/family role conflict in former jobs might measure success in terms of achieving a balance of work and family responsibilities.[10] On the other hand, studies have shown that men define success in terms of achieving goals.[11]

Company age and industry Women-owned businesses are also smaller because of the industries chosen. More women-owned businesses are in the service industries and are often smaller than those in other industries such as manufacturing and wholesaling.[12]

One of the most important factors that affects company size, though, is the age of the business. Women-owned businesses are younger establishments. Many start out as part-time ventures, and most small businesses take time to grow. Since many women-owned businesses were started within the past 30 years, it is logical that they would be smaller when compared to all existing businesses.

Possible obstacles Many people believe that women-owned businesses could grow larger if they were given equal access to capital. Female entrepreneurs typically start businesses with less capital than their male counterparts. One study showed that start-up funds for women averaged $15,000, while for men the average was $36,000. One explanation for the discrepancy is that, as stated previously, women tend to start service businesses, which often require less capital than those in other industries. Moreover, if the service business is operated from the home, little start-up financing may be needed.[13]

Many believe, though, that women do not have equal access to capital when they need it. According to one survey, more than half of the women entrepreneurs found it difficult to obtain financing to start their businesses. Most of them used their own savings to start the companies. The executive director of the Kansas Women's Business Center stated, "Access to capital has been a recurring concern for women business owners."[14] Women of color face even greater difficulties in obtaining needed funding.[15]

For several possible reasons, then, the lack of adequate capital may limit the rate of growth. To generate more financing for female entrepreneurs, several banks have developed loan programs for women. In addition, several microloan programs are available through local development corporations or through non-profit foundations. Also, the Small Business Administration has a special loan-guarantee program for female entrepreneurs.

Breaking the Tradition

While the majority of women-owned businesses are concentrated in the retail and service sectors, and many of them are small, this is only a part of the picture. It would be a great disservice to female entrepreneurs if we did not discuss those who have started and operated businesses that became large corporations and those that are in nontraditional industries. The Women Presidents Organization (WPO) is comprised of women business owners who own businesses that gross at least $2 million in annual sales (or $1 million for service businesses). Their members' businesses have an average $12 million in annual sales and employ 113 people. Their members include Paula Innis who owns a technology-based digital printing facility and Margaret Johnson, whose consulting firm has been growing at an annual rate of 79 percent.[16] A survey by Strategic Surveys International found that the WPO businesses increased in revenue even when the economy was poor. The survey indicated that the owner was generally "a service-oriented business woman in the prime of her career."[17]

Women are also starting many businesses in nontraditional industries such as construction and transportation. Within a seven-year period, growth in the construction industry of women-owned businesses increased 30 percent and growth in the transportation, communication, and public utilities grew 28.1 percent.[18]

Women Entrepreneurs in Other Countries

The number of female entrepreneurs is increasing in many countries across the globe. One study in India found that women entrepreneurs comprised 10 percent of all Indian entrepreneurs but were expected to total 20 percent by 2009.[19] In the United Kingdom, women-owned businesses now total 26 percent of all businesses. The CEO of an organization that assists U.K. women-owned businesses stated, "The U.K. economy is experiencing a rapid surge of companies being started and run by women."[20]

In Africa, women comprise the majority of the "small-scale economy." This includes small companies and microenterprises. This small-scale economy generates 40 percent of the gross domestic product of the country. In Uganda, women are the majority of the country's businesspeople in farming and in small- to medium-sized firms.[21]

Women entrepreneurs are thus having an impact worldwide and will continue to do so in the future. This will have an increasing impact on the economy and employment of countries and will help to stimulate economic development in many areas of the world.

MINORITY ENTREPRENEURS

Small business ownership has always provided opportunities for minorities and immigrants; however, in recent years, there has been substantial growth in minority-owned businesses, including those owned by African Americans, Hispanics, and Asian Americans.

> **Minority entrepreneurs –** include ethnic entrepreneurs, immigrant entrepreneurs and entrepreneurs for minority populations.

Though the term *minority entrepreneurs* is used, it is somewhat misleading because these businesspeople are not a homogeneous group. Some researchers prefer to distinguish between three subgroups—ethnic entrepreneurs, immigrant entrepreneurs, and minority entrepreneurs. The reason for this distinction is that the groups do not necessarily face the same issues when starting a business. Immigrant entrepreneurs are those who recently arrived in the country and often start a business as a means of survival. Ethnic entrepreneurs are those who "interact among people sharing common national background or migration experience." But ethnic entrepreneurs are not always immigrants. For example, a family whose ancestors arrived many years ago may operate a store that serves more recent immigrants. They serve an ethnic population, but they themselves are not recent arrivals. Finally, a minority entrepreneur would include any individual not of the majority population. This includes African Americans, those of Hispanic or Latin ancestry; Asian, Pacific Islanders, American Indians, and those of Alaska native descent.[22]

African American Entrepreneurs

African Americans in the United States were entrepreneurs as early as the late 1700s and 1800s. One entrepreneur, James Forten, owned a firm that manufactured sails for ships; he was one of the most successful businessmen in Philadelphia.[23] One of the first female African American entrepreneurs to become successful was born to sharecropping ex-slaves in 1867. Madam C. J. Walker was an orphan by age 7, a wife at 14, a widow at 20, and a business owner by 38. By age 50 she was the first female African American millionaire.[24] One writer states, African Americans have overcome "staggering odds to become entrepreneurs. They had little in the way of capital, education, or business training," and faced racism, much of it legislated.[25] However, by the early 20th century, African American businesses started to cater to the black community instead of the white community, and this created business districts within black neighborhoods. Many grocery stores, barber shops, and other small businesses began to flourish.

Within the past few decades, there has been a substantial increase in the number of businesses owned by African Americans. By 2010, the number is expected to reach 2.2 million.[26]

Asians and Pacific Islanders

Asian Americans have been successful in many industries, from hotels to high-technology companies in Silicon Valley. The Asian American Hotel Owners Association (AAHOA), which started in 1989, has grown from 100 to 8,000 members. It is the fastest growing hospitality organization in the United States.[27]

In the high-tech boom of the late 1990s, Asian Americans started many successful companies and owned a substantial portion of all high-tech firms in Silicon Valley. With the problems that occurred in the dot-com industry, many experienced turbulent times. However, many have weathered the storm and have survived to become well-established businesses.

Korean Americans have the highest self-employment rate of any ethnic or racial group, including whites. More than 1 of every 10 Korean Americans is a business owner. The rate for Caucasian Americans is 1 in 15 and for African Americans 1 in 67. While many businesses have fled the inner city, thousands of Korean Americans have remained and started businesses. They attribute their success to hard work, financial support from fellow immigrants, free labor from family members, and a cultural tradition of pride and self-reliance.[28]

Hispanic

The Hispanic culture comprises many subgroups, including Mexicans, Cubans, Spaniards, Puerto Ricans, and others from South America. Among Hispanic groups, Mexicans owned the greatest number of firms.[29]

The first Cuban refugees who came to Miami in the 1960s and 1970s were mostly middle-class immigrants, and many had saved enough money to start businesses. As more Cubans and Haitians entered Florida during the 1980s, the Cuban entrepreneurs, connected by both language and culture, experienced substantial market increase and excellent economic gains.[30]

As a result of the success in the restaurant industry by Hispanics, a generation of Hispanic food service entrepreneurs is being born. As many have found the capital and obtained the education and training to become their own bosses, they have opened well-patronized restaurants. Some own many franchises such as Applebee's, On the Border, Little Caeser's, and Burger King.[31]

Other Hispanic entrepreneurs have entered less traditional industries. Lionel Sosa, owner of his own publicity corporation, is one of the most successful Hispanic entrepreneurs in the United States. Sosa has written a book, *El Sueno Americano: Como los Latinos Pueden Triunfar en los Estados Unidos (The American*

Dream: How Latinos Can Succeed in the United States), which outlines the 12 essential characteristics of a successful Hispanic businessperson.[32]

American Indians and Alaska Natives

According to the Economic Census, the number of American Indian and Alaska Native–owned businesses in the United States increased 84 percent within a five-year period. This compares with a 7 percent increase for all U.S. firms. Thus, the rate of entrepreneurship among this group has increased substantially. Sales receipts among these businesses increased 179 percent over the same five-year period, generating $34.3 billion in revenue. Alaska has slightly more than 10 percent of the businesses; many also exist in California, Texas, Oklahoma, and Florida.[33]

Obstacles and Opportunities

Many minority entrepreneurs face unique obstacles. A lack of access to capital is often cited as a problem. A *Wall Street Journal* survey found that for African Americans, lack of access to capital and credit was given as the biggest obstacle to growth.[34] Carl J. Schramm, president and CEO of the Ewing Marion Kaufman Foundation of Kansas City, states, "Access to capital is one of the biggest hurdles for any entrepreneur—and even more so for minority entrepreneurs."[35] A working paper from the Federal Reserve found that one-third of Hispanic companies had been turned down for a loan and more than half of black-owned firms have been turned down.[36] However, studies suggest that many minority firms are exceptionally profitable. The Kaufman Foundation study found that venture capital funds that make significant investments in minority business realize rates of returns that are equal to, or greater than, that of traditional venture capitalists.[37]

Racism remains a significant factor for minority entrepreneurs despite improvements in race relations in the United States. The *Wall Street Journal* survey cited earlier found that two-thirds of African American entrepreneurs stated that discrimination is as common in the business community as in society in general.[38] One entrepreneur who describes himself as a "white Hispanic" with an Anglo-Saxon last name stated that it was better for him to hide his Hispanic heritage when working with potential customers. He feels that the instant they realize he is Hispanic, the business deal and his credibility start to disappear.[39]

The future for minority business appears to be excellent, though. Many factors point to a promising future, two of which are an increasing minority population and an increase in entrepreneurship among ethnic groups. By the year 2050, it is estimated that one of every four people living in the United States will be Latino. The number of Asians will also increase, so Latinos and Asians combined will comprise one of every three U.S. residents.[40] This will provide increasing target markets for those businesses that cater to minority populations.

A study by the Kaufman Foundation shows an interest in entrepreneurship among many ethnic groups. The study found that African Americans are "50 percent more likely to start a business than whites. Black men between 25 and 35 years of age with some graduate education start more businesses than any other group in the country. Latinos are 20 percent more likely to start a business than whites. Furthermore, minority teens were more interested in starting businesses than white teens."[41] Therefore it seems that for many minorities, the road to success will be through self-employment.

WOMEN AND MINORITY ENTREPRENEURS AND THE BUSINESS PLAN

Although many entrepreneurs have difficulty convincing bankers and investors to provide financing, women and minority entrepreneurs may have to be even more convincing and persistent. It is extremely important to stress entrepreneurial qualifications in the management section of the business plan, including education, work experience, and entrepreneurial personality traits.

SUMMARY

In recent years, women have been forming businesses at a rapid rate. There are many reasons for the increased number of female entrepreneurs, including dissatisfaction with corporate life and a desire for an entrepreneurial challenge. Although many women-owned businesses are small, others have grown to be large and successful and are operating in industries that were previously male-dominated.

Minority-owned businesses also increased substantially in recent years. Many researchers prefer to separate "minority entrepreneurs" into three separate groups—ethnic entrepreneurs, immigrant entrepreneurs, and minority entrepreneurs. Many minority entrepreneurs face obstacles such as a lack of capital and racism. However, with the increasing minority population in the United States and an increased interest in entrepreneurship among many ethnic groups, the future for these businesses looks promising.

DISCUSSION QUESTIONS

1. List possible reasons why women-owned businesses are, on average, smaller than businesses owned by men.

2. One writer for *Inc.* magazine wrote that African American entrepreneurs were "returning to tradition" by becoming entrepreneurs. What information supports this statement?

3. What factors do Korean Americans cite as contributing to their entrepreneurial success?

ENDNOTES

1. Toddi Gutner, "Finally Credit Where Credit Is Due," *BusinessWeek*, June 26, 2000, 250; Clare Ramsey, "Number of Women Entrepreneurs on Rise," *Knight Ridder Tribune Business News*, September 12, 2003, 1.

2. Clare Ramsey and Anita Szoke, "Women Entrepreneurs Gain Economic Clout. But Still Lack Access to Credit," *Knight Ridder Tribune Business News*, May 25, 2004, 1.

3. Center for Women's Business Research, "Biennial Update on Women-Owned Business Documents Substantial Economic Impact," press release, April 28, 2004, http://www.nfwbo.org/media center/4-28-2004/4-28-2004.htm.

4. Ibid.

5. Dorothy P. Moore and E. Holly Buttner, *Women Entrepreneurs* (Thousand Oaks, CA: Sage Publications, 1997), 27.

6. Meg Lundstrom, "Mommy Do You Love Your Company More Than Me?" *BusinessWeek*, December 20, 1999, 175.

7. "Women Start Businesses to Test Ideas," *The St. Louis Post Dispatch*, February 26, 1998, D10.

8. Ellen Wojahn, "Why There Aren't More Women in This Magazine," *Inc.*, July 1986, 46.

9. Catherine Romano, "It Looks Like Men Are from Mars. Women Are from Venus," *Management Review*, 1994, 7.

10. Holly E. Buttner and Dorothy P. Moore, "Women's Organizational Exodus to Entrepreneurship: Self-Reported Motivations and Correlates with Success," *Journal of Small Business Management*, January 1997, 34–36.

11. Romano, 7.

12. *2000 Statistical Abstract of the United States* (Washington, DC: U.S. Department of Commerce, Bureau of the Census), http://www.census.gov/csd/mwb.

13. Center for Women's Business Research, "Key Facts," http://www.nfwbo.org/key.html.

14. Joyce Smith, "Health Care, Capital, Economy Top Concerns of Women Business Owners," *Knight Ridder Tribune Business News*, September 25, 2003, 1.

15. Gerda Gallop-Goodman, "A Fund for Female Ventures," *Black Enterprise*, July 2000, 52.

16. Women's President Organization, "Membership Criteria," http://www.womenpresidentsorg.com/how_to_join/criteria.htm.

17. Martha Firestone, "Reasons for Optimism About Women in Business," *Journal Record*, October 17, 2002, 1.

18. Center for Women's Business Research.

19. "Seminar on Women Entrepreneurs," *Chennai*, March 4, 2004, 1.

20. Glenda Stone, "BT Increases Support for UK Women Entrepreneurs," *The British Journal of Administration Management*, Spring 2003, 8.

21. Margaret Snyder, "Bridging the Research Gap: A Profile of Women Entrepreneurs in Uganda," *International Trade Forum*, 2003, 22.

22. Radha Cheganti and Patricia Greene, "Who Are Ethnic Entrepreneurs?" *Journal of Small Business Management*, April 2002, 126; Information Development Group, "Minority Entrepreneurs: A Review of Current Literature," http://www.answerbusiness.net/bridg.

23. John Sibely Butler, "Black Entrepreneurship. The Sequel," *Inc.*, October 1996, 31.

24. Laurie M. Grossman, "Expanding Horizons," *The Wall Street Journal*, April 3, 1992, R5.

25. John N. Ingham, "Build Businesses, Creating Communities: Residential Segregation and the Growth of African American Business in Southern Cities, 1880–1915," *Business History Review*, Winter 2003, 639.

26. The State of Small Black Business," *Black Enterprise*, November 1997, 65–73.

27. Asia American Hotel Owners Association, http://www.aahoa.com.

28. Pauline Yoshohashi, "How the Kims of L.A. and Other Koreans Made It in the U.S.," *The Wall Street Journal*, June 16, 1992, 1.

29. "Minority-Owned Business Enterprises," 1997 Economic Census, http://www.census.gov.

30. Ingrid Abramovitch, "Seize the Moment," *Success*, June 1994, 23.

31. Milford Prewitt, "Hispanics Find Job Niche in Restaurant Industry," *Nation's Business News*, February 1, 1999, 41–46.

32. Jose M. Fornes, "El Sueno Americano: Como los Latinos Pueden Triunfar en los Estados Unidos," *Library Journal*, January 1999, 80.

33. "Minority-Owned Business Enterprises."

34. Eugene Carlson, "Battling Bias," *The Wall Street Journal*, April 3, 1992, R1.

35. Michael Puente, "Cash Flow Woes," *Chicago Post-Tribune*, http://www.post-trib.com/news/race0922.html.

36. No Author, "Minority Firms Access to Capital," National Center for Policy

Analysis,   http://www.ncpa.org/pd/
economy/pdo321006.html.

37. Timothy Bates and William Bradford,
"Minorities and Venture Capital,"
http://www.kaufman.org/pdf/minorities
_vc_report.pdf.

38. Eugene Carlson, "Battling Bias," *The
Wall Street Journal*, April 3, 1992, R1.

39. Randy Crump, "Commentary: Is There
Enough Room at the Bottom?" *The
Daily Reporter*, March 26, 2004, 1.

40. John   Micklethwait   and   Adrian
Wooldridge, *The Right Nation* (East
Rutherford, NJ: Penguin Press, 2004),
239.

41. http://www.kaufman.org.

Chapter 7

Home-Based Businesses

LEARNING OBJECTIVES

- $ To realize that home-based businesses were common before the Industrial Revolution.

- $ To identify the reasons for the increasing number of home-based businesses.

- $ To understand the advantages and disadvantages of home-based businesses.

- $ To be aware of the legal, insurance, and tax issues applicable to home-based businesses.

THE REBIRTH OF COTTAGE INDUSTRIES

Before the development of the railroads and communication systems in the United States, the country's economy depended on people working at home. The number of these businesses, referred to as *cottage industries*, decreased during the past century as industrial parks and office complexes became more common. However, the trend has now come full circle, and home-based businesses are once again becoming very common.[1]

The number of home-based businesses is growing rapidly; government studies have estimated that home-based businesses comprise more than 50 percent of all firms and generate more than $300 billion in revenue.[2]

Home-based businesses are not distributed evenly across the United States, although there is no obvious explanation for the differences. Hawaii, Utah, and Wyoming have the highest percentage of businesses in the home, compared to non-home-based businesses. The states with the highest proportion of home-based businesses with employees are relatively rural—Arkansas, New Hampshire, Washington, and Vermont.[3]

> **Cottage industries** – industries in which the labor force works from home.

REASONS FOR GROWTH

The increase in popularity of home businesses is due to many factors, including the increasing use of the Internet, recessions and corporate downsizing, greater concern for family issues, and the improving image of home-based businesses.

Increasing Use of the Internet

The Internet has changed the lives of people and revolutionized the way many enterprises conduct business. Home-based businesses, often operated by the entrepreneur without additional employees, can now market products globally. For example, Joan Abbe operates Chocolate Expression out of her home in Lake St. Louis, Missouri. Using her Web site, she markets specialty chocolate gifts to businesses. Her products have been sold in many countries around the world.[4]

Auction sites, such as eBay, have also provided many opportunities for home-based entrepreneurs. According to Meg Whitman, president and CEO of eBay, "The success of e-commerce is the success of millions of invisible pioneers in garages and spare bedrooms from New York to St. Louis, from LA to Sioux City."[5] She estimates that more than 430,000 Americans are making a substantial part of their income by selling on the eBay site.[6]

Recessions and Corporate Downsizing

Whenever the economy goes through a recession, many people who are laid off decide to start a business. During the late 1980s and early 1990s, when a recession occurred, the number of self-employed people increased. And from 2002 to 2003 when the economy again recovered slowly, the National Association of the Self-Employed saw its membership increase by 25 percent. Half of the organization's members now operate home-based businesses.[7]

During recessions and downsizings, businesses are started not only by those who lose their jobs but also by some of the employees who survive the first round of layoffs. The morale of the remaining employees is often poor because they have seen friends lose their jobs. In addition, their workload often increases as the company tries to do more work with fewer people. Finally, some employees are afraid that they will lose their jobs if there is another round of layoffs. For example, Austin Monroe, Jr., worked as an electrical engineer at Rockwell International. However, when layoffs occurred, he started his own home-based business. He explains his career move by saying, "I wanted to get out before I got dumped."[8] For many reasons then, recessions and corporate downsizings have caused people to start home-based businesses.

Greater Concern for Family Issues

Many people have been establishing home-based businesses because of the desire for greater balance between work and family life. Surveys indicate that the new generation of workers is not willing to work long hours at a company at the expense of family time. A home business may provide more time with family members.

Other people work at home so children do not have to be placed in full-time day care. Spending time with children, especially when they are young, is a deciding factor for many home-based entrepreneurs. More home-based entrepreneurs have children ages 18 and younger than self-employed people who have offices outside the home.

Improving Image of Home-Based Businesses

The attitudes of society are changing as working at home becomes more commonplace. In years past, home-based businesses were stigmatized as second-class businesses. Potential customers were concerned about the professionalism and quality of entrepreneurs who were home-based. The general attitude was that they were not good enough to have a "real business." Home-based entrepreneurs would try not to mention that they did not have an office in a commercial location. "Ten years ago, if you were working out of your home, it was like you had some sort of disease," says Don Vleck, a former vice president of Domino's Pizza, who now works from his home advising companies on executive efficiency.[9] Now entrepreneurs have found that their clients' skepticism concerning professionalism and quality has changed to envy of their freedom.

ADVANTAGES AND DISADVANTAGES OF HOME-BASED BUSINESSES

Operating a home-based business has many advantages and disadvantages. Let's consider some of those benefits and obstacles.

Advantages

No commuting For many Americans, commuting to work is time consuming, stressful, and expensive. It is common for people to spend an hour or two every workday just to get to and from work. The wasted time spent sitting in a car or on public transportation could be better spent on work or family activities. Commuting has also been shown to lead to health problems. The stress and pollution are thought to contribute to a higher rate of heart disease. Finally, the price of gasoline has fluctuated in recent years, and many people find the increasing costs to be a huge drain on the family budget. Home-based entrepreneurs do not have to endure any of these problems. Their work is always a few steps away.

Lower Wardrobe Costs

For many corporate employees, the purchase and maintenance of clothing are a burden. Shopping for work attire is costly, time consuming, and often seen as a chore. Many people feel required to wear clothing they do not especially like, only because it is considered "appropriate dress" for their office. In addition, if the clothing must be dry cleaned, they endure another costly weekly expense.

While some home-based entrepreneurs may need good clothing to meet clients, they may not need as many outfits and they may have more choice in what to wear. Home-based entrepreneurs who do not frequently meet clients (for example, software developers and eBay sellers) may be happily sitting at home in blue jeans while they are working.

Flexible Hours

Many home-based entrepreneurs love the flexibility of working at any hour of the day. For some, work can be completed at 4 a.m. as easily as 10 p.m. If the entrepreneur is trying to raise a family, working while the children are asleep is a wonderful advantage.

Disadvantages

Although a home-based business has many advantages, not everyone is suited for this type of life, and the family's cooperation is an important factor. Some of these personal and family considerations are discussed next.

Loss of structure "Losing the structure of a daily routine is a big deal for most people," says syndicated columnist Joyce Brothers. "This is a big reason why going into business for yourself is tougher than most people think."[10] In a home-based business, there is less structure than if the entrepreneur has an office or business that has specific operating hours. There is little structure, no boss, no one to notice if you start working late or watch television in the middle of the day. For this reason, a home-based worker must be self-disciplined. Many people who are successful at home are those who are outgoing self-starters who enjoy going out to market their business. Kathleen Van De Zande, a home-based business owner, states, "Staying dedicated to the growth of your business is a tough thing to do alone. There is no one else there who needs the business to succeed."[11]

Isolation One of the biggest problems encountered by the home-based entrepreneur is isolation. Particularly in the early stages of the business before a good customer base is established, the entrepreneur's ability to combat isolation may mean the difference between success and failure. There are no chats at the water cooler or hallway conversations.[12] Rollene Saal left her job as editor-in-chief of Bantam Books to start a literary agency from home. Although she has a successful business, she misses the support of the office and found the first two years difficult. She summarizes her feelings by saying, "You miss your chums." If a person needs constant interaction, a home-based business is not a good idea.[13]

Long hours with no separation between work and home Although home-based businesses may seem to be a way to make money in your spare time, this is rarely the case. According to an article in *Kiplinger's Personal Finance Magazine*, the most successful home entrepreneurs have not only a good idea and a passion for their business but also a tendency toward workaholism.[14]

The lack of separation between work and home makes it easier to become a workaholic. One entrepreneur stated, "You don't go home from work. You're always at work—you go to bed with work."[15] Kathy Lynch, a spokesperson for Boston College, says that when home-based workers are in the home, "they are surrounded by work. It's hard to turn it off."[16] Omar Wasow, founder of New York Online, found his rapidly growing home-based business taking over his apartment. He states, "An expanding home-based business can be really corrosive and frustrating if you're not careful."[17]

Family interruptions Although balancing work and family life is often a major factor in deciding to start a home-based business, the entrepreneur often has unrealistic expectations. Those who expect young children to play quietly all day without interrupting their mother or father find that the home business arrangement does not work as easily as they had anticipated. Plans must be made to try to accommodate children and business demands.

HOME-BASED FRANCHISES

For many years, most franchises were in industries such as fast food, in which location was a key ingredient of success. Now home-based franchises are being developed as franchisors hope to capitalize on the home business trend. According to the International Franchise Association there were 93 different home-based franchises to choose from in 2004. These franchises include home-inspection service, travel agencies, and wedding consultants.[18]

Home-based franchises combine the flexibility of a home-based business with the experience of the franchisor. For example, Corliss Clark-Barnes purchased a Computer Tots franchise, a company that provides computer classes for preschool children. The franchisor sends a monthly packet containing successful marketing ideas of the Computer Tots franchises and publishes a newsletter that reports on the latest issues and trends in education. Corliss says she looks forward to the monthly packets and is happy that the franchisor provides a support network.[19]

But these are not for everyone. Michael Baum, executive vice president of a franchise development company, describes the ideal home-based franchisee as one who loves sales and is self-motivated, able to work alone, committed, disciplined and willing to follow the franchisor's plan.[20] While this is similar to the advice for all home-based entrepreneurs, the need to follow the franchisor's plan may not be acceptable to entrepreneurs who are extremely independent.

All franchises must be investigated carefully, as we noted in chapter 5. Many home-based franchises do not succeed or produce far less income than the entrepreneur originally expected.

IS YOUR HOME-BASED BUSINESS LEGAL?

Zoning laws – local ordinances that restrict the use of property for specific purposes.

Although the interest in home-based businesses has increased dramatically, zoning laws in many communities have not recognized this shift. Many entrepreneurs who plan to start a home-based business find that their communities will not allow it. Paul and Sarah Edwards, authors of self-employment books and hosts on entrepreneur radio network, say that most bans on home-based businesses were put into place decades ago to shelter neighborhoods from smoke, dirt, and noise generated by factories. These rules do not recognize the change to today's high-tech and service-oriented industries. [21]

Some cities do not completely ban home-based businesses but often prohibit employees other than family members and/or limit the square footage of a home that can be used. Stillwater, Oklahoma, had these restrictions until the city revised its laws. In large metropolitan areas such as Chicago, each municipality sets its own rules. In one suburb of Chicago, the city closed two home-based day care centers that had employees and refused a request from a lawyer who wanted to hire a secretary.[22]

Some cities require home-based business owners to fill out special forms, and some of the requirements depend on the business. Robert Tarutis started Tarutis Communications Group, Inc., out of his home in Waltham, Massachusetts, and found that he didn't need a business permit. If he had customers going in and out of the home, though, he would have had to apply for a zoning variance.[23]

Property is usually zoned in one of four ways—residential, commercial, industrial, or agricultural. A home-based business is usually legal in all but residential zoning. It is sometimes possible to obtain a waiver or variance from the city to operate a home-based business in an area where it is normally restricted. For example, Wesley Morrison wanted to operate a desktop publishing company from his apartment in Philadelphia and was informed that it was illegal. He spent an entire afternoon convincing city employees that his business would not be noisy and disturbing to the other apartment dwellers. Eventually, he obtained a variance.[24]

Other entrepreneurs find that the zoning ordinances are inflexible and that they cannot obtain a variance. Faced with this situation, many decide to operate illegally. One entrepreneur had been restoring antique furniture for friends and relatives as a hobby for many years. Eventually through word of mouth, his business increased to a level at which he wanted to make his hobby into a legal business. Unfortunately, zoning laws would not allow this type of business in the home and no variance could be obtained. Therefore, he continues to operate his "hobby" without a business license.

Entrepreneurs who live in condominiums, townhouses, apartments, and private subdivisions may also find that there are restrictions placed by the property associations and management. Therefore, in addition to the zoning restrictions, it is necessary to check leases, subdivision bylaws, and other contracts.

UTILITIES, INSURANCE, AND TAXES

Before opening a home office, entrepreneurs should also consider utility and insurance ramifications. Many homes are not equipped to handle such utility needs, and these requirements must be considered if the office is to operate efficiently. For example, Ray Ruth, a computer consultant who works from his home in Connecticut, suggests that you start planning for a home-based business by calling an electrician. He found that whenever his room air conditioner turns on, the computer equipment slows down.[25] The power needed by office equipment may be too great for the existing wiring, and precious time may be wasted.

Home-based businesses have special insurance needs and are usually not covered by regular homeowner's insurance. In fact, most homeowner's policies specifically exclude coverage for any type of business activity. Therefore, if a fire is traced to an office machine, the entire homeowner coverage could be voided.[26] And if employees or customers come to the home, additional liability insurance

---

A SURVEY BY THE INDEPENDENT INSURANCE AGENTS OF AMERICA REVEALED THE FOLLOWING:

Percentage of home-based businesses not properly insured ----- 60

Percentage of home-based entrepreneurs who mistakenly thought they were covered under another policy ------------------44

Percentage unaware that insurance was needed ----------------------6

Source: Adapted from "IIAA Survey Shows Most In-Home Businesses Are Not Properly Covered," *Rough Notes*, June 1997, 20.

FIGURE 7–1   Insurance lacking for home-based businesses.

---

may be needed.[27] In a survey of home-based entrepreneurs, many were found to be underinsured. (See Figure 7–1.)

Some insurers are willing to issue an endorsement that will extend home coverage to the home business. Typically, there is an additional fee, but it's usually under $600. If the home-based business does not qualify for an endorsement, the entrepreneur should purchase a regular commercial policy providing the same coverage as any basic business policy.[28]

The Taxpayer Relief Act of 1997 brought welcome changes to the tax laws for many home-based entrepreneurs. Prior to that time, someone who spent most of the day at his or her customers' locations could not take a tax deduction for a home office. A key issue in determining the legality of the tax deduction was where the entrepreneur spent most of his or her working time. If that time was not in the home office, no tax deduction was allowed. This was detrimental to many businesses such as lawn care, pest control, and air conditioning and heating repairs.

But this act (which took effect in the 1999 tax year) allows entrepreneurs to qualify for the deduction even if they use their home office mainly for administrative tasks and do the bulk of their work on the road. In order for the entrepreneur to qualify, the following two conditions must apply:

$ The taxpayer uses the office for administrative or management activities.
$ The taxpayer does not conduct "substantial" administrative or management activities anywhere else.

The U.S. Small Business Administration says the new law is expected to save small business owners as much as $2.3 billion over 10 years.[29]

The home office deduction is advantageous in the short run; however, many are not aware that there may be a tax liability if the home is sold. If the home has been depreciated as part of the tax deduction and the entrepreneur sells the home, a capital gains tax may be due.[30]

Therefore, entrepreneurs should check with their tax advisor if they are planning to sell the home in the coming years.

THE GROWTH DECISION

If a home-based business is successful, the entrepreneur may need to decide whether to scale back the business or relocate to commercial space. When employees are hired, the lack of privacy becomes a factor if they are using spare bedrooms, bathrooms, and so forth. Marth Gay, who runs a research business in Fort Washington, Pennsylvania, had her office off her bedroom until an employee stole $50 from her underwear drawer. She moved her office twice within the same house to try to maintain privacy. She then moved the office to the third floor of the home explaining that she wants to be "as far away from the living space as I can get."[31]

Terri Alpert operated Professional Cutlery Direct LLC from her home for two years. But her laptop computer, five phone lines, and basement full of inventory could not keep up with the company's growth. When she realized she could not add new product lines because she did not have room, she decided to move.[32]

Many entrepreneurs choose another option: they limit growth by increasing prices or by contracting work out to others rather than give up privacy or move to a commercial space. Others try to compromise by keeping an office at home while also opening an office or warehouse at another location. One entrepreneur who started a book publishing company from her southern California home opened an office in Los Angeles after her company outgrew her garage, but she opted to stay behind and run the business from home.[33]

THE HOME-BASED BUSINESS IN THE BUSINESS PLAN

If a business will be home-based, this should be stated in the business plan in the location section. If the business plan will be presented to banks or potential investors, it should be noted that the business location complies with local and state laws. For businesses that will need a business license, the entrepreneur should indicate that he or she is aware of the requirements and that the license will be secured if funding is received. Also, it is a good idea to identify the company's insurance agent and state whether insurance in addition to the regular homeowners' insurance will be needed.

SUMMARY

Home-based businesses were common before the Industrial Revolution. After that time, most people began to work for large corporations, and the number of home-based businesses sharply declined. In recent years, there has been a resurgence because of the increasing use of the Internet, recessions and corporate downsizing, greater concern for family issues, and the improving image of home-based businesses. Operating a home-based business has many advantages and disadvantages, and the entrepreneur is advised to consider the pros and cons of working from home before starting the business.

DISCUSSION QUESTIONS

1. Identify the factors that have led to the increase in home-based businesses.
2. Identify advantages and disadvantages that should be considered when starting a home-based business.
3. Why do some communities prevent home-based businesses?

ENDNOTES

1. George Beiswinger, "The Home Office: A Practical Guide," *D&B Reports*, January/February 1994, 38.

2. Odette Pollar, "Homeward Bound," *Successful Meetings*, April 1998, 101–103.

3. JoAnne H. Pratt, "Home-based Businesses: The Hidden Economy," http://www.sba.gov/advo/research.

4. Lacey Burnette, "Chocolate Expressions Is Sweet Business for Lake St. Louis Woman," *The St. Louis Post-Dispatch*, July 25, 2000, 3.

5. "Small Business Is the Real Internet Story," *Business Wire*, May 6, 2004.

6. Ibid.

7. National Association for the Self-Employed, http://www.nase.org.

8. Adrienne S. Harris, "Hot Franchises You Can Run from Your Home," *Black Enterprise*, September 1993, 64.

9. John Grossmann, "Meeting's at 9. I'll Be the One in Slippers," *Inc.,* May 19, 1998, 47–48.

10. James Morrow, "House Calls," *Success*, February 1998, 67–68.

11. Caimetta Coleman, "Home Alone," *The Wall Street Journal*, October 14, 1994, R20.

12. Ibid.

13. Louise Washer, "Home Alone," *Working Woman*, March 1993, 46.

14. Ronaleen R. Roha and Ed Henry, "These Home Businesses Are Smoking," *Kiplingers Personal Finance Magazine,* March 1998, 142–149.

15. Morrow, 67–68.

16. Susan Stronger Clarke, "Home-Based Workers Put in Longer Hours, Study Shows," *The San Diego Tribune*, February 26, 2001, C3.

17. Morrow, 67–68.

18. Jan Norman, "Examine Fees, Growth Potential of Home-based Franchise, Experts Suggest," *Knight Ridder Tribune Business News,* July 18, 2004.

19. Harris, 64.

20. Harris, 60.

21. Julie Fanselow, "Zoning Laws vs. Home Businesses," *Nation's Business*, August 1992, 35; and Paul and Sarah Edwards, "Are You Wondering About Your Next STEP to Become Self-Employed," http://www.workingfromhome.com.

22. Martha Irvine, "Not Welcome," *The Wall Street Journal*, October 14, 1994, R22.

23. Jill Andresky Fraser, "Home Grown," *Inc.,* December 1999, 92–108.

24. Fanselow, 35.

25. Stephanie N. Mehta, "Power and More Power," *The Wall Street Journal*, October 14, 1992, R6.

26. Beiswinger, 38.

27. Ibid.

28. Fraser, 92–108.

29. Joan Pryde, "Easier Deductions for Home Offices," *Nation's Business*, March 1998, 39.

30. Mary L. Sprouse, "Three Ways to Make the 1997 Tax Law Work for Your Small Business," *Money,* February 1998, 32.

31. Washer, 47.

32. Fraser, 92–108.

33. Washer, 50.

Family Businesses

LEARNING OBJECTIVES

$ To become aware that most of the businesses in the United States are family-owned.

$ To understand the advantages and disadvantages of being an entrepreneurial couple.

$ To understand the alternatives for the entrepreneur's children to enter the business.

$ To comprehend the issues that need to be addressed in a succession plan.

WHAT IS A FAMILY BUSINESS?

Family business – a majority of ownership of control lies within a family, and two or more family members are directly involved in the business.

The term *family business* is defined in a number of ways. The U.S. Small Business Administration defines a family business as one in which a majority of the ownership or control lies within a family, and in which two or more family members are directly involved.[1] However, when the Massachusetts Mutual Life Insurance Company completes its annual survey of family businesses, it defines a family business as a firm that meets any one of the following criteria:

$ "In addition to the owner or co-owners of the business, other family members work in the day-to-day operations of the business.
$ The owner intends to pass on his or her ownership position to a close relative.
$ The owner considers the firm to be a family business (self-described)."[2]

Family businesses play a substantial role in the U.S. economy. According to the Family Firm Institute in Brookline, Massachusetts, family businesses account for 78 percent of all new job creation and 60 percent of the nation's employment. More than 80 percent of all business enterprises in North America and the majority internationally are family-owned. In addition, nearly 35 percent of the Fortune 500 companies are family firms.[3] Some large corporations that began as family businesses and are still controlled by their founding families are Ford, Johnson & Johnson, Marriott, Motorola, Nordstrom, Philip Morris, and Wal-Mart.[4] In Canada, one of the largest businesses, Cara, is a family-owned company that operates 1,200 restaurants and employs 39,000 workers.[5]

ADVANTAGES AND DISADVANTAGES

Family businesses have unique advantages when everyone works well together. These advantages include stability, trust, resilience, positive public perception, speed, and the ability to sacrifice for the long haul.[6]

However, family businesses have a unique set of problems because family issues often spill over into the business operations. In addition, the success of a family and a business are based on different criteria. Dan Bishop, president of the National Family Business Association, states, "A family is based on emotion, nurturing, and security, but a business revolves around productivity, accomplishment, and profit."[7] John Messervey, director of the National Family Business Council, believes that family harmony is essential. Messervey says, "Most people have the part about making money down pat. It's the part about the family that tends to unglue them."[8] In this section, we will first consider entrepreneurial couples and then discuss the issues that arise when children enter the family business.

ENTREPRENEURIAL COUPLES

Having your spouse as a business partner is becoming a popular idea. Entrepreneurial couples are one of the fastest growing segments of the business population. The National Federation of Independent Businesses estimates that 1.2 million U.S. businesses are operated by husband and wife entrepreneurial teams. That figure is actually a low estimate, though, because it only includes businesses

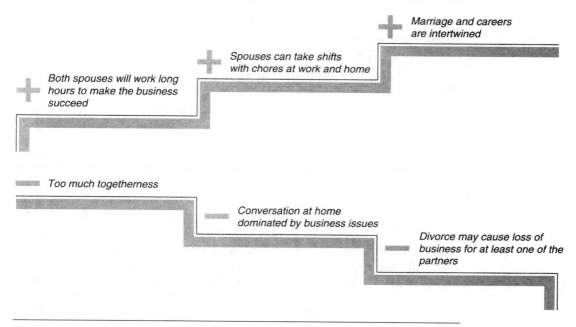

Too much togetherness

FIGURE 8–1   Advantages and disadvantages of entrepreneurial couples.

that have employees. Many husband-wife teams own businesses but do not have any employees.[9] Entrepreneurial couples own businesses that range from small mom-and-pop operations to companies owning billions in assets.

Entrepreneurial couples find the experience both rewarding and stressful (see Figure 8–1). As an article in *Fortune Small Business* stated, "Neither building a business nor sustaining a happy marriage is easy—and trying to do both at once can seem an impossible dream."[10] Particularly in the early years of the company, when cash flow is limited, the partner–spouse arrangement can be a tremendous asset. It is very common for the husband and wife to work long hours for less pay than any employee would tolerate. Spouse partnerships can also balance work and family life successfully, once the business is much larger. Often, one spouse will work an early shift and the other spouse will work a later shift. While this type of arrangement has advantages, the obvious disadvantage is that the amount of personal time the couple spends together is limited. Time must be set aside to relate as husband and wife, not just as business partners.

A more common situation is for the husband and wife to work together in the business all day long. Some couples find that this is too much togetherness. Unlike couples who have separate lives and careers during the day, entrepreneurial couples may find that when they come home, they have nothing to say to each other. There is nothing new to report, no need to say, "Guess what happened at the office?" An even more common problem is that discussions about work take place at home and often consume a major portion of the time the couple spends communicating. Anton Rush, who owns a PR firm with his wife, Jane Applebee, states, "We've been known to talk about work in the middle of the night. I'd estimate it invades 80 percent of our conversation."[11] For this reason it is important to establish time to discuss personal issues, such as those that

---

Establish a time—at least once a month—to nurture the personal relationship.

Reserve a separate time to discuss ownership or business issues.

Practice healthy confrontation by describing the spouse's observed behavior and then discussing personal feelings.

Find a family business consultant to help resolve conflicts.

Source: Henry D. Landes and Ellen Frankenberg, "Case Study: A Business Threatens a Couple," *Nation's Business,* June 1998, 72.

FIGURE 8–2   Advice for entrepreneurial couples.

---

concern the couple's relationship, or the marriage will suffer. Figure 8–2 provides some advice.

Many of the suggestions for regular partnerships are especially true for entrepreneurial couples. Sharing power and decision making is a concern for all partners, but husbands and wives often find this a problem area. Experts usually suggest assigning specific areas of responsibility and having a written agreement detailing what type of decisions need both partners' approval. Sometimes there is a natural division of responsibility. For example, Terry and Stella Henry started a long-term care and assisted-living facility in California. Since Stella is a registered nurse, she is responsible for patient care and employees. Terry is responsible for business and finance matters.[12] Frances Cook, the managing director of a career-management consulting firm, says the couple's skills must be compatible—different but complementary. Each person must respect what the other contributes.[13]

It is also critical for the couple to have the same goals and share the same vision for the company. They must agree on whether the company should grow slowly or quickly, when new product lines should be added, and so forth. One of the most publicized entrepreneurial couples, Doug and Susie Tompkins of Esprit de Corps, could not agree on the direction for their $800 million clothing company. While Doug wanted to maintain the youthful look of the clothing, Susie argued that customers' tastes were changing and a more mature look was required. This indecision, along with many other marital and business problems, caused the company severe financial problems.[14]

A final issue is the effect of a divorce. A divorce may result in the financial ruin or forced sale of a company even if only one spouse was the owner/operator of the business and the other spouse had a career elsewhere. For entrepreneurial couples, a divorce is even more complicated. Nine states are considered *community property states*, in which essentially all assets and liabilities acquired during a marriage are split 50-50. This includes the business venture. The other 41 states are considered *equitable-distribution states*, where the courts divide assets and liabilities accumulated during the course of the marriage according to family circumstances and state guidelines. In both situations, the entrepreneur must come up with cash to pay the spouse for his or her percentage. If cash is not available and a payment plan cannot be agreed upon, the entrepreneur may have to sell the company to raise the cash. If an entrepreneurial couple gets divorced, it must be determined which spouse will leave the company if the former husband and wife no longer wish to work together. Because of these problems, it is suggested that all entrepreneurs develop a prenuptial agreement if the business exists when they get married or a postnuptial agreement if the business is started

Community property state – state in which all assets and abilities acquired during a marriage are split 50-50 if a divorce occurs.

Equitable distribution state – a state in which courts divide assets and liabilities of a marriage according to family circumstances and state guidelines.

after they are married.[15] One consultant states, "It all gets so anti-entrepreneurial. You work and work to build something . . . and then, because a personal relationship has failed, you find yourself in this totally negative situation . . . And doing negative things isn't something you—or the company—can recover from overnight."[16]

BRINGING IN THE CHILDREN

As with entrepreneurial couples, businesses operated by the owner and the children range from small shops to extremely large firms. For example, the mutual fund industry, worth almost $2 trillion, is operated by many family businesses. Some of the most successful funds have been managed by the same family for decades or generations.[17]

Many entrepreneurial families eventually bring the children into the business. Often, from an early age, children help out with the company activities, and the business is part of their lives. It may seem, then, that the transition from parent to child would be a simple, natural step, but this is rarely how it happens. Only about one-third of family businesses are successfully transferred to the second generation, and only 10 to 20 percent are transferred to the third generation.[18] Less than 13 percent of family businesses stay in the family for more than 60 years.[19] This failure of transition to the next generation occurs for several reasons. First, many children do not want the family business, which requires long hours and a substantial commitment that many children choose not to assume. The children may also have different interests; just because the father or mother liked a certain occupation does not guarantee that their children want the same career. Finally, children often want to go in a different direction in order to prove themselves, not wanting to live in the parent's shadow.

A second reason why businesses are not successfully transferred is sibling rivalry. For example, Becky Whatley had worked at her father's printing business for a number of years when her brother graduated from college and joined the company. Even though her brother was new to the company, her father made him sales manager and paid him the same amount of money as Becky. Fortunately, they were able to work through their feelings of rivalry, and today they are partners. Many other siblings find that their rivalry is so strong that it ruins the company.[20]

Even if sibling rivalry is not an issue, the transition to the next generation is often difficult. For the entrepreneur, it is usually agonizing to relinquish the management of his or her company (his or her "baby"). Arnold Daniels, president of Praendex Inc., had numerous problems when he tried to give control to his sons. He realizes now that he "was looking for somebody who would do exactly what I do, the way I do it." He was not willing to listen to their ideas. For Daniels, the solution finally came when he delegated control to his daughter, who had a very successful public relations career outside the family business. Her conciliatory personality meshed better with her father's personality, and he was more willing to listen to her ideas.[21]

This reluctance to transfer management to the second generation has a lot to do with the characteristics of the classic entrepreneur, says Joachim Schwass, a professor of family business at Switzerland's IMD Business School. "They are not willing to let go of control and not sufficiently aware of what they need to do to prepare the next generation."[22]

The transition to the next generation can also be complicated if the company was founded by a partnership. Taylor-Morley, Inc., a home-building company, was founded by two men who worked well together. The company grew from a small start-up into a large firm grossing $110 million annually. However, when the company was transferred to their sons, the sons of the partners did not have a good working relationship, and legal battles and operational problems quickly developed.[23]

The Succession Plan

Succession – the process of transferring leadership of a business to the new generation.

The process of transferring leadership to the next generation is known as *succession*. In order for a successful transfer to occur, the entrepreneur must transfer more than just the company assets and operations. Kay B. Wakefield, a Portland attorney who specializes in family business, states, "The easiest part of a succession plan is transferring the hard assets; the most difficult part is transferring leadership and values."[24] This should not occur quickly. Instead, a process referred to as the *succession plan* should be carried out over a long period of time with a well-designed strategy. The plan details how succession will occur and how to know when the successor is capable of taking over company management.[25] Lack of planning for the succession is one of the major reasons why transfers are often not successful.

Whatever the decision of the founder, his or her plans regarding succession should be made clear. The children should know if they will take over management or if the business will be sold to an outsider. If they spend years working in the business only to find it sold to an outsider, they may have trouble finding positions in other companies. On the other hand, if the children are not told that they will take over some day, they often leave the family business only to find that their parents feel hurt because "the children did not show an interest in the company." For this reason, plans should be made clear and should be stated early enough so that the children are able to make good career decisions. Unfortunately, most entrepreneurs (about 63 percent) wait until retirement age or even later to begin their succession plan.[26]

The succession plan addresses many issues that help both the entrepreneur and the second generation plan for the future. Some of the concerns that should be resolved are discussed next.

Should the Company Be Sold to an Outsider or Employees?

While many business owners assume that the company should be passed on to the children, they should also consider the option of selling to an outside party or to employees. Entrepreneurs may be surprised to know that many children of wealthy entrepreneurs are happy that the wealth was not handed to them. John Katzman's parents own Kaz, Inc., the New York City company that invented the electric vaporizer. He says that parental wealth is just that—parental wealth. "My parents made it pretty clear that I didn't have money; they had money." He is now glad that the distinction was made; he has since started his own college-exam coaching program. Because he grew up rich, Katzman says, "I started life on the 30-yard line. Do I really need somebody to kick it into the end zone for me?"[27]

Employee stock ownership plan – employees own stock in the company that employs them.

Many entrepreneurs realize that the employees were an important factor in the success of the business, and they reward the employees' efforts by transferring some or all of the ownership to them. This is often accomplished through an *employee stock ownership plan (ESOP)* in which the stock that was owned by the entrepreneur is purchased by the company and is then transferred to the employees. Generally, some employees are appointed to a board of directors that then makes company decisions. Bob Daggs, owner of GRC, decided to transfer ownership through an ESOP because he felt that his sons needed time to learn more about the business and he saw employees as part of a "larger family." Therefore, he used an ESOP to sell 51 percent of the company to the employees and eventually plans to transfer his 49 percent to his sons and other family members.[28]

HOW AND WHEN SHOULD THE COMPANY BE TRANSFERRED?

The entrepreneur has many choices when transferring ownership of the business. The ownership may be transferred to family members as a gift, or it may be sold to them. The company may be transferred while the entrepreneur is still living, or it may be transferred upon his or her death. Some transfers are combinations of several options. However, because of the tax implications of these decisions, legal and financial advice is essential.[29]

Active Versus Inactive Family Members

When there are several children in a family, it is common for some to be active members who work in the business and others to have no interest at all. Although this is not of concern when the entrepreneur is still running the company, problems concerning stock ownership often develop when the second generation takes over. Some families believe it's only fair to give each child an equal portion of the stock. While this results in equal treatment, it often causes problems, since children who are not active in the daily operations of the company, sometimes called *inactive family members*, still have decision-making power.

If the entrepreneur has enough other assets, such as a house and publicly traded stocks and bonds, these can be given to the inactive family members and the business can be given to those who will be running it. For many entrepreneurs, however, the value of the business far exceeds the value of all other assets and this business-nonbusiness split still would not result in a distribution that is equal in monetary terms.

Active family member – person who works in the family business.

Inactive family member – person who does not take part in the daily operations of the family business.

Low Entry Versus Delayed Entry

The *low-entry strategy* recommends that children begin working at the company in an entry-level position so that they can work their way up and learn all aspects of the business in the process. This way they can develop skills that are important for the business, as well as the relationships with customers and employees that are formed in the process. One disadvantage of this strategy, however, is that the entrepreneur is often not good at training his or her own children, and conflicts often result. In addition, the children do not have any outside experience on which to draw, and this may limit their ability to develop new ideas.

The *delayed-entry strategy* recommends that children work outside the company to learn new ideas and be successful in their own careers. They can then rejoin the company in a management position. Those who favor this approach state that it contributes to family employees' self-esteem, gives them credibility among nonfamily managers, and brings new ideas to the company.[30] Problems may still

Low-entry strategy – recommendation that children begin working in the family business in an entry-level position, often at a young age.

Delayed-entry strategy – recommendation that children work outside the family business and then rejoin it in a management position.

arise, however, because the child lacks the specific expertise or understanding that the company needs. Employee morale is also a concern when family members are brought in at a higher level than long-time employees.[31]

Each entrepreneur must consider his or her own situation, that of the business, and that of the children before deciding which approach is best. While some business consultants recommend that the children *always* work outside the company for at least three years, each family and each business is different. It is a personal decision as well as a business decision, and only the entrepreneur and the children can determine what is best.

Hiring and Compensation Policy

The entrepreneur must decide whether any and all family members will be hired and whether they will be paid market rates or higher. Most experts advise that family members should not be hired unless they meet the same criteria as outside employees. The entrepreneur must ask, "Would I hire this person if we were not related?" There should be no false jobs for false applicants. Family members must have a genuine interest in the firm and must make genuine contributions in a real, well-defined job. Pay should be based on merit and should be based on market rates. If a family bonus is given, it should remain separate from regular pay.[32]

SHOULD THERE BE A FAMILY COUNCIL AND ADVISORY BOARD?

Family council – a meeting of family members to discuss business issues and problems.

Many family business experts recommend a *family council*, a meeting of family members to discuss business issues and any problems that are occurring. This helps to stimulate discussion and prevent small problems from growing into large ones. The family council meets on a regular basis and may include all family members that work in the business as well as those who are inactive and the spouses of family members.

Advisory board – a group of family and nonfamily employees as well as outside advisors.

An *advisory board* often has family members as well as nonfamily members who work in the business. In addition, it usually includes advisors who are not a part of the company. These outside advisors may include other entrepreneurs, financial experts, university business faculty, and others who provide objective guidance for the family.

Choosing a Successor from Active Family Members

Problems may arise if several children want to manage the company. The parent must then decide if one child will be made president while others are given lesser positions, or if all children will share power equally. Appointing one child as president may result in hurt feelings, but equal power sharing does not always work. The owner of a construction firm who had inherited the company from his father decided to retire and give equal authority to his three sons who were active in the business. The brothers could not agree on management decisions and within a year of their ownership, the company was liquidated. In hindsight, the father believes that if he had appointed the most qualified son as president and had given him more authority than the others, the company liquidation might have been prevented.

This type of decision should be made clear to everyone as soon as possible. This may help to decrease sibling rivalry and uncertainty surrounding the future of the business. It also decreases the uncertainty of each child's career. Many owners of both large and small businesses, however, do not want to choose one child over the other. Dennis Jaffee, a professor at Saprook Graduate School, states that the successor feels like he is getting some special recognition from the family. "What's being given out in the family is esteem and respect." [33] This is a difficult decision for parents and an emotional time for the children.

THE FAMILY BUSINESS AND THE BUSINESS PLAN

The role of family members should be addressed in the management section of the business plan. Active members should be identified, and the compensation of family members should be addressed. In addition, if a family council or advisory board exists, this beneficial information should be included in the plan. Finally, if a succession plan exists, it should definitely be stated. As the entrepreneur ages, the succession plan will become more of a concern for bankers and investors.

SUMMARY

Most of the businesses in the United States are family-owned. Entrepreneurial couples and other family businesses face unique rewards and challenges. With the right mix of entrepreneurial spirit and family cohesion, a family business is a powerful economic force as well as a rewarding way of life. Steve Zuckerman, the president of a third-generation family firm, states, "Dad worked hard. He taught me honor, affection, and values." [34] If the family business can generate a profit and at the same time provide a positive environment for the children, it is a substantial accomplishment for the entrepreneur. Family businesses are likely to remain a powerful economic force and a rewarding way of life.

DISCUSSION QUESTIONS

1. From the children's perspective, what would be the advantages and disadvantages of growing up in a family in which one parent owns a business and the other works as an employee in another firm? What would be the advantages and disadvantages of having both parents work in the family business?

2. Why is it important to establish a hiring and compensation policy for family members?

3. What is the difference between the low-entry and the delayed-entry strategy? Which do you believe is best? Why?

4. What problems arise if a succession plan is not clearly stated?

ENDNOTES

1. "Transferring Management in the Family-Owned Business," http://www.sba.gov/sbainfo/manage-a-business/trans.txt.

2. Northeastern University's Center for Family Business, http://www.fambiz.com.

3. "Some Facts on Family Firms," *National Underwriter,* October 5, 1998, 10.

4. Nicholas Stein, "The Age of the Scion," *Fortune,* April 2, 2001, 121.

5. Mark Brown, "Inside An Empire," *Canadian Business,* May 24–June 6, 2004, 61.

6. George W. Rimler and Don Ingersoll, "How to Professionalize the Family Firm," *Air Conditioning, Heating & Refrigeration News,* June 19, 2001, 1.

7. Rich Babl, "All in the Family," *Business News,* Winter 1994, 9–11.

8. Ibid.

9. Ann Fisher, "Is Your Business Running Your Marriage?" *Fortune Small Business,* March 2003, 64.

10. Ibid.

11. Jim Davies, "Sleeping Partners," *Management Today,* London, October 1998, 112.

12. Fisher, 64.

13. Davies, 112.

14. Peter Waldman, "Flagging Spirit," *The Wall Street Journal,* March 16, 1988, 1.

15. Jill Andresky Fraser, "Divorce-Proofing Your Company," *Inc.,* September 1, 1998, 92.

16. Ellen Wojahn, "Divorce," *Inc.,* March 1986, 55–64.

17. "It's Just a Family Tradition," *The St. Louis Post-Dispatch,* November 7, 1993, E1.

18. William S. White, Timothy D. Krinke, and David L. Geller, "Family Business Succession Planning: Devising an Overall Strategy," *Journal of Financial Services Professionals,* May 2004, 67.

19. John Bedosky, "Planning a Successful Family Business Succession," *Trusts and Estates,* April 2002, 47.

20. Katherine O'Brien, "How to Succeed in Business," *American Printer,* April 1998, 60.

21. Curtis Hartman, "Why Daughters Are Better," *Inc.,* August 1987, 41–46.

22. Stein, 120.

23. Jack Naudi, "A House Divided," *St. Louis Post-Dispatch,* October 1, 2004, Cl.

24. Sharon Nelton, "Timeless Insights through Oral Histories," *Nation's Business,* March 1998, 72.

25. "Transferring Management in the Family-Owned Business."

26. Wendy M. Beech, "Keeping It in the Family," *Black Enterprise,* November 1998, 98.

27. Ellen Wojahn, "Share the Wealth, Spoil the Child," *Inc.,* August 1989, 64.

28. Bob Daggs, Mort Ockenfels, and Marcy Ockenfels, "Should You Leave the Company to Your Kids?" *Inc.,* May 1997, 121.

29. White, Krinke, and Geller, 67.

30. Sharon Nelton, "The Need to Clarify Expectations," *Nation's Business,* November 1998, 61.

31. Jeffrey A. Barach, Joseph Gantisky, James A. Carson, and Benjamin A. Doochin, "Entry of the Next Generation: Strategic Challenge for Family Business," *Journal of Small Business Management,* April 1988, 49–56.

32. Babl, 9–11.

33. Tom Nawrocki, "Family Affair: The Emotional Issues of Succession Planning," *Journal of Financial Planning,* July 2005, 34.

34. Babl, 9–11.

New Product Development

Chapter 9

LEARNING OBJECTIVES

$ To become aware that new product development is a high-risk endeavor.

$ To be able to explain why small companies can develop new products more easily than large companies can.

$ To know several ways of brainstorming for new product ideas.

$ To be able to identify the factors needed for a successful new product.

$ To comprehend the types of legal protection available for new products.

Consider the following challenges:

1. Identify a product that has had no major improvements in the past 20 years.
2. Dream up a concept that serves customers so well it changes people's lives.

While these challenges may at first seem difficult, after a short time ideas usually develop. For example, for more than 100 years, the engine under the hood of an automobile remained essentially the same. Wolfgang Armbrecht, director of innovation at BMW, states, "The internal combustion engine as we know it will become a thing of the past."[1] Hybrid gasoline-electric cars are already on the market and selling well. Many people believe that the car of the future will run on hydrogen. Hydrogen is the most abundant element in the universe.[2] Many people believe that if engine can be made to run on hydrogen, it will revolutionize the way we use power not only for cars but also for homes and businesses.

Many small businesses are started after the entrepreneur develops an idea for a new product or service. Although high-technology products get a lot of publicity, many highly successful, low-tech products and services have become successful. For example, Laurence Schwartz, founder of Rumpus Toys, develops low-tech toys. These toys include Harry Hairballs, a cat whose stomach contains fish bone, slippers, and hair balls, and Gus Gutz, whose stuffed organs are removable.[3]

A HIGH-RISK VENTURE

New product development is a high-risk endeavor, since many new products and services fail. Even large companies with experienced research and development departments create many flops. Consider the following examples:

Coca-Cola introduced Surge, a caffeinated drink for teens and young adults. Despite the fact that Coca-Cola has an incredible distribution system and spent million of dollars on advertising, the product failed to reach the projected sales volume.[4]

3M, known for its success with innovative products, developed a PC disk called Floptical. Despite the fact that it stored 15 times more data than a floppy disk, it was not successful.[5]

An enormous number of new products are brought to market every year— sometimes more than 25,000. That's 486 new products per week, or 69 per day.[6] Many are not successful. However, the actual failure rate of new products is disputed. A commonly quoted statistic is that 80 to 96 percent of all new products fail.[7] However, a study of 11,000 new products found that 56 percent of the products that reached the market were still being sold five years later, a failure rate of 44 percent. Other studies have found a failure rate of only 35 percent. These statistics are probably different from each other because of the differing measures that were used by each study. For example, some studies may have counted all new product ideas under development, whereas others may have counted only those that were test-marketed or marketed nationwide.[8] Nonetheless, in almost all cases, the product did not live up to expectations in some respect— performance in use, sales volume, profitability, distributor acceptance, or effect on corporate image.[9]

STRENGTHS AND WEAKNESSES OF SMALL COMPANIES

Small companies and individual entrepreneurs have an advantage in new product development because they are not caught up with all of the rules and regulations of large companies.[10] The bureaucratic problems that plague large corporations are less likely to occur at a small business. Decisions are made much more quickly, and the entrepreneur is often more aware of customer needs.

One of the biggest weaknesses of small businesses, however, is the lack of financial backing. Large companies may lose enormous sums of money when a new product fails, but the companies have sufficient financial resources to absorb the loss. A small business, on the other hand, usually has very limited financial resources, and just the research and development costs of the product may exceed the funds available. If the product is not successful, it may cause the bankruptcy of the small business and/or the entrepreneur. Small businesses do not have the luxury of making a big mistake.

DEVELOPING A NEW IDEA

There are many ways to develop a new idea for a product or service, but most of us find it difficult to create new concepts. Some of the most common ways are described next (see Figure 9–1).

$ *Recognize a need.* Many small businesses begin because the entrepreneur recognizes a need in the marketplace that is not being served. For example, because of the increasing number of immigrants, many entrepreneurs have seen a need to develop businesses to cater to this target market. Also, some mothers have become successful entrepreneurs developing products for children after they realized there was nothing on the market to fill a specific need.

$ *Improve existing products.* As stated at the beginning of this chapter, it may be helpful to identify products that have had no major improvements in recent years and then try to develop some needed changes. Many products in a normal classroom are good examples—rubber bands and staplers might be candidates for improvements.

$ *Combine industries.* Nolan Bushnell, developer of the first home video game, believes that creating a new idea may just require taking something that is standard in one industry and applying it to another. Bushnell had worked at amusement parks during college and was able to combine his knowledge of the amusement industry with computers.[11] Combining industries, often referred to as *blurring boundaries*, is a common trend. Consider, for example, the Mall of America in Minnesota. It is not only a shopping mall; it is an amusement park and a tourist attraction. Similarly, antimicrobial socks not only keep your feet warm but also eliminate foot odor by killing bacteria.[12]

> **Blurring boundaries –** the process of combining two different industries to create a new industry.

$ *Recognize trends.* Consider demographic trends such as the aging of the baby boomers. Recognize the fast pace of American lifestyles and design products to make life easier. Bushnell also believes that knowledge of human nature is critical and that it is important to know what customers want before they even know they want it.[13]

$ *Be aware of everything.* Many ideas surround us on a daily basis, but most people are so busy with their normal lives that they are not truly aware of everything.

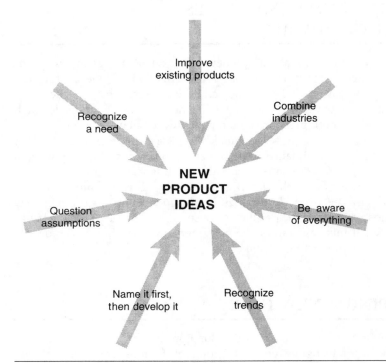

FIGURE 9–1   How to develop new product ideas.

One example that many of us have experienced is the thistle blossoms or "burrs" that cling to our jeans when we run through the woods. While most of us consider this an annoying problem, Georges de Mestral was inspired by these blossoms to create Velcro.[14]

$ *Question assumptions.* One amusing and useful technique for developing new ideas is to take a product or service and question all of the assumptions we normally make about these products. First, list all of the assumptions, then negate, eliminate, or think of the opposite of each of these facts.[15] One student used this method to develop a new type of Chinese restaurant. Most Chinese restaurants have no children's menu, no drive-through window, and few desserts. Changing these factors created a new kind of restaurant. Another recent example of this technique is Pizza Hut's development of the stuffed crust pizza. One commonly accepted fact is that most people eat the crust of the pizza last. What would make someone want to eat it first?

$ *Name it first, then develop it.* While the normal procedure for new product development is to develop a product and then think of a name for it, it is sometimes helpful to reverse that process. For example, think of a game called Winding Blinding Bats and then decide what that game would be.[16]

These methods are only a few of the many alternatives conducive to developing new product ideas. It should be obvious that many concepts will not be viable and may be ridiculous. However, during brainstorming sessions, ideas should not be closely scrutinized. These sessions are to create ideas; critical evaluation is a separate process.

KEY FACTORS FOR SUCCESS

The failure rate of new products even by large corporations is proof that there is no easy way to determine if a product will succeed. Although many attempts have been made by companies and academics to improve the success rate, no magic formula has yet been discovered. One study of new products at Hewlett-Packard's Medical Products Group tried to identify some of the essential factors that led to success or failure. The study found that if only one or two key factors were wrong, product failure could result.[17] Some of the key factors are discussed next.

$ *Conduct adequate market research.* This is essential if an entrepreneur wants to prevent a product failure. However, this step is often ignored. In fact, manufacturers with 500 employees or fewer tend to completely avoid market research, competitive analysis, pricing, or trends work before launching a product.[18] Often the cost is an important consideration. While contracting with a well-recognized research firm could easily cost as much as $10,000, there are ways to test-market products using cheaper methods, such as craft shows or trade shows. Customer response can then be gauged. One restaurant test-marketed a new food product by setting up carts in theater lobbies and intermission areas of summer concerts.[19]

$ *Satisfy a need.* One essential requirement of new products and services is that they must satisfy a real need of the customers.[20] Many entrepreneurs are so thrilled about their idea that they cannot be objective enough to determine if it fills a real need of the consumer. Doug Hall, a new product development consultant, states, "The vast majority [of new products] just don't offer people anything different."[21] Chet Kane, president of new-product specialists Kane, Bortree, and Associates, states, "Companies develop products based on their growth or competitive needs and not the consumers' needs."[22]

$ *Have a high product advantage.* One study of 200 moderate- to high-technology new-product launches found that the number one success factor was a unique superior product—one with higher quality, new features, and higher value in use. High-product-advantage products succeeded 98 percent of the time.[23]

$ *Get quality, pricing, and customer experience right the first time.* If quality is poor or pricing is too high when the product is introduced, the product may fail before it has a chance to succeed. Large corporations have found this to be true. General Foods tried to market refrigerated dinners that cost as much as $7, but consumers didn't buy them. Clorox tried to market single-use (but pricier) detergent pouches but failed to attract customers.[24] The Peugeot 607 was described as feeling like "an imitation of a luxury car," not the real thing.[25]

In the article in *Management Review*, Eric Berggren and Thomas Nacher contend that the entire customer experience must be right the first time. If it is difficult to purchase or use it, customers will not continue to buy the product. Peapod, an online grocer, constantly improves its Web site so a customer's first-use experience will encourage repeat buying.[26]

$ *Use the right channels of distribution.* A critical decision for all designers and manufacturers of new products involves the channels of distribution through which the products will be sold. There are many options available; however, not all of the distribution channels will be equally effective in generating sales. The wrong choice might cause a financial failure.[27] Choices are discussed next.

CHOOSING A DISTRIBUTION CHANNEL

Distribution channels – marketing institutions and interrelationships responsible for the flow of goods and services from producer to consumer or industrial user.

Direct marketing – system of marketing by which an organization communicates directly with customers to generate a response and/or transaction.

Wholesaler – an intermediary between a producer and a retailer.

Manufacturers' representatives or agents – self-employed salespeople who sell others' products to retailers or wholesalers and are paid on a commission basis.

Merchant wholesalers or agent wholesalers – intermediaries who help connect producers and buyers.

Distribution channels are the marketing institutions and interrelationships responsible for the physical and title flow of goods and services from producers to consumer or industrial user.[28] Companies develop distribution strategies to ensure that their products are available in the proper quantities at the right time and place.[29] Many options are available to someone who develops a new product:

$ *Direct marketing. Direct marketing* is a system of marketing by which an organization communicates directly with customers to generate a response and/or transaction.[30] In the consumer market, this occurs through several methods. The first is through direct contacts between buyer and seller such as with Avon, Mary Kay Cosmetics, or Amway. The second is through catalogs such as L.L. Bean and Lillian Vernon or other direct-mail literature. The increasing use of technology has also added direct marketing options such as the home shopping services available through cable television.[31] Finally, direct marketing through an Internet site is possible.

$ *Wholesalers.* In consumer goods industries, it is common for the producer to sell to a *wholesaler*, who in turn sells to a retailer. The retailer then sells to the final consumer. For small companies with limited resources, a wholesaler is helpful in reaching hundreds of retailers nationwide.[32]

$ *Agents.* If wholesalers are necessary, the entrepreneur must determine how to reach them. The individual entrepreneur may find it impossible to contact and service the wholesalers without additional help. In many cases, *manufacturer's representatives* (or *agents*) contact the wholesaling or retailing companies and are paid a commission on their sales. Other agents, known as *merchant wholesalers* or *agent wholesalers*, are often used when products are produced by a large number of small businesses. The agents seek a market for the producer's goods or may help the buyers find sources of supply.[33]

In the service industries, most contact is direct between the service provider and the customer. Agents are sometimes used, as with insurance agents and travel agents. However, because the item being sold is usually intangible, a less complicated distribution system exists.

Berggren and Nacher state that "seemingly superior products fail because a company's channel partners have no incentive to market or appropriately support them."[34] It is important that entrepreneurs understand that companies in the distribution channel incur added costs when stocking a new product. These costs include initial costs such as training staff, but also ongoing costs like handling returns and running promotions. Entrepreneurs must help the company in the distribution channel with these activities or the product may not succeed.[35]

Factors Influencing the Distribution Decision

When choosing a distribution channel, the following questions should be considered.[36]

$ *Will the product be sold in the consumer or industrial market?* Most industrial products are sold through direct sales; consumer products may also use this route, although they are often sold through retailers.

$ *What is the geographic location and number of customers?* If the customers are located throughout the country, direct sales would be more complex than if they are in a small geographic area. Although direct sales would be possible, it would take more time and money to develop the network.

$ *What are the product characteristics?* Perishable products must move quickly through channels. Complex, high-technology items are often sold through person-to-person sales.

$ *What are the entrepreneur's resources?* If the entrepreneur has the financial re-sources to have a sales force or to market the product directly to the final con-sumer, this may be an alternative. However, because of limited resources, many small businesses use intermediaries who have financial resources and a market-ing network that is far more efficient than the small business's own system.

$ *How do competitors sell their products? Will the marketing intermediaries ade-quately promote the new product?* Entrepreneurs must consider how their com-petitors sell products and whether the marketing intermediaries will promote the new product if it decreases sales of competing products. If the intermediaries will not promote the product adequately, the entrepreneur may decide on a different approach.[37]

Obstacles to Securing Distribution Channels

Although many distribution channels are available, entrepreneurs often find it dif-ficult to get their product to market. For example, many who go directly to whole-salers or retailers with new products find that the intermediaries are not interested in taking on a new product. Entrepreneurs must realize that large retailers such as Wal-Mart, Target, and others are constantly bombarded with new products, and they do not want to stock and display a product if it will not sell. Many want proof of a demand for the product—a successful market test—before they carry the item. It is often difficult to persuade someone to carry it even for a market test.

Many entrepreneurs with new product ideas are also surprised to find that direct marketing channels, such as catalogs or home shopping services, require a minimum inventory level before they will market the product. One entrepreneur who developed a new baking device was told that she could not advertise her product in a home shopping service unless she could prove she had an inventory of at least 10,000 units. (The home shopping service did not want customers to order the product and then be told it was not in stock.) Because the entrepreneur did not have the financial resources to produce 10,000 units without a guarantee of sales, she could not use this marketing channel.

Some retailers will not accept a new product unless the entrepreneur can guarantee a minimum level of advertising to create demand among customers. Often this minimum is far in excess of the financial resources of the small firm.

Finally, because of the large number of new products, limited retail space, and the cost of inventorying new items, many retailers charge fees for carrying new products. Called *slotting fees*, they can range into tens of thousands of dol-lars. Other fees may be charged if a new item does not meet sales projections. These additional fees are based on the costs of removing items from inventory and the lost revenue from the item. Retailers may also ask for an annual renewal fee to continue carrying an item, as well as trade allowances or other discounts.[38] Obviously, for a new small business, these fees may be prohibitive. Many entre-preneurs find that these fees make it impossible to get their items on store shelves.

Slotting fees – charges by retailers for carrying a new product.

LICENSING

If an entrepreneur develops a new product but does not have the time or funds to manufacture and distribute it, a licensing arrangement may be the answer. The entrepreneur licenses another company to manufacture and sell the product in exchange for a fee.

Licensing is common in many industries, including the toy industry. The Toy Manufacturers of America estimates that 40 percent of all toys sold are licensed products.[39] However, that does not mean that it is easy to get a new toy licensed and distributed. Many of the licensed toys are based on well-known characters such as Barney, Batman, or the *Star Wars* characters. It is much more difficult for an inventor to get a company interested in a licensed product. Don Debelak, author of *Bringing Your Product to Market*, estimates that only 300 to 500 people per year are successful in licensing a product. Debelak states, "Companies that know how to market products usually have plenty of their own product ideas to introduce and will take on only truly novel, innovative products."[40]

LEGAL PROTECTION OF NEW PRODUCTS AND SERVICES

Nondisclosure document – contract stating that the signator will not discuss the idea with anyone else or use it for personal gain.

If an entrepreneur develops a new product or service, a major concern is that others will try to develop similar items. This comes about quickly when the entrepreneur needs advice and/or expertise during the research and development phase and when a prototype (the original model) is developed. Even discussing the idea with others may result in the concept being stolen.

A simple form known as a *nondisclosure document* is often used in the early stages of development. Anyone who must be made aware of the idea is asked to sign the nondisclosure document, which states that the signator will not discuss the idea with anyone else, nor use the idea for personal gain.

Patents

Patent – the grant of a property right to the inventor(s) issued by the U.S. Patent and Trademark Office.

A U.S. *patent* for an invention is the grant of a property right to the inventor(s), issued by the U.S. Patent and Trademark Office. The patent excludes others from "making, using, offering for sale, selling," or "importing" the invention in the United States. *Utility patents* are granted for any new useful process, machine, article of manufacture, or useful improvements. *Design patents* are granted for new, original, and ornamental designs of manufactured articles. Finally, horticultural *plant patents* may be granted for new varieties of plants.[41]

In order for an invention to be patentable, it must be new as defined by patent law. If the invention has been described in a printed publication anywhere in the world, or if it has been in public use or on sale in this country before the date that the applicant made the invention, or more than one year before the patent is applied for, a patent cannot be obtained. Thus if the inventor describes the invention in a printed publication, uses the invention publicly, or places it on sale, he or she must apply for a patent before one year has gone by; otherwise any right to a patent will be lost.[42] Only the inventor may apply for a patent, with certain exceptions. A person who makes a financial contribution is not a joint inventor and cannot be named in the application as an inventor.[43]

As shown in Figure 9–2, the number of patents issued since 1980 has risen steadily.

Problems with patents Patents often do not provide as much protection as the inventor originally believes. Unfortunately, competitors can sometimes circumvent patents by making minor changes in the design of new products and then selling them as different from the patented products. And, since ideas are not patentable, an idea for a new business such as selling balloon bouquets instead of flowers is easily copied once the first person starts operating. Even if a patent is obtained, this only gives the patent holder the right to a court fight. Obtaining patents and fighting infringement are often a costly process. Also, a patent does not protect the inventor from claims that his or her product infringes on an existing patent. Although patent searches can be completed before applying, such a search will not identify patents that are pending. Therefore, it is not an absolute guarantee that the product is unique. Finally, a U.S. patent does not provide protection in foreign countries. In some countries, it is possible to obtain a *patent of importation*, which provides temporary protection. However, a permanent patent must be obtained in every country in which protection is desired.

> **Patent of importation –** provides temporary patent protection in a foreign country.

Patent searches on the Internet One of the first steps required is to complete a search of existing patents to determine if one exists on a similar product. Prior to the invention of the Internet, this could only be done in libraries or by hiring a search firm. With the development of the Internet, a substantial amount of patent information is available free of charge. The U.S. Patent and Trademark Office (http://www.uspto.gov) has full texts of patents on its Web site. The European Patent Office (EPO) also offers the full text of patents for free on its Web site at http://www.european-patent-office.org.[44]

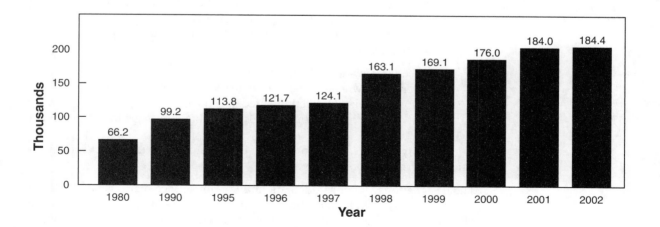

Source: U.S. Census Bureau, *Statistical Abstract of the United States: 2003,* http://www.census.gov/prod/2004/pubs/03statab/business.pdf.

FIGURE 9–2   U.S. Patents issued, selected years 1980 to 2002.

Copyrights

> **Copyright** – protection provided by federal laws for intellectual works.

A *copyright* is a form of protection provided by the laws of the United States to the authors of "original works of authorship," including literary, dramatic, musical, artistic, and certain other intellectual works such as software. In addition, copyrights may be obtained on pantomines and choreographic creations, pictorial, graphic, and sculptural works; motion pictures and other audiovisual works; and architectural accomplishments. A copyright gives the owner of the copyright the exclusive rights to reproduce the work and to prepare any other material derived from the work. For any works created after January 1, 1978, the work is automatically protected for the life of the author plus 70 years. In some cases, such as an anonymous work where the author is not known, the copyright will extend for a longer period (95 or 120 years) but the term will be based on the date of the publication or creation since the author's birth date is not known.[45]

Copyrights may not be obtained on information that is common property and that does not contain original authorship. Therefore, items such as calendars, height and weight charts, and rulers may not be copyrighted.[46]

A copyright is secured automatically when the work is created, and a work is created when it is fixed in written copy, videotape, microfilm, cassette tapes, or other tangible form. No publication or registration in the copyright office is required to secure a copyright. A copyright registration made with the Register of Copyrights in Washington, D.C., is a legal formality to make a public record of the copyright. However, before an infringement suit may be filed in court, registration is necessary for works of U.S. origin.[47] More information is available at http://www.copyright.gov.

Trademarks

> **Trademark** – a word, symbol, name, or device that a business uses to identify its goods and distinguish them from others.

A *trademark* is a word, symbol, name, or device that a business uses to identify its goods and distinguish them from those of others. (A service mark is similar in that it is used to distinguish the services of one provider from another.) The mark is granted when the design is used; however, an application can be filed as long as there is intent to use it. As with copyrights, it is not essential to register a trademark or service mark with the Patent and Trademark Office; however, it does provide several benefits:

$ notice nationwide of the trademark owner's claim
$ evidence of ownership of the trademark
$ ability to invoke jurisdiction of federal courts
$ ability to use registration as a basis for obtaining registration in foreign countries
$ ability to file registration with the U.S. Customs Service to prevent importation of infringing foreign goods[48]

The designations "™" for trademark and "SM" for service mark usually indicate that a company or individual claims rights to the mark. These designations are often used before a federal registration is issued. There are no federal regulations governing the use of these designations; however, there may be state or local laws.[49] The federal registration symbol "®" may be used once the mark is actually registered with the U.S. Patent and Trademark Office. Even if an application is pending, the symbol may not be used before the mark is officially registered.[50]

In addition to the federal trademark laws, state trademark statutes exist and are not preempted by federal laws. State registrations are less expensive and easier to obtain than federal registration. It is advisable to obtain state trademark registrations in the principal states where the mark is used.[51]

One of the biggest problems with trademark law is that it is often vague and confusing, making it difficult to determine if trademark infringement will result. For example, when Compaq computers were developed, the inventors were told by their lawyers that the name might infringe on the trademark of a cable-switching company named Compac. The inventors decided to keep the Compaq name anyway because they believed it was a good name. No lawsuit resulted.[52] On the other hand, Lone Star Steakhouse and Saloon has been involved in a number of lawsuits concerning the rights to use the Lone Star mark.[53]

Trade Secrets

If a business has a process or information that cannot be patented, copyrighted, or trademarked, the entrepreneur may still wish to keep the information confidential. In this situation, a *trade secret* may be helpful. Employees are asked to sign a statement that they will not disclose the information. This becomes a legal contract and violation of that contract is illegal.

> **Trade secret** – a legal protection for information that cannot be patented, copyrighted, or trademarked.

The theft of a trade secret has been and still is subject to a civil lawsuit in many states and to criminal action in some states. However, now the theft of a trade secret may also be subject to federal criminal action. With the passage by the U.S. Congress of the Economic Espionage Act of 1996, the theft of a trade secret is now a federal criminal offense. A person convicted under this law can be fined and imprisoned, and an organization can be convicted and fined.[54]

In order to make a trade secret contract binding, the entrepreneur should first define what is to be protected as narrowly as possible. If common information is included in the contract, it may be declared void. Second, the number of people who are asked to sign it should be limited. If every employee is asked to sign the document, the agreement becomes less enforceable. Finally, employees should sign the agreement when they are first employed. It is better if the entrepreneur can prove that the employee received something as a condition of signing the agreement. Therefore, if the entrepreneur waits until the employee has worked for the company for many years, the contract may not be upheld. Asking the employee to sign the document as a condition of a promotion or raise, however, may be upheld.[55]

NEW PRODUCT DEVELOPMENT AND THE BUSINESS PLAN

If the new business is dependent on a new product that has been developed or will be developed, a thorough explanation of the stage in the development process must be given in the business plan. If any copyrights, trademarks, patents, or trade secrets will be obtained, that information should be explained in the legal section of the plan.

Since new product development is a risky and time-consuming endeavor, banks will usually not be interested in reviewing business plans requesting financing for the early stages of the process. Often, a business plan based on new products must be submitted to investors, or the entrepreneur must use his or her own funds. Banks will be more likely to provide financing once the product is developed and the entrepreneur can demonstrate that a demand for the product exists.

SUMMARY

New product development is a high-risk endeavor, since many new products and services fail. Small companies can develop products more easily than large companies can because they are less bureaucratic and can react quickly to market changes. Small businesses, though, are hindered by a lack of financial resources and obstacles such as minimum inventory levels and slotting fees. In addition, the entrepreneur may need to obtain a patent, copyright, trademark, or trade secret to provide legal protection for the new product.

DISCUSSION QUESTIONS

1. Identify two products or services that have failed (do not use the ones listed in this chapter). Why do you think they did not succeed?
2. Choose an item that is used in everyday activities (chair, desk, toaster, and so on). List all of the assumptions you can identify that are associated with this product. Then vary those assumptions to create new product ideas.
3. When cheaper, look-alike products are created to compete with original products, the look-alike items are often called *knock-offs*. Identify some products for which knock-offs have been created. Through library research, identify any legal action that was taken.
4. Many experts state that in order to be successful, a new product has to be the first of its kind on the market. Do you agree? Why or why not? Give examples to support your answer.

ENDNOTES

1. Curtis Rist, "Drivers Start Your Engines," *Discover*, June 2001, 80.
2. Ibid.
3. Karl Taro Greenfeld, "Mattel: Some Assembly Required," *Time*, October 25, 1999, 58–59.
4. Bruce Tait, "The Failure of Marketing Science," *Brandweek*, April 8, 2002, 20.
5. Eric Berggren and Thomas Nacher, "Why Good Ideas Go Bust," *Management Review*, February 2000, 32.
6. Michelle Wirth Fellman, "Forecast: New Products Storm Subsides," *Marketing News*, March 30, 1998, 1.
7. "Fizzlers," *The St. Louis Post-Dispatch*, April 16, 1995, E1.
8. Christopher Power, Kathleen Kerwin, Ronald Grover, Keith Alexander, and Robert Hof, "Flops," *BusinessWeek*, August 16, 1993, 76.
9. Thomas T. Semon, "New Product Failure Is a Bogeyman," *Marketing News*, January 1, 1996, 11.
10. "Making It New," *Sales and Marketing Management*, February 1993, 50.
11. Paul Chu, "Brainstorms," *Success*, October 1993, 30.
12. Chris Bynum, "Haute and Cool," *The* [New Orleans] *Times-Picayune*, August 8, 2000, F1.
13. Chu, 30.
14. Bryan W. Mattimore, "Eureka," *The Futurist*, March–April 1995, 34.

15. Ibid.

16. Ibid.

17. Power et al., 76.

18. Fellman, 1.

19. Nancy Levenburg and Tom Dandridge, "Can't Afford Research? Try Miniresearch," *Marketing News*, March 31, 1997, 19.

20. Power et al., 76.

21. "Making It New," 50.

22. "Fizzlers."

23. Philip Kotler and Gary Armstrong, *Principles of Marketing*, 7th ed. (Upper Saddle River, NJ: Prentice-Hall, 1996), 313.

24. "Fizzlers."

25. Cathryn Espinosa, "Inside Job—There's Something Missing from the New Peugeot 607," *The* [London, UK] *Daily Telegraph*, May 5, 2001, 10.

26. Berggren and Nacher, 32.

27. Power et al., 76.

28. Louis E. Boone and David L. Kurtz, *Contemporary Marketing* (Fort Worth, TX: Dryden Press, 1992), 398.

29. Ibid.

30. George E. Belch and Michael A. Belch, *Introduction to Advertising and Promotion* (Homewood, IL: Irwin, 1995), 11.

31. Ibid., 348.

32. Boone and Kurtz, 404.

33. Ibid.

34. Berggren and Nacher, 32.

35. Ibid., 415.

36. Boone and Kurtz, 404.

37. Ibid., 415.

38. Ibid., 411.

39. Stacy Botwinick, "Aiming for the Bull's-Eye," *Discount Merchandiser*, February 1998, 36–40.

40. Don Debelak, *Bringing Your Product to Market* (New York: Wiley, 1997), 63–64.

41. U.S. Patent and Trademark Office, "How to Get a Patent," http:// www.uspto.gov/web/patents/howtopat.htm.

42. U.S. Patent and Trademark Office, "Novelty and Other Conditions for Obtaining a Patent," http://www.uspto.gov/web/offices/pac/doc/general/novelty.htm.

43. U.S. Patent and Trademark Office, "Who May Apply for a Patent," http://www.uspto.gov/web/offices/pac/doc/general/apply.htm.

44. Paul Blake, "The Arrival of Free Patent Information," *Information Today*, March 1998, 19–20.

45. U.S. Copyright Office, http://www.copyright.gov/circs/circ1. html#hlc.

46. U.S. Copyright Office, "Copyright Basics," http://www.loc.gov/copyright/circs/circ1.html.

47. *Copyright Basics* (Washington, DC: U.S. Government Printing Office, 1994), 2–8.

48. U.S. Patent and Trademark Office, "Frequently Asked Questions and Trademarks," http://www.uspto.gov/web/offices/tac/tmfaq.htm.

49. Ibid.

50. Ibid.

51. Howard A. Davis, "Understanding Trademark Law," *Food Management*, April 1998, 81–84.

52. Robert McMamis, "Name Calling," *Inc.*, July 1984, 67–74.

53. Ibid.

54. Stephen S. Hodgson, "Intellectual Property Theft Emerging As Hot Issue in U.S. Oil and Gas Industry," *Oil & Gas Journal*, February 9, 1998, 26–27.

55. *Inc.'s Managing People: 101 Proven Ideas for Making You and Your People More Productive* (Boston: *Inc.*, 1992), 100.

Chapter 10

Business Growth and the Entrepreneur

Rapidly growing companies have been the subject of studies for many years. Researchers have tried to identify the factors that cause some businesses to grow rapidly while others remain small or grow slowly. Most researchers agree that growth is not automatic and is not the result of chance or good luck. It is instead the result of "positively motivated business intentions and actions on the part of the owner-manager."[1] The entrepreneur's characteristics, educational level, knowledge of business, and continued learning all affect the growth potential of the business.[2]

A company's growth is also affected by internal company factors, the resources available, and external factors. If poor market conditions exist or if government regulation limits growth, the entrepreneur's efforts may not be as successful.[3]

BUSINESS GROWTH AND MANAGEMENT SKILLS

Although it is commonly believed that company growth follows a simple linear progression, with sales and company size consistently expanding, often it is not that smooth. Some firms grow and then backslide while some skip growth stages that others experience.[4] Though not always smooth, business growth stages can nevertheless be categorized. One study by John Eggers and Kim Leahy identified six stages of business development: conception, survival, stabilization, growth orientation, rapid growth, and maturity. Eggers and Leahy also found that within each stage, the entrepreneur's leadership style and necessary skills were forced to change.[5] This is because the problems faced during the start-up phase are not always the same ones the entrepreneur must tackle when the business has grown. Some of the biggest problem areas and, therefore, some of the skills needed by owners of growing companies are personnel management, financial management, and marketing.[6]

Personnel Management

The management problems of small businesses change greatly as the company grows. One study found that in the early years of the business, the entrepreneur's management problems focused on the entrepreneur's time management, goal setting, and performance measurement. As the business grew, time management continued to be an issue but finding, retaining, and motivating qualified employees became a major concern.

Control in a small business is usually informal.[7] When there are only a few employees, job descriptions and rules and regulations are often not written down because the entrepreneur is closely involved in every aspect of the company and he or she can easily oversee everything. However, if the company grows, the entrepreneur must move from direct supervision of a few employees to indirect management when the number of employees increases.[8] Figure 10–1 shows the typical changes that occur in the organizational chart as the company grows. Although this may appear to be a simple process, it is often a difficult transition for the entrepreneur and the employees.

Small businesses require employees to wear many different hats, but as the business grows this often changes. As additional personnel are added, loss or anxiety may occur among the original group of employees because someone else is now taking care of "their" issues. In some cases, employees may not be able to

Simple Structure

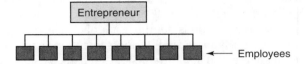

Limited Growth Structure

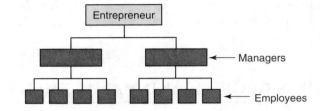

Departmental Structure

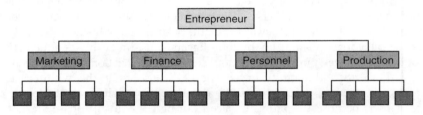

FIGURE 10–1   Organizational charts as a company grows.

adjust to the growth and changes experienced by restructuring job functions. They not only lose control of tasks, they lose a sense of importance.[9]

Many entrepreneurs tend to *micromanage* their businesses, trying to remain involved in every aspect of the company's operations even as it grows. But this can inhibit growth because it does not allow employees room for advancement and may result in high turnover. Sometimes, micromanagement occurs because the entrepreneur, believing that the company cannot afford top-quality personnel, hires people at a lower level and constantly manages them. Aldonna Ambler, president and CEO of Ambler Growth Strategy Consultants, states, "Hiring someone with aptitude costs a bit more but can make your company much more money in the end."[10]

Small companies must also realize the need for training their employees. Often it is informal, on-the-job learn-as-you-work training. However, as the company grows, the entrepreneur must anticipate what skills the employees will need to do their jobs and plan for training needs. If training is not provided, the jobs will outgrow the skills of the employees. This happened in Esprit de Corp., the apparel company that grew from a tiny dressmaking shop to an international clothing company in 15 years. An employee with little retailing background was soon heading the retail division and a secretary was promoted to product manager and given responsibility for negotiating international contracts.[11] Neither had any training for the job he or she was given.

Micromanaging – involvement in all aspects of the company even as it grows.

Financial Management

Cash flow problems are likely in rapidly growing businesses. To generate more sales, the company has to produce more inventory, spend more on labor, and possibly increase overhead expenses. When a company incurs short-term costs that it cannot meet while in the pursuit of growth, this is known as *overtrading*. The lack of working capital can cause profit margins to drop. This happened to the Body Shop, a successful cosmetics company. Phenomenal growth was soon followed by a steep drop in profit margins. Similarly, the Sock Shop grew rapidly, opening many new outlets, only to experience severe financial problems and a steep drop in the company's stock price.[12] The entrepreneur must carefully watch the cash flow, or growth will not be sustained.

> **Overtrading** – a situation in which a company incurs short-term costs that it cannot meet while in the pursuit of growth.

Because of the need for cash to fuel the growth, raising capital becomes an issue in the growth phase. Often this cash is needed in the form of equity since the company cannot borrow the large amount of cash that is necessary. Surrendering equity in a company becomes a personal issue for the entrepreneur. It turns the "hands-on" owner/entrepreneur into someone who is no longer the sole decision maker and full financial risk holder. The entrepreneur now answers to a group of investors and potentially a board of directors.[13]

Managing accounts receivable is also an issue. When companies are small, the entrepreneur often focuses on sales, without good controls on collecting payments in a timely manner. As the company generates more business, entrepreneurs often find that the sales volume is great but accounts receivable collection is not. At that point, it becomes obvious that it may be better to forgo a sale than to make one that will not result in payment.

Marketing

Marketing is also an ongoing concern for entrepreneurs, but as with management and finance, the specific issues may change. One study found that cost-effective advertising was a problem for start-ups and for mature businesses, but the mature businesses were also concerned about competition from big businesses and needed to find new opportunities.[14]

Entrepreneurs often start businesses in growing industries and the industry growth helps to propel the growth of the individual businesses. But as more businesses enter the industry, competition becomes intense. Demand for the product may also slow, and the company's sales may reach a plateau. Efforts must then be made to find new products and/or new markets, or the business will stagnate.

MATCHING THE COMPANY AND THE ENTREPRENEUR

The entrepreneur needs different skills in different phases of the company's life cycle, and there are several options for addressing these needs. The entrepreneur can develop all of the skills that are necessary (personnel management, financial management, and so on), train existing employees, or bring in professionally qualified managers.[15] But many entrepreneurs find that their personalities can never allow them to feel comfortable delegating much responsibility.

Ronald E. Merrill and Henry D. Sedgwick, authors of *The New Venture Handbook*, recommend tailoring the size of the company to the entrepreneur's personality. Some of their recommendations are described next.[16]

$ *Craftsperson.* If the entrepreneur does not trust people easily or prefers not to delegate, then a one-person business should be considered. Although this will limit the size of the business, it may be the best choice.

$ *Coordinator.* Outsourcing, or subcontracting, many functions may also allow the entrepreneur to have a large business without many employees. For example, Merrily Orsini, owner of My Virtual Corp., has 135 active associates who work on projects such as copyediting, word processing, and graphic design. However, she has only one full-time employee. She outsources work to the best candidate she can find whenever a project is received.[17]

$ *Classic entrepreneurial management.* Another technique often used by entrepreneurs is to hire employees but monitor and supervise everything closely. This style, known as the *classic style*, works only if the entrepreneur admits that he or she controls everything and makes that clear to employees.[18]

$ *Employee teams.* If the entrepreneur feels comfortable delegating substantial responsibility to other people, the company may grow by hiring an employee team, by bringing in a few other partners, or by bringing in partners for a big-team venture.

The key to success is to match the style of management with the entrepreneur's personality. If the preferred style is craftsperson, coordinator, or classic, the company should not be too complex. If the business is simple enough, the company can grow with these styles. If the business becomes too complex, it will grow successfully only if the entrepreneur is comfortable in giving up some control.[19]

THE AMERICAN DREAM/THE AMERICAN NIGHTMARE

Although many people believe the American dream is to start a business that becomes large and successful, for some entrepreneurs this is the American nightmare. There are many reasons why success may lead to dissatisfaction. Some of the most common are given next.

The Challenge of a New Business

One of the most exciting times for an entrepreneur is the start-up or early ownership phase. Building a company from the idea stage takes creativity and vision and is a great challenge. Even for the entrepreneur who buys an existing business with plans to improve it, the early ownership phase requires innovation and presents the entrepreneur with exciting goals to be accomplished. For these reasons, the early years of business ownership are usually very rewarding. However, once the start-up phase is over and the company is past the survival stage, the level of challenge may seem to decrease. Despite the constant problems to be solved, this is often not as enjoyable as developing the company.

The Loss of the Family Atmosphere

If the company is small, in the first few years the family atmosphere is an enjoyable experience for both the entrepreneur and employees. The entrepreneur knows the employees, works directly with each of them, and closely manages the daily company operations. His or her direct involvement is usually crucial for the survival of the business. As the company grows, however, the atmosphere of the company changes. The entrepreneur no longer works directly with all of the employees, and it may be more difficult to maintain the "family atmosphere." This is often a source of discontent for both the company founder and the original group of employees.

Keith Dunn discovered this problem the hard way when he started McGuffey's Restaurant. After working at large restaurants for many years, he planned to open one where the employees would enjoy working as much as the customers would enjoy eating. When he opened his first restaurant in Asheville, North Carolina, the employees had many benefits, including the freedom to give away free appetizers and desserts. A special camaraderie existed among the employees, and the restaurant was a huge success.

Two years later, Dunn and his partners opened two more restaurants, assuming that the success of the first would be repeated. They were surprised to find that the new restaurants were not as successful: in addition, many problems developed at the first restaurant. Sales at the original outlet dropped 15 percent and employee turnover skyrocketed. Three years later, sales continued to decline, restrooms were not maintained, and employee turnover was 220 percent. After attempts to solve the problems were unsuccessful, Keith Dunn and his partners each assumed ownership of separate outlets so the small, family atmosphere could be restored.[20]

THE CHANGING ROLE OF THE ENTREPRENEUR

As stated earlier, the skills the entrepreneur needs will change as the business grows. He or she should no longer be involved in daily tasks but instead should concentrate on management and motivation. Despite the need for strong leadership and management skills, however, the entrepreneur often feels trapped in a less important role. Once other managers and salespeople are hired, the entrepreneur's job is less well defined. A common complaint at this point is, "I don't know what my job is anymore. I used to be the head salesperson and cheerleader for my company, but now I've got a sales manager who does that. What's my job?"[21]

Another problem that often occurs is that a business grows much larger and faster than the entrepreneur expected, which conflicts with personal goals. For example, Carolyn Blakeslee founded ArtCalendar, a publication that lists grants, art shows, and other articles of interest to artists. She began the company believing that it would be a part-time venture that she could operate from her home while raising her new baby. For the first few years, the company experienced a growth rate of more than 100 percent per year, and the business consumed much more of her time than expected. She felt torn between a desire to grow the company and a desire to spend more time with her child. She admits that she "has a perfectionist streak" and "can see what the magazine ultimately could be." On the other hand, balancing both a full-time, demanding job and a child was not what she wanted when she started the business. In such a situation, crucial decisions regarding personal and company goals need to be made.[22]

OPTIONS FOR GROWTH

If the entrepreneur becomes unhappy with growth or finds that outside management skills are needed, he or she has several options, some of which are discussed next.

Keep the Company Small

When faced with a growing company, the entrepreneur often makes a conscious decision to limit company growth or even reduce the company size. Although the potential exists to own a large business, the entrepreneur forgoes the financial rewards in favor of a smaller, simpler one. By limiting the customer base, the number of hours of operation, the number of outlets, and so on, the business remains at a given level for the entrepreneur's entire career.

Rediscover the Entrepreneurial Spirit

Some entrepreneurs adjust to the growing business and use their skills to build a company that is strong enough to let the founder be entrepreneurial again. This may be accomplished within the same company.

Entrepreneurs may develop a company to a mature phase and then hire a good team of managers to run the business on a daily basis. The entrepreneur can then use his or her skills to decide where the company is going next and what opportunities should be pursued. One entrepreneur says she believes that entrepreneurs should know their own strengths and build on them.[23] Mary Kay Ash, founder of Mary Kay Cosmetics, gave similar advice to entrepreneurs. Her advice was to "stay in the area that you do best" and find qualified people to handle the other tasks.[24]

The entrepreneurial spirit can also be rediscovered by keeping the larger business and starting a second one. This allows the founder to experience the challenge of a start-up while maintaining the larger, more profitable business. In one small study of entrepreneurs who had been self-employed for more than six years, 44 percent indicated that they owned more than one company.[25]

Cash In

Other entrepreneurs at the same stage may have different reactions. Cashing in is always an option, but even then there are several alternatives.

Some entrepreneurs realize that they do not want sole responsibility for the company's management but they still want to be involved. For many, the solution is to sell a portion of the company to a key employee. One entrepreneur who started an auto repair firm sold a portion of the company to an employee when the business became too large and time-consuming for one person to handle. This provided additional management expertise and also gave the entrepreneur more time for family and leisure activities.

Others decide to sell the business to an outsider and take a break from self-employment. One owner of a rapidly growing automotive equipment company found the business overwhelming. He chose to sell to another entrepreneur and then accepted a job at an engineering firm.

Still others sell one business and start another. One veterinarian's successful animal hospital became too demanding. His solution was to sell the practice to another veterinarian and start a muffler repair shop instead.

GROWTH AND THE BUSINESS PLAN

The growth of the company is shown in the business plan through the financial projections. The entrepreneur must project future sales, expenses, and profit, and this is closely tied to growth plans. The projected growth of the company must seem achievable to bankers and investors or they will think the entrepreneur is being overly optimistic. Many entrepreneurs have failed after expanding too rapidly, so the business plan must show consistent but manageable growth.

SUMMARY

As a business grows, the skills the entrepreneur needs will change. The move will be from direct to more indirect management as the number of employees increases. Both personnel management and financial management are critical factors for a growing business. Many entrepreneurs become dissatisfied when a company grows because the family atmosphere no longer exists, the challenge of the start-up is gone, and the entrepreneur's role becomes less well defined. One recommendation is to match the size of the company with the personality of the entrepreneur. If the company becomes too large, he or she may choose to make the company smaller, start other ventures, or cash in.

DISCUSSION QUESTIONS

1. What is outsourcing? Why does it lower start-up costs? Why does it make management simpler? What would be the disadvantages of outsourcing?

2. Do you think it is possible for a small business to grow quickly and still retain the family atmosphere? Why or why not?

3. How does the entrepreneur's role change as a company grows?

4. What options does an entrepreneur have if he or she becomes unhappy with the growth of the company?

ENDNOTES

1. Alison Morrison, John Breen, and Shameen Ali, "Small Business Growth: Intention, Ability, and Opportunity," *Journal of Small Business Management*, October 2003, 417.

2. Ibid.

3. Ibid.

4. John H. Eggers and Kim T. Leahy, "Entrepreneurial Leadership," *Business Quarterly*, Summer 1995, 71–76.

5. Ibid.

6. Gwen Richtermeyer, "Problems Entrepreneurs Face," http://www.missouribusiness.net/bridgproblems_entrepreneurs_face.pdf.

7. Nerys Fuller-Love and R.W. Scapens, "Performance-Related Pay: A Case Study of a Small Business," *International Small Business Journal*, July/September 1997, 48–63.

8. Ibid.

9. Larry A. Atherton, "A Leap of Faith: Growing Outside the Entrepreneurial Shell," *The National Public Accountant*, September 2000, 49–51.

10. Linda Formichelli, "Letting Go of the Details," *Nation's Business*, November 1997, 50–52.

11. Peter Waldman, "Flagging Spirit," *The Wall Street Journal*, March 16, 1988, 1.

12. Robert Outram, "Turn Down That Order," *Management Today*, October 1997, 112–113.

13. Atherton, 49–51.

14. Richtermeyer.

15. Fuller-Love and Scapens, 48–63.

16. Ronald E. Merrill and Henry D. Sedgwick, "To Thine Own Self," *Inc.*, August 1994, 50.

17. Samuel Fromartz, "Extreme Outsourcing," *Fortune Small Business*, June 2001, 36–42.

18. Merrill and Sedgwick, 50.

19. Ibid.

20. Joshua Hyatt, "The Odyssey of an Excellent Man," *Inc.*, February 1989, 62.

21. Michael Barrier, "The Changing Face of Leadership," *Nation's Business*, January 1995, 41.

22. Leslie Brokaw, "Can Carolyn Blakeslee Have It All?" *Inc.*, September 1991, 78.

23. Barrier, 42.

24. "*Entrepreneurs*," a film produced by Nathan Tyler Productions, 1985.

25. Robert C. Ronstadt, *Entrepreneurship* (Dover, MA: Lord, 1984), 109.

Global Business

Chapter 11

LEARNING OBJECTIVES

$ To become convinced that small firms should consider exporting and importing.

$ To appreciate the range of approaches that may be used to enter foreign markets.

$ To know that there are widely accepted procedures for reducing the risk of doing business with an individual or firm in another country.

$ To be aware of the wide range of government programs to assist entrepreneurs interested in exporting.

The U.S. economy is huge and growing. For most small businesses it provides ample opportunity for growth and prosperity. Although most U.S. small businesses are blessed by large and active markets, things are changing in such a way that international elements can be seen even in what would appear to be remote parts of the economy. Competition from foreign companies has increased in recent years and seems likely to continue. In this chapter we describe why international trade has become so important to our economy and what an entrepreneur can do to cope with the threats and capitalize on the opportunities found in the new global economy.

As World War II was coming to an end, a group of leaders from the Allied countries met to develop strategies for preventing such future calamities. One important cause of the war seemed to be the economic devastation of the 1930s. That decade, known as the Great Depression, saw the development of trade barriers in all of the major industrial nations. They were erected in the hope of protecting jobs at home by keeping out foreign-made goods. While the barriers usually succeeded in keeping out imports, they also meant the loss of markets for international producers. Those losses brought pressures for further retaliatory measures, which took the form of additional trade barriers, each of which had a further chilling effect on trade. The United States, known in recent years for its liberal trade policies, was an active participant in this process; with the passage of the Smoot-Hawley Act of 1930, an enormous barrier to trade in the form of dramatically increased tariffs was erected.

The end-of-the-war leadership summit started the world toward an international trading system designed to encourage free trade between nations. Perhaps the most important step toward free trade has been the long-term reduction in tariffs. In 1950 tariff rates of 15 to 25 percent were common, even among the world's most active trading nations. Currently tariffs are below 4 percent, the goal set by the World Trade Organization in the early 1990s.

Along with the reduction in tariffs, technological change has encouraged world trade. The astounding developments in communications technology and improvements in transportation have made the world a smaller place in many ways. Communications with even remote locations are nearly instantaneous and inexpensive relative to years past. The development of the jet engine for aircraft has dramatically reduced the time needed to get anywhere in the world. No longer does it require weeks to get people or materials to isolated parts of the world; we can typically do it in a day or two.

Taken together, the change in the political climate and the many breakthroughs in technology have had an enormous effect on how business takes place. Great distances are neither a barrier nor an obstacle to competing effectively. So we now face the prospect of a company we have never heard of, from a country about which we know very little, being a real threat in our domestic market. Perhaps the best advice for a company faced with this kind of threat is to change from being passive to being active. Being active, in this context, means investigating the opportunities provided by exporting and importing; we discuss both in this chapter.

Trade barriers – measures by which a country discourages or prohibits goods from other countries entering its markets.

Tariff – tax levied on imports, often to discourage importation.

EXPORTING

While the United States has the largest economy in the world, it represents only about 5 percent of the world's population. To reach the other 95 percent, a business must sell outside the country, a prospect that not all companies find appealing.

We discuss exporting as it is currently practiced here in the United States; the decision by an entrepreneur to start exporting; getting established in an overseas market; procedures to get the product into the hands of the foreign customer; and the process by which the entrepreneur gets paid.

The Current Situation

In comparison to most industrialized nations, the United States has been rather ineffective in competing in export markets. In recent years the United States has consumed considerably more than it has produced. That has resulted in a large and growing deficit in international trade. Put differently, we import huge amounts of goods from all over the world, then we export considerably less of our production. One of the factors contributing to this unimpressive level of exporting can be found in the reasons why small businesses engaged in little exporting activity. We discuss some reasons why small firms should export and then describe the country's poor performance in exporting, relative to its leading economic competitors. Finally, we identify some things that keep small businesses from competing internationally.

> **International trade deficit** – amount by which a country's imports of goods and services exceeds its exports.

Among the many reasons to start exporting is the impressive growth of international trade. While world output rose an impressive 40 percent during the period 1980 to 1994, world trade went up by an even more impressive 80 percent. Even the world's fastest-growing economies do not have growth rates to match expansion of trade between countries. Furthermore, it appears the impressive growth rate will continue for the foreseeable future due in part to the efforts of the World Trade Organization to make exporting easier and to the establishment of treaties such as the North American Free Trade Agreement (NAFTA). Exporting is an expanding element of our economy, one that promises to give future opportunities to many entrepreneurial firms.

One attraction of exporting is that it often provides companies with a way to use excess capacity. Such cases involve a company whose sales constitute only part of what the company is capable of producing. Finding a new market, in this example an international one, allows the firm to improve the use of its production facilities and, as a result, to boost its financial performance.

One set of circumstances under which a firm may turn to international markets as an addition to domestic demand is when the domestic market has started its decline. This happens in the mature phase of the product life cycle, during which the members of the industry frequently engage in price competition to keep their market share. International markets in which the product has not yet reached the mature phase can provide profitable opportunities for the firm that knows how to serve those markets.

Another case in which exporting may be a useful strategic option is for companies with seasonal product lines. Consider a manufacturer of skiing equipment. Sales of the gear require that the retail outlets be served at such time that they will be ready when the first buyer comes in. Some manufacturers have capitalized on the fact that in South America the skiing season comes during the North American summer. Developing that export market allows the manufacturer to maintain a more even level of production and thereby make better use of production facilities. The same logic holds, of course, for summer recreational gear and for many kinds of agricultural products.

Another argument for getting into exporting is that "they" are in the U.S. market. The "they" are, of course, foreign competitiors. Because of all of the forces that encourage international trade, they are likely in your market for the long term. One promising way of dealing with this "invasion" is to establish markets outside the country, thereby reducing dependence on the U.S. market.

Companies in industries that have been targeted by international companies usually find that the competition gets difficult. The foreign company has been attracted by the size of the U.S. market and has as a high priority gaining a significant share of the market. The strategy used to get this share frequently includes setting a low price. This price is often so low that financial losses result, but the company is willing to subsidize U.S. operation with profits from its home market. This strategy may even be one that involves the illegal practice known as *dumping*. Dumping, while running counter to regulations of the WTO, is commonly practiced. Under these circumstances, a "counterinvasion" strategy may make sense.

A final reason for considering the move into international markets is that the growth rates in some of the developing countries are impressive. They mean that the markets are becoming increasingly important. Consider the significance of the growth rate of the United States in comparison with those of three large countries with much lower levels of economic wealth. During 2004 the United States recorded an average increase in gross domestic product (GDP) of nearly 4.0 percent. That is a solid performance, but considerably less than the two largest countries on the globe; India's increase was 7.3 percent, and China's was a remarkable 9.5 percent. While it is true that the economic activity in each of these nations is still far below that of the United States, growth rates such as these mean that things are changing and that these markets are worth investigating for any firm that wants to grow beyond its domestic market. Indeed, many economic analysts say that the developing world, as it is called, is going to be the scene of some of the most exciting action in the future.

With all these reasons to export, it would seem that most businesses would be doing it, or at least looking into the prospect. That is far from the case; very few U.S. businesses export. Partly as a result of this limited participation in international trade, the country has suffered chronic balance of trade problems. Throughout most of the 20th century the United States exported more than it imported; without exception the country had a positive trade balance. Things changed rather dramatically in the early 1970s, however, and for the past 30 years or so, the United States has had nothing but trade deficits. The country is currently running at nearly $600 billion per year in balance of trade deficits; that is, it imported in 2004 $600 billion more in goods and services than it exported.[1] Is this a ruinous level? No. U.S. annual economic activity (gross domestic product or GDP) is about $10 trillion, so the negative trade balance is only a very small percentage of the country's overall economic activity, approximately 6 percent.[2] Is it a troublesome level? Yes it is; the way the United States pays for goods and services it gets from the rest of the world is either to sell its goods to them, to borrow, or to pay with the wealth it holds. The first alternative is clearly the most viable in the long run.

The trade deficit problem has captured the attention of the press and the public, and U.S. politicians have responded with the introduction of a variety of programs at federal and state levels to encourage firms to export. As you will see in our descriptions of some of these programs, help in various forms is available to a small business that wants to export. Despite this help and despite the many important reasons to enter international markets, not many firms do. Let's examine some of the obstacles hindering them.

Many firms have concluded that there is no need to go beyond the borders of the United States in search of sales. The rationale is, "We have not yet expanded

> **Dumping –** the practice by which a company sells its product internationally for less than its costs or at a price below what the company charges in its home market.

to the West Coast; why would we want to go to Asia?" This attitude is at once understandable and myopic. The United States is, indeed, a very large market, and serving it well is beyond the capabilities of any small firm. The myopic element is that some parts of the world may actually be easier to compete in and may also provide greater profit potential. But an official in a Department of Commerce agency charged with building interest in exporting once commented, "American companies have a mind set when it comes to selling that stretches from the Atlantic to the Pacific but no farther."[3]

In addition to the view that the U.S. market is large enough to deserve the firm's full attention, many entrepreneurs are reluctant to get into exporting because of the complications associated with the process. Doing the research needed to evaluate markets in other countries, organizing the channels of distribution, getting the product to the foreign market, and finally getting paid are steps that can prove difficult. In a word, many entrepreneurs simply do not know how to export. In this chapter we explain the process and identify some sources of assistance for firms interested in expanding into the international market.

The Decision to Start Exporting

Perhaps the most basic concern in reaching the decision about exporting is the determination of the export potential of a firm's products. If the products have met with limited success in the domestic market, introducing them into a new market is not likely to change things. With successful products, the potential brightens considerably, and the issues of precisely what features make the products unique and attractive to current customers and what those features will mean in other markets become relevant. Some products have appeal closely linked to U.S. culture. For example, many baseball bats are sold in the United States, but trying to sell them to Austrians or Brazilians may not work no matter how hard we try.

Other products have widespread interest, the kind that easily crosses borders. Among the more obvious examples of consumer products with universal interest are Levi's jeans, McDonald's fast food, and Coca-Cola. In addition to these consumer products, countless items sold to businesses and other organizations have appeal with no linkage to the culture. A more efficient electric motor, a faster computer, a more effective vaccine, and a more durable fabric are examples of products with global market potential.

In addition to a close examination of its product line, the company must look closely at its own culture and priorities. Why is exporting even being considered? What does the firm hope to gain from exporting? What demands will the exporting effort place on the company's other resources? Are these costs or burdens matched or exceeded by the benefits the company anticipates? Is exporting consistent with the other goals of the company? The point of this analysis is to identify the impact of exporting on the company. See Figure 11-1 for a summary of management issues involved in the export decision.

Developing an Export Plan

After a company has determined that at least some of its products have export potential, that it has the resources needed for the task, and that exporting fits into its overall mission, an export plan must be written. The purposes of the plan are to assemble the facts, constraints, and objectives and to create an action plan. In

Export plan – document identifiying the international markets a company plans to enter, the products it will compete with, the way in which it will enter the overseas market(s), and the objectives it has for exporting.

Management Objectives
- What are the company's reasons for pursuing export markets? Are they solid objectives (increasing sales volume or developing a broader, more stable customer base), or are they frivolous (the owner wants an excuse to travel)?
- How committed is top management to an export effort? Is exporting viewed as a quick fix for a slump in domestic sales? Will the company neglect its export customers if domestic sales pick up?
- What are management's expectations for the export effort? How quickly does management expect export operations to become self-sustaining? What level of return on investment is expected from the export program?

Experience
- With what countries has business already been conducted, or from what countries have inquiries already been received?
- Which product lines are mentioned most often?
- Are any domestic customers buying the product for sale or shipment overseas? If so, to what countries?
- Is the trend of sales and inquiries up or down?
- Who are the main domestic and foreign competitors?
- What general and specific lessons have been learned from past export attempts or experiences?

Management and Personnel
- What in-house international expertise does the firm have (e.g., international sales experience, language capabilities)?
- Who will be responsible for the export department's organization and staff?
- How much senior management time (a) should be allocated and (b) could be allocated?
- What organizational structure is required to ensure that export sales are adequately serviced?
- Who will follow through after the planning is done?

Production Capacity
- How is the present capacity being used?
- Will filling export orders hurt domestic sales?
- What will be the cost of additional production?
- Are there fluctuations in the annual workload? When? Why?
- What minimum order quantity is required?
- What would be required to design and package products specifically for export?

Financial Capacity
- What amount of capital can be committed to export production and marketing?
- What level of export department operating costs can be supported?
- How are the initial expenses of export efforts to be allocated?
- What other new development plans are in the works that may compete with export plans?
- By what date must an export effort pay for itself?

Source: A Basic Guide to Exporting, 1998 Edition (Washington, DC: Department of Commerce and Unz & Co., Inc.).

FIGURE 11–1   Management issues involved in the export decision.

order to structure the company's efforts to enter exporting, the plan must address questions such as the following:

1. Which products should be developed for export?

    Having export potential is not the same thing as being export-ready. Some modifications are almost always needed to adapt products to foreign markets. Who will be the user, and what does that necessitate in the way of technical design and instructions? For example, household appliances throughout Europe require a different voltage than in the United States, so a U.S. manufacturer would face the need to modify the units headed for Europe to meet the voltage standard there. Furthermore, if the exporter hopes to sell in more than one European country, additional changes are needed because the plugs are not uniform throughout the European market. Some of the modifications are essential, some simply advisable. Some are big, involved, costly; others are minor. But it should not be assumed that exporting will require nothing more than putting a foreign address on the label.

2. Which country or countries are targeted?

This is a critical question, and one that is difficult to answer. Before we describe the process by which country markets are evaluated, here is one piece of advice: Start small. Any entrepreneur who has not participated in international trade should probably stick to just one market at the outset. The chance of making mistakes is high; the cost of those mistakes can be minimized using the one-market strategy. Furthermore, the learning that takes place during entry into the first market will make the task of entering additional countries less troublesome.

Even with the restricted scale of starting, the question of which country is to be targeted remains critical. How do we select the country? What are the important criteria for making the choice? How do we gather information? Because there is no surefire method by which foreign markets can be selected, many companies would probably do well to stick close to home and go into Canada and/or Mexico. Canada is by far the largest buyer of U.S. goods and services; in 2003 the United States exported $161 billion to Canada—more than its second-largest customer (Mexico at $97 billion) and third-largest customer (Japan at $54 billion) combined. The proximity of the Canadian and Mexican markets, and the degree to which U.S. goods are already being used, make them likely prospects for any company starting to export.

Another factor determining the attractiveness of a foreign market is the ease of entry of products into the country. That is, what kind of barriers will be encountered as the product enters the country? These barriers may take the form of excessively high tariff rates, bureaucratic complications, stringent technical standards, and unreasonable quality assurance.[4] An extreme example of a country's entry requirements discouraging imports can be seen in the case of tulip bulb suppliers from the Netherlands trying to get the bulbs into Japan. The Japanese customs inspectors insisted on cutting each bulb in half.[5] Consequently, no matter how good the Japanese tulip market may have been, these inspection procedures created a barrier that meant Japan was not a viable option for bulb exporters from the Netherlands.

Political stability is another factor to consider in making the choice about which market to enter. In countries with governments and economies that are undergoing stress, some important changes in the way business is conducted could develop. For example, a repressive government may bring on revolution that may be accompanied by demands to "kick the foreigners out." Even something far less dramatic—change in tariff rates, for example—can make an important difference in the attractiveness of the country as a market. In summary, an unstable government makes a country less attractive than it otherwise might have been. Most companies will enter markets plagued with uncertainty only if the rewards are great enough to pay for taking the risk.

A Web site developed and maintained by the U.S. Chamber of Commerce, the Small Business Administration, and the insurance company, American Insurance Company (AIG), serves as an excellent introduction to the risks of doing business overseas. The site, http://assessyourinternational risk.org, describes common risks and the ways of protecting against them through better understanding and through insurance specifically written with those risks in mind.

3. What price shall we charge?

This is among the most important practical issues to be covered in an export plan. One key consideration in the determination of price is the company's objectives in competing in the foreign market. Some firms will enter a market with an eye toward the long run, so they will concentrate on establishing themselves, often sacrificing early profits. The strategy is to develop a favorable image in the market and use that image to capture market share and customer loyalty. Such an approach suggests keeping the price low where possible. An alternative objective is to make as much money as is reasonably possible from the time the company enters the market. This objective obviously leads to different pricing decisions than those made with the long-term objective described earlier.

Rather than using the objectives of the firm to determine price, we can follow the alternative of letting the costs of doing business internationally drive the process. Selling a product in a country other than the one in which it is produced brings with it additional costs. Frequently, for example, the product requires modification, packaging usually costs more than for domestic sales, dealing with the paper work required by some countries can be very involved, and good communications require maintaining long distance networks of contacts. See Illustration Capsule 11-1 for one entrepreneur's description of the costs his company encounters in its international markets.

Getting Established in an International Market

A company that has decided to enter the international market must then decide how it will get its products to its overseas customers. There are two basic approaches: indirect, which involves another individual or company, and direct, where the firm does the job on its own.

Indirect exporting Many entrepreneurs find that indirect exporting suits their needs because it involves less time, effort, and resources than would doing all of the required tasks independently. First-time exporters frequently decide to turn over much of the exporting process to an export management company (EMC). An EMC can best be described as an export specialist that will act as the international marketing department for the firm. EMCs can provide market research, develop distribution networks, establish valuable contacts for the firm, and identify troublesome aspects of dealing with certain countries. For this wide range of expertise the entrepreneur will pay, of course, but EMCs represent an option that most companies with no experience in exporting should consider.

The value of the service provided by the EMC varies considerably, being determined by its experience and capabilities. Some EMCs specialize in certain areas of the world; others have a particular industry as their concentration. Still others have specialties that emphasize a specific industry within a certain part of the world. For example, one EMC may cover South America, and another may

> **Export management company (EMC)** – used by many companies new to international business as a means of outsourcing various elements of the exporting process.

ILLUSTRATION CAPSULE 11-1

COSTS FACED IN INTERNATIONAL SALES

Any entrepreneur planning to sell overseas had better recognize the many types of additional costs that will be encountered. Ed Mayorga, the CEO of R&E Electronics of Wilmington, North Carolina, has known what those costs are, because he had encountered them. His experience has led him to make pricing decisions for overseas markets that carefully reflect the costly complications of exporting. The additional cost factors he has identified include the following:

1. **Longer collection times.** The time between shipments of any payment for export orders is always longer for foreign sales than for domestic. This delay means cash shortages, which must be covered by taking out loans. The interest on those loans is an expense of doing international business.
2. **Insurance.** Two types of situations must be covered by insurance. The first is for nonpayment by the customer; the second covers situations when the transaction is disrupted by war, insurrection, or similar calamity. Obviously both types of insurance cost money and, in the case of countries undergoing political unrest, the costs can be significant. Consequently, Mr. Mayorga's firm must get a quote on insurance of both types before the final price of the product can be given.
3. **Taxes.** In may international transactions, the entrepreneur is required to pay taxes to the foreign government. As a means of avoiding this liability, Mr. Mayorga requires that payment, in dollars, be sent to his company's headquarters.
4. **Administrative burden.** International orders are typically more involved than domestic orders, requiring more forms and greater staff attention. The costs of the additional time, effort, and staffing should be reflected in the price of the product.

Source: Adapted from Andresky Fraser, "Pricing to Cover Export Costs," *Inc.*, March 1992, 103.

---

handle building materials; but a third may concentrate on the building materials industry within South America. All things equal, a firm would likely get best results from an EMC that has experience both in the region the firm hopes to enter and in the appropriate industry.

Another type of organization that a firm entering the international market may choose to use is an international trading company. Such a company provides an even broader array of services than does an EMC. These firms are frequently extremely large and have capabilities in transportation, financing, production, and marketing. Trading companies have a rich tradition in Japan and an important role in that country's international trade efforts.

Other types of indirect exporting relationships include companies that act as "finders" for overseas customers; buyers for foreign users; and export merchants who buy from the manufacturer and then sell, ship, and invoice in their own name. Finally, there are manufacturers, already in international sales, who take on products of other companies for sale in the markets they serve. Regardless of which of the various options of indirect exporting a firm selects, the task should be less involved than doing it on its own.

The direct option is nonetheless the right choice for some exporters, so we will now discuss its various forms.

Direct exporting In direct exporting the company itself carries out the marketing of its product in the foreign market. A firm that decides not to avail itself of the services of an outside agency or specialist must create a means for getting its product marketed and into the hands of customers. Some of the more commonly used channels are described next.

Sales representatives are used by many firms because such arrangements are simple and straightforward. The representatives are independent agents who are paid on a commission basis, an arrangement that reduces the firm's financial risk. The firm supports the representative with training, promotional literature, and samples in much the same way as it would for employee salespeople. Because the sales representative does not take title to the goods, the independence of both the firm and the representative is maintained.

Distributors are merchants who purchase the goods from the manufacturer for resale. Typically, a distributor will carry inventory and supply of spare parts, and will have the capability to service customer needs. This is a closer more formal relationship than that between the firm and a sales representative, and it usually includes a contract that specifies considerations such as payment terms, territories, and the period of the relationship.

Some firms have no outside group between them and their retailers—that is, they deal directly with the retail outlets that handle their product. This can be a demanding arrangement in cases where there are many retailers and their needs are difficult to fulfill. Exacerbating these problems is the complication of long distances between the manufacturer and the outlets. For consumer products, dealing directly with retailers may be an unwieldy arrangement, with too many outlets for the exporter to serve adequately. For some industrial products, on the other hand, this channel of distribution may work well, because service may improve by eliminating the intermediary. It also provides the advantage of putting the firm in closer contact with the consumer.

The final channel of distribution to be discussed here puts the exporter in direct contact with the end user. For this arrangement to be workable, there must be a few large buyers. Example of the kinds of customers for whom this arrangement might be satisfactory are government, schools, hospitals, and large businesses. Such organizations would likely have large enough needs to warrant attention directly from the exporter.

Getting Paid

Exporting, by definition, involves a supplier in one country selling something to a buyer in another. Not only are the two parties members of different countries, they are from different cultures. To complicate matters even further, the buyer and seller often have to proceed without the benefit of having dealt with one another on a face-to-face basis. Many questions are on the mind of the seller; counterpart questions are on the mind of the buyer. The buyer wonders if the quality will be high; the seller worries about some unusual requirement causing the buyer to reject the shipment. The seller wonders what kinds of questions regarding use of the product may arise; the buyer is concerned about the kind of after-sale service the seller will provide if there's trouble.

Beyond these issues is the most important of all the questions about the transaction: How will payment be handled? The heart of the concern is trust. Consider the situation you would face if you had just sold an order to a buyer from another continent. Chances are you do not know this person from anything other than your dealings during the transaction. The buyer speaks a different language, may have an ethical code governing business transactions that is different from yours, and lives in a country with a legal system about which you know very little. How comfortable will you be with the prospect of shipping the order and then waiting for payment to arrive in two, three, or perhaps six months? One way of eliminating any discomfort you may suffer in this situation is to specify that payment be received prior to shipment. Before we go too far in pursuing this solution, we have to consider the buyer. Will the buyer worry about sending payment before the goods have been received? Of course, the buyer has the same doubts you do. Differences in country, culture, language, legal system, and so on will make the prepayment proposal unacceptable.

What is needed for transactions to proceed between buyers and sellers in different parts of the world is a system that allows both the seller and the buyer to put aside concerns about whether the other party can be trusted. Such a system has been developed, and it is an integral part of international trade. At its heart is a standard procedure, understood and accepted by traders throughout the world, that involves the use of an intermediary, or third party, standing between the seller and buyer. Let us describe the basic elements of the process by which international transactions proceed.

To illustrate the use of international payment procedures we will provide an example of a U.S. exporter selling 100 tons of wheat to an importer in Germany, a flour mill. After the deal has been made, the flour mill arranges for its bank in Frankfurt to issue a promise to pay on its behalf. The Frankfurt bank issues the promise, known as a *letter of credit*, because it knows the importer and is satisfied that it will pay. The fact that a bank, and probably a large reputable one at that, has issued the promise provides the kind of assurance the exporter needs to release the wheat for shipment to Germany. The bank, as a third party, has provided the exporter with what it needs to set aside any questions it may have about whether it trusts the flour mill to pay.

> **Letter of credit** – document issued by the bank of an international buyer and sent to the bank of the seller to assure payment to the seller, upon satisfactory execution of the terms of the sales contract.

So the bank's involvement has dealt with any reservations the exporter may have had, but what about the flour mill? As importer, it may be worried about the way the transaction gets handled. Specifically, will it be concerned about the bank paying the exporter and then billing the mill for wheat that never makes it to Germany? The process protects the importer from this happening by requiring the exporter to relinquish the title to the grain as part of the step the exporter must complete in order to be paid. The title is sent after the grain has been shipped, using a document called a *bill of lading*. (Remember that the exporter ships only after having seen the letter of credit its customer has gotten the bank in Frankfurt to issue.) Accompanying the bill of lading is a request for payment, called a *draft*. Upon receipt of the draft, the bank pays the exporter and sends the title for the wheat to the importer. The importer then pays off its bank loan; the process has run its course.

Before leaving this topic, we should point out that this description is an oversimplification intended to show how the process protects the interests of both sides by using a bank as intermediary. As this process is actually practiced in international trade, it consists of 14 steps, and a U.S. bank would get involved.

Government Assistance

Because exporting can be a complex process and because many people are worried about the balance-of-trade difficulties of the United States, numerous government programs to encourage exporting have been developed in recent years. We will review some of the most important. For a useful preview of the steps in reaching overseas markets, go to http://www.export.gov/exportbasics/index.asp. The site gives the "Exporting Basics Life Cycle" of some essential steps, from a self-assessment of whether exporting is a good decision, to research guidance, to ways of finding and developing trade contacts, to using freight forwarders, to arranging to follow up on transactions.

An essential early step in the exploration of exporting is information gathering. The International Trade Administration (ITA) of the Department of Commerce is an important source of support for any company interested in exporting. At its home page, http://www.trade.gov/, are links to many useful groups, including ITA'S Trade Information Center (TIC). The TIC is the central source of information on international trade programs offered through 20 federal government agencies.

The programs and services of these agencies are identified and described in the TIC'S Export Programs Guide to Federal Export Assistance. The guide, available on the Web at http://www.itd.doc.gov/td/tic/, was written to help businesses decide whether and how to start exporting. The following is a description of some of the topics it covers.

General export counseling and assistance The ITA is dedicated to opening markets for U.S. products and providing assistance and information to exporters. The ITA's offices include the U.S. & Foreign Commercial Service (US&FCS) network, consisting of 104 domestic Export Assistance Centers (discussed next) and 158 overseas offices. The mission of the US&FCS is to support U.S. firms—especially small- and medium-sized companies—in their efforts to increase exports.

In cooperation with the Small Business Administration (SBA) and the Export-Import Bank of the United States (Ex-Im Bank), the Department of Commerce has established a network of Export Assistance Centers. These centers, located in major metropolitan cities throughout the country, are "one-stop shops" that provide small- and medium-sized firms with hands-on export marketing and trade finance support. Trade specialists at the centers can (1) identify the best markets for products; (2) develop an effective market entry strategy based on information generated from overseas commercial officers; (3) facilitate the implementation of these strategies by advising clients on distribution channels, key factors to consider in pricing, and relevant trade shows and missions; and (4) assist with trade finance programs available through federal, state, and local public sources and private-sector entities.

The Department of Commerce has also developed a nationwide network of organizations of local business community leaders who volunteer their time, supplying specialized expertise to small- and medium-sized businesses interested in exporting. Among other services, the District Export Councils organize seminars on various topics, host international buyer delegations, design guides to help firms export, and put exporters on the Internet.

In addition to these general export counseling programs offered through the Department of Commerce, help is available through the Small Business Administration. The Office of International Trade (OIT) works with other federal agencies and public- and private-sector organizations to encourage small businesses to expand their export activities. OIT's activities include various financing support for small business exporters, including *ExportExpress,* a program designed to help entry into an overseas market, a working capital program, and one to facilitate expansion or deal with competition from imports. Another SBA program, the Export Legal Assistance Network (ELAN), provides free initial consultations to new-to-export businesses on export-related matters.

Industry-specific export counseling and assistance The Department of Commerce assists entrepreneurs who need information on world trade in a particular industry. The Trade Development (TD) office has specialists who work directly with firms to identify trade opportunities and obstacles by product or service, industry, and market. In addition to these services provided directly to companies, TD conducts trade missions, organizes trade fairs, and gives marketing seminars. TD experts are organized into six major industry sectors:

Technology and aerospace

Basic industries

Textiles, apparel, and consumer goods

Service industries

Environmental technology exports

Tourism

Country-specific export counseling and assistance In contrast to programs that concentrate on certain industries, several federal programs and services have as their focus specific countries. Specialists at TIC provide counseling on Asia, Western Europe, Latin America, NAFTA, and the Near East. Country-specific counseling is available on standards, intellectual property protection, government procurement, laws, regulations, distribution channels, business travel, opportunities and best prospects for U.S. companies in individual markets, customs procedures, and commercial difficulties encountered in doing business abroad.

Trade contact and market research programs Many entrepreneurs entering exporting will find the programs of ITA to be helpful. The International Partner Search provides a customized search that helps identify well-matched agents, distributors, licensees, and strategic alliance partners. The Gold Key Service offers help to firms planning to visit a country. The service includes orientation briefings, help in developing a marketing strategy, introductions to prospective customers or partners, interpreters, and follow-up efforts. The Market Research service offers both general and customized assistance related to a client's products or services. The service, available on a quick turnaround basis, varies in cost depending on the scope of the work.

Export financing, insurance, and grants Another important group of federal services listed in the Export Programs Guide are those dealing with financing, insurance, and grants. Among the principal participants in these initiatives are the Ex-Im Bank, the SBA, the Department of Commerce, the Department of Agriculture, the Trade and Development Agency (TDA), and the Overseas Private Investment Corporation (OPIC). These services are only a part of what is available to the prospective exporter, courtesy of the federal government. There are many other federal programs and state and local services as well. An entrepreneur hoping to start exporting need not go it alone. The first step in the process should be a call to the Trade Information Center at 800-872-8723 (800-USA-TRADE) or a visit to its home page at http://www.export.gov/tic.

IMPORTING

The United States is one of the largest exporters in the world; as to importing, it is by far the biggest, importing well over $1 trillion in goods and services annually. While multinational corporations dominate this segment of the economy, entrepreneurs also play an important role. We explore some of the basic elements of importing, organizing our discussion into three topics: finding the product to import, getting it into the country, and selling it when it becomes available.

Finding Products to Import

Two basic routes into importing can be identified. We will call them *sourcing* and *opportunity spotting*. The sourcing route is one in which the entrepreneur searches internationally for sources of a product that is already available domestically. The purpose of the search is to uncover sources of the product that offer lower cost or superior quality. Many Pacific Rim countries are noted for their ability to sell quality goods at low price. Entrepreneurs who find a market that is not well served by domestic producers often will initiate a search for new suppliers to enter the market. If these new suppliers are foreign companies that do not have a U.S. base of operations, an opportunity for an import entrepreneur exists.

In addition to lower cost than those of domestic suppliers, the foreign suppliers may offer better quality. This can take many forms—superior design, appearance, or some other element—and if it is important to buyers, an opening for importing exists. Neither French wine nor precision machine tools from Germany compete on price, but compete they do because many buyers of these products see them as providing something beyond what competing American products offer. Developing sources outside the country is done for a variety of reasons. Starting a business on this basis requires thorough knowledge of the market being served, the ability to do industry research on a global scope, an understanding of international trade, and familiarity with importing processes.

Opportunity spotting is perhaps less systematic than sourcing and seems to be more oriented toward consumer products. The process is triggered by someone being attracted to an item that is not available in the United States. Frequently, as people travel or look through magazines or similar literature from foreign sources, they encounter something new or unusual and wonder why the item is not available in the United States. Some entrepreneurs turn that question into an opportunity to start a new importing business. The possibility of using the rich experiences provided by travel as a spring board into the importing business has prompted the publication of a book, *How to Be an Importer and Pay for Your World Travel*.[5] The book is based on the idea that there is an opportunity to make money while doing many of the things you would do anyway on a trip. The authors refer to the process as the "Importing Game" to portray the fun and adventure that this undertaking promises. The next step involves the individual bringing home samples of the product to see if buyers agree that the product has some appeal.

Getting the Goods into the Country

Once the decision about what goods to deal in has been made and the transaction has taken place, we must arrange to get them into the country. This means clearing them through the U.S. Customs Service. The process consists of a number of steps: entry, inspection, appraisal, classification, and liquidation.

Entry of the goods requires the following documents:

1. A bill of lading, airway bill, or carrier's certificate. These documents specifying the importer as purchaser show that the shipper has accepted the merchandise and has contracted to deliver to its destination.
2. A commercial invoice, obtained from the seller, which shows the value and description of the merchandise.
3. Entry manifest, an itemized list of cargo entering the country.
4. Packing lists, if applicable.

Inspection of the shipment determines the value of the goods, the accuracy of the invoice, whether the shipment contains prohibited articles, and whether the goods have met other federal requirements, such as indication of country of origin.

Because the value of the goods determines the amount of duty levied on the shipment, an accurate appraisal is important. Generally the transaction value—that is, the amount shown on the invoice—serves as the appraisal value. However, if the Customs Service determines that figure to be inaccurate, another will be used.

The Customs Service uses the Harmonized Tariff Schedule of the United States (HTSUS) as a basis for classifying imported products and thereby establishing the duty to be charged. The HTSUS is divided into various sections and chapters dealing separately with merchandise in broad product categories. The tariff schedule includes several rates of duty for each item general rates for most-favored nations; "special" rates for many developing nations; and "Column 2" rates for imports not eligible for general or special rates.

The HTSUS rate and the value set in the appraisal step determine the amount of duty that must be paid. This final step in the entry process is known as *liquidation*.

Selling the Goods

Once the goods have cleared customs, they are available to the entrepreneur importer. We will now examine some ways by which the entrepreneur can dispose of them. Many entrepreneurs who import because of contacts with an international source with lower costs or better quality than those of the domestic competition (the sourcing route described earlier) will have no problem because they will be filling orders. The issue for them is not whether the product is being used but which source provides the best price/value combination. With entrepreneur importers who locate items during foreign travel or research, the issues of who will buy the merchandise and how it should be distributed are crucial.

The simplest way to sell imported goods is to family, friends, and associates. If you bought some sweaters from Peru, you may find that just by wearing one, interest and sales will develop. If the sweaters are exceptional, the next phase may involve contact with a retail outlet. Typically this will be a friend, or perhaps a friend of a friend. Another way to develop this channel is, of course, to make direct contact, a sales call. Once you have one store as a customer, you will likely get others because store owners talk with other store owners. In addition to conventional retail outlets, shops operated by charitable organizations may be useful. The arrangement between the importer and the outlet is often one by which the goods are not purchased by the shop, as is the usual procedure, but simply displayed until they are bought. When the sale takes place, the importer gets the money after giving the store a commission. This is known as placing goods on consignment and has the advantage of providing the store with a risk-free opportunity to sell the merchandise. The disadvantage to the importer is the delay in getting paid.

Some products may best be distributed by placing ads in newspapers or magazines. This, of course, requires establishing a means for interested people to respond and following up on those responses. A similar method is direct mail. Using direct mail in a cost-effective manner requires careful attention to mailing list details—who is included, how the list was compiled, and how old the entries are.

Another means of distribution involves renting a booth or table at an event that attracts prospective buyers. The event can be a flea market for moderately priced consumer items, a trade show for industrial products, or a convention at which a variety of office and professional goods may attract interests.

GLOBAL BUSINESS AND THE BUSINESS PLAN

It is important to include plans for exporting and importing in the business plan even if it is only a small part of the company's sales. Bankers and investors will want to know that the entrepreneur really understands how to operate in a global market if that will be a part of the business operations. The questions listed above concerning management objectives, experience, pricing, and so on are a critical part of the business plan and demonstrate the entrepreneur's knowledge of the global market.

SUMMARY

Global business provides both threats and opportunities for small firms. As a result, entrepreneurs should engage in careful exploration of foreign markets. The decision whether or not to export is one that demands careful information gathering and analysis. Fortunately for the entrepreneur involved in the decision, many sources of assistance are available. Because many people have recognized the importance of small businesses competing effectively in overseas markets, a variety of programs of federal and state government offices have been developed to ease the entry into those markets.

DISCUSSION QUESTIONS

1. Describe the contract between the U.S. trade balance during the first 70 years of the 20th century versus that of the period since 1970.
2. Why are so few small businesses involved in exporting or importing?
3. Distinguish between direct and indirect approaches to entering international markets and give examples of each.
4. What is the Department of Commerce's Trade Information Center?

5. Give reasons why a U.S.-based entrepreneur would be well advised to start exporting efforts with either Mexico or Canada.

6. Describe the process by which merchandise enters this country from another.

ENDNOTES

1. *2005 Statistical Abstract of the United States* (Washington, DC: U.S. Department of Commerce, Bureau of the Census).

2. Ibid.

3. Christopher Knowles, "The New Entrepreneurs," *Fortune*, June 6, 1988, 87–102.

4. Charko W. Hill, *International Business*, 2nd ed. (Boston: McGraw-Hill, 1997), 160.

5. Mary Green and Stanley Gillmar, *How to Be an Importer and Pay for Your World Travel* (Berkeley, CA: Ten Speed Press, 1993).

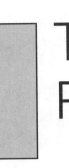

The Business Plan

INTRODUCTION

LEARNING OBJECTIVES

$ To understand the many topics that should be addressed in a business plan.

$ To realize business plans are helpful for both start-ups and existing businesses.

$ To be able to write a business plan that could be submitted to a bank or investor for financing.

WHAT IS A BUSINESS PLAN?

A *business plan* is a comprehensive document that helps an entrepreneur analyze the market and plan a business strategy. A business plan is often prepared by an existing company to ensure that future growth is properly managed. If the plan is prepared for a start-up, it helps the entrepreneurs avoid costly mistakes. In addition to being useful as a planning document, the business plan often is necessary for obtaining financing. Banks', venture capitalists', and investors' usually require a business plan in order to help them make their investment decisions. A well-written business plan provides evidence of the entrepreneur's ability to plan and manage the company.

> **Business plan** – a comprehensive document that helps an entrepreneur analyze the market and plan a business strategy.

HOW DO PLANS FOR EXISTING BUSINESSES AND START-UPS DIFFER?

Although the plan for an existing business and the plan for a start-up examine the same factors, the focus varies slightly. With the existing business, the plan states the current situation, where the company wants to be in three to five years, and what it will take to reach those goals. For a start-up, more emphasis is often placed on the first few years, with less emphasis placed on the future years. For example, an existing business plan may state:

> The current location of Smith Sisters' Furniture includes 5,000 square feet of selling space, a 2,000-square-foot warehouse, and an 800-square-foot office. In order to reach the projected sales figures, the company will need at least 8,000 square feet of selling space plus a 3,000-square-foot warehouse and 1,000 square feet of office space. The company will therefore move within the next year to a larger location within the same community.

A new business, though, may state:

> Smith Sisters' Furniture has leased space in the new Sanford Mall in Springfield. This location has 5,000 square feet of selling space in addition to a 2,000-square-foot warehouse and an 800-square-foot office. The company has signed a three-year lease for this location.

WHAT IS INCLUDED IN THE BUSINESS PLAN?

In the sections that follow, the business plan format is outlined and helpful checklists are provided. Common mistakes are also listed for some topics. This information is designed to prevent you from making some of the costly errors that entrepreneurs often make. If you follow the format and answer the questions in the checklists, you will have a comprehensive planning document that can also be used to obtain financing.

A business plan includes the following major topic headings:

$ Executive Summary

$ Mission Statement

$ Business Environment

$ Marketing Plan

$ Management Team

$ Financial Data

$ Legal Considerations

$ Insurance Requirements

$ Suppliers

$ Risks

$ Assumptions/Conclusions

EXECUTIVE SUMMARY

Executive summary – two-page overview of the most important facts in the business plan.

Because the business plan is usually a lengthy document, an executive summary is necessary. The *executive summary*, which is approximately two pages long, provides the reader with an overview of all of the most important facts contained in the plan. Although the executive summary is placed in the front of the business plan, it is actually easier to write it *after* you have written the entire business plan. Then portions of each section can be used to write a paragraph or two about each of the major topics. The Executive Summary Checklist will help you write your executive summary.

Discussion Questions

1. Suppose an entrepreneur tells you she has been successful and has never written a business plan. She asks you why she should write one. How would you respond?
2. When entrepreneurs seek financing, financial institutions often require a business plan before making a decision. Why is this a requirement?
3. How does a business plan for a start-up differ from a plan for an existing business?
4. What is the purpose of the executive summary of a business plan?

EXECUTIVE SUMMARY, MISSION STATEMENT, AND THE BUSINESS ENVIRONMENT

Learning Objectives

$ To be able to write an executive summary for a business plan.

$ To be able to formulate a mission statement for a business.

$ To comprehend the impact of the external business environment.

Mission Statement

Mission statement – a concise, well-defined explanation of the purpose of the business and the management's philosophy.

The *mission statement* is a concise, well-defined explanation of the purpose of the business and the management's philosophy. Many experts suggest that the mission statement should be 50 words or less because that restriction on length forces the entrepreneur to be focused.[1] Although mission statements vary,

CHECKLIST: EXECUTIVE SUMMARY

☐ Briefly describe the proposed business and product or service it will provide.
☐ Describe the most important trends in the industry.
☐ Describe the type of advertising and promotion that will be implemented.
☐ Give the sales and profits for the past three years (if it is an existing company). Give projected sales and profits for the next three years (for both existing businesses and start-ups).
☐ Describe the education and relevant work experience of the owners and key management personnel.
☐ Include any important legal considerations such as exclusive agreements, customer contracts, and patents.
☐ Include any other information that you believe the reader should know in order to understand the business operation.

common elements include a description of the products or services offered and the management philosophy of the company's owner. Celestial Seasonings, Inc., which sells herbal teas, once stated its mission on the back of each box of tea as follows:

> We believe in making the most delicious and natural teas that nurture your body and uplift your soul. We believe our products must be superior in quality, of good value, beautifully artistic, and philosophically inspiring. We are an independent company in Boulder, Colorado, striving to fulfill these beliefs without taking ourselves too seriously.[2]

Nonprofit organizations also have mission statements to guide the activities of the members. The mission of the National Wildlife Foundation is stated as follows:

> To educate, inspire, and assist individuals and organizations of diverse cultures to conserve wildlife and other natural resources while protecting the Earth's environment to promote a peaceful, equitable, and sustainable future.[3]

The mission statement provides direction for the company and prevents the company owners from diversifying into areas that do not serve the original company purpose. For this reason, the mission statement should be written as the first step in developing the business plan. The Mission Statement Checklist will help you write your mission statement.

The Business Environment

As stated in Chapter 2, successful entrepreneurs constantly analyze the business environment and its impact on the company. This analysis is an important first step in determining whether a business can survive and grow. The business

CHECKLIST: MISSION STATEMENT

☐ What is the purpose of your business?
☐ What products and services will be offered?
☐ What is your management philosophy?

environment is composed of three factors—national trends, industry trends, and local trends.

What national trends will affect your business? National trends often have a dramatic impact on the consumer's buying habits. Although small changes occur all the time, major shifts in the market will affect the survival of the company. Each business will be affected by different trends, so the entrepreneur must decide which trends will have the greatest impact on the business. Changes that may affect a company's survival would include the following:

$ *Demographic shifts.* Changes in the demographic composition of the country have a huge impact on many businesses. These changes create increased demand for some products and services while at the same time greatly reducing the demand for others. Two of the major trends that will affect companies in the future are the aging population and the increasing minority population.

In the late 1990s, senior citizens, age 65 and older, made up less than 13 percent of all Americans. By 2030, this group will make up more than 20 percent of the population—there will be about as many people age 65 and older as there are people age 18 and younger. This will increase the demand for retirement communities, single-portion food packaging, leisure travel, and other goods and services.[4]

Also, as stated in Chapter 6, the minority population in the United States is expected to increase substantially in the next several decades. This will certainly create changes in demand for products and services and may also change marketing methods to reach those customers.

$ *An increase in the number of women working outside the home and an increase in the number of stay-at-home fathers.* Figure B-1 shows the percentage of married women in the workforce who have very young children. For many years, this percentage continued to increase and the need for day care facilities dramatically increased. However, as the chart shows, this percentage has decreased in recent years. In addition, the number of

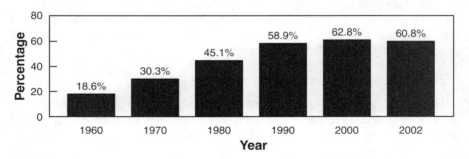

Source: 2000 Statistical Abstract of the United States (Washington, DC: U.S. Department of Commerce, Bureau of the Census), 409; and *2003 Statistical Abstract*, http://www.census.gov/prod/2004pubs/03statab/labor.pdf.

FIGURE B–1   Labor force participation rate of married women with children under age 6.

stay-at-home fathers has continually increased. These combined trends may have a negative impact on day care demand in future years.

$ *Legislative trends.* The federal government, as well as state and local governments, passes laws that have a major impact on businesses. Many small auto repair shops were affected by the Federal Clean Air Act, which requires that autos in many cities pass emissions tests to get the car registration renewed. The equipment for testing emissions is expensive and many small shops could not afford to purchase it, thus preventing them from completing inspections. This eliminated a major source of business for small shops, while the large service facilities that could afford the equipment increased revenues.

Demographic changes, lifestyle changes, and legislative trends are just a few of the many trends that may affect a company. Each entrepreneur must decide which trends will affect his or her business most. For example, a business that sells products to law enforcement personnel would be affected by national crime legislation. For other businesses this law may not have a direct impact on sales. The checklist on page 149 lists some of the trends that affect businesses and provides some possible sources of information.

What industry trends will affect your business? It is also important to research the trends in the industry you are entering. It is common to see industries with large increases or decreases in sales, major shifts in how the businesses operate, or upheavals caused by technological changes. Consider, for example, the personal digital assistant (PDA) industry. PDA sales are dropping while sales of smart phones are increasing. Rapid changes in technology are likely to make the original PDAs obsolete.

It is not only the high-tech industries that go through upheavals. As shown in Figure B-2, the total number of grocery stores decreased during the 1990s although the number of superstores that carry a large variety of grocery and non-food items increased more than 36 percent.[5]

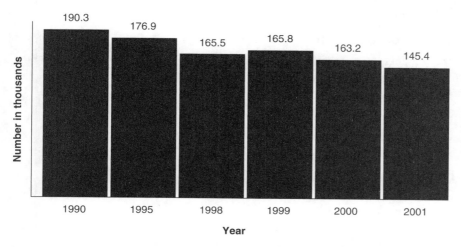

Source: U.S. Census Bureau, *2003 Statistical Abstract of the United States,* http://www.census.gov/prod/2004pubs/03statab/domtrade.pdf.

FIGURE B–2   Number of grocery stores.

The following are examples of other industry trends:

$ An entrepreneur thinking of starting a waste-hauling business should consider the number of landfills that are closing and the higher costs for insurance and dumping fees. These trends could have a negative impact on the company's profitability.

$ An optometrist who is thinking about opening a private practice should consider the trend for franchised outlets that promise glasses in an hour. For most other businesses, however, this trend would not be important. Laser surgery is also having an impact on the industry.

$ For a mechanic who is planning to open an auto repair shop, the trend toward computerized cars and the need for high-technology diagnostic equipment affect the amount of money needed up front. Not only will start-up costs be higher than in the past, but additional equipment will be necessary once the business is in operation.

One of the best sources of industry information is national trade associations. These organizations often compile data regarding trends and risks of industries. The Business Environment Checklist lists questions to be answered concerning the industry and gives possible sources of information.

What local trends will affect your business? It is also important to consider trends in the community in which the business will locate. Local trends often have more of an impact on a business than national trends. Factors that may be considered include the following:

$ The economy of the community

$ The attitude of the community toward the type of business proposed

$ The increase or decrease of the community's population

The Business Environment Checklist lists some of the local factors that may affect a business. These and others should be considered when completing an analysis of the business environment.

Discussion Questions

1. Why would an entrepreneur complete a business plan before opening a business? Why would the owner of an existing business prepare a business plan?
2. What is the purpose of a mission statement?
3. What national trends would affect a home health care service?
4. Because of pollution and trash problems, some states have passed laws banning disposable diapers. What effect would this have on small businesses?

Endnotes

1. *How to Really Write a Business Plan,* a film produced by the Goldhirsh Group (Fort Worth, TX: Dryden Press, 1994).
2. Celestial Seasonings, Inc., Boulder, CO.
3. National Wildlife Foundation, Washington, DC.
4. Philip Kotler and Gary Armstrong, *Principles of Marketing,* 7th ed. (Upper Saddle River, NJ: Prentice-Hall, 1996), 75–76.
5. U.S. Census Bureau, *Statistical Abstract of the United States, 2003,* http://www.cenesus.gov/prod/2004pubs/03statab/domtrade.pdf.

CHECKLIST: BUSINESS ENVIRONMENT

National Trends

- ☐ Demographic changes
- ☐ Legislative actions
- ☐ Technological changes
- ☐ Health care reform
- ☐ Two-income families
- ☐ The economy and interest rates
- ☐ Faster pace of life

The following sources may be helpful in identifying national trends:

Census of the Population (http://www.census.gov)
Lists demographic data for states, counties, and cities

Census of Businesses (http://www.census.gov)
Identifies the types of businesses, the number, and the size of businesses in each state, county, and city

Business Conditions Digest
Gives information on prices, employment, wages, and other economic factors

Industry Information

- ☐ Is this industry dominated by large or small firms?
- ☐ What is the failure rate in this industry?
- ☐ Is this a new industry or one that is well established?
- ☐ What is the typical profitability in this industry?
- ☐ What are the trends in this industry?

The following sources provide industry information:

Encyclopedia of Associations
Lists the name and telephone number of national trade associations

Annual Statement Studies
Provides financial information such as average markups and profits for many industries

Dun and Bradstreet's Key Business Ratios
Provides financial information for many businesses

U.S. Industrial Outlook
Analyzes trends for more than 200 industries

Standard and Poor's Industry Surveys
Provides industry surveys and company analyses

Community Information

- ☐ Is the population in the community increasing or decreasing?
- ☐ What is the attitude of the community toward your business? Is it positive, negative, or neutral?
- ☐ Will the community help provide any financing for your business or help in getting it started?
- ☐ Is the local economy strong or in a recession?

Sources of local information may include the local chamber of commerce, the local economic development office, city hall, and other government agencies.

The Business Plan

MARKETING

LEARNING OBJECTIVES

$ To be able to write a detailed description of how a company will compete in the marketplace.

$ To be able to provide a comprehensive explanation of a company's products and services.

$ To understand how to complete a competitor analysis and develop a competitive advantage for a company.

WHAT IS INCLUDED IN THE MARKETING SECTION?

The mission statement you have developed briefly describes the products or services the company will offer. The marketing section of the business plan provides a detailed description of how the company will compete in the marketplace as it sells those products and services.

The marketing section includes the following:

$ A more detailed description of the products and services

$ An analysis of the competition

$ An examination of the pricing structure

$ An explanation of the company's credit policy

$ An explanation of the competitive advantage

$ A profile of the target market

$ A site analysis

$ A promotional plan

What Is Your Product or Service?

A detailed description of the company's products and services is important for two reasons. First, it helps you thoroughly develop the concept, requiring you to move from the idea stage to something more tangible. Second, it helps the reader of your business plan better understand your business. If you plan to sell a product the description should include the size, weight, shape, packaging, and quality. If you plan to sell a service, describe all of the services you will offer and explain the typical procedures you will follow.

If your business will be a franchise, the information in the previous paragraph should be accompanied by a history of the franchise, information on the ownership of the franchise corporation, and the number of existing franchised outlets. If the franchise corporation provides training prior to opening or on an ongoing basis, this is also an important fact to include since it improves your chances of success.

The Product or Service Checklist will help you describe your product or service.

Who Are Your Competitors?

Almost every small business faces competition from both large and small companies. It is important to know the competition thoroughly in order to develop your competitive strategy. An analysis of the competition can be completed by determining their strengths and weaknesses and examining specific aspects of their operation. Do they have a large product line? Do they have poor service? Are they strong or weak financially? Do they have a stable workforce or is there a high turnover?

It is important to consider both direct and indirect competition, since many entrepreneurs underestimate their competition. For example, if an entrepreneur plans to start an Italian restaurant, he or she often only considers the number of Italian restaurants in the area. However, other full-service restaurants are direct competitors, even if they sell Greek food or Chinese food. Indirect competitors include any businesses that sell prepared food, including fast-food restaurants and grocery stores with takeout menus.

CHECKLIST: PRODUCT OR SERVICE

Describe Your Product:
- ☐ Size
- ☐ Shape
- ☐ Ingredients/Materials
- ☐ Colors
- ☐ Weight
- ☐ Speed
- ☐ Packaging
- ☐ Texture

What Services Will You Offer?
- ☐ Personalized attention
- ☐ Guaranteed response time
- ☐ Custom ordering
- ☐ Trial offers
- ☐ Money-back guarantee

Is Your Business a Franchise?
- ☐ How long has the franchise corporation been operating?
- ☐ Who owns the franchise corporation?
- ☐ How many franchised outlets currently exist?
- ☐ Does the franchise corporation provide training?
- ☐ Does the franchise corporation provide ongoing assistance once you are in business?

The Competitor Analysis Checklist will help in analyzing the competition. It may not be possible to answer all of the questions about all of the competitors. Therefore, the entrepreneur should identify three to five major competitors and then answer as many questions as possible concerning them.

Discussion Questions

1. If an entrepreneur is thinking of opening a laundromat, identify two ways to determine the number of competing laundromats in the area. In addition to other laundromats, what else may be competition?

2. If an entrepreneur plans to start a nursery to sell shrubs, fertilizers, and gardening utensils, what should be considered as competing businesses?

3. If an entrepreneur wants to identify manufacturers in the midwestern United States that manufacture fertilizer, identity two references in the library that may be helpful.

PRICING

Learning Objectives

$ To understand the difference between pricing objectives and pricing policies.

$ To be aware of all of the factors that must be considered when establishing prices.

CHECKLIST: COMPETITOR ANALYSIS

- ☐ Identity your main competitors by name.
- ☐ If your business is a retail or service business: How far away are the competitors from your business?
- ☐ If your business is wholesale or manufacturing: How do the competitors' trading areas compare with yours?
- ☐ Identify the strengths and weaknesses of your competitors by using the following checklist.

How is your competitor's. . . ?

☐ Product selection			
	Large	Average	Small
☐ Market share			
	100%	50%	0%
☐ Product quality			
	Good	Average	Poor
☐ Quality of service			
	Good	Average	Poor
☐ Amount of advertising and promotion			
	Heavy	Average	Very little
☐ Pricing			
	Higher than most	Average	Lower than most
☐ Workforce turnover			
	Very stable	Average	High
☐ Workforce knowledge			
	Good	Average	Poor
☐ Financial condition			
	Very profitable	Average profits	Incurs losses
☐ Level of debt			
	Low	Average	High
☐ Equipment			
	New (state of the art)	Average	Obsolete
☐ Production capacity			
	Operating at full capacity		Has excess Capacity

- $ To understand that methods of determining prices vary by industry.
- $ To realize that shipping costs must be included in the pricing decision.

What Is Your Pricing Objective?

It is important to determine what you want to accomplish with your pricing structure. The goals to be achieved with your pricing structure are known as your *pricing objectives.* Typical pricing objectives may be as follows:

- $ To achieve a specific dollar amount of profit (for example, $10,000 in annual profit)

> **Pricing objectives** – goals to be achieved with the pricing structure.

$ To achieve a profit level as a percentage of sales (profit should be 5 percent of sales)

$ To capture a specific share of the market (5 percent of total market potential)

$ To reach a certain sales volume ($250,000 in sales)

Pricing objectives should be specific and quantifiable so that at the end of the year, you can determine if the goals were met.

What Are Your Pricing Policies?

Once pricing objectives have been established, you should then determine your *pricing policies.* Pricing policies are general pricing guidelines that you will follow to achieve your goals. Typical pricing policies may include the following:

$ Will you run sales to take advantage of the different seasons or to eliminate seasonal merchandise?

$ Will you try to match competitors' prices?

$ Will you use coupons to attract customers?

$ Will you give employees discounts on merchandise they purchase?

> **Pricing policies** – general pricing guidelines that are followed to achieve company goals.

How Will You Determine Your Prices?

Entrepreneurs often use a simplified approach to pricing without realizing that pricing is an important part of the marketing strategy. Many factors must be considered before prices are established. Some of the considerations are as follows:

$ *Costs.* The pricing structure must cover all costs and provide an acceptable profit margin. If you are selling a product, you must consider your costs to purchase the product from your suppliers. If you provide a service, you must determine the labor costs. The costs to purchase the product and the costs of wages to perform a service are known as *direct costs.* All other costs incurred in running the business, such as rent, utilities, other wages, and supplies, must be considered. These are your *indirect costs.* The pricing structure must be designed to cover direct and indirect costs and provide a profit.

Ed Galvin, a partner in the Chicago office of Coopers & Lybrand, states, "Small firms often have a false sense of what it actually costs them to deliver a product or service." Sometimes this is due to an accounting system that does not provide adequate information. However, Galvin has found that even when adequate information is available, business owners often do not factor into their prices their costs for things such as inventory storage, packaging, freight, and product returns. There is more emphasis on getting the sale than making the proper margin.[1]

$ *Competitors' prices.* The competitors' prices cannot be ignored, since customers will consider prices when making their purchase decision. In the previous section of the marketing plan, we provided a method to analyze the competitors. When setting prices, this analysis must be considered. If your competition has poor service, a smaller product selection, and so on, you will be justified in charging a higher price than that competitor. Conversely, if the competition has many advantages compared to your business, you may have to offer a lower price in order to compete effectively.

$ *Effect on demand.* The demand for a product is often affected by the price. If customers demand less as the price increases and demand more as the price decreases, this is known as an *elastic demand.* For some products and services, however, the demand does not change much if prices change. This is known as an *inelastic demand.* Clothing has an elastic demand, whereas the demand for salt is somewhat inelastic. Most of us would buy more clothes if prices decreased, but we would not buy more salt just because the price was lowered.

> **Elastic demand** – when demand for a product increases as price decreases, and demand decreases as price increases.

> **Inelastic demand** – when demand for a product does not change if prices increase or decrease.

Small businesses must find a way to differentiate their products so that customers are willing to pay a high price. Galvin of Coopers & Lybrand recommends identifying your company's strengths compared to the competitors'—better product, better supply, better delivery time, and so forth. "If you talk about quality, you can usually drive profit up."[2]

$ *Image.* For many products, a higher price actually results in higher sales, since customers often equate quality and price. If you want customers to perceive your product or service as a high-quality item, a higher price is best. One self-employed photographer found that demand for his services increased after he raised his prices. When his prices were too low, customers assumed that the quality of his work was equally poor.

$ *Channels of distribution.* If you sell through intermediaries—wholesalers, manufacturers, representatives, and so forth—they will affect your pricing in two ways. First, your product has to be priced so that their margins will motivate them to sell your product. Second, the effect of the intermediary's markups on the final selling price must be considered.[3] Often this analysis helps determine which channels of distribution will be viable and which will not.

$ *Compatibility.* Pricing should work in conjunction with everything else you are trying to achieve as a company.[4] It must be compatible with the marketing objectives, sales goals, image, production goals, and so forth. This decision should not be made in a vacuum.

Industry Markups

It is common in many industries to calculate an average *markup* or *gross margin,* although the method for calculating these varies by industry. There are many sources for obtaining industry markups. Reference books include *Annual Statement Studies* by Robert Morris and Associates and the *Almanac of Business and Industrial Financial Ratios* published by Prentice-Hall. Industry associations also may be helpful.

> **Markup or gross margin** – the profit made on each sale before operating expenses are subtracted.

Retail In Figure B-3, markup is equated with the gross margin percentage. This is known as markup on selling price and it is the method that most retailers use. The calculation is shown in the following example.

An entrepreneur who owns a retail clothing store buys shirts for the store that cost $20 each. These are sold in the store for $35 each. Thus, the profit is as follows:

$$\begin{array}{r} \$\,35 \\ \underline{-20} \\ \$15 \end{array}$$

$15 profit/$35 price = 0.42. So markup on selling price is 42 percent. Another type of markup known as markup on cost is determined as follows.

$15 profit/$20.00 cost = 0.75. So markup on cost is 75 percent.

See Figures B-4 and B-5.

Wholesale Price competition by wholesalers is often intense, and therefore pricing must be considered carefully. Wholesalers use a system of markups similar to that of retailers, except that the wholesaler buys in large quantities and the prices of each shipment may vary widely. Some wholesalers average the cost of items, while others use a last-in/first-out or first-in/first-out method. Examples are given in Table B-1.

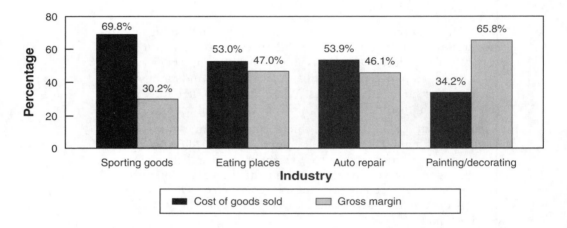

FIGURE B–3   Average markups for selected industries.

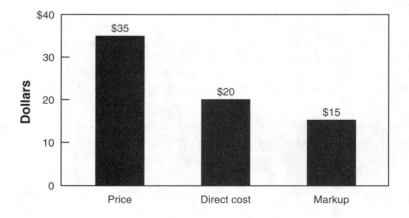

FIGURE B–4   Price, direct cost, markup.

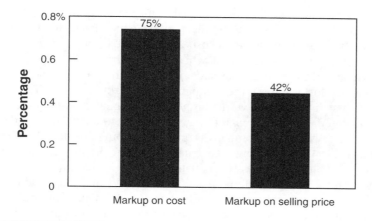

FIGURE B–5 Retail markups.

TABLE B–1 Pricing by wholesalers

Shipment #1—10,000 items at $4 each
Shipment #2—15,000 items at $5 each

Average Cost Method
If an order for 5,000 items is received, the average cost is determined as follows:

$$\frac{(10,000 \times \$4) + (15,000 \times \$5)}{25,000 \text{ total items}} = \frac{40,000 + 75,000}{25,000}$$

$$= \frac{115,000}{25,000}$$

$$= \$4.60$$

If the manufacturer adds a 25 percent markup on cost, the selling price would be:

$$\$4.60 \times 1.25 = \$5.75$$

First-In/First-Out Method
If an order for 5,000 units is received, 5,000 of the first 10,000 items are taken from inventory at a cost of $4.00 each. If the 25 percent markup on cost is used, the selling price would be:

$$\$4.00 \times 1.25 = \$5.00$$

Last-In/First-Out Method
If an order for 5,000 units is received, 5,000 of the last 15,000 items are taken from inventory at a cost of $5.00 each. If the 25 percent markup on cost is used, the selling price would be:

$$\$5.00 \times 1.25 = \$6.25$$

Service, construction, and manufacturing As stated previously, the retail industry uses the wholesale cost of the item in the calculation of markup. The cost of the item is considered the only direct cost (the cost included in cost of goods sold). However, in service, construction, and manufacturing businesses, labor is also an expense that must be considered. For example, if a construction company builds an office complex, the cost of the labor may be equal to the cost of the materials (steel, bricks, and so on). Similarly, when a manufacturing firm produces a product, both labor and material costs are substantial. In a consulting firm, the material costs may be insignificant while the labor costs are substantial. If the workers in any of these companies are not engaged in productive activity (if they are on breaks, for example), the company is not making money. Therefore, the price that is charged for any work completed must be high enough to cover the labor and material costs as well as to pay for any unproductive time and all overhead expenses. This is the company's true cost of doing business. Because many small businesses do not know their true costs, their pricing structure may not cover costs, let alone provide an adequate profit.

The formula shown in Table B-2 was developed by Alan F. Hauff, a small business program specialist with the University of Missouri Continuing Education and Outreach Program. This practical, step-by-step formula has been used successfully for more than 20 years to help small manufacturers, service firms, and construction companies project their costs of operation and assist them in setting prices based on those costs. The following terminology is used:[5]

Direct labor. Labor used to produce a product or service.

Indirect labor. Labor used to provide supporting services (e.g., accounting, clerical, custodial, management, customer service, purchasing, sales, warehousing).

Direct materials. Materials used in the final product or service. Expenses associated with their shipping, handling, and/or storage should be included in the overall cost.

Business expenses (also called *overhead*). Includes *all expenses* found on the income statement except for direct labor and direct material costs (salaries and wages for indirect labor, cost of outside services, supplies, repairs, advertising, travel, accounting, legal, rent, telephone, utilities, insurance, taxes, interest, depreciation, and so on).

Overhead percentage. Compares business expenses to direct labor in the form of a percentage.

Profit. The difference between total business income and total business expenses.

Shipping Costs

Shipping costs must be considered by all entrepreneurs before setting final selling prices. Failure to consider shipping costs will result in much less profit than expected. Some of the more common methods of determining shipping costs include:

$ *F.O.B. seller.* A common method of shipping products is "free on board seller"—often shown as *F.O.B. seller*—which means that the buyer pays all shipping costs. Also, the title to the goods passes to the buyer as soon as the seller delivers the goods to the shipper. Thus, if any items are damaged while being shipped, the buyer is responsible for negotiating with the shipper; the seller is not responsible for damaged goods.

$ *F.O.B. buyer.* If goods are shipped "free on board buyer"—F.O.B. buyer—the seller pays all shipping costs and is responsible for damaged goods. Thus, the actual cost of the goods is less for the buyer if this method is used. Because of this, entrepreneurs should be sure to obtain shipping costs before comparing prices quoted for any items purchased.

$ *Zone pricing.* With *zone pricing,* the seller establishes geographical territories, and all customers within a territory pay the same shipping costs. Because

---

Direct labor – labor used to produce a product or service.

Indirect labor – labor used to provide supporting services.

Direct materials – materials used in the final product or service.

Overhead – includes all expenses except for direct labor and direct material costs.

Overhead percentage – compares business expenses to direct labor in the form of the percentage.

Profit – difference between total business income and total business expenses.

TABLE B-2   True cost and pricing

Calculating the Overhead Percentage

Formula:

$$\frac{\text{Annual business expenses}}{\text{Annual direct labor cost}} = \text{Annual overhead percentage}$$

Step 1: Determine the average direct labor wage per hour.

Employee	Hourly Wage
John	$ 7.50
Mary	$ 8.00
Cristina (owner)	$10.00
Total	$25.50 / 3 employees

Average direct labor wage per hour = $8.50

Step 2: Estimate the total work days available in the work year for direct labor employees.

Calendar days		365 days
Less nonwork days:		
Weekends (52 × 2 days each)	104 days	
Holidays	7 days	
Vacation	10 days	
Miscellaneous		
(injury, illness, etc.)	12 days	
Total nonwork days		−133 days
Total work days available		232 days

Step 3: Estimate billable direct labor *hours* in the work year for each employee.

Total work days available	232 days
Hours available in work day	× 8 hours
Work hours available per year	1,856 hours
Less: nonbillable time for preparation, job changes, breaks, cleanup, meetings, etc. (approx. 1.5 hours per day × 232 days)	−348 hours
Billable direct labor hours	1,508 hours per employee

Step 4: Estimate billable direct labor dollars for the work year.

2 full-time employees × 1,508 hours per year	3,016 hours
1 owner × 754 hours per year	754 hours*
Total direct labor hours	3,770 hours
Total direct labor hours	3,770 hours
Average direct labor wage (from Step 1)	× 8.50 per hour
Billable direct labor dollars	$32,045

*Billable hours for the owner were estimated at half that of a regular employee.

Step 5: Estimate nonbillable direct labor *dollars* for the work year. (This is the cost of labor for days off, breaks, meetings, etc.)

Work hours available in a work year (2,080 hours × 3 employees)	6,240 hours
Less: Billable hours (from Step 4)	3,770 hours
Nonbillable direct labor hours	2,470 hours
Average "direct labor" wage (from Step 1)	× 8.50 per hour
Nonbillable direct labor dollars	$20,995

(continued)

TABLE B-2   (*continued*)

Step 6: Estimate all business expenses for the work year. (This is total annual operating expenses shown on the income statement minus any direct labor dollars that are included in that figure. If all direct labor is in cost of goods sold, do not subtract any dollar amount.)

"Total operating expenses" shown on the income statement	$102,470
Billable direct labor dollars from Step 4	−32,045
Total business expenses	$ 70,425

Step 7: Calculate the annual overhead percentage.

$$\frac{\text{Annual business expense}}{\text{Annual direct labor}} = \text{Annual overhead percentage}$$

$$\frac{\$70,425}{\$32,045} = 2.2 \ (220\%)$$

This means that for every dollar billed to the customer as direct labor, the business must collect an additional $2.20 from the customer to pay its administrative and operational (business) expenses.

Step 8: Use the overhead percentage to calculate the real cost of direct labor.

Average direct labor wage	$ 8.50
Overhead @220%	
2.2 × $8.50	$18.70
Direct labor cost	$27.20

Step 9: Determine the charge per labor hour that customers should pay.

If you want the markup on selling price (gross margin) to be 15 percent, the charge per labor hour is determined as follows:

$$\frac{\$27.20}{1.0 - 0.15} = \frac{\$27.20}{0.85} = \$32.00$$

If you want the markup on cost to be 15 percent, the charge per labor hour is determined as follows:

$$\$27.20 \times 1.15 = \$31.28$$

Step 10: Determine your prices.

Service Firms

Assume you own a home-cleaning service and supplies are included in the overhead costs. You estimate that to clean a home it will take two people working for one hour. Using the markup on selling price, the charge to the customer would be:
2 hours × $32.00 = $64.00

Manufacturing Firms

Assume you own a manufacturing firm and it takes 18 minutes to produce a product. The direct material cost per product is $4.00. The cost for the product would be calculated as follows:

$$\text{Labor cost per minute} = \frac{\$27.20}{60 \text{ minutes}} = 45 \text{ cents per minute}$$

Production time	= 18 minutes
45 cents × 18 minutes	= $8.10 cost per item for labor

Therefore, the total cost to make the product is:

Direct labor cost	$ 8.10
Direct material cost	4.00
Total Cost	$12.10

Using markup on selling price, the charge to the customer would be:

$$\frac{\$12.10}{1.0 - 0.15} = \frac{\$12.10}{0.85} = \$14.24$$

TABLE B-2   (*continued*)

Construction Firms

Assume a project is estimated to take 3 employees 100 hours each and the material costs are estimated at $8,000. Total costs for the project would be:

Labor costs = 3 × 100 hours = 300 hours × $27.20 $ 8,160
Material costs $ 8,000
Total costs $16,160

Using the markup on selling price, the charge to the customer would be:

$$\frac{\$16,160}{1.0 - 0.15} = \frac{\$16,160}{0.85} = \$19,012$$

Step 11: Evaluate this price in conjunction with the total marketing strategy.

Remember that the price developed must be considered as a part of the total marketing strategy. How does this price compare to your competitors' prices? How will this affect the company image? What effect will this price have on demand for your product or service? All of these factors must be considered when setting the final price.

Source: Alan F. Hauff, *Pricing for Success* Seminar. Adapted with permission.

CHECKLIST: PRICING

☐ What is your *pricing objective*, or the goal to be achieved through pricing? A certain level of profit, a specific market share, to reach a certain sales volume?
☐ What is your average markup? (Specify a percentage.)
☐ If you are a retailer, is this markup on cost or markup on selling price? If you are a service firm, what are your labor and material costs per hour? What is your price per hour?
☐ If you are a manufacturer, what are your total direct costs? What are your total fixed costs? How many units do you plan to produce?
☐ If you are a wholesaler, will you use average cost, first-in/first-out, or last-in/first-out?
☐ What is the typical markup in this industry? How will your prices compare to competitors'?
☐ What are your pricing policies—general pricing guidelines? For example, will you run seasonal sales? Will you try to match competitors' prices? Will you use coupons? Will you give employees discounts on merchandise purchased?
☐ Will you use any of the following strategies?

- *Introductory prices*—low prices used to gain entry into the market
- *Skimming*—setting a high initial price and then gradually lowering it
- *Price-lining*—grouping inventory into categories and then setting the same price for all items in each category
- *Odd-ending*—prices set at odd numbers such as $1.99, $3.95, and so on
- *Loss leader*—selling one or a few items below cost in order to attract customers
- *All-one-price*—Setting every item equal to the same price
- *Bundling*—grouping items together and selling them for less than if each item were purchased separately

☐ Have you determined the shipping costs for the goods you will order? What are the terms—F.O.B. seller, F.O.B. buyer, and so on? Was this included when you established your sales price? Will you ship goods to your customer? If so, who pays the shipping costs?

actual shipping costs to each customer vary, the seller will not have the same profit margin on all products sold. Thus, a wholesaler or manufacturer who is thinking of establishing zone pricing must define the geographic areas so that the average of all sales in a territory will result in the profit margin desired.

$ *Uniform-delivered.* If customers pay shipping costs, the seller may not be price competitive if products are shipped over long distances. This limits the seller's trading area and prevents the seller from expanding. Therefore, in some cases, the seller uses a method known as *uniform-delivered,* in which all customers pay the same shipping cost. As with zone pricing, this results in varying profit margins for the seller.

The Pricing Checklist will help you determine your prices.

Discussion Questions

1. In addition to costs, competitors' prices, elasticity, and image, what other factors would affect prices?
2. Companies that use bid pricing often find that their gross profit margin is lower than expected. Identify several factors that could cause a lower-than-expected profit margin.
3. Use the bundling pricing concept to develop new pricing structures for a university or college.
4. Using the price-lining concept to develop a pricing strategy for some items that may be found in a hardware store.

Endnotes

1. Roberta Maynard, "Taking Guesswork Out of Pricing," *Nations Business,* December 1997, 27–29.
2. Ibid.
3. Michael D. Mondello, "Naming Your Price," *Inc.,* July 1992, 80–83.
4. Ibid.
5. Alan F. Hauff, *Pricing for Success* Seminar.

CREDIT TERMS TO CUSTOMERS

Learning Objectives

$ To understand the relationship between credit terms and sales volume.

$ To be able to explain the difference between consumer credit and trade credit.

$ To comprehend consumer credit and trade credit terminology.

In many industries, it is common to extend credit to customers, allowing them a specified time to pay for the goods and services they have received. The main purpose in extending credit is to increase sales; therefore, it is often an important part of a company's marketing strategy.

> **Consumer credit** – credit extended from retail stores to the final consumer.

There are two general categories of credit—consumer credit and trade credit. *Consumer credit* is extended from retail stores to the final consumer. *Trade credit* is extended from one business to another (for example, from a wholesaler to a retailer). Typical terms are as follows:

$ *Net 30*. No discounts are given for early payment, and full amount is due within 30 days of the invoice.

$ *2/10 net 30*. Credit terms are often specified in this manner, giving the customer a maximum of 30 days to pay the bill but offering a 2 percent discount if the bill is paid within 10 days of the purchase. If no discount for early payment is offered, the terms would just be stated as "net 30."

$ *2/10 net 30 E.O.M.* The customer has 30 days to pay the bill and will receive a 2 percent discount if it is paid within 10 days. The E.O.M. means that the 30 days and the 10-day periods do not begin until the end of the month. Therefore, the actual payment period is longer than it appears. For example, if the purchase is made on May 5, a 2 percent discount may be taken if the bill is paid by June 10, or the full amount is due by June 30.

There are several types of consumer credit, including the following:

$ *Installment accounts. Installment accounts* allow a customer a long time (often several years) to pay big-ticket items. The required monthly payment includes both the repayment and interest. This type of financing is common for furniture and appliance stores as well as car and boat dealers.

$ *Open charge accounts.* An *open charge account* allows the customer a specified length of time to pay (often 30 days). The full amount is due at the end of the 30-day period, and interest is usually not charged. These accounts are more common in smaller stores in rural areas.

$ *Revolving charge accounts.* A *revolving charge account* allows the customer a specified amount of credit. The customer may make purchases at any time as long as the purchases do not exceed the credit limit. Monthly payments are required and usually include an interest charge. Credit cards are a type of revolving charge account. However, with a credit card the seller obtains cash for the purchase from the credit card company quickly if the final consumer has not paid the charge card company for the item.

Even companies that do not offer typical credit must make decisions regarding how customer payments will be made. For example, home remodeling companies and fence companies must decide whether to have customers pay part of the bill before work begins or just pay the full amount when the job is completed. Since many customers are wary of paying cash up front, this decision could greatly affect sales.

Several factors that should be considered when developing a credit policy are discussed next. The Credit Policy Checklist should also be helpful.

> **Trade credit** – credit extended from one business to another.

> **Installment accounts** – allow a customer a long time to pay for big ticket items.

> **Open charge accounts** – allow the customer a specified time to pay.

> **Revolving charge accounts** – allow the customer a specified amount of credit.

CHECKLIST: CREDIT POLICY

☐ What are your credit terms to your customers?
☐ How does this compare to the terms offered by competitors?
☐ Will you accept checks?
☐ Will you accept credit cards? If so, which ones?
☐ Will you use a check verification system or a credit reporting agency? If so, what are the costs for these services?

The Industry and Your Competitors

Within each industry, there are established credit policies and it is difficult to deviate from the norm without affecting your sales volume. For example, a common practice in business-to-business sales is to extend 30 days' credit but to offer a discount of 2 percent if the bill is paid within 10 days. (This is written as "2/10 net 30.") If a company tries to operate without extending any credit, and instead requires a cash payment immediately, the company's sales volume would suffer.

The industry norm may change over time, however. For example, the grocery industry used to require all customers to pay by cash or check. However, in recent years, many have started to accept credit and debit cards. Although there is a cost to the company to offer these services, the additional forms of payment should result in increased sales.

The Customers

Extending credit is a wise business decision only if the customer is likely to pay the bill. Before extending certain types of credit, it is common to "run a credit check" by contacting credit reporting agencies and obtaining the credit rating of the potential customer. For businesses, the most common source for credit ratings is Dun & Bradstreet, Inc. For individual consumers, credit reporting agencies such as TransUnion are often used. Although there is a cost to the business to obtain these ratings, it prevents extending credit to a customer who is unlikely to pay.

The Company's Cash Flow

One of the biggest disadvantages of extending credit is that the business does not immediately receive the cash for the goods or services rendered, and this decreases the amount of money the company has to operate. Many small companies find that extending credit results in higher sales but less cash on hand. In the financial section of the business plan, the cash flow projection shows the effect of credit on cash flow.

Discussion Questions

1. What factors have caused grocery stores to accept charge cards?
2. Although extending credit usually helps increase sales, it also results in added costs. What are some of the disadvantages and costs of extending credit?
3. Suppose an entrepreneur is trying to decide whether to offer terms of 2/10 net 30 or 2/10 net 30 E.O.M. How would his or her decision affect the company?

COMPETITIVE ADVANTAGE

Learning Objectives

$ To be able to identify a competitive advantage for a company.

$ To understand the many factors that can be used as a competitive advantage.

Every business must have a *competitive advantage*, something that differentiates it from similar businesses. The competitive advantage must be carefully developed because it is the reason why customers will buy from you instead of buying from your competitors. Typical competitive advantages may include the following:

> **Competitive advantage** – a unique feature of a company that differentiates it from competitors.

$ *Quality.* If you can provide a better product or service than that which is currently offered, customers will often buy it even if it costs more. Many small businesses, including Ben and Jerry's Ice Cream and Patagonia (clothing and sports gear), have become successful by following this strategy.

$ *Price.* If you can offer a product or service at a lower price, your business will appeal to bargain hunters who want to keep their costs low.

$ *Location.* Many small businesses are successful because they are more conveniently located than their competitors. Convenience food stores, including 7-Eleven franchises and independent mom-and-pop stores, have been successful because of location. Customers buy products from these stores even though the cost is usually more than at a full-line grocery store. Convenient locations are one of the major reasons for their success.

$ *Selection.* A wide product selection is often successful in attracting customers. A wide product selection may allow you to serve several groups of customers. As we noted in the section on industry trends, the grocery superstores that carry a large selection have increased in number while the number of grocery stores in general has decreased. Companies in many industries use a large product selection as their competitive advantage.

$ *Service.* Small businesses can often provide more personalized service than large businesses. Particularly when a business is small, the owner can work directly with the customers and ensure customer satisfaction.

$ *Speed/turnaround time.* Especially in the United States, customers expect fast delivery of a product or service. The pace of life continually increases and yesterday's standards are soon outdated. We have moved from regular mail delivery to overnight delivery, fax machines, and most recently, electronic mail. If you can take any existing product or service and provide a faster turnaround time, customers will respond.

You should also consider combining several competitive advantages. Many entrepreneurs build their businesses on only one competitive advantage and are

CHECKLIST: COMPETITIVE ADVANTAGE

☐ What is your competitive advantage?

Quality	Selection
Price	Service
Location	Speed/Turnaround

☐ Explain how you will achieve the competitive advantage. How will you have better quality? What will make your service better? Why is your location better? How will you be able to sell at a lower price and still make a good profit?

Try to combine several of the advantages listed here, if possible.

successful. However, if you can combine them (for example, excellent quality and large selection), you will have an even better chance of beating the competition.

See the Competitive Advantage Checklist for guidelines on determining your competitive advantage.

Discussion Questions

1. Identify colleges or universities in your city or state. What is the competitive advantage for the college or university you are attending? What are the competitive advantages for the others? What other competitive advantage could your school develop?

2. Identify a business that competes on speed or turnaround time.

3. Identify a business that sells through mail-order catalogs. Identify several competitive advantages of that company.

4. In addition to the competitive advantages listed, name other factors that could be used as competitive advantages.

MARKET SEGMENTATION

Learning Objectives

$ To be able to explain segmentation methods.
$ To know how to separate potential customers into groups with similar needs.

How Will You Segment Your Target Market?

> **Market segmentation or niche marketing** – separating customers into groups with similar needs or characteristics.

No business can serve everyone, and small businesses with limited resources usually concentrate on a specific customer base. You can identify your target markets by separating the customers into groups with similar needs. This is known as *market segmentation* or *niche marketing*. Your target market(s) can be segmented in several ways; some of the more common ways are described next.

> **Geographic segmentation** – grouping customers by place of residence or place of work.

$ *Geographic.* Often customers can be described in terms of their residence or place of work. Some information concerning various geographical areas is available from the U.S. population census taken every 10 years. Many public libraries will have the census data on file. For example, an entrepreneur planning to start a home improvement company may describe the target market as follows:

> *The initial target market of Improvements Unlimited will include all of the homeowners in 99325, 99326, and 99327 ZIP codes. Within these ZIP codes, the average home value exceeds $200,000, and the average age of the homes is 40 years. Once the business is established, additional ZIP codes will be targeted.*

> **Demographic segmentation** – grouping customers by characteristics such as age, income, or gender.

$ *Demographic.* Often customers are described by demographic characteristics such as age, income, or gender. Figure B-6, for example, shows the average annual dollar amount a person spends in the United States on reading material, segmented by age. Figure B-7 shows the average annual dollar amount a person spends in the United States on entertainment, segmented by age. Information of this type is used by companies to select their target group of customers.

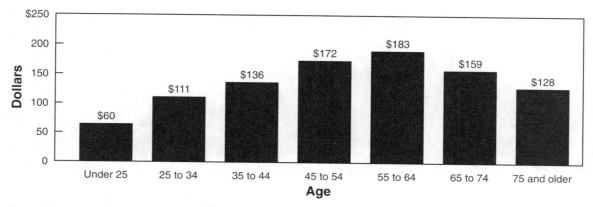

Source: U.S. Census Bureau, *2003 Statistical Abstract of the United States,* http://www.census.gov/prod/2004pubs/03statab/arts.pdf.

FIGURE B–6   Annual individual expenditures on reading material by age.

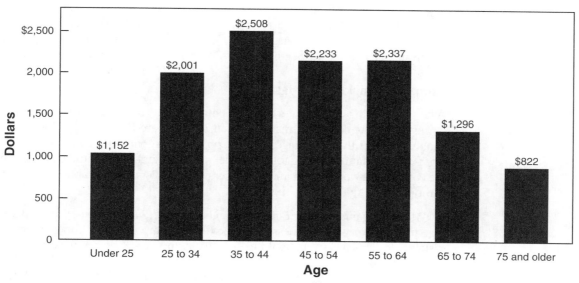

Source: U.S. Census Bureau, *2003 Statistical Abstract of the United States,* http://www.census.gov/prod/2004pubs/03statab/arts.pdf.

FIGURE B–7   Annual expenditures on entertainment by age.

$ *Benefit.* Entrepreneurs will often find that different groups of customers buy their product or service for different reasons. Grouping customers according to their reasons for purchasing the product or service is known as *benefit segmentation.* For example, while a jogger buys athletic shoes because of the comfort and support they provide, a teenager often buys athletic shoes as a status symbol. Similarly, one person may purchase a dog

> **Benefit segmentation** – grouping customers according to their reasons for buying a product or service.

because it will provide unconditional love; another person may buy a dog to provide safety and security. Some of the common benefits customers purchase include convenience, status, security/safety, sociability, romance, entertainment, comfort, durability, and self-indulgence. Many other benefits are possible.

$ *Usage rate.* In many industries, a small group of customers buys the largest amount of a product or service. Grouping customers by how often they use a product or service is known as *usage-rate segmentation*. A recent study analyzed consumers who ate soup and categorized them into heavy users (ate soup more than once a week), light users (ate soup more than once a month), and nonusers. The study found that personality and lifestyle characteristics were distinguishing factors. Heavy users were socially active, creative, optimistic, witty, and less stubborn than light and nonusers.[1]

> **Usage-rate segmentation** – grouping customers by how often they use a product or service.

$ *Psychographic. Psychographic segmentation* is a method of grouping customers based on values and/or lifestyle. For example, research shows that people who visit zoos are societally conscious and likely to be the traditional family-oriented type.[2] Studies of pet owners find that people who own cats value independence.

> **Psychographic segmentation** – grouping customers based on their values and/or lifestyle.

Entrepreneurs should carefully define their target market because this will ensure that marketing efforts are targeted to potential customers and will not be wasted. It also helps the business owner focus all of his or her efforts in the proper direction. See the Market Segmentation Checklist for segmentation guidelines.

Common Marketing Mistakes

When developing the business concept, entrepreneurs often make the same types of mistakes. The common mistakes discussed next are failing to develop a sustainable competitive advantage, taking a product or service orientation instead of a benefit orientation, failing to clearly define the target market, underestimating the competition, planning based on excessive optimism, and establishing prices without knowing the effect on demand.

Marketing mistake #1: Failing to develop a sustainable competitive advantage In order for your business to succeed, your competitive advantage must be sustainable. This means it should be one that competitiors do not have and cannot easily copy.

Small companies that try to compete by offering a lower price may find that a large competitor can undercut their prices. Similarly, offering a service such as "free delivery" can be easily copied by competitors. In order to survive, a small business must not be as good as other businesses—it must be better in some unique way.

Marketing mistake #2: Focusing on the product or service instead of the benefit. It is often difficult for entrepreneurs to realize that customers do not buy products or services but instead buy the benefits provided by the product or service. Customers don't buy Domino's Pizza because the company sells pizza; they buy it because it satisfies their hunger and it is also convenient. When consumers buy cars, they are purchasing more than an automobile. They may buy a Volvo not only because it provides transportation but also because it is prestigious and designed for safety.

CHECKLIST: MARKET SEGMENTATION

How will you segment your market?

Geographically
☐ What geographic area will you serve?

Demographically
☐ Give age, sex, race, income, etc.

By benefit
☐ What benefit are your customers buying? Status, security or safety, convenience, romance, sociability, entertainment, comfort, self-indulgence, durability, other?

By usage rate
☐ What percentage of your customers account for the largest portion of your sales? How do these customers differ from those who are not frequent customers?

Psychographically
☐ What is the lifestyle of your customers? Are they outgoing, introverted, scholarly, party-loving, athletic, family-oriented, other?

MOST COMMON MARKETING MISTAKES

☐ Failing to develop a sustainable competitive advantage (the "Cheap Hamburger" mistake)
☐ Focusing on the product or service instead of the benefit (the "Domino's Sells Pizza" mistake)
☐ Failing to clearly define the target market (the "Everything to Everybody" mistake)
☐ Underestimating the competition (the "No Other Business Like Ours" mistake)
☐ Planning based on excessive optimism (the "We Can't Be Beat" mistake)
☐ Establishing prices without knowing the effect on demand (the "Cut Prices to Make More Money" mistake)

Determining the benefit the customer wants is extremely important when developing the business concept: If customers buy benefits, the business must be designed to provide those benefits.

Marketing mistake #3: Failing to clearly define the target market The business cannot be all things to all people, yet many entrepreneurs cannot clearly identify their customers. A student who developed a party-entertainment business targeted to women defined her target market as "all women over age 18." This is such a broad definition that it would include women throughout the world of all incomes and lifestyles. In fact, her target market was women within a specific geographic area, with a specific income level, and who would be classified as more liberal than conservative.

Marketing mistake #4: Underestimating the competition One of the most common mistakes made by entrepreneurs is that they underestimate the competitor's ability to draw customers away from the proposed business. Entrepreneurs often believe that if the competitor's business is not exactly like theirs, it will not be a major threat. For example, an entrepreneur planning to open an Italian restaurant stated in the business plan, "This restaurant will not have competition; there are no other Italian restaurants within five miles." There were, however, many other types of restaurants that hungry customers would consider. While the Italian food would be a competitive advantage, strong competition from the other restaurants cannot be ignored.

Marketing mistake #5: **Planning based on excessive optimism** Entrepreneurs are often so enthusiastic about their idea that they cannot be objective. They are so convinced that their idea is great that they do not see the pitfalls. This leads to overly optimistic sales projections and unrealistic planning. The best way to avoid this mistake is to discuss your idea with those you trust—relatives, business advisors, and friends. They will be able to provide you with an objective opinion.

Marketing mistake #6: **Establishing prices without knowing the effect on demand** Many entrepreneurs decide to set prices low or run sales without knowing the industry well enough to understand the effect on consumer behavior. This often just lowers profits without increasing demand. It is important to research prices in the industry and talk with others who know the industry well before pricing policies and guidelines are established.

Discussion Questions

1. Using benefit segmentation, segment the market for personal computers used at home.
2. Explain how the information in Figures B-6 and B-7 could be used by an entrepreneur.
3. Using psychographic segmentation, segment teenagers.
4. In addition to the benefits listed on page 169, identify two benefits that customers may purchase.
5. What does it mean if a competitive advantage is "sustainable"?

Endnotes

1. Brain Wansink and Sea Bum Park, "Methods and Measures That Profile Heavy Users," *Journal of Advertising Research,* July/August 2000, 61–72.
2. George E. Belch and Michael A. Belch, *Introduction to Advertising and Promotion* (Homewood, IL: Irwin, 1995), 25.

LOCATION

Learning Objectives

$ To understand the difference between required criteria and desirable criteria.
$ To be able to identify specific location criteria for different industries.
$ To be aware of business incubators and the services they provide.

What Is Your Ideal Location?

One of the first steps in choosing a site is to describe the ideal location by developing two lists—required criteria and desirable criteria. *Required criteria* are those that must exist; if the location does not have all of the required criteria, it should not be considered as an option. The *desirable criteria*, however, are those that you would like to have but are not essential for the success of the business. For example, a fast-food business may have required criteria that include a population density of more than 30,000 people within a two-mile radius and a traffic count of more than 20,000 cars per day passing the site. Desirable criteria may include lenient sign laws, low tax rates, and proximity to a major shopping center.

Each industry has unique location factors. Factors that are important for a retail site are often irrelevant to a manufacturing firm. Zoning laws, however, are a factor for every business and should be researched early in the site selection process. These laws are established by communities to control the type of businesses that are opened and to ensure that the community development occurs in a well-planned manner. Each piece of property is zoned in one of four ways:

$ Residential (homes/apartments/condominiums)

$ Commercial (office space, retail, and so on)

$ Industrial (manufacturing)

$ Agricultural (farming)

Within each category, there are additional classifications. For example, the commercial category would include different codes for office space, restaurants, and retail outlets. If a site is not zoned for the type of business the entrepreneur wishes to open, the local government will determine if the property should be rezoned to the new classification. Thus, local governments can prevent the entrepreneur from opening the business if they decide not to rezone the property. For this reason, zoning laws should be researched early in the planning process.

See the Location Checklists to help you select a location. The following is a brief description of the factors listed.

Will Your Business Be Home-Based?

As stated in Chapter 7, many entrepreneurs choose to operate their businesses from home. If the business will be home-based, this should be explained in the location section of the business plan. Information should also be given concerning insurance coverage that will be needed, planned renovations, or upgrading of utilities. Zoning considerations should also be addressed so the banker or investor knows the home-based business will not violate zoning ordinances.

Is Your Business Retail or Service?

Retail businesses and service businesses that have customers come to them, such as auto repair and dry cleaners, should consider the same factors when comparing sites for a business. For these businesses, an excellent location is essential for

Required location criteria – features that must exist in order for a site to be chosen.

Desirable criteria – features that are preferred but not essential for a site to be chosen.

CHECKLIST: LOCATION OF A HOME-BASED BUSINESS

☐ Business Address _____
☐ Have you checked the zoning?
☐ What additional insurance will be needed?
☐ Will renovations be necessary? If yes, describe.
☐ Are the current utilities adequate? If not, what needs to be done?

CHECKLIST: LOCATION OF A RETAIL OR SERVICE BUSINESS

☐ Business Address_____
☐ Have you checked the zoning? Can a property be rezoned if necessary?
☐ What is your trading area?
☐ Provide the demographic data for your trading area, giving age, sex, race, income, and occupation.
☐ What is the average traffic count in front of the outlet?
☐ What is the average speed of the traffic passing the outlet?
☐ Is there anything hindering accessibility, such as medians, one-way streets, congested traffic, or a difficult entrance? Is there anything helping accessibility, such as more than one entrance or a location near major highways?
☐ Do adjacent businesses serve the same customers as your business? Do adjacent businesses have similar operating hours? Do they attract many customers?
☐ When you are approaching the site, is it visible from 400 feet? 200 feet? 100 feet? Are there any signs, trees, buildings, or other objects that hinder visibility?
☐ What are the sign laws in the community? Is the size and type of sign restricted?
☐ What are the parking ordinances? What is the minimum number of parking spaces you need for the size of your store? Is there a parking lot or will customers park on the street? How many parking spaces are available?

CHECKLIST: LOCATION OF A MANUFACTURING PLANT

☐ Business Address_____
☐ Have you checked the zoning? Can a property be rezoned if necessary?
☐ What is the labor climate? Is there a high level of union activity? What are the average wage rates? What is the work ethic of the residents? How are absentee rates of employees in neighboring businesses? What are the turnover rates?
☐ Does the company need to be near raw materials or customers?
☐ Have you investigated utility access and rates?
☐ What are the tax rates?
☐ Are transportation facilities adequate?
☐ Have you checked environmental regulations?
☐ What is the quality of life in the area?

success. However, service businesses that go to their customers do not always need to be concerned about their location. For example, although some home remodeling companies have excellent retail locations that are used as a showroom and an office, other home remodeling companies are successfully operated out of the entrepreneur's home.

The following questions are important when starting a retail or service business that needs a good location.

Trading area – a geographically defined area in which your target market is located.

$ *What is your trading area?* The *trading area* is a geographically defined area in which your target market is located. This will be affected by a number of factors, including the type of business, the number of competitors, and the type of facility (regional mall, neighborhood shopping center, freestanding building). While the trading area for some convenience food stores is less than a mile, the trading area for a clothing store in a regional mall may be 10 miles or more. In determining trading area, the entrepreneur should ask, "How far will the average customer drive to come to this store?" Typical trading areas may be obtained from trade associations or other industry data. If you cannot find the information from industry data, an entrepreneur in a similar business may be willing to estimate the trading area for you.

$ *Do you have demographic information?* Once the trading area has been established, the demographics of the population within the trading area should be determined. Demographic information can be obtained from the U.S. Census data available in many libraries or online. Demographic information that may be helpful includes the density (how many people within the trading area) and the age, sex, income, and profession of the residents. The demographics of several areas can be compared to the target market data to determine which area is best for the business.

Table B-3 shows typical demographic information that is available by ZIP code from the U.S. Census Web site at http://www.census.gov.

$ *Can you research traffic counts?* The *automobile traffic count* (the number of cars passing the site each day) is available from the city or county street department. If the road is maintained by the state, the traffic count would be available from the state highway department. Traffic counts of several sites should be compared, however, as this is not sufficient to determine whether it is a positive or negative factor. For example, suppose you are planning to open an independent hamburger/fast-food restaurant, and, when comparing two possible sites, site A has a traffic count of 10,000 cars per day and site B has a traffic count of 12,000 cars per day. While site B obviously has a higher traffic count, how do you know if 12,000 cars is sufficient to be successful? One valuable comparison is to look at existing successful businesses in the same industry and obtain the traffic counts for those sites. If all of these businesses have locations with traffic counts in excess of 20,000, your location with only 12,000 cars per day may not be adequate.

Automobile traffic count – the number of cars passing a site each day.

$ *What is the speed of the traffic?* The speed of the traffic may be a positive or negative factor. In general, within an urban area, a slower traffic speed is better because it gives the motorists more of a chance to slow down and stop in. (This does not apply to highway locations.) If the traffic is passing rapidly by the business, the motorists may pass the business without seeing it, or they may not have a chance to stop on an impulse. As a rule, a speed limit of less than 35 miles per hour is a positive factor.

TABLE B–3 Sample of demographic information available from the U.S. Census

Austin, Texas (ZIP Code 78731)

Total population (Living in ZIP code 78731)	24,059
Median age	37.4 years
Median household income	$62,404
Median family income	$97,638
Median value of single family owner-occupied homes	$260,700

Source: http://www.Census.gov. American Factfinder, Fact Sheet.

$ *How accessible is each site? Accessibility* refers to the ease with which a customer can get to the business. Positive factors may include a stoplight within one block, a corner lot, or more than one entrance or exit. Negative factors include a divided street or a complicated entrance.

$ *What are the adjacent businesses?* Adjacent businesses will have a substantial impact on the sales of a retail business. If adjacent stores cater to the same target market as the proposed business, this will have a positive impact because the neighboring stores will help attract customers. For example, a women's clothing store next to a women's shoe store is an excellent combination. A women's shoe store next to an auto parts store would not be ideal. You should also determine if adjacent businesses maintain similar operating hours, since this is helpful in maintaining constant customer traffic throughout the day.

$ *Is the visibility good? Visibility,* or how easily the business can be seen from a distance, is often a critical factor for a retail or service business. Factors that affect the visibility of a business include whether the business is parallel or perpendicular to the road, if the building sits close to the road or farther back, whether business signs or large trees obstruct customers' view, and what impact community sign laws may have. *Sign laws* are often established by communities to maintain a certain appearance. If the sign laws are restrictive, this can substantially reduce a company's visibility.

Rather than subjectively stating that visibility is "good" or "bad," you should determine the distance (in feet or yards) from which the building or sign can be seen. This allows you an objective comparison—for example, "site A is visible from 400 feet, whereas site B is only visible from 150 feet."

$ *Have you researched parking ordinances?* Communities often have laws concerning parking requirements for retail businesses. These laws specify a minimum number of parking places determined by the number of square feet in the store. You should check these ordinances when planning a business so that problems do not arise after a lease has been signed. For example, if you plan to open a restaurant, the number of tables (and therefore the number of customers you can serve) may be restricted by the number of parking spaces outside.

Is Your Business a Manufacturing Firm?

A site analysis for a manufacturing firm is just as important as for a retail firm, but the criteria are very different. The factors discussed in this section are often considered when completing a site analysis for a manufacturing firm.

$ *What is the labor climate?* Because manufacturing firms usually require a large labor force, labor factors are an important criterion. Labor factors include the following:
- The level of union activity (a high level of unionization is considered a negative factor)
- The average wage rates
- The "work ethic" of the residents (low absentee rates and turnover rates are positive factors)

$ *Does the company need to be near raw materials or customers?* Manufacturers often need to be located near their source of raw materials because transportation costs of these materials are very high. Other manufacturers find it necessary to be located near customers in order to serve them better or

---

Visibility – how easily a site can be seen from a distance.

Sign laws – laws restricting the type and size of sign a business may erect.

Labor climate – workforce factors including union activity, wage rates, and work ethic.

because transportation costs of the finished product are greater than the transportation costs of the raw materials. For some manufacturers, neither factor is an overriding concern and the factory is located halfway between suppliers and customers.

$ *Have you investigated utility access and rates?* Manufacturing firms often use high levels of utilities, and therefore access to those utilities is essential. If the utility lines are not readily available, the cost to develop the property may be too high. Also, utility rates vary substantially among communities and should be researched.

$ *Is transportation adequate?* Manufacturing firms need access to a variety of transportation systems, including rail lines, airlines, water/barge traffic, and trucking. The type of transportation that is needed depends on many factors, including the type of manufacturing and whether the company is close to raw materials or customers.

$ *What are the tax rates?* Local taxes for manufacturing firms vary substantially among communities, and therefore manufacturers should investigate the types of taxes that are assessed and the rates for each. Communities try to attract manufacturers that employ many people and offer tax abatements or reductions as an incentive to locate in the community. Manufacturers should inquire about tax abatements by contacting the local department of revenue or the local economic development office. Tax abatements are often viewed as an indication of the community's support of the manufacturing company.

$ *What are the environmental regulations?* Manufacturers must check environmental regulations, since these laws may prohibit certain types of manufacturers from locating in certain areas. Companies that produce toxic chemicals, air pollution, and other hazards may find site selection difficult. Paper mills, for example, would find a market in some areas, but local or state environmental laws prohibit them from operating. Waste disposal is also a concern; if landfills are too far away, disposal costs may be unusually high.

$ *Have you considered the quality of life?* Quality of life has become more important for companies in recent years. Quality of life refers to a variety of factors that make life in the community a pleasant experience. These factors include the following:
  • Cultural and sports events
  • Recreation facilities
  • Access to airports
  • Quality of the roadways
  • Quality and variety of educational institutions
  • Health care/hospital systems
  • Crime rate
  • Weather

While quality of life is not the most important factor in site selection, if two communities meet all other criteria, the quality of life in each may be the deciding factor.

Is Your Business a Wholesaling Operation?

Wholesalers serve retail outlets and are therefore affected by economic factors that would decrease retail activity. Within a community, however, there may be several possible locations since the business does not rely on its customers coming to the site. Some of the factors that should be considered are as follows:

$ *Is the community financially stable?* Because wholesalers sell to retailers, any factors that decrease retail activity would also decrease the wholesaler's revenue. A wholesaler should therefore look for a community with stable income that has a diverse number of industries. Communities that rely on only one or two large businesses are risky, since a downturn in one of the large businesses could severely affect the financial health of the entire community.

$ *Are the retail stores financially strong?* The wholesaler should consider the number and the financial health of the retail outlets. Factors to consider include the turnover of the retail businesses, the length of time they have been in business, and the trends in activity (growth or decrease) in the past five years.

$ *Do other wholesalers serve your industry?* Wholesalers usually try to locate in an area that has many retailers but few other wholesalers who serve the same industry. If there are other wholesalers serving the industry's needs, it may be very difficult to enter the market.

$ *Should the business be in the city or in an outlying area?* If rent costs in the middle of the community are too high, wholesalers have the option of locating at the edge of town. As long as the transportation system is adequate, the goods can be shipped to retailers quickly and efficiently from surrounding locations. Wholesalers therefore have the option of paying lower rent costs for a more rural location while still serving their customers' needs.

Incubators

Business incubators are facilities that provide start-up firms with affordable rent and services. Incubators are large facilities subdivided into smaller spaces, each occupied by a different business. The rent is often below market rates, and services may include financing assistance, shared use of equipment such as copiers and fax machines, shared use of a conference room and loading-dock facilities, and even management consulting services.

The camaraderie of being in an incubator is also helpful for many entrepreneurs. James Robbins, director of the Environmental Business Cluster incubator, has found that many entrepreneurs come to the incubator somewhat isolated. Being in a building with other entrepreneurs offers them access to a broader range of ideas and advice.[1]

> **Business incubators** – facilities that provide start-ups with affordable rent and services.

CHECKLIST: LOCATION OF A WHOLESALING BUSINESS

☐ Business Address_____
☐ Have you checked zoning? Can a property be rezoned if necessary?
☐ Are transportation facilities adequate?
☐ Is the community financially stable?
☐ Are the retail stores financially strong?
☐ Do other wholesalers serve your industry?
☐ Should your business locate in the city or in an outlying area?

According to the National Business Incubation Association, 1,000 incubators are currently operating in North America, up from 12 in 1980.[2] Many are sponsored by governments and nonprofit organizations and are established for economic development purposes. Others are affiliated with colleges and universities or are joint efforts among governments and nonprofits.

Despite the increasing number of incubators being developed, the demand for incubator space is usually quite high and incubators are selective about the tenants they admit. Some specialize in high-technology businesses; others are designed only for women- or minority-owned businesses. Even the incubators that allow all types of businesses may have rigorous application procedures and require a business plan before they consider admitting a tenant.[3] Many incubators do not want mom-and-pops that do not plan to create jobs, develop new technologies, or strengthen the local economy.[4]

Incubators are not designed for long-term leases but, instead, are meant to help start-ups in the early, difficult years. Most incubators require that tenants "graduate," meaning that the company can be a tenant only for three to five years. The company is then expected to join the "real world" and pay market rent in regular commercial space.

In recent years, for-profit incubators have become common. Many of the new incubator owners are not experienced in running this type of business and cannot provide the assistance that start-ups need. In addition, many of them want an equity stake in the start-ups they nurture. Therefore, entrepreneurs must be very careful in scrutinizing and selecting an incubator.[5]

Common Location Mistakes

Despite the fact that different industries need to consider different location criteria, entrepreneurs often make the same mistakes when choosing a site. The most common of these mistakes are listed next.

Location mistake #1: Choosing a location because it is close to home Most entrepreneurs start a business within the metropolitan area in which they live, and many choose a location close to home to minimize commuting time. While this is a logical decision, you should not choose the location solely because it is close to home. The location of the business is often a critical factor in the business's success, and a longer commute may be well worth the inconvenience.

Location mistake #2: Choosing a location because it is the cheapest Many entrepreneurs fall into the trap of choosing a location based on price. While price is a consideration, it should not be the priority. Trade-offs often exist; locations are often cheap because they have poor visibility or are inconveniently located. What is saved by choosing a cheap location may be paid for in higher costs (such as renovations) or lower sales.

Location mistake #3: Choosing a location because it is the only one available During poor economic times, there are often many available sites from which to choose. The entrepreneur has the advantage in bargaining with landlords and developers, and there is no pressure to make a hasty decision. In good economic times, however, good locations are often hard to find, and the landlords and developers have the bargaining advantage. Faced with this situation, many entrepreneurs jump at the first location that becomes available instead of waiting for the right site. Strict adherence to the list of required criteria will prevent hasty decisions from occurring.

Discussion Questions

1. Consider the location of your school. What is the average trading area? Analyze the accessibility and visibility. What businesses nearby cater to the same customers?

2. What demographics would indicate an area that is best for a pharmacy? What demographics would be the least desirable for a pharmacy?

3. The federal government mandates maximum pollution levels for cities that are determined by combination of auto and factory emissions. If you were planning for a rapidly growing city, how would this affect your strategy?

4. Identify retail stores for which you make a special trip. Then identify the types of retail stores that are convenience-oriented (that is, you stop there on your way to the other places).

   Make two lists as follows:

   Special Trip   **Convenience**

Endnotes

1. Douglas E. Caldwell, "Profile: James Robbins, When He Sheets, Companies Win," *Silicon Valley San Jose Business Journal,* July 2, 2004.

2. National Business Incubation Association, "Business Incubation FAQ," http://www.nbia.org.

3. "Get Thee to a Hatchery," *Nation's Business,* March 1997, 50.

4. "For More Information . . ." *Money,* November 1996, 30.

5. Chad Chadwick, "Build a Better Business Incubator through Branding," *Advertising Age,* October 16, 2000, 50.

PROMOTION AND SALES

Learning Objectives

$ To understand the different types of promotion a company may use.
$ To be able to identify the factors that must be considered when establishing a sales force.

One of the biggest mistakes an entrepreneur can make is to underestimate the amount of promotion that is necessary for success. A business with the best products and services will still fail if the customers are not informed and persuaded. For this reason, a promotional plan is crucial to the success of the business.

What Types of Promotion Will You Use?

Promotion may take many forms, including the following (see also the Promotional Methods Checklist):

> $ *Direct marketing. Direct marketing* includes direct mail; mail-order catalogs; direct selling; telemarketing; direct-response ads through mail, broadcast and print media, and the Internet.[1]
>
> $ *Advertising. Advertising* consists of nonpersonal messages directed at a large number of people. Advertising is carried out through media such as radio, television, and newspapers.

Direct marketing – a marketing method that includes direct mail, catalogs, direct selling, telemarketing, and direct-response ads.

$ *Sales promotion. Sales promotion* consists of marketing activities that provide extra value or incentives to the sales force, distributors, or the ultimate consumer. Sales promotions are developed to increase sales.[2]

$ *Publicity and public relations. Publicity* is company information released as news on radio, on television, or in newspapers. Publicity is designed to create an awareness of the company and its products. *Public relations* consists of community activities of a company designed to create a favorable impression with the public.

The combination of direct marketing, advertising, sales promotion, publicity, and public relations is called the *promotional mix.*[3]

> **Promotional mix –** The combination of direct marketing, advertising, sales promotion, publicity, and public relations.

What Are Your Promotional Goals?

The entrepreneur must decide what type of promotion will work best for the business. The first step in this process is to develop promotional goals (see the Promotional Goals Checklist). Some of the most common promotional goals would be to increase sales (or, for a new business, it may be to reach a specific level of sales the first year), to generate customer awareness, to differentiate the product or service by showing how it is better than the competition, and to eliminate seasonal merchandise. In order to be effective, these goals should be specific and measurable. For example, if a company wants to increase sales, the promotional goal may be "to increase sales in 2006 by 10 percent over the 2005 sales level." Or, for a new business, the goal may be "to reach a sales volume of $300,000 during the first year of operation." Then, at the end of the year, the entrepreneur can determine if the goals were met, and the promotional goals for the following year can be increased and changed as necessary.

What Is Your Promotional Budget?

It is also important to determine the advertising budget. Many entrepreneurs use a method known as "all you can afford," in which they pay all of their other bills and then advertise if there is money left over. This will not produce good results since advertising will be sporadic and will not necessarily be enough to achieve the advertising goals. The best approach is to determine the goals and then estimate how much advertising will be needed to reach those goals. This is known as the *objective and task method.* Later in this section, a monthly planning guide will be provided to help develop the advertising budget. The information on the following pages discusses the various promotional methods available to small business owners.

Sales and Direct Marketing

See the Sales and Direct Marketing Checklist for a summary of the following considerations.

Will you have a sales force? The best salesperson for a business is often the entrepreneur. No one knows the product or service better; no one is more committed to the company. However, in many cases, additional salespeople are needed for the company to grow. In fact, the entrepreneur should think of every employee who interacts with customers as a salesperson, since that employee's actions will affect the customer's opinion of the company. Employees who are hired specifically for the sales function, however, must be trained in sales techniques and product knowledge. Inside salespeople help customers who come to

CHECKLIST: PROMOTIONAL METHODS

What Types of Promotion Will You Use?

☐ Sales and/or direct marketing   ☐ Advertising
☐ Publicity/public relations   ☐ Sales promotion

CHECKLIST: PROMOTIONAL GOALS

What Are Your Promotional Goals?

☐ To reach a specific sales volume
☐ To increase sales
☐ To increase awareness
☐ To inform customers of a sale
☐ To eliminate seasonal merchandise

CHECKLIST: SALES AND DIRECT MARKETING

☐ Will you have inside salespeople, outside salespeople, or both?
☐ Will you hire only experienced salespeople, or will you hire inexperienced personnel and train them?
☐ How will the inside salespeople be compensated? How will the outside sales force be compensated? (Salary only, salary plus commission, or straight commission?)
☐ How often will you make sales calls with each salesperson?
☐ How will customer accounts be divided among the sales force? (geographically, by industry, by company size, and so on)
☐ Will you use telemarketing? Will you have your own telemarketing staff? How will they be compensated?
☐ Will you hire an outside telemarketing firm? What is the cost for those services?
☐ Will you use direct mail, catalogs, or direct-response ads through mail, broadcast, or print media?

the business or who call the business. Outside salespeople make personal calls to the customers businesses or homes.

If a sales force exists, the entrepreneur will have several functions as a sales manager, including recruiting, training, allocating customer accounts among the sales force, supervising, compensating, and evaluating their efforts. These are discussed next.

How much experience will the sales force need? The entrepreneur must decide whether to hire experienced salespeople or hire inexperienced employees and train them. The type of person hired should depend on the product or service to be sold and the length of the sales cycle. A technical product or service may require a salesperson who can serve as a consultant as well as a salesperson. In addition, some products with a short sales cycle are sold and delivered almost immediately. Other products that have a long sales cycle are sold only after many sales calls. A salesperson who likes immediate feedback should be hired for the short sales cycle product or service, since that type of person would become frustrated with a long cycle.

Although an experienced salesperson may require greater compensation, training an employee to be a good salesperson is very time-consuming. The entrepreneur must decide if he or she has adequate time and skills to devote to the training process. Sales training tapes and classes are available through many companies and may be a valuable resource for the entrepreneur.

How will you allocate customer accounts? The entrepreneur must also decide how to allocate customer accounts among the sales force. Some of the more common ways of allocating accounts are as follows:

$ *Geographically:* by assigning each salesperson a territory that has an equal sales potential

$ *By industry:* dividing accounts into groups such as retailers, wholesalers, and manufacturers

$ *By company size:* assigning smaller customer accounts to one salesperson and larger accounts to another

The allocation method used should be one that results in an efficient use of the salesperson's time while also providing an equitable distribution of accounts.

How will you supervise the sales force? The supervision of the sales force often includes holding sales meetings, making sales calls with personnel, resolving problems, and providing company information to the sales force. The supervision should provide the sales force with adequate support without excessive control.

How will compensation be determined? Compensation may be in the form of a straight salary, a salary plus a commission, or straight commission. While the salary provides more financial stability for the sales forces, it does not provide an incentive for excellent performance. A straight commission may seem attractive to the company, since no compensation is paid unless a sale is made; however, this provides no financial security to the sales force, and morale may suffer. A combination of salary plus commission often works best for both the company and the sales force.

How will you evaluate performance? The entrepreneur and the sales force should meet to establish sales goals that are reasonable and achievable. Goals should not be set solely by the entrepreneur and then given to the sales force, since the sales force may not agree with the goals and will not strive to achieve them. Sales goals may include a dollar volume of sales, a specific number of new accounts to be opened, or a specified number of sales calls to be made each month. The salesperson's performance can then be measured against these objectives.

Will you use telemarketing? *Telemarketing,* or telephone sales, is used by many companies to sell products or to make the initial customer contact and set up appointments. Telemarketing is much cheaper than personal sales calls to the customer's location because there is less time spent traveling and waiting. Entrepreneurs may hire an employee for telemarketing purposes or may hire a professional telemarketing firm on an as-needed basis.

Will you use direct-response ads? Direct-response ads are a type of direct marketing. It is called *direct-response marketing* because the company advertises a product and provides a method for the customer to immediately purchase the product. This may be done through a toll-free telephone number, a catalog order form, or other similar method. More about this type of promotion is included in

Telemarketing – telephone calls used to make a sale or set up appointments for salespeople.

Direct-response marketing – a marketing method that advertises a product and provides a method for the customer to immediately purchase the product.

the Advertising section later in this chapter, which covers types of advertising, including direct mail, radio, and broadcast and print media. The checklist on page 180 is designed to help the entrepreneur who will have a direct marketing program.

SALES PROMOTION

Learning Objectives

$ To be able to explain the difference between consumer-oriented and trade-oriented sales promotion.

$ To understand the different types of sales promotion methods that a company can use.

Sales promotions are classified as consumer-oriented or trade-oriented. *Consumer-oriented sales promotions* are targeted to the ultimate user of the product or service, whereas *trade-oriented sales promotions* are targeted to the marketing intermediaries such as wholesalers, distributors, and retailers.[4]

Consumer-oriented promotions are often used with advertising to encourage customers to buy a particular brand. They may also be used by retailers to encourage consumers to shop at a particular store. Consumer-oriented promotions include the following:[5]

> **Consumer-oriented sales promotions** – sales incentives targeted to the ultimate user of the product or service.

> **Trade-oriented sales promotions** – sales incentives targeted to marketing intermediaries such as wholesalers, distributors, and retailers.

$ Samples

$ Refunds and rebates

$ Contests and sweepstakes

$ Coupons

$ Cents off/dollars off

$ Event sponsorships

$ Premiums

$ Bonus packs

Trade-oriented promotions are designed to encourage distributors and retailers to carry a product or to make extra efforts to sell the product. Trade-oriented promotions include the following:[6]

$ Trade allowances

$ Point-of-purchase displays

$ Contests and dealer incentives

$ Trade shows

$ Training programs

$ Cooperative advertising

The Sales Promotion Checklist will help you plan sales promotion activities.

Discussion Questions

1. Direct marketing has become more popular in recent years and is used more frequently than in the past. What trends in society might have caused the increase in use?

CHECKLIST: SALES PROMOTION

☐ Will you use sales promotions?
☐ Will they be trade-oriented or consumer-oriented?
☐ What is the objective of your sales promotion?
  ☐ To encourage customers to try a new product
  ☐ To encourage customers to continue buying a product
  ☐ To increase consumption
  ☐ To fight competitors' marketing efforts
  ☐ To gain greater product distribution
  ☐ To encourage retailers to promote and/or display a product
  ☐ To increase the level of product inventory carried by a retailer
☐ What is the cost of each trade promotion? What is the total annual cost of all of the promotions?

2. Identify types of businesses for which door hangers would be an effective form of advertising.

3. Develop three consumer-oriented sales promotions for a small hardware store.

4. Many small businesses never establish promotional goals. What is the advantage of setting objectives?

5. Many small businesses do not set an advertising budget but instead advertise only when extra funds are available. What is the likely result of this approach?

6. Although an entrepreneur is often a good salesperson, managing a sales force often is a difficult task. How do the skills needed to be a good salesperson differ from the skills needed to be a good sales manager?

Endnotes

1. George E. Belch and Michael A. Belch, *Introduction to Advertising and Promotion* (Homewood, IL: Irwin, 1995), 11.
2. Ibid., 12.
3. Ibid., 9.
4. Ibid., 12.
5. Ibid., 477.
6. Ibid.

ADVERTISING

Learning Objectives

$ To understand the difference between informative, persuasive, and reminder advertising.

$ To be able to identify different types of media.

$ To be aware of all of the factors that must be considered when writing an advertising plan.

What Type of Advertising Will You Use?

Advertising is usually an essential part of the promotional plan for a new business. *Informative advertising,* which explains the company's products and services, is helpful building the initial customer base. *Persuasive advertising* often compares the new company to the competition and is used to convince the customer that the new company is superior to the competition. Once the company is well established, *reminder,* or *maintenance, advertising* is used to sustain an awareness of the company.[1]

> **Informative advertising** – advertising that explains the company's products and services.

> **Persuasive advertising** – advertising that compares one company's product or service to another company's.

> **Reminder or maintenance advertising** – advertising used to sustain awareness of the company.

Media

Which media will be most effective? One of the most important decisions in the promotional plan is the selection of the media that will be used. Choices of media are shown in Table B-4.

    Print media include newspapers, magazines, directories, direct mail, and flyers, whereas broadcast media include radio and television. *Outdoor advertising* is also a popular medium for many companies. Billboards may be purchased in two forms—*poster panels,* which are preprinted panels that are affixed to billboards,

---

TABLE B–4　Types of media

Media	Type	Example
Print Media		
Newspapers	Metropolitan	*The New York Times*
	Community	*Ladue News*
	Specialty	*The Business Journal*
Magazines	Consumer	*Redbook, Life*
	Trade	*Wood and Wood Products*
Directories	General	Yellow Pages
	Specialty	Women's Yellow Pages
Direct mail	Catalog	L.L. Bean
	General mailer	Publishers Clearing House
	Group mailing	Direct-mail firms
Flyers	Door hangers	Domino's coupons
	Person-to-person	
Broadcast Media		
Television	Network	ABC, CBS, NBC
	Cable	HBO, ESPN
	Independent	Local stations
Radio	Network	Clear channel
	Independent	Local stations
Outdoor Advertising		
Billboards	Poster panel	
	Painted bulletin	
Transit	Buses	
	Taxis	
Other		
Trade shows	Local	
	National	

and *painted bulletins*, which are billboards on which advertising is directly painted. Painted bulletins are generally more expensive than poster panels but may generate a greater response. Outdoor advertising also includes *transit advertising* on buses, cabs, and subways. Other types of advertising, such as local and national trade shows, are the main promotional method in many industries, and companies can reach many potential buyers by having a booth at a show.

In choosing media, entrepreneurs should choose those that will reach a large number of people in the target market for a reasonable cost without wasting advertising dollars on people who are not potential customers. For example, if the target market is lawyers in the Chicago metropolitan area, it would not be sensible to use the *Chicago Tribune*. Although some lawyers may see the ad, most of the people reading the paper would not be in the legal profession and advertising dollars would be wasted. A better choice would be a direct-mail campaign sent only to lawyers in a trade journal for Chicago lawyers.

When choosing the media, the entrepreneur should consider the questions in the Evaluating Media Checklist.

Which media will reach the most customers? The number of people who will see or hear the ad is referred to as the *reach* of the medium. Television, radio, metropolitan newspapers, national magazines, and outdoor advertising all have excellent reach. The reach of each medium can be determined as follows:

> **Reach** – the number of people who will see or hear an ad.

$ *Television.* The number of viewers for television programs is determined by the Nielsen ratings, which estimate the number of viewers for programs using sample households throughout the country. The number of viewers for a program can be obtained by calling the station that airs the program.

$ *Radio.* Information concerning the number of listeners of a radio station can be obtained by calling the station or through research groups such as Arbitron and Birch.

$ *Newspapers and magazines.* The number of people who receive a newspaper or magazine is known as the *circulation.* Each newspaper and magazine can provide information on the circulation and the readership profiles (age, income, and so on) of the typical customer. The reach of a magazine may be understated, however, since it is common for people to pass magazines along to friends or relatives. Circulation figures for magazines should be checked to determine if the figure includes only those who subscribe or other *pass-along readers.*

> **Circulation** – the number of people who receive a newspaper or magazine through subscription or newstand purchase.

> **Pass-along readers** – readers who do not subscribe to a publication but who receive it from a friend or relative.

$ *Outdoor advertising.* The number of customers reached through outdoor advertising is known as a *showing.* The entrepreneur must first decide what percentage of the target market he or she wishes to reach; the advertising company will then help determine how many billboards need to carry the ad in order to reach that number of people. For example, if the entrepreneur wants to reach 50 percent of the people in the target market, this would be referred to as a #50 showing.

> **Showing** – the number of people reached through outdoor advertising

$ *Trade shows. Trade shows* are often used by manufacturers and wholesalers to reach their customers. Trade shows are conventions at which the manufacturers or wholesalers rent booths and display their products. The reach of trade shows varies widely; some national trade shows are well attended, and participation is almost necessary for success in the industry. Other trade shows may be poorly attended, though, and the cost for a booth cannot be justified.

> **Trade shows** – conventions at which the manufacturers or wholesalers rent booths and display their products.

$ *Direct mail and flyers.* The reach of direct mail and flyers is controlled by the entrepreneur. The entrepreneur may choose to mail an ad to only a small number of people or to every household in the metropolitan area. Similarly, flyers may be hung on doors only in certain neighborhoods, or they may be passed out to everyone who passes a certain street corner. The excellent control of the reach of direct mail and flyers is one of the major advantages of these two media.

$ *Directories.* The reach of directories is controlled by the company that produces the directory, although the entrepreneur may have several options. For example, an ad in the Yellow Pages for a particular city will reach every household that has a telephone. However, the entrepreneur may choose to advertise only in the Yellow Pages for a particular county, thus reducing the reach and the cost of the ad.

How often will you run the advertising? The number of times a customer sees or hears an ad is referred to as the *frequency*. The frequency for various media varies.

> **Frequency –** the number of times a customer sees or hears an ad.

$ *Newspapers, radio, and television.* The number of ads is specified in advance, and discounts may be available for purchasing more than one ad. In order to be effective, however, it may be necessary to repeat the ad many times (high frequency).

$ *Magazines.* Magazines are similar to newspapers in that the number of ads is specified by the entrepreneur. While newspapers are quickly discarded, readers often keep magazines and page through them several times. The reader of the magazine may therefore see the same ad more than once.

$ *Direct mail and flyers.* The frequency for direct mail and flyers can also be controlled by the entrepreneur. Many companies place flyers on doors on a monthly basis, whereas other companies do so sporadically. Similarly, catalogs may be mailed monthly, quarterly, or semiannually.

$ *Directories.* An ad in a directory may be seen several times by a customer or not at all, depending on the number of times the customer refers to that section of the directory. The frequency may also be increased by placing an ad in several places within the same directory. For example, a company that sells crafts and gifts may be listed under retail craft stores and retail gift stores.

$ *Trade shows.* The frequency of a trade show is very limited, as most customers who attend the show would see the booth only once or twice. However, most companies provide brochures or other written material to customers who are interested, and the frequency may therefore be increased.

CHECKLIST: EVALUATING MEDIA

- [ ] How many people in the target market will see or hear the ad?
- [ ] How many times will they see or hear it?
- [ ] Where will the potential customers be when they see or hear the ad?
- [ ] Will they be distracted?
- [ ] How much advertising will be wasted on people who are not potential customers?
- [ ] How much will the advertising cost?

$ *Outdoor advertising.* Billboards and transit advertising have an excellent frequency because people will see the ad many times while traveling around the city. A billboard on a highway may be seen by a customer every day on the way to work. Similarly, ads on buses will be seen by people who travel along part of the same route every day. The excellent frequency of outdoor advertising is one of its major advantages.

Will the customer be distracted? *Delivery* refers to where the customer is when the advertising message is heard. This is important because the customer may be distracted and the advertising will be ineffective. Consider, for example, the following reasons that would cause distractions and ineffective advertising.

> **Delivery** – the customer's location when the advertising message is heard.

$ *Television and radio.* Television viewers and radio listeners may leave the room when ads come on. They may also be distracted by a ringing telephone or a crying baby. During weekday mornings, when there is a lot of activity in the home, the effectiveness of a television ad will be decreased.[2] Furthermore, viewers now use the remote control to "channel surf," switching to other stations when advertising begins.

$ *Outdoor advertising.* Someone driving down the highway in heavy traffic may be carefully watching the road and may not see the billboard. Furthermore, if many billboards and signs are located near each other, the likelihood of a viewer seeing a particular ad is decreased.

$ *Direct mail and flyers.* Parents often arrive home from work, grab the mail, and hurry into the home to fix supper. Direct-mail pieces or flyers may be discarded without ever being read. Many people view direct mail as "junk mail" and do not take the time to read it.

$ *Trade shows.* Attendance at some shows is so heavy that getting to a booth becomes difficult. If this occurs, attendees may choose to avoid the crowd and will never pass some of the booths.

$ *Multiple media.* Many people page through newspapers and magazines at the same time they are watching television or listening to the radio. Some advertising messages are likely to be missed.

How selective is the medium? *Selectivity* refers to the people who receive the advertising message and whether they are in the target market. The previous example of trying to reach lawyers in the Chicago area by advertising in the *Chicago Tribune* is an example of why selectivity is important. If the medium chosen reaches too many people outside the target market, advertising dollars will be wasted.

> **Selectivity** – whether the people who receive the advertising message are in the target market.

$ *Newspapers.* Metropolitan newspapers generally have poor selectivity, whereas small community papers will reach a more specific target market. Community newspapers are an excellent medium for many small businesses that cater to local residents. Small clothing stores, auto repair shops, and pet stores often find that ads in community newspapers produce results.

$ *Magazines.* Many magazines have excellent selectivity because they cater to customers with specific interests. Consumer magazines such as *Country Living* cater to individuals with an interest in the "country" style of homemaking; trade magazines such as *CADENCE* are written for people who use computer-aided design software at work. Selectivity allows the magazine advertiser to reach a specific group of people without wasting advertising dollars on those who are not interested.

$ *Direct mail and flyers.* Direct mail can be very selective if the entrepreneur carefully chooses the mailing list. Some direct mail, such as a booklet of coupons for local companies, is best mailed to all homes in nearby ZIP codes. However, if an entrepreneur wants to reach all of the women in Texas who have earned a master's degree and drive a car worth more than $35,000, it may be necessary to have a marketing firm custom-design a list.

$ *Directories.* General directories such as the Yellow Pages do not have good selectivity because they are delivered to everyone who has a telephone. If a hobby shop places an ad in the Yellow Pages, it will be delivered to many residents who will never need a hobby shop. More specialized directories are often published—for example, a directory of companies that serve a specific industry or a specific target market. Before advertising in any directory, however, entrepreneurs should determine how many people receive the publication and whether those people are potential customers.

$ *Trade shows.* The selectivity of trade shows is usually excellent. Trade shows often limit attendance to those who can prove they own a business or are employed in the industry. Trade shows that are targeted to the general public, such as the Home and Garden Show, usually only attract those who are truly interested, since an entrance fee will discourage those who are not.

$ *Outdoor advertising.* Outdoor advertising has very poor selectivity because many people will pass a billboard or see an ad on a bus even though they are not potential customers. For example, although billboards are often used to advertise tourist attractions, many people, such as business travelers and local residents, drive past the advertising who would not visit the attraction.

Selectivity must be considered when determining the cost to reach potential customers. The following example illustrates how only those in the target market should be considered when determining advertising costs.

When Will You Advertise?

Every entrepreneur should develop an advertising plan for each year in advance. This results in more consistent advertising and should result in more effective advertising. Before setting the advertising schedule, however, it is important to consider seasonality.

DETERMINING THE COST OF ADVERTISING

Name of the newspaper	*Urban Times*
Total circulation	100,000
Number in target market reached	15,000
Cost of ad	$500
Cost per potential customer	3.3 cents

Example: An entrepreneur wants to advertise clothing to women with a household income of more than $50,000. One of the newspapers is the *Urban Times*, which has a total circulation (men and women) of 100,000 people. Only 15,000 women who receive the paper meet the minimum income criteria. The cost of the ad would be $500. The cost per potential customer is $500/15,000, or approximately 3.3 cents per customer.

TABLE B–5   Sample advertising plan for January

Medium: Urban Times

Size of ad: 3" × 5"
Number of ads this month: 4
Message: Quality clothing at clearance sale prices
Cost for each ad: $350
Total number in target market reached: 15,000
Total ad cost for this medium: $1,400

Medium: KXYZ Radio

Size of ad: 30 seconds
Number of ads this month: 8
Message: The shop for those with discriminating taste
Cost for each ad: $150
Total number in target market reached: 4,000
Total ad costs for this medium: $1,200

Medium: Direct mail to 1,000 homes

Size: 8 1/2" × 11"
Number: 1,000
Message: Personal invitation to attend early clearance sale
Cost for each mailer including postage: 45 cents
Total number in target market reached: 1,000
Total ad cost for this medium: $450
Total advertising costs for this month: $3,050

Some products such as laundry detergent are purchased throughout the year and do not vary much with the seasons. For these products, a constant level of advertising is logical. Most products, however, have peak selling seasons as well as slower times. In those instances, methods known as *flighting* or *pulsing* might be used. *Flighting* uses heavy promotion during peak selling seasons, with no advertising during slow times. *Pulsing* maintains a low level of constant advertising but has much higher levels of advertising during peak seasons.[3]

> **Flighting** – a method that uses heavy promotion during peak selling seasons.

> **Pulsing** – a method that maintains a low level of constant advertising but has higher levels during peak seasons.

A sample monthly plan for a retail clothing store is shown in Table B-5. The plan lists the following:

Media
Size of the ad
Number of ads to be run during the month
Message of each ad
Cost for each ad
Total number in the target market reached by the ad
Total cost for each medium
Total monthly cost

This information should then be used to develop a monthly advertising plan, as shown in the Planning Advertising Checklist.

Discussion Questions

1. Why do successful businesses such as McDonald's still spend a large amount on advertising?

2. Identify the types of business that generally advertise on billboards. Identify one type of business that should not advertise on a billboard and state why a billboard would be a poor choice.

3. Suppose you own an ice cream store in a freestanding building in Chicago and your annual advertising budget is $5,000. For each month, identify the amount of money you would spend advertising.

4. For the ice cream store in question 3, which medium would be a good choice? Which medium would be a poor choice?

5. Identify businesses for which direct mail would be the most cost-effective method of advertising.

Endnotes

1. Louis E. Boone and David L. Kurtz, *Contemporary Business*, 7th ed. (Fort Worth, TX: Dryden Press, 1992), 526.

2. Peggy Swisher, "One Touch Sell," *Successful Meetings*, January 2001, 21.

3. George E. Belch and Michael A. Belch, *Advertising and Promotion* (Homewood, IL: Richard D. Irwin, 1995), 333.

CHECKLIST: PLANNING ADVERTISING

For each month, complete the following checklist to help determine your total advertising budget.

(Month)_____ Advertising Plan

(Medium)_____

☐ Size of ad_____
☐ Number of ads this month_____
☐ Message of the ads _____
☐ Cost for each ad _____
☐ Total number in target market reached_____
☐ Total ad costs for this medium_____

(Medium) _____

☐ Size of ad_____
☐ Number of ads this month_____
☐ Message of the ads_____
☐ Cost for each ad_____
☐ Total number in target market reached_____
☐ Total ad costs for this medium_____

(Medium)_____

☐ Size of ad_____
☐ Number of ads this month_____
☐ Message of the ads_____
☐ Cost for each ad_____
☐ Total number in target market reached_____
☐ Total ad costs for this medium_____
☐ Total advertising costs this month $_____

Marketing Online

In an article in *Inc.* magazine, David H. Freedman warns that the Web was supposed to level the playing field between large and small companies, but this has not happened. "'Small companies'" Web sites are often buried from view in a sea of competitive sites."[1] Just as in the regular marketplace, small businesses face stiff competition from large competitors as well as many small ones. Traditional small businesses proceeded cautiously in entering the Internet economy, but many now conduct business over the Internet. Despite the numerous competitors, many small businesses are finding that an Internet presence is an essential part of their marketing strategy.

Small businesses have many alternatives for online marketing. A company may wish to establish its own site, but it must be able to pay the up-front and maintenance costs. It is also essential to promote the site heavily and have an easy-to-remember address.[2] If a company's business is limited to a local area, a regional Internet bulletin board may be useful. Bulletin board systems specialize in online services that center on a specific topic or group. Small businesses may sponsor a bulletin board that caters to the company's target market.[3]

The entrepreneur may also want to consider purchasing space from an Internet shopping mall. Many Internet service providers now offer Internet commerce applications and hosting services in an effort to distinguish themselves from competitors. Technology writer Laura Kujubu suggests that

> For small businesses, online malls and commerce service providers may provide a useful combination of infrastructure and marketing services, enabling these stores to get customers they would have a difficult time attracting in other ways. They also help small businesses minimize the costs of online commerce.[4]

Some trade associations also have Web sites that allow businesses to post products and services.[5]

Microsoft and Yahoo! have both launched products designed to catapult millions of small businesses into the Internet economy. These Internet giants sell a range of software, and low-level commerce consultancy services help to get small businesses online.[6]

Small businesses may also want to consider e-mail marketing. Online marketing through e-mail is becoming a popular method of reaching a targeted audience. However, research shows that consumers read only about one-third of all e-mail messages received. The rest get deleted without ever being opened. Internet users are annoyed by spam, and they worry that this unsolicited e-mail may be sent with attachments or links to Web sites that could expose their computers to viruses and other destructive programs. Small businesses can respond to these concerns by using *permission-based e-mail*. These businesses ask for customers' permission to send e-mail conveying product and sales information and offering special deals. For example, a restaurant in a business district may invite lunchgoers to drop their business cards into a fish bowl for a chance to win a free meal in a monthly drawing and then use the e-mail addresses on those cards to send them coupons and information on daily specials. At its Web site, a business may ask visitors to type in their e-mail address in return for regular updates and coupons. Customers are more likely to respond when they have requested an offer. Therefore, small businesses should get consumers' permission to send the e-mail, keep the message simple and personalized, and only send e-mails when they have something important to say.[7]

Permission-based e-mail – marketing messages sent to consumers at their request.

The Web has also created numerous microbusinesses, started by entrepreneurs who sell items on auction sites such as eBay. Many of these businesses are operated part-time from someone's home and serve as a second income for the entrepreneur. Because of the extremely low overhead, these businesses have a competitive advantage over brick-and-mortar businesses. As Freedman noted, "We may increasingly find ourselves living in a sort of 'eBay economy,' in which businesses face tremendous pressure whether to invest heavily in sharply distinguishing themselves or to dramatically shed costs and switch competencies to beat microbusinesses at their own game."[8]

Discussion Questions

1. The Web was supposed to level the playing field between large and small businesses, but this has not happened. Why not?
2. Consider the e-mail marketing that you currently receive. What e-mails do you read? What e-mails do you delete without opening? What factors influence your decision?
3. *Inc.* writer David Freedman referred to an "eBay economy." What is an eBay economy?

Endnotes

1. David H. Freedman, "Can You Survive the eBay Economy?" *Inc*, March 2000, 88–95.
2. "The DMA Releases Best Practices in Interactive Marketing Study," *Direct Marketing*, December 1997, 10.
3. Gary Armstrong and Philip Kotler, *Marketing* (Upper Saddle River, NJ: Prentice-Hall, 2000), 498.
4. Laura Kujubu, "The Return of the Shopping Mall," *Info World,* February 1, 1999, 1.
5. Carolyn M. Brown, "Setting Up Shop in an Incubator," *Essence,* March 1997, 134.
6. Michael Kavanagh, "Microsoft and Yahoo! Target Small Business," *Market Week,* March 11, 1993, 31.
7. Michael Pridermore, "Chart Your Path," *Target Marketing,* June 2001, 46–48.
8. Freedman, 88–95.

PUBLIC RELATIONS AND PUBLICITY

To understand learning objectives.

$ To understand the goal of public relations is to create a favorable impression with the public.

$ To realize the goal of publicity is to increase awareness of a company and to present company information as news.

$ To know the use of public relations and publicity may be a very cost-effective way to promote the company and its products.

Public relations and publicity can be used to promote a business even if a company has a very limited advertising budget. *Public relations* consists of company activities designed to create a favorable impression with the public. Public relations includes activities such as sponsoring youth sports teams, joining the local chamber of commerce, and donating time (or money) to charitable organizations. *Publicity* refers to activities that are designed to increase the awareness of a company and present company information as news. Publicity often includes feature stories in local newspapers, interviews on local radios, and spot features on local or cable television stations. Many entrepreneurs have built a successful business by creatively using publicity and public relations as their primary promotional strategy. The Publicity and Public Relations Checklist offers ideas on the steps to take to outline a public relations and publicity plan.

> **Public relations** – consists of community activities of a company designed to creates a favorable impression with the public.

> **Publicity** – company information released as news on radio, on television, or in newspapers.

WILL YOU SELL YOUR PRODUCTS OVERSEAS?

A final consideration in the marketing plan is whether you will sell products overseas. If so, this is an important topic to be addressed in the marketing section. It is important to state the countries that will be targeted, why those countries were chosen, and the distribution channels that will be used to sell the products in the foreign countries. A checklist of some items is shown below; however, a more detailed list can be found in Chapter 11.

Discussion Questions

1. Choose a specific type of business, such as a hardware store or laundromat, and identify one example of publicity and one example of public relations the company could use. (Do not use examples given in this section. Develop ones that are unique to the business you have chosen.)

2. Identify all of the publicity items that could be developed concerning a company's employees (in addition to employee promotions and company anniversary dates).

3. Find an example of publicity or public relations used by a small firm in your area.

CHECKLIST: SELLING PRODUCTS OVERSEAS

- [ ] What products will be exported?
- [ ] What countries will be targeted? Why?
- [ ] What channel of distribution will you use?
  Export management company?
  Independent agents?
  Distributors?
  Selling direct to retailers?
  Selling direct to customers?
- [ ] Will you use letters of credit?
  (See Chapter 11 for more questions)

CHECKLIST: PUBLICITY AND PUBLIC RELATIONS

☐ Will you sponsor a youth sports team? If so, identify which one.
☐ If you plan to join local business organizations such as the Chamber of Commerce, identify those organizations.
☐ If you will donate time or funds to charitable organizations, identify them.
☐ What company activities can be used for publicity? Will you write an article for the local newspaper concerning the grand opening, expansion plans, new products that are developed, employee promotions, employee anniversaries (10 years with the company), and so on? Are any company activities interesting enough to be featured on local radio or television stations?

The Business Plan

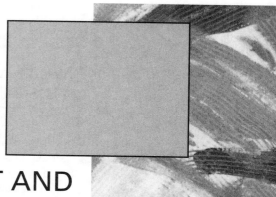

MANAGEMENT AND PERSONNEL

LEARNING OBJECTIVES

$ To understand how to write the management section of the business plan.

$ To be aware of the laws affecting the hiring and promotion of employees.

$ To be able to explain the difference between an employee and a subcontractor.

The Management and Personnel Checklist summarizes the considerations discussed in this section.

WHAT ARE YOUR QUALIFICATIONS TO OPERATE THIS BUSINESS?

Even the best business idea is useless if the entrepreneur and employees do not have the skills necessary to implement a plan of action. The management and personnel section of the business plan details the human resources that will be needed to operate the business.

The qualifications of the owner are critical to the success of the business. The business plan should contain a resumé of the owner as well as a paragraph describing his or her education, work history, industry training, management experience, and entrepreneurial personality traits. It is important to convince the banker or investor that the entrepreneur has the knowledge and training to succeed, because financiers often state that they loan money to people, not to businesses.

The qualifications of key employees should also be given. For example, if an entrepreneur plans to open a restaurant and plans to hire several chefs, the previous experience of those chefs is important. Similarly, the background information of managers and key salespeople should be provided. For all other employees, resumés are not required, but the entrepreneur must determine the type and number of jobs that will be needed and the skills that the employees will need.

If this is a family business, state the family members who will be employed in the company and their relationship to the owner.

HAVE YOU COMPLETED JOB DESCRIPTIONS?

Job analysis – identifies the important elements of a job (skill, education, etc.)

Job description – includes the tasks to be performed and the minimum education and work experience required.

The first step in the hiring process is the completion of a *job analysis*, which identifies the important elements of the job. A detailed *job description* should then be completed for two reasons: It tells the employee what you expect, and it tells you what you expect.[1] All too often, entrepreneurs are not satisfied with an employee's performance, yet the employee was never given an accurate description of what was expected. And job descriptions minimize unjustified firings and the discrimination lawsuits that often result.[2]

Job descriptions should focus on specific tasks (an employee is required to proofread documents) rather than on physical attributes (he or she must have 20/20 vision).[3] The more explicit the description, the better. For example, it is better to say, "Must operate a personal computer using both AutoCad and Word" than to say, "Must be able to use a computer."[4] The job description should provide the employee with a good idea of what is expected, but it is best not to state specific percentages, such as "25 percent answering phones, 50 percent typing," because jobs often change.[5] Similarly, there should be some flexibility written into the description so that it does not limit additional duties or special projects. The phrase "and other duties as assigned" is written into many job descriptions to provide this flexibility.

For entrepreneurs who want a basic format to use, job description software and reference books are available. However every company will have special needs, and a standardized job description should be customized to be effective.

HAVE YOU ESTABLISHED THE EMPLOYEES' WAGE RATES?

The compensation that will be paid to employees must also be determined. Entrepreneurs should determine the average wages paid for the type of jobs they are offering. This information can be obtained from the local state employment office.

Legislation increased the national minimum wage to $5.15 per hour in 1997, and recent efforts to raise that minimum have been foiled. States have the right to implement a minimum wage law, and if state and federal laws differ, the higher standard applies.[6] Companies that do not comply with minimum wage laws may be required to pay back pay as well as fines and penalties. As of 1993 the courts began to impose fines of up to $1,000 for every employee who was not paid proper minimum wage or overtime.[7] When combined with the back pay that is due, this may be a huge amount for a small business; therefore, it is in the company's best interest to comply with the law.

Workers must be identified as nonexempt or exempt. This must be based on the laws established by the Fair Labor Standards Act of 1938 (revised in April 2004). *Nonexempt employees* must be paid at least the minimum wage rate and should receive overtime pay at a rate of not less than one and one-half times their regular rates of pay after 40 hours of work in a work week.[8] To be classified as *exempt* and not receive overtime pay, an employee must be in one of the following categories: executive, administrative, professional, computer, outside sales, or highly compensated employee. In order to qualify for these exemptions, certain criteria must be met. These criteria are listed in Table B-6.

> **Nonexempt employees –** must be paid at least the minimum wage rate and overtime pay after 40 hours of work in a week.

> **Exempt employees –** employees who are not paid for overtime pay.

Unfortunately, the guidelines have always been somewhat vague and open to interpretation. Consider, for example, the administrative exemption that states discretion must be exercised with respect to matters of significance. What constitutes discretion? What is a matter of significance? Because of this lack of specificity, companies may call an employee an executive or administrator and not pay overtime. The employee, though, may see things differently and sue for overtime pay. In recent years, many companies have paid millions of dollars to settle lawsuits concerning overtime pay. Lawsuits have involved not only low-paid workers but also those in higher-paying management positions.[9]

The Fair Labor Standards Act was modified by the *Equal Pay Act of 1963,* which requires "equal pay for equal work." This part of the law prohibits companies from paying women less than men if they hold equal jobs. Jobs are considered equal if they require equal skill, effort, and responsibility and have similar working conditions. The Supreme Court has ruled that the jobs do not need to be identical in order for an employee to sue for wage discrimination.[10]

> **Equal Pay Act –** federal law that requires equal pay for equal work.

WHAT BENEFITS WILL YOU PROVIDE TO YOUR EMPLOYEES?

Although small businesses may not be able to offer as many benefits as large corporations, the entrepreneur must decide what, if any, benefits will be offered and which employees will be entitled to them. This includes not only benefits such as medical insurance but basic considerations such as holidays, vacation, sick days, and funeral leave. Written policies concerning each of these will ensure that the rules are applied equally.

TABLE B–6   Qualifying as an exempt employee

The following criteria must exist for an employee to qualify for the executive exemption:
- Compensation on a salary basis of not less than $455 per week
- Primary duty of managing the enterprise or a department
- Regularly supervising at least two or more full-time employees
- Having the authority to hire, fire, and promote other employees

To qualify for the administrative exemption, the employee must meet all of the following:
- Compensation on a salary basis at a rate not less than $455 per week
- Primary duty of office or nonmanual work related to the management of the company operation or customers
- Exercising discretion and independent judgment with respect to matters of significance

The requirements for a professional exemption are
- Compensation on a salary basis of not less than $455 per week
- Primary duty requiring advanced knowledge and consistent exercise of discretion and judgment
- Advanced knowledge in science or learning
- Acquisition of knowledge through a prolonged course of specialized instruction

To qualify for a computer employee exemption, the employee must
- Be compensated on a salary basis of not less than $455 per week or an hourly basis of at least $27.63 per hour
- Be employed as a computer systems analyst, computer programmer, software engineer, or similarly skilled worker
- Have a primary duty that meets specific criteria, including application of systems analysis techniques, designing, modifying, or testing computer programs

To qualify for an outside sales exemption, the employee must
- Have a primary duty of making sales and obtaining orders or contracts for paying customers
- Be regularly engaged away from the employer's place of business

Highly compensated employees are exempt if they perform office or nonmanual work and are paid $100,000 or more annually. This must include at least $455 per week; it cannot be paid in several large amounts.

Source: U.S. Department of Labor, http://www.dol.gov/esa/regs/compliance/whd/fairpay/fsl7a_overview.htm.

In addition to these benefits, social security and unemployment compensation are required by law for many employees. These benefits are considered taxes and are discussed in the legal section of the feasibility study.

HAVE YOU COMPLETED A TYPICAL WORK SCHEDULE?

In order to determine how many people will be needed in each job classification, it is helpful to develop a work schedule for a typical week. This consists of identifying how many hours the shop will be open and the number and type of employees that need to be working at specific times. Since most businesses have busy seasons and slow seasons, it is helpful to complete a schedule for both periods. A typical work schedule for a retail store is shown in Figure B-8.

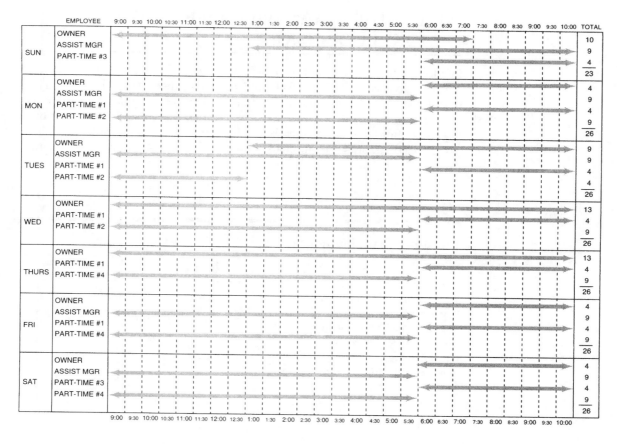

SCHEDULE FOR OWNER, ASSISTANT MANAGER, AND 4 PART-TIME WORKERS

TOTAL HOURS:	OWNER	57
	ASSIST. MGR	45
	PART-TIME #1	20
	PART-TIME #2	22
	PART-TIME #3	8
	PART-TIME #4	27

FIGURE B–8   Sample work schedule.

HAVE YOU COMPLETED AN ORGANIZATIONAL CHART?

An organizational chart is a graphic representation of the lines of authority in the company. If the company consists only of the entrepreneur, there is certainly no need for an organizational chart. However, if there are employees, an organizational chart is advisable. As stated in Chapter 6, when there are only a few employees, the organizational chart is a simple structure—for example, when all of the employees report directly to the owner. As the company grows, the owner cannot supervise all the staff, and an additional manager or supervisor is necessary. This results in an organizational chart with at least three levels—the entrepreneur, the managers, and all other employees. When a company becomes even larger and has several managers, the company may be organized along departmental lines.

WHAT OTHER LAWS WILL AFFECT YOUR PERSONNEL DECISIONS?

In addition to the Fair Labor Standards Act discussed earlier, the federal government has enacted laws to protect employees from dangerous work environments, discrimination in hiring and promotion, and payment of substandard wages. Although very small businesses are exempt from these federal laws because of the regulatory burden it would impose on them, state laws may apply.

The federal laws are summarized in the following sections and are briefly listed in Table B-7.

TABLE B–7   Employment laws

Laws	Applies to
Title VII of the Civil Rights Act Prohibits discrimination because of race, color, national origin, religion, or sex in all employment practices	Companies with 15 or more employees for 20 weeks in the current or preceding year
Equal Pay Act Amended Title VII to require equal pay for comparable work	Same as above
Civil Rights Act	Same as above
Americans with Disabilities Act Prevents discrimination because of a disability in all employment practices	Same as above
National Labor Relations Act Establishes employees' right to unionize	All companies
Taft-Hartley Act Prohibits unfair labor practices by unions	All companies
Age Discrimination in Employment Act Prohibits discrimination against people between ages 40 and 70	Companies with 20 or more employees
Family and Medical Leave Act Provides up to 12 weeks of unpaid leave for employees who need time for family matters	Companies with 50 or more employees
Occupational Safety and Health Act Ensures safe and healthful working conditions	All businesses
Worker's Compensation Enacted by each state: provides medical costs and lost wages due to job-related injuries	Varies by state
Immigration Reform and Control Act	All businesses
Immigration Act Prevents illegal aliens from working in the United States	All businesses

Occupational Safety and Health Act

The Occupational Safety and Health Act (OSHA) was passed in 1970 to ensure safe and healthful working conditions. OSHA regulations apply to almost all small businesses because the guidelines are applicable to any business that has one or more employees.

> **Occupational Safety and Health Act (OSHA)** – intended to ensure safe and healthful working conditions.

Title VII of the Civil Rights Act and the Age Discrimination in Employment Act

Title VII of the Civil Rights Act was passed in 1964 to prevent discrimination in employment based on race, religion, color, national origin, or sex. The law has recently been amended to include discrimination against pregnant women; people with AIDS, cancer, or physical and mental disabilities; and people who are recovering from or being treated for substance abuse. The Civil Rights Act of 1991 allows employees who feel they have been discriminated against to sue for punitive damages as well as back pay. These laws apply only to businesses that have 15 or more employees for 20 weeks in the current or preceding year.

> **Civil Rights Act** – prohibits discrimination in employment based on race, religion, color, national origin, or sex.

For those businesses covered, the discrimination laws affect hiring, firing, and promotions. The only time sex or race may be specified in a want ad is when the job requires either a male or female or a person of a particular race; this is referred to as the *bona fide occupational qualification.* (Generally, these jobs are rare. A recent example is that women are excluded from a few military positions such as the special forces, primarily because they usually cannot meet the physical requirements.) Job ads must also be placed to reach the largest number of qualified applicants.[11]

> **Bona fide occupational qualification** – a legal job requirement stating a specific race or sex.

The *Federal Age Discrimination in Employment Act* (1967) prohibits employers from discriminating against people ages 40 to 70. While most people are aware that blatant discrimination is illegal, many do not know that this law also affects the wording of want ads. Ads stating that the company has a "young, dynamic staff" may discourage older workers; conversely, ads should not state that the job would be "excellent retirement income."[12]

> **Federal Age Discrimination in Employment Act** – prohibits employees from discriminating against people ages 40 to 70.

Americans with Disabilities Act

The *Americans with Disabilities Act (ADA)*, enacted in 1990, prohibits discrimination in employment, accommodations, transportation, and communication. The laws concerning discrimination in employment do not apply to companies with fewer than 15 employees. For companies that are covered by the law, however, job ads, interviews, and the workplace are affected. Under the ADA, it is not a violation to refuse to hire or consider a person with a disability if he or she cannot perform the "essential functions" of the job. The employer, however, must be able to distinguish between essential and nonessential functions. The employer cannot discriminate against an "otherwise qualified individual with a disability" if he or she can perform the essential job functions (even if reasonable accommodations are needed).

> **Americans with Disabilities Act** – prohibits discrimination in employment, accommodations, transportation, and communication.

Because of the ADA, interviewers must refrain from asking questions concerning health, disabilities, workers' compensation claims, medical history, and medical exams. Applicants cannot be asked how they became disabled; questions about the prognosis of the disability are also prohibited.

Table B-8 lists some of the topics that should not be discussed during interviews because of discrimination laws that protect job applicants.

TABLE B–8   Job interview topics to avoid

Do not ask questions about:
    Personal finances
    Religious preferences
    Marital status
    Age
    Race
    Previous residence
    Ability to speak a foreign language unless it is directly related to the job
    Child care arrangements
    Car ownership
    Previous worker's compensation claims
    Arrest record, unless job-related
    Union membership or opinions about unions
    Health, disabilities, medical history, and medical exams
    Political affiliation

Sources: Debbie Eide Niculescu, "Legal Developments Affecting the Selection Process," *Supervision*, May 1993, 5; and George D. Webster, "Hiring Do's and Don'ts," *Association Management*, November 1992, 100.

Immigration Laws

> **Immigration Reform and Control Act and Immigration Act of 1990** – enacted to prevent illegal aliens from working in the United States.

The *Immigration Reform and Control Act* (1986) and the *Immigration Act of 1990* were enacted to prevent illegal aliens from working in the United States. Prior to these laws, if an illegal alien was found to be working in a company, the worker was deported but the company was not held accountable. Companies must now complete an Employment Eligibility Verification Form (also known as an I-9 form) for each employee. This form, shown in Figure B-9, is designed to provide documentation that the employee is legally eligible to work in the United States. The company must retain the form at the business location for at least three years after the employee is hired. Substantial fines may be imposed if these records are not complete.

Family and Medical Leave Act

> **Family and Medical Leave Act** – requires companies with 50 or more employees to provide employees unpaid leave for family matters.

The *Family and Medical Leave Act* became law in 1993. Companies with 50 or more employees must provide up to 12 weeks of unpaid leave to employees who need time for family matters. Time may be needed as a result of the birth or adoption of a child, an illness in the family, or other family emergencies.

National Labor Relations Act and Taft-Hartley Act

> **National Labor Relations Act (Wagner Act)** – requires employees to bargain in good faith with union representatives and prevents employers from interfering with union activities.

Although many small businesses are not affected by union activity, many industries, including construction and textile manufacturing, may be unionized. The *National Labor Relations Act of 1935*, also known as the *Wagner Act*, requires employers to bargain in good faith with employee union representatives and prevents employers from interfering with union activities.

The Taft-Hartley Act of 1947 forbids unfair labor practices by unions such as requiring that employers pay for services that have not been completed or requiring excessive union dues.

U.S. Department of Justice
Immigration and Naturalization Service

OMB No. 1115-0136

Employment Eligibility Verification

Please read instructions carefully before completing this form. The instructions must be available during completion of this form. **ANTI-DISCRIMINATION NOTICE:** It is illegal to discriminate against work eligible individuals. Employers CANNOT specify which document(s) they will accept from an employee. The refusal to hire an individual because of a future expiration date may also constitute illegal discrimination.

Section 1. Employee Information and Verification. To be completed and signed by employee at the time employment begins.

Print Name: Last	First	Middle Initial	Maiden Name

Address (Street Name and Number)		Apt. #	Date of Birth (month/day/year)
City	State	Zip Code	Social Security #

I am aware that federal law provides for imprisonment and/or fines for false statements or use of false documents in connection with the completion of this form.

I attest, under penalty of perjury, that I am (check one of the following):
☐ A citizen or national of the United States
☐ A Lawful Permanent Resident (Alien # A_____)
☐ An alien authorized to work until ___/___/___
(Alien # or Admission #) _____

Employee's Signature	Date (month/day/year)

Preparer and/or Translator Certification. *(To be completed and signed if Section 1 is prepared by a person other than the employee.) I attest, under penalty of perjury, that I have assisted in the completion of this form and that to the best of my knowledge the information is true and correct.*

Preparer's/Translator's Signature	Print Name
Address (Street Name and Number, City, State, Zip Code)	Date (month/day/year)

Section 2. Employer Review and Verification. To be completed and signed by employer. Examine one document from List A OR examine one document from List B and one from List C, as listed on the reverse of this form, and record the title, number and expiration date, if any, of the document(s)

List A	OR	List B	AND	List C
Document title: _____		_____		_____
Issuing authority: _____		_____		_____
Document #: _____		_____		_____
Expiration Date (if any): ___/___/___		___/___/___		___/___/___
Document #: _____				
Expiration Date (if any): ___/___/___				

CERTIFICATION - I attest, under penalty of perjury, that I have examined the document(s) presented by the above-named employee, that the above-listed document(s) appear to be genuine and to relate to the employee named, that the employee began employment on *(month/day/year)* ___/___/___ and that to the best of my knowledge the employee is eligible to work in the United States. (State employment agencies may omit the date the employee began employment.)

Signature of Employer or Authorized Representative	Print Name	Title
Business or Organization Name	Address (Street Name and Number, City, State, Zip Code)	Date (month/day/year)

Section 3. Updating and Reverification. To be completed and signed by employer.

A. New Name (if applicable)	B. Date of rehire (month/day/year) (if applicable)

C. If employee's previous grant of work authorization has expired, provide the information below for the document that establishes current employment eligibility.

Document Title:_____   Document #: _____   Expiration Date (if any): ___/___/___

I attest, under penalty of perjury, that to the best of my knowledge, this employee is eligible to work in the United States, and if the employee presented document(s), the document(s) I have examined appear to be genuine and to relate to the individual.

Signature of Employer or Authorized Representative	Date (month/day/year)

Form I-9 (Rev. 11-21-91)N Page 2

FIGURE B–9   Employment eligibility verification form (I-9 form) *(continued).*

LISTS OF ACCEPTABLE DOCUMENTS

LIST A		LIST B		LIST C
Documents that Establish Both Identity and Employment Eligibility	**OR**	**Documents that Establish Identity**	**AND**	**Documents that Establish Employment Eligibility**

LIST A
Documents that Establish Both Identity and Employment Eligibility

1. U.S. Passport (unexpired or expired)

2. Certificate of U.S. Citizenship *(INS Form N-560 or N-561)*

3. Certificate of Naturalization *(INS Form N-550 or N-570)*

4. Unexpired foreign passport, with *I-551 stamp or* attached *INS Form I-94* indicating unexpired employment authorization

5. Alien Registration Receipt Card with photograph *(INS Form I-151 or I-551)*

6. Unexpired Temporary Resident Card *(INS Form I-688)*

7. Unexpired Employment Authorization Card *(INS Form I-688A)*

8. Unexpired Reentry Permit *(INS Form I-327)*

9. Unexpired Refugee Travel Document *(INS Form I-571)*

10. Unexpired Employment Authorization Document issued by the INS which contains a photograph *(INS Form I-688B)*

OR

LIST B
Documents that Establish Identity

1. Driver's license or ID card issued by a state or outlying possession of the United States provided it contains a photograph or information such as name, date of birth, sex, height, eye color, and address

2. ID card issued by federal, state, or local government agencies or entities provided it contains a photograph or information such as name, date of birth, sex, height, eye color, and address

3. School ID card with a photograph

4. Voter's registration card

5. U.S. Military card or draft record

6. Military dependent's ID card

7. U.S. Coast Guard Merchant Mariner Card

8. Native American tribal document

9. Driver's license issued by a Canadian government authority

For persons under age 18 who are unable to present a document listed above:

10. School record or report card

11. Clinic, doctor, or hospital record

12. Day-care or nursery school record

AND

LIST C
Documents that Establish Employment Eligibility

1. U.S. social security card issued by the Social Security Administration *(other than a card stating it is not valid for employment)*

2. Certification of Birth Abroad issued by the Department of State *(Form FS-545 or Form DS-1350)*

3. Original or certified copy of a birth certificate issued by a state, county, municipal authority or outlying possession of the United States bearing an official seal

4. Native American tribal document

5. U.S. Citizen ID Card *(INS Form I-197)*

6. ID Card for use of Resident Citizen in the United States *(INS Form I-179)*

7. Unexpired employment authorization document issued by the INS *(other then those listed under List A)*

Illustrations of many of these documents appear in Part 8 of the Handbook for Employers (M-274)

Form I-9 (Rev. 11-21-91) N

FIGURE B–9   *(continued)*.

CHECKLIST: MANAGEMENT AND PERSONNEL

☐ Include a paragraph describing the education, work experience, and entrepreneurial personality traits of the owner(s). Emphasize any management experience and any experience in the industry of the proposed business. Include complete resumés if they are available. Also include resumés of key personnel.

☐ Explain in paragraph form the type of employee positions that will be filled and the pay and benefits that will be provided. Then complete the following chart to show all personnel needed:

Job Title	Number Needed	PT/FT (Part-/Full-Time)	Salary or Hourly Pay	Benefits

☐ What paid holidays will the company observe? Which employees will be entitled to holiday pay?

☐ How will vacation time be accrued? Which employees will have paid vacations? (Full-time and part-time, or only full-time?)

☐ What is your policy concerning sick days? Are paid sick days available to full-time and part-time or only full-time employees?

☐ What is your policy concerning funeral leave? How many days are granted? For which relatives?

☐ How many employees will you have? Will your hiring and firing policies be legally governed by:
    ☐ Title VII of the Civil Rights Act?
    ☐ Age Discrimination in Employment Act?
    ☐ Americans with Disabilities Act?
    ☐ Family and Medical Leave Act?

☐ Complete an organizational chart.

☐ Complete a work schedule for a typical work week.

☐ Is this a family business?
    ☐ If so, state which family members will be employed and give their relationship to the owner(s).

Workers' Compensation

Workers' compensation provides payment for job-related injuries and lost wages. It is federally mandated but is administered by the states. Therefore, the laws concerning the size of businesses vary from state to state. More information on workers' compensation is included in the insurance section of the business plan.

> **Workers' compensation** – provides payment for job-related injuries and lost wages.

State Laws

Although many federal employment laws do not apply to businesses with fewer than 15 employees, state laws often are more stringent. Although Title VII of the Civil Rights Act prevents discrimination in companies with 15 or more employees, many states have discrimination laws that apply to companies with far fewer employees. For example, in Missouri, discrimination laws apply to companies with six or more employees, whereas Missouri's workers' compensation laws apply to companies with five or more employees. Therefore, it is important that all entrepreneurs check both federal and state labor laws.

DO YOU HAVE EMPLOYEES OR SUBCONTRACTORS?

Subcontractors – self-employed individuals who perform services for other companies.

Many entrepreneurs try to avoid the regulations and taxes associated with employees by calling the employees "subcontractors." Since *subcontractors* are self-employed, they receive no benefits and they are responsible for their own employment and social security payments. However, just because the employer and worker agree on a subcontractual arrangement does not make it legal. The Internal Revenue Service has established standards to determine whether a worker is an employee or subcontractor. If a company has not paid taxes on a worker that was called a subcontractor, and the IRS determines that the worker was an employee, the company may be held liable for back taxes. More than 20 different standards are applied to determine whether a worker is an employee or subcontractor. However, there are six main issues:[13]

1. Does the business control the manner in which the work is performed?
2. Does the worker have a special or unique skill?
3. Is the service provided by the worker an integral part of the business?
4. Is there a degree of permanence in the working relationship between the worker and the business?
5. Is there opportunity for loss or profit to the worker?
6. Does the individual have an investment in equipment or materials necessary for the work?

A subcontractor must be able to decide work location, time of work, scheduling, and the way in which the work is completed. It is best if compensation is based on results or completion of the job with quality specifications or timing of completion stated.[14] If compensation is based only on the number of hours worked, the worker is more likely to be considered an employee.

Entrepreneurs must be careful in establishing a "subcontractor" arrangement. Because the laws are vague, it is often difficult to determine whether a worker is an employee or subcontractor. Legal counsel is definitely advisable.

Discussion Questions

1. Why would job descriptions minimize unjustified firings and discrimination lawsuits?
2. The federal government has passed many laws that prevent discrimination in hiring and firing practices, although many small businesses are exempt from these laws. Discuss the advantages and disadvantages of granting exemptions for small businesses.
3. Give an example of a job position that may be classified as a subcontractor. Give an example of a job position that could not be justified as a subcontractor.
4. What is the difference between an exempt and nonexempt employee?

Endnotes

1. W. Stephen Brown, "Failing to Train and Coach New Hires Is Failing to Manage," *Supervision,* March 1994, 10.
2. Stephen F. Ruffino, "An Ounce of Prevention," *Small Business Reports,* February 1994, 10.
3. Ibid.

4. Debbie Eide Niculescu, "Legal Development Affecting the Selection Process," *Supervision,* May 1993, 7.

5. Joseph D. O'Brain, "Beware of False Advertising When Hiring," *Supervisory Management*, November 1993.

6. U.S. Department of Labor, "Minimum Wage Laws in the States—August 1, 2005," http:www.dol.gov/Esa/minwage/america.htm.

7. Joan Oleck, "Bending Wage and Hour Laws Just Got Riskier," *Restaurant Business*, October 10, 1993, 32.

8. U.S. Department of Labor, "Handy Reference Guide to the FAIR Labor Standards Act," http://www.dol.gov/esa/regs/compliance/whd/hrg.htm.

9. Adam Geller, "Salaried Employees Are Suing for Unpaid Overtime," *St. Louis Post Dispatch*, August 4, 2002, EI.

10. Charles R. Kuehl and Peggy A. Lambing, *Small Business Planning and Management* (Fort Worth, TX: Dryden Press, 1994), 488.

11. George D. Webster, "Hiring Do's and Don'ts," *Association Management*, November 1992, 100.

12. Ibid.

13. John S. Sturges, "When Is an Employee Truly an Employee?" *HRMagazine,* October 1993, 56.

14. Ibid.

The Business Plan

START-UP COSTS AND FINANCING

LEARNING OBJECTIVES

$ To comprehend the difference between start-up costs and ongoing expenses.

$ To be able to list common start-up costs.

$ To be aware of the different sources of financing.

$ To understand the difference between debt and equity financing.

If the business plan is going to be used to obtain financing, the financial section is one of the most important. Mistakes in this section may prevent you from obtaining funds even if all other parts of the business plan are excellent. The financial section includes the following topics:

$ Start-up costs

$ Business financing

$ The projected income statements
- Opening-day balance sheet
- Projected income statements
- Projected cash flow statements

$ The break-even point

Start-up costs are costs that are necessary to open the business. Most of these costs will be incurred before the company opens for business. Start-up costs for businesses vary by industry, but the following categories are common for most businesses.

$ *Inventory. Inventory* consists of any items you will buy and resell to customers. Estimates of inventory costs can be obtained from companies that will be your suppliers.

$ *Furniture and fixtures. Furniture and fixtures* include office desks and chairs, shelving, counters, display cases, and so forth. Estimates of costs can be obtained from retailers of these items.

$ *Machinery and equipment.* This category includes computers, cash registers, copiers, fax machines, and special industry items such as manufacturing equipment or construction equipment. Entrepreneurs should identify the companies from which they would purchase the machinery and equipment and obtain costs for each item. See the Furniture and Fixtures, Machinery and Equipment Checklist for help in identifying these costs.

$ *Prepaid expenses.* It is often necessary to pay for services before the company is open for business. These *prepaid expenses* may include legal fees, insurance for the first six months of operation, grand opening advertising, and so forth. Determine what expenses must be paid before the company opens and obtain an estimate for each.

$ *Training costs for employees.* When the doors open for business, the employees must know how to perform their jobs efficiently. For this reason, it is usually necessary to hire and train employees before the first day of operation. If they are hired a week or two before opening, they may receive a paycheck before any sales are generated.

$ *Deposits.* Many entrepreneurs forget to include deposits in their start-up costs, only to find that this amounts to thousands of dollars. Deposits may include the following:
- *Lease deposit.* This is almost always required if a building or space is leased. The deposit is usually equal to two months' rent. Exact deposit amounts can be obtained from the landlord.
- *Utility deposits.* The utility companies (gas, electric, and telephone) may require a deposit before service is connected. Utility companies will provide estimates of the required deposit.

> **Start-up costs** – initial costs necessary to open a business.

> **Inventory** – items on hand that a company buys or manufactures for resale.

- *Taxes.* Many states require a sales tax deposit for taxes that will be due, especially if the firm will collect sales tax. Contact the state department of revenue to identify required tax deposits.

$ *Renovations and/or building purchase.* Unless the business is operated from the home, there will be costs associated with the site. If a location is leased, renovations may be required. Renovations to leased property are called *leasehold improvements.* If the facility is purchased, the sales price is a start-up cost and renovations may also be needed.

$ *Working capital.* For most businesses, it takes at least several months to develop a good customer base. During this time, the sales volume is usually not sufficient to pay all of the bills. *Working capital* is a cash reserve to cover monthly expenses until the cash coming into the company every month is equal to or greater than the amount of bills that need to be paid. In general, the working capital amount should cover at least three to six months' expenses. See the Start-up Costs Checklist for help with these calculations.

> **Leasehold improvements** – renovations to leased property.

> **Working capital** – case reserve used to cover expenses until the cash received equals or exceeds bills to be paid.

CHECKLIST: FURNITURE, FIXTURES, MACHINERY, AND EQUIPMENT

Furniture and Fixtures

Item	Quantity Needed	Price Each	Total Prices
Sample:			
Desk	3	$150	$450
Shelving	7	$100	$700
___	___	___	___
___	___	___	___
___	___	___	___
___	___	___	___
___	___	___	___
___	___	___	___
		Total for Furniture and Fixtures	$____

Machinery and Equipment

Item	Quantity Needed	Price Each	Total Prices
Sample:			
PC and software	1	$1,200	$1,200
Telephone/fax combination	1	$600	$600
___	___	___	___
___	___	___	___
___	___	___	___
___	___	___	___
___	___	___	___
___	___	___	___
		Total for Machinery and Equipment	$____

CHECKLIST: START-UP COSTS

- ☐ Inventory
- ☐ Furniture and fixtures   _____
- ☐ Machinery and equipment   _____
- ☐ Prepaid expenses
    - ☐ Insurance
    - ☐ Grand opening advertising   _____
    - ☐ Legal fees   _____
    - ☐ Accounting fees   _____
    - ☐ Employee wages   _____
    - ☐ Other (specify)   _____
- ☐ Total prepaid expenses   _____
- ☐ Deposits
    - ☐ Lease
    - ☐ Utility   _____
    - ☐ Tax   _____
    - ☐ Other (specify)   _____
- ☐ Total deposits
- ☐ Building and renovation   _____
    - ☐ If purchased
        - ☐ Sales price   _____
        - ☐ Construction and renovation   _____
    - ☐ If leased
        - ☐ Leasehold improvements   _____
- ☐ Total location costs
- ☐ Working capital   _____

	Cost per month
☐ Owner's salary	_____ × 3 = _____
☐ Employees' salary	_____ × 3 = _____
☐ Employee taxes	_____ × 3 = _____
(approximately 11 percent of owner and employee wages)	
☐ Rent	_____ × 3 = _____
☐ Advertising	_____ × 3 = _____
☐ Utilities	_____ × 3 = _____
☐ Supplies	_____ × 3 = _____
☐ Telephone	_____ × 3 = _____
☐ Legal and accounting fees	_____ × 3 = _____
☐ Loan payment	_____ × 3 = _____
☐ Repairs and maintenance	_____ × 3 = _____
☐ Auto and travel expenses	_____ × 3 = _____
☐ Inventory	_____ × 1 = _____
(If customers do not pay cash for purchases, this amount will be needed to replace inventory until payment is received.)	
☐ Miscellaneous	_____ × 3 = _____
☐ Other (specify)	_____ × 3 = _____

- ☐ Total working capital
- ☐ Total start-up costs

HOW WILL THE BUSINESS BE FINANCED?

The financing section of the business plan should identify the type of financing that will be used because this may have a financial impact on you and the company. For example, if a large amount of money is borrowed, the company will have substantial loan payments every month, which could be a burden for a new company. If you use personal assets as collateral for a loan, you could lose them if the business does not succeed. Money that is borrowed, known as *debt financing*, must be repaid with interest. The interest rate for business loans is generally determined by the *prime rate*, a benchmark rate that fluctuates depending on the economic conditions in the country. Small businesses are often charged a rate of 1 to 3 points more than prime. Therefore, if prime is 4 percent, a loan to a small business may have a rate as low as 5 percent or as high as 7 percent.

The length of time you have to repay the loan depends on the asset that is purchased with the loan proceeds. If the asset is a building, you will have a long time (15 to 30 years) to repay the loan. If the loan will be used to buy a delivery van, the loan will be repaid over three to five years.

If you plan to obtain private investors or partners, or if friends and relatives will provide funds, you must consider how they will be compensated for their investment. Some investors and partners want only a financial return, whereas others want to take an active role in making company decisions. Investors, partners, and others who provide financing in exchange for ownership are called *equity investors*.

A brief explanation of financing alternatives follows. Several sources of debt financing will first be discussed. Then sources of equity financing will be examined.

> **Debt financing –** financing that must be repaid.

> **Prime rate –** a benchmark interest rate that fluctuates with economic conditions.

> **Equity investors –** provide financing in exchange for ownership.

Debt Financing

Bank loans According to the Small Business Administration, "access to credit is vital for small business survival, and a key supplier of credit to small firms is the commercial banking system."[1] However, not all banks actively seek small business customers and entrepreneurs may find their business plan rejected at one bank while being enthusiastically accepted at another. For this reason, the Small Business Administration produces an annual Small Business Lending report that shows which banks are meeting the credit needs of small firms and which banks are investing elsewhere. This helps small businesses save time and shop efficiently for credit.[2]

When considering a request for a small business loan, the bank will consider many factors. These factors are listed in the Bank Financing Criteria Checklist.

Federal government financing programs The federal government has several financing programs for small businesses. The Small Business Administration (SBA) is a federal agency that provides many services to small businesses. The agency has many types of loans available to small businesses. Because the funds for loans are provided through the federal budget, the amount of funding varies from time to time. In the past 20 years, the number of SBA-approved loans has ranged from a low of 17,000 to more than 60,000 per year.[3] Additional information on SBA loans can be obtained from the SBA Web site at http://www.sba.gov.

State and local government financing programs State governments as well as county and city governments often have loan programs to encourage

CHECKLIST: BANK FINANCING CRITERIA

1. *Is there a market for the business?*
2. *What do you have for collateral?* Collateral consists of items that the bank will sell if the loan cannot be repaid. This usually includes business assets such as your furniture and fixtures, as well as personal assets such as your home. Items will not be considered at full market value but will instead be discounted by 50 to 80 percent depending on the item. Homes are discounted by 75 or 80 percent of the value business inventory that is more difficult to sell may be discounted by 50 percent. For example, suppose you own a home that could be sold under normal conditions for $100,000. You currently owe $30,000 on the original purchase price. The collateral value for a business loan would be as follows:

Market value of home	$100,000
Discount factor	× 80%
	= 80,000
Current amount owed	− 30,000
Collateral value	$50,000

3. *How much money will you be investing in the company?* If it is an existing company, how much money did you invest in the past? How much of the profits have been reinvested in the company? It is common for a bank to require the entrepreneur to invest at least 20 percent of the total start-up costs. Therefore, if total start-up costs are $100,000, the entrepreneur would have to invest $20,000 cash and the bank would loan $80,000.
4. *Do you have a good credit record?* Have you paid personal bills such as your credit cards and car payment on time? If you are requesting a loan for an existing company, the bank may check both your personal and company credit record.
5. *Do you have the education and experience needed to manage this company?* What is your educational background? Have you had any special training or trade school instruction? Have you worked in this industry before? What were your responsibilities?
6. *Are general economic conditions in the area good or bad? Is the local economy growing or is the economy in a recession?*
7. *Does the company have the ability to repay the loan?* One of the most important factors a bank will consider is whether the company will generate enough profits to repay the loan. If the company is a start-up, the bank will use the financial projections in the business plan for its analysis. The projections must be realistic yet show enough cash flow to repay the loan. If the company is an existing business, the bank will consider both the profits earned in the past three years and the figures in the financial projections.

---

businesses to locate in their area. These may be general-purpose loans available to any small business or they may be specialized. For example, loan programs have been available to companies in the recycling industry, companies hurt by decreases in the federal defense budget, and companies that will employ many people. Each government establishes its own program and eligibility criteria.

Finance companies Finance companies often provide loans to companies that cannot get financing through banks. They are often willing to finance businesses that are considered a high risk, those in industry with high failure rates, or those that are in a marginal financial condition. The interest rate charged by finance companies, however, is generally higher than the rate charged by banks.

> **Finance companies** – provide debt financing to higher-risk companies that banks may not finance.

Equity Financing

Personal funds Personal funds include any money invested from savings accounts and checking accounts. Many financial institutions and investors expect the entrepreneur to invest some personal funds if he or she is also seeking financing from others.

Private investors Private investors may include friends and family members, wealthy individuals, and partners. Friends and family members are often willing to provide funds, but family relations may be strained or ruined if the business does not succeed or if there are disagreements about how it should be operated.

Some wealthy individuals invest in small businesses, hoping to earn a high rate of return when the company becomes successful. These individuals are often referred to as *angels* because of the financial assistance they provide. Because entrepreneurs often do not know how to find investors, and the investors do not know how to find entrepreneurs, many matching services have been started. Many states or municipalities have established databases for that purpose.

Many networks can also be found on the Internet under "investor network" or "capital network." Entrepreneurs should research a network before paying any fees to ensure that it is a reputable firm that has actually helped other entrepreneurs to obtain funds.

> **Active partner –** a partner who works in the business.

Partners Partners may be *active partners* who work in the business; others, known as *silent partners*, invest money and own a part of the company but do not help run it on a daily basis. More information on partnerships can be found in the legal section of the business plan.

> **Silent partner –** invests in a company but is not actively involved on a daily basis.

Venture capital firms *Venture capital firms* are companies that invest money in small businesses that have a potential to achieve extremely rapid growth and generate large profits. These firms generally prefer to invest in companies that can generate a rate of return of 25 to 40 percent compounded annually and go public within five to seven years after the investment by the venture capital firm. They also look for companies that have an excellent management team.

> **Venture capital firm –** company that invests money into small businesses that have high growth potential.

Venture capital firms often specialize in a specific industry such as biotechnology, data communications, and health care; therefore, entrepreneurs seeking venture capital should research the firms to determine which invest in their industry. The willingness of venture capital firms to invest in businesses is also affected by tax rates on capital gains. When the company goes public and the stock is sold, the firm will pay capital gains taxes on the sale of the stock. Therefore, if the venture capitalist knows that the tax rate is low, he or she may be more willing to invest. If the sale of stock is subject to a large tax, however, the cash that the venture capitalist will retain is much less and the investment is not as attractive.

An entrepreneur should also realize that since venture capital firms provide equity capital, he or she must often give up substantial ownership. A typical investment by a venture capital firm would be approximately $5 million, and it would be common for the firm to request at least 40 percent ownership in return for this investment. However, in some situations, the firm may require controlling interest (more than 50 percent), in which case the entrepreneur no longer makes the final decisions concerning the company. The advantage for the entrepreneur, though, is that the company will grow very quickly with the infusion of the funds, and the stock owned by the entrepreneur may be worth millions of dollars.

> **Private stock sale –** sale in which the stock is sold to family, friends, and acquaintances.

> **Public stock sale –** sale in which the stock is offered to the general public.

Stock sales *Stock sales* may be either *public* (stock is sold through the stock market to everyone) or *private* (stock is sold to individuals such as families,

CHECKLIST: FINANCING

1. What are your total start-up costs? $_____
2. How much will you invest from personal funds? $_____
3. How much will you obtain in other equity? $_____
   - ☐ Family and friends
     $____ invested for____percent ownership
     Dividends paid? Yes____ No____
     ____ percent of profit
     paid quarterly____ annually____
   - ☐ Private investors
     $____ invested for____percent ownership
     Dividends paid? Yes____ No____
     ____ percent of profit
     paid quarterly____ annually____
   - ☐ Venture capital
     $____ invested for____percent ownership
     Dividends paid? Yes____ No____
     ____percent of profit
     paid quarterly____ annually____
   - ☐ Silent partners
     $____ invested for____percent ownership
     Dividends paid? Yes____ No____
     ____percent of profit
     paid quarterly____ annually____
   - ☐ Other investors (specify) ____
     $____ invested for____percent ownership
     Dividends paid? Yes____ No____
     ____percent of profit
     paid quarterly____ annually____
4. How much will you borrow? $____ $_____
   - ☐ Friend and family $____ ____
     Borrowed for____ years at____percent interest
     Monthly payments of $____
   - ☐ Bank loan $____ ____
     Borrowed for____ years at____percent interest
     Monthly payments of $____
   - ☐ Finance companies $____ ____
     Borrowed for____ years at____percent interest
     Monthly payments of $____
   - ☐ Other (specify) $____ ____
     Borrowed for____ years at____percent interest
     Monthly payments of $____

(Note: #1 = #2 + #3 + #4.)

friends, and acquaintances). Public stock sales require more regulation and are more difficult to accomplish than private stock sales, although laws have been passed to minimize the regulatory burden. Through the Uniform Limited Offering Registration (ULOR) and the Small Corporate Offering Registration (SCOR), an entrepreneur may sell up to $1 million in stock and still be exempt from federal stock sale regulations. Each state must approve this process and establish its own rules, so entrepreneurs should check with the state attorney general for details.

The Cost of Financing

The business plan must also state how debt financing will be repaid and what will be given in exchange for equity funds. For loans, the plan should state the number of years over which the loan will be repaid and the interest rate. For equity, the percentage ownership must be stated along with other payments. It is common to reward investors with *dividends*, which are periodic payments based on the company's net profit. The business plan should therefore state both percentage of ownership for investors and dividends that will be paid (see the company's Financing Checklist).

> **Dividends** – periodic payments to investors based on the company's net profit.

Discussion Questions

1. Why would an entrepreneur prefer debt financing over equity financing? In what situations would equity financing be better than debt financing?

2. The federal, state, and local governments have established financing programs to help small businesses. However, many people believe that this interferes with the free market system. Give arguments supporting government assistance for small businesses. Then give arguments stating why this would be considered interference in the free market system.

3. Consider the criteria listed for a bank loan. Which of the criteria is most likely to be an obstacle for an entrepreneur seeking bank financing?

Endnotes

1. Small Business Administration, "1999 Small Business Lending in the United States," http://www.sba.gov.

2. Ibid.

3. U.S. Census Bureau, *1997 Statistical Abstract of the United States* (Washington, DC: U.S. Department of Commerce, Bureau of the Census), 549; and http://www.sba.gov/cgi-bin/loan-approvalsal.pl.

The Business Plan

PROJECTED FINANCIAL STATEMENTS

LEARNING OBJECTIVES

- $ To understand the different methods of accounting.
- $ To be able to prepare an opening-day balance sheet.
- $ To be able to prepare a projected income statement.
- $ To comprehend the concept of cash flow and be able to complete a projected statement of cash flow.

The projected financial statements that are included in the business plan are the opening-day balance sheet, the projected income statements, and the projected cash flow statements. Before describing these, a discussion of accounting methods is necessary because several different methods are used to develop financial statements.

ACCOUNTING METHODS

Cash Basis

Cash basis of accounting – records a sale when payment is received from the customers and records an expense when the bill is paid.

The cash basis is the simplest method and easiest to use. The *cash basis* records a sale when payment is received from the customer and records an expense when the bill is paid. For some businesses, especially service businesses that do not extend credit, this method works well and can be used for management purposes and for tax purposes. However, the cash basis does not always provide an accurate picture of the financial status of the company. Also, for companies that extend credit to their customers, the cash basis does not work well because the cash received from customers is not necessarily an accurate reflection of sales. Collections from customers may lag behind sales, making sales appear lower than they actually are.

Accrual Basis

Accrual basis of accounting – records sales when they are made and records expenses when they are incurred.

The *accrual basis* records sales when they are made and records expenses when they are incurred. This method is not as simple as the cash method but gives an accurate picture of the financial health of the company. For companies that carry inventory and/or those that extend credit, the accrual basis is the best method to use.

Completed-Contract Method

Completed-contract method – records revenue as a project progresses and records a corresponding amount of expenses.

Some firms, such as construction companies, work on projects that extend over many months. In these instances, it would give an inaccurate portrayal of the company if no expenses or income were recorded until the project was completed. For this reason, a method known as the *completed-contract method* is used. The customer is often billed as the project progresses (for example at increments of 25, 50, and 75 percent completion), and corresponding amounts of expenses for materials and labor are recorded at the same time. This presents a more accurate picture of the income and expenses than if the cash or accrual method were used.

BALANCE SHEET

Balance sheet – compares the possessions of a company and the debts it owes on a specific day.

The *balance sheet* compares the possessions of a company and the debts it owes on a specific day. Therefore, while the income statement records profit or loss over a period of time, the balance sheet shows the financial situation on a certain day.

Assets

Assets – company's possessions, including tangible or intangible items.

A company's possessions, called *assets,* may be tangible items such as machinery and equipment, or they may be intangible assets such as a patent or goodwill. On the balance sheet, assets are divided into several categories—current, fixed, and other.

Current assets are those that are easily converted into cash and include the following:

$ *Cash.* All cash on hand in the business and in the business checking and savings accounts is recorded.

$ *Accounts receivable.* If a company extends credit and customers owe for purchases, this is a company asset because it is money that will be received in the future.

$ *Inventory.* All items available for resale are current assets. In a manufacturing firm, the inventory may be separated into two categories—raw materials and finished goods.

$ *Supplies.* All supplies such as shop supplies, office supplies, and bags and boxes for customers' packages would be included.

$ *Prepaid expenses.* The prepaid expenses listed in start-up costs are considered a current asset.

Fixed assets are items that are more permanent in nature and are used in the business. These include the following:

$ *Machinery, equipment, furniture, fixtures.* All items listed in your start-up costs in these categories would be fixed assets.

$ *Land and buildings.* If you purchase land and a building or if you construct a building, this would be shown in the amount of the price paid or the construction costs.

$ *Renovations.* If you spend money for renovations to leased property, this is considered a business asset even though you do not own the property.

$ *Vehicles.* This includes all company cars, trucks, and so on.

A company may have assets that do not fall into these categories. For example, if you are required to pay deposits for leases or utilities, the money is often held for several years before it is returned. For this reason, it is not considered a current asset and is therefore placed in a category called *other assets*. Similarly, a company may have intangible assets such as goodwill or patents; these are included as other assets.

Liabilities

The *liabilities* section of the balance sheet includes all debts the company owes. As with the assets, the liabilities are categorized. Liabilities are classified as *current* (those that must be paid within 12 months) and *long-term* (those that are due more than one year after the date of the balance sheet).

Current liabilities are as follows.

$ *Accounts payable.* All bills due for inventory and supplies are included in *accounts payable.*

$ *Accrued expenses.* Bills due for utilities and other miscellaneous expenses are considered *accrued expenses.* Also, if employees are paid every two weeks and wages are owed to them when the balance sheet is prepared, these would be included.

$ *Notes payable.* Any short-term loans that are due within 12 months from the date of the balance sheet are considered a current liability. Loan payments include both principal (loan repayment) and interest. Only the principal is recorded on the balance sheet.

TABLE B–9 Calculation of current and long-term portions of a loan

Loan Amount	Payback	Interest	First-year Payment	First-year Current Portion	Long-term Debt
$10,000 (van)	3 years	10%	$4,020 1,000 interest 3,020 principal	$3,020	$6,980 ($10,000 – $3,020)
$20,000 (equipment)	4 years	12%	$6,584 2,400 interest 4,184 principal	$4,184	$15,816 ($20,000 – $4,184)
$100,000 (building)	15 years	10%	$13,147 10,000 interest 3,147 principal	$3,147	$96,853 ($100,000 – $3,147)

$ *Current portion of long-term debt.* Even if a loan is to be repaid over several years, a portion of the loan is due within the next year. That principal portion due within the next 12 months is considered the *current portion of long-term debt.* For example, if loan principal of $10,000 is due over a five-year period, and $3,000 of that amount is due within the next year, the $3,000 is considered the current portion of the long-term debt.

> **Long-term liabilities** – debts that are due more than 12 months from the date of the balance sheet.

Long-term liabilities are debts or portions of debts that are due more than 12 months from the date of the balance sheet. Sample loan amounts with estimated monthly payments, current portion, and long-term portion are shown in Table B-9. The current portion of the debt is subtracted from the total. This is shown in the table as well as on the sample balance sheet in Figure B-10.

> **Equity** – assets minus liabilities.

Equity

Another category on the balance sheet is called the *equity, net worth,* or *capital account.* This account represents the difference between the assets and liabilities. Total assets minus total liabilities must equal net worth or equity. The equity includes all of the money the entrepreneur has invested from personal funds as well

> **Retained earnings** – an accumulation of all profits and losses the company has generated.

as retained earnings. *Retained earnings* is an accumulation of all profits and losses of the company from the day it began until the day the balance sheet is prepared. If the company makes a profit, retained earnings (and, therefore, equity) increases; if the company loses money, retained earnings (and, therefore, equity) decreases. Although the total equity figure does not necessarily represent the market value of the company, it is an important figure because financial institutions often compare the total liabilities to the total equity if the company applies for a loan.

OPENING-DAY BALANCE SHEET

The opening-day balance sheet will correspond to the start-up costs of the business. For example, suppose start-up costs for a gift shop total $140,000, as shown here:

Inventory	$60,000
Furniture and fixtures	15,000

Assets

Current assets:

Cash (working capital)	$20,000	
Supplies	2,000	
Prepaid expenses	4,000	
Inventory	60,000	
Total current assets		$86,000

Fixed assets:

Furniture and fixtures	$15,000	
Machinery and equipment	10,000	
Renovations	25,000	
Total fixed assets		$50,000

Other assets	$4,000	
Deposits		$4,000
Total assets		$140,000

Liabilities

Current liabilities

Current portion of long-term debt	$10,540	
Total current liabilities		$10,540

Long-term liabilities

Note payable	$100,000	
Less: current portion	10,540	
Total long-term liabilities		$89,460
Total liabilities		$100,000

Equity		$40,000
Total liabilities and equity		$140,000

FIGURE B–10   The gift shop opening-day balance sheet.

Machinery and equipment	10,000
Prepaid expenses	4,000
Supplies	2,000
Deposits	4,000
Building renovations	25,000
Working capital	20,000
Total start-up costs	$140,000

The owner plans to invest $40,000 of her own money and borrow $100,000 from the bank for seven years at 10 percent interest. The monthly payments would be approximately $1,712. The first-year total loan payments would be $20,540 and would include $10,000 in interest and $10,540 in principal. The opening-day balance sheet for this company is shown in Figure B-10.

PROJECTED INCOME STATEMENT

The income statement is completed on a periodic basic and records sales, cost of goods sold, expenses, and profit or loss.

$ *Sales.* On the income statement, the *sales* of a company may be listed as "sales," "income," or "revenue," depending on the type of company. If the statements are completed on an accrual basis, this represents the sales that have been generated, not necessarily those for which payment has been received.

$ *Cost of goods sold. Cost of goods sold* includes any costs for products, materials, or labor that are directly related to the sale. In a retail firm, cost of goods sold is the cost paid to suppliers for inventory. In service firms such as housecleaning or maid service businesses, the product cost is small, but labor is a major part of the cost of goods sold. In construction firms, both labor and materials costs are often included for different firms. Some of the more common calculations are shown in Figure B-11.

$ *Gross margin. Gross margin,* or *gross profit,* is the difference between sales and cost of goods sold. It shows the markup on the sales or activity of the company. For example, if a company has sales of $100,000 and cost of goods sold of $60,000, the gross margin would be $40,000. Thus, it could be said that the company has a markup on sales of 40 percent ($40,000/$100,000).

$ *Operating expenses. Operating expenses* include ongoing expenditures that occur in the process of selling and managing the company. As a company grows, the operating expenses may have subcategories such as "selling expenses" and "general and administrative expenses."

Sales – revenue a company has generated during a specific period of time.

Cost of goods sold – includes any costs for products, materials, or labor directly related to the sale.

Gross margin or gross profit – the difference between sales and cost of goods sold.

Operating expenses – ongoing expenditures that occur in the process of selling and managing a company.

Cost of Goods Sold for a Retail Gift Shop
Beginning inventory
+ Purchases
+ Freight
− Ending inventory
= Cost of goods sold

Cost of Goods Sold for a Construction Firm
Direct material
+ Direct labor
= Cost of goods sold

Cost of Goods Sold for a Manufacturing Firm
Beginning inventory of raw material
+ Purchases
+ Freight-in
− Ending inventory of raw material
+ Direct labor
= Cost of goods sold

FIGURE B–11   Cost-of-goods-sold calculations for various industries.

Sales	$_____
Cost of goods sold	
Beginning inventory	$_____
+ Purchases	+_____
+ Freight	+_____
− Ending inventory	−_____
= Cost of goods sold	$_____
Gross margin	$_____
Expenses:	
Officer's salary	$_____
Employee wages	_____
Accounting/legal	_____
Advertising	_____
Rent	_____
Depreciation	_____
Supplies	_____
Utilities	_____
Telephone	_____
Interest	_____
Repairs	_____
Taxes	_____
Insurance	_____
Miscellaneous	_____
Credit card fees	_____
Dues/subscriptions	_____
Total expenses	$_____
Net profit	$_____
Income taxes	_____
Net profit after taxes	$_____
For planning purposes, compute the following:	
Net profit	$_____
Less: Income taxes	_____
Less: Loan principal*	_____
Net cash	$_____

*Discussed in section on cash flow.

FIGURE B–12   Sample income statement for a corporation.

There is one major difference on the income statement between a proprietorship and a corporation owner. The corporation owner's salary is a tax-deductible expense. The money that is taken by a proprietor or a partner is not a tax-deductible expense and is not shown on the income statement. The sample income statements for a corporation (Figure B-12) and a proprietorship or partnership (Figure B-13) show this difference.

Sales	$_____
Cost of goods sold	
Beginning inventory	$_____
+ Purchases	+_____
+ Freight	+_____
− Ending inventory	−_____
= Cost of goods sold	$_____
Gross margin	$_____
Expenses:	
Employee wages	_____
Accounting/legal	_____
Advertising	_____
Rent	_____
Depreciation	_____
Supplies	_____
Utilities	_____
Telephone	_____
Interest	_____
Repairs	_____
Taxes	_____
Insurance	_____
Miscellaneous	_____
Credit card fees	_____
Dues/subscriptions	_____
Total expenses	$_____
Net profit	$_____
Less: Income taxes	_____
Less: Self-employment tax	_____
Net profit after taxes	$_____

Note that the owner's wages have not been subtracted anywhere on the income statement. However, the money must come out of the business; therefore, the following format is recommended for planning purposes.

Net profit	$_____
Less: Income taxes	_____
Less: Self-employment tax	_____
Less: Owner's wages	_____
Less: Loan principal	_____
Net cash	$_____

FIGURE B–13   Sample income statement for a proprietorship or partnership.

Net profit – gross margin minus operating expenses.

$ *Net profit. Net profit* is equal to gross margin minus operating expenses. The full amount is not available to the entrepreneur, however, since income taxes and other cash outlays must be deducted from this sum.

A sample income statement for Fine Wines, Inc., a retail shop, is shown in Figure B-14.

CASH FLOW

Many entrepreneurs are surprised to find that a "profitable" business may not be able to pay all of the bills that come due. This is caused by several factors. First, several bills must be paid out of the profit the company makes. These bills do not appear as expenses on the income statement, but they must be paid nonetheless. Several other factors (the extension of credit to customers, seasonality, and so forth) also affect the cash balance of a company. These factors are discussed next. See also Table B-10, which contrasts the cash flow statement with the income statement.

$ *The proprietor's or partner's salary.* As stated earlier, these are not expenses and do not appear as tax-deductible operating expenses. They do drain cash out of the company, however.

$ *The principal paid on a loan.* As stated in the section on financing start-up costs, a loan repayment consist of two parts, the actual loan repayment (principal) and the interest. Notice that the sample income statements in Figure B-12 through B-14 show the interest as an operating expense. The principal is not included; it must be paid out of profits.

$ *Increases in inventory.* If a store begins the year with $100,000 in inventory and ends the year with $125,000 in inventory, the increase does not decrease profit. The inventory purchases are added in "purchases" in cost of goods sold but the increase is subtracted in "ending inventory." The net effect on profit is therefore 0. The example in Figure B-15 shows financial information for two stores that are identical except that one increases inventory and the other keeps inventory constant. Notice that the net profit is identical, but Store #2 purchased (and must pay for) $50,000 more inventory than Store #1. Thus, cash will be affected by inventory increases, but the profit will not change.

$ *Accounts receivable.* The lag between the time a sale is made and the time the money is collected (which creates accounts receivable) from the

TABLE B–10   The income statement versus the cash flow statement

Income Statement (Accrual Method)	Cash Flow Statement
Shows sales as they are generated.	Shows sales as "Cash in" only when the money is received.
Depreciation is shown.	If depreciation is included as an expense, it must be added back in since it is not a cash expense.
Interest on the loan is listed.	Both interest and principal are included (often combined on one line titled "Loan Payment").
Beginning inventory and ending inventory are included in the calculation of cost of goods sold.	Inventory purchases are recorded as the bills are paid.
A proprietor's salary is not shown as an expense.	A proprietor's salary is shown as the money is withdrawn.

Sales	$700,000
Cost of goods sold	
Beginning inventory	$125,000
+ Purchases	+530,000
+ Freight	+ 10,000
− Ending inventory	− 115,000
= Cost of goods sold	$550,000
Gross margin	$150,000
Expenses:	
Officer's salary	$ 22,000
Employee wages	34,500
Accounting/legal	1,500
Advertising	9,200
Rent	23,500
Depreciation	5,100
Supplies	3,200
Utilities	6,250
Telephone	2,300
Interest	6,400
Repairs	1,300
Taxes	6,200
Insurance	2,500
Miscellaneous	1,500
Credit card fees	7,100
Dues/subscriptions	500
Total expenses	$133,050
Net profit	$ 16,950

FIGURE B–14   Sample income statement, Fine Wines, Inc.

	Store #1	Store #2
Sales	$200,000	$200,000
Cost of goods sold		
Beginning inventory	$100,000	$100,000
+ Purchases	+ 75,000	+125,000
+ Freight	+ 5,000	+ 5,000
− Ending inventory	−100,000	−150,000
= Cost of goods sold	$ 80,000	$ 80,000
Gross margin	$120,000	$120,000
Expenses	100,000	100,000
Net profit	$ 20,000	$ 20,000

Note that the profit of both stores is identical; however, Store #2 has $50,000 more in inventory purchases ($125,000 compared to $75,000). Thus, if both companies start with an equal amount of cash, Store #2 will have much less cash than Store #1.

FIGURE B–15   Inventory purchases and profit.

customer will have a definite impact on the cash balance of the company. If the company must pay for labor and/or materials costs to complete a job but must wait 30 or 60 days to receive the customer's payment, this will cause cash shortages.

$ *Seasonality.* Most businesses have peak sales seasons and other times when sales are slow. This results in periodic cash shortages even though the company is profitable for the year as a whole.

$ *Depreciation.* Depreciation is one factor that affects profitability but does not affect cash. When fixed assets are *depreciated*, a portion of the total cost is shown as an expense each year. However, this is not necessarily the same amount as the payments on the asset. For example, an entrepreneur may buy a van for $20,000 by paying a $10,000 down payment and financing the balance for five years. The payments would be based on the $10,000 balance, but the full $20,000 cost would be depreciated over five years. For this reason, companies with a high depreciation expense often show a small profit or even show a loss, but since there is no depreciation "payment," the company may have adequate cash.

> **Depreciation** – an expense that records a portion of the cost of a fixed asset in each accounting per 100.

CASE STUDY: THE TRAVEL SCHOOL

The following is an illustration of projected financial information for a new business, The Travel School. The example includes start-up costs, the opening-day balance sheet, the projected income statement, and the projected cash flow. The business, a corporation, was established to provide training for travel agents and airline reservationists. Because it is a service (training), there is no cost of goods sold or inventory. Several factors should be noted. First, notice the connection between the start-up costs and the balance sheet (see Figure B-16), as discussed in the previous section. The categories in the cash flow projection are not identical to the categories on the income statement (see Figure B-17). Also note that the working capital of $55,700 shown in start-up costs is the beginning cash amount on the cash flow projection (Figure B-18).

Discussion Questions

1. What is the difference between a current asset and a fixed asset?
2. Consider the three accounting methods discussed in this section. How do they vary? Why would a company choose one method over another?
3. Why does the opening-day balance sheet correspond to the start-up costs?
4. Identify three industries in which labor should be recorded as part of cost of goods sold.
5. If a proprietorship shows a net profit of $10,000 and a corporation shows the same net profit, why are the companies not equally profitable?
6. What is the difference between an operating expense and a start-up cost?
7. Why would a profitable business not be able to pay its bills?
8. If a company shows a loss each year but has a very large depreciation expense, is that company in financial trouble? Why or why not?
9. Although most businesses should have three to six months of working capital, many new businesses need much more even if they are profitable. What factors would increase the amount of working capital a company needs?

Start-up Costs

Working capital	$55,700
Supplies	3,900
Grand opening advertising	2,000
Legal fees	2,000
Computers and software	16,400
Phone system	1,600
Furniture and fixtures	8,400
Total start-up costs	$90,000
Owner's investment	40,000
Amount borrowed	$50,000

Opening-Day Balance Sheet

Current assets:		
Cash	$55,700	
Supplies	3,900	
Prepaid advertising	2,000	
Prepaid legal fees	2,000	
Total current assets		$63,600
Fixed assets:		
Computers and software	$16,400	
Phone system	1,600	
Furniture and fixtures	8,400	
Total fixed assets		$26,400
Total assets		$90,000
Current liabilities:		
Current maturity of long-term debt	$8,523	
Total current liabilities		$8,523
Long-term liabilities:		
Notes payable	$50,000	
Less: Current maturity	8,523	
Long-term liabilities		$41,477
Total liabilities		$50,000
Equity:		
Common stock	$40,000	
Retained earnings	0	
Total equity		$40,000
Total liabilities and equity		$90,000

FIGURE B–16   The Travel School start-up costs and opening-day balance sheet.

BREAK-EVEN POINT

Learning Objectives

$ To be able to identify fixed and variable expenses.

$ To comprehend the concept of contribution margin and how to calculate it.

$ To understand and know how to determine the break-even point for a company.

Sales	$185,000
Expenses:	
Rent	$36,000
Telephone	1,500
Advertising	12,000
Insurance	2,400
Equipment leases	7,800
Office supplies	1,200
Car phone lease	780
Officer's salary	24,996
Employee wages	51,000
Employee taxes	8,360
Accounting and legal	6,000
Repairs and maintenance	2,400
Auto expense	1,200
Depreciation	5,280
Interest	4,000
Total expenses	$164,916
Net profit	$20,084
Less: Income taxes	3,013
Profit after taxes	$17,071

FIGURE B–17   The Travel School projected income statement (first year).

$ To realize if the break-even point is very high, the business may not be feasible.

$ To know how it is helpful to calculate both the sales volume and the number of customers needed to break even.

What Is Your Break-Even Point?

It is helpful to the entrepreneur to calculate the *break-even point*, the minimum amount of sales necessary for the company's survival. Often when the break-even point is calculated, it is obvious that the business is not feasible. For example, one entrepreneur who planned to open a women's clothing store calculated that he would need to sell a minimum of $1,000 per day in order to survive. Based on his location and the size of the proposed store, he knew that this was not possible and he did not open the business. Thus, calculating the break-even point may prevent an entrepreneur from making a costly mistake.

Break-even point – the minimum amount of sales necessary for the company's survival.

Have You Identified Fixed and Variable Expenses?

One of the first steps needed to determine the break-even point is to separate the company's expenses into two categories—fixed and variable. *Fixed expenses* are those that are not affected by the sales volume of the company. For example, if a company's lease agreement states that the rent will be $3,000 per month, the company will pay this amount every month no matter what the sales volume is. Thus, it would be a fixed expense. Conversely, if the lease agreement states that the rent will be 7 percent of sales, the rent is then a *variable expense* because it will increase

Fixed expenses – expenses that do not fluctuate with the company's sales volume.

	Feb.	March	April	May	June	July	August	Sept.	Oct.	Nov.	Dec.	Jan.
Beginning cash	$55,700	$41,921	$31,230	$21,659	$17,112	$14,054	$12,736	$12,375	$11,865	$25,188	$27,760	$23,229
Cash in	218	1,606	2,726	7,500	10,464	12,204	14,636	14,657	28,540	17,039	9,961	10,027
Cash available	$55,918	$43,527	$33,956	$29,159	$27,576	$26,258	$27,372	$27,032	$40,405	$42,227	$37,721	$33,256
Cash out:												
Rent	$3,000	$3,000	$3,000	$3,000	$3,000	$3,000	$3,000	$3,000	$3,000	$3,000	$3,000	$3,000
Telephone	125	125	125	125	125	125	125	125	125	125	125	125
Advertising	1,500	1,000	1,000	750	750	750	1,000	1,500	1,500	750	750	750
Insurance	1,200	0	0	0	0	0	1,200	0	0	0	0	0
Equipment lease	650	650	650	650	650	650	650	650	650	650	650	650
Office supplies	50	50	50	50	75	75	100	100	150	150	175	175
Car phone	65	65	65	65	65	65	65	65	65	65	65	65
Officer's salary	2,083	2,083	2,083	2,083	2,083	2,083	2,083	2,083	2,083	2,083	2,083	2,083
Employee wages	3,000	3,000	3,000	3,000	4,250	4,250	4,250	5,000	5,000	5,000	5,000	6,250
Employee taxes	480	480	480	480	680	680	680	800	800	800	800	1,200
Accounting/legal	500	500	500	500	500	500	500	500	500	500	500	500
Repairs/maintenance	200	200	200	200	200	200	200	200	200	200	200	200
Auto	100	100	100	100	100	100	100	100	100	100	100	100
Loan payment	1,044	1,044	1,044	1,044	1,044	1,044	1,044	1,044	1,044	1,044	1,044	1,044
Total cash out	$13,997	$12,297	$12,297	$12,047	$13,522	$13,522	$14,997	$15,167	$15,217	$14,467	$14,492	$16,142
Cash balance	$41,921	$31,230	$21,659	$17,112	$14,054	$12,736	$12,375	$11,865	$25,188	$27,760	$23,229	$17,114

Note: This cash flow does not show a cost for inventory purchases because it is a service business and does not carry inventory. If a business buys and sells inventory, the cost for purchases must be shown under "Cash out."

FIGURE B–18   The Travel School projected cash flow (first 12 months, beginning in February).

or decrease with the sales volume. Similarly, if an employee receives a salary of $1,500 per month, this is a fixed expense; if the employee is also paid a commission based on sales, that part would be variable.

The distinction between fixed and variable is often vague. For example, we stated that the employee's monthly salary of $1,500 is a fixed expense. However, if sales are too low, the employee would be laid off; therefore, it might be argued that this is a variable expense. For business plan purposes, it is helpful to calculate the break-even point based on the income statement you have projected. Thus, if you projected employee wages at $1,500 per month with no commissions on the income statement, consider that a fixed expense. Most expenses such as rent, utilities, insurance, and equipment lease costs should be considered fixed.

> **Variable expenses** – increase or decrease with fluctuations in sales.

What Is Your Contribution Margin?

Another step in the break-even calculation is determining the contribution margin. The *contribution margin* is calculated by dividing gross profit by the sales volume. This can be calculated on a per-unit basis, or it can be determined by looking at the projected income statement.

> **Contribution margin** – gross profit divided by sales margin.

For example, refer to the income statement for the Fine Wines store in Figure B-14. Sales are estimated at $700,000, cost of goods sold is estimated at $550,000, and the gross margin (gross profit) is estimated at $150,000. Assume that all expenses are fixed except for supplies expense of $3,200 and credit card fees of $7,100. These two expenses are variable expenses. Then, the contribution margin would be calculated as follows:

Cost of goods sold is 78.57 percent of sales (550,000/700,000). Supplies expense is .46 percent of sales (3,200/700,000). Credit card fees are 1.01 percent of sales (7,100/700,000). Therefore, the total variable expenses are .7857 + .0046 + .0101 = .8004. The contribution margin is 100 percent − 80.04 percent = 1.00 − .8004 = .1996 or 19.96 percent.

Notice that for service businesses such as The Travel School, the companies do not show a cost of goods sold. Therefore, the sales volume and the gross profits are the same.

Calculating the Break-Even Point

The break-even point is determined by dividing fixed expenses by the contribution margin. For example, the Fine Wines store shows total expenses of $133,050 for the first year. However, since the supplies expense and the credit card fees are variable expenses, the fixed expenses are determined by subtracting the variable expenses from the total expenses. Therefore, fixed expenses are $133,050 − $3,200 − $7,100 = $122,750. We have already determined that the contribution margin is .1996; therefore, the break-even point is $122.750/.1996 = $614,980. If the company's sales volume the first year is $614,980, the net profit will be $0. If sales are higher than the break-even point, the company will make a profit; if sales are lower, the company will incur a loss.

For The Travel School, total expenses are $164,916. If all of these expenses are fixed except for office supplies of $1,200, fixed expenses total $163,716 ($164,916 − $1,200). Since there is no cost of goods sold, the break-even point is $163,716 (equal to the fixed expenses).

How Many Customers Are Needed to Break Even?

It is helpful to determine how many customers per day are needed to reach your break-even point. The first step is to determine how much a typical customer will spend each time he or she makes a purchase. Although it will vary from one customer to the next, the entrepreneur must determine the average dollar amount for each customer. For example, the Fine Wines store may sell one customer a bottle of wine for $10 and another customer may buy several bottles of more expensive wine for a total purchase of $45. The average would be $27.50 ($10.00 + $45.00 = $55.00/2 = $27.50). Since the break-even point is $614,980 and the average customer spends $27.50, it will take 22,363 customers per year ($614,980/$27.50) to survive. If the store is open 360 days per year, 62 customers per day will be needed to reach the break-even point (22,363 customers/360 days)

For some businesses, there is no need to calculate an average because each customer will spend the same amount. For example, The Travel School offers only one program for $2,000. Thus each customer will spend exactly $2,000. Since the break-even point is $163,716 and each student pays $2,000, approximately 82 customers will be needed the first year to break even ($163,716/$2,000 = 81.8).

See the Determining the Break-Even Point Checklist for assistance.

Discussion Questions

1. Completing a break-even analysis early in the business planning process may save the entrepreneur a lot of wasted effort. Why?

2. Why is it helpful to calculate both the sales volume and the number of customers needed to reach the break-even point?

3. What is the difference between a fixed and a variable expense?

CHECKLIST: DETERMINING THE BREAK-EVEN POINT

☐ 1. Categorize all of your operating expenses as "fixed" and "variable."
Sample:

Expense	Fixed	Variable
Rent	$3,000/Yr	
Office supplies		$1,200/Yr
_____	_____	_____
_____	_____	_____
_____	_____	_____
Total	_____	_____

☐ 2. Determine your contribution margin.
    ☐ a. Projected sales for the first year
    ☐ b. Projected cost of goods sold for the first year
    ☐ c. Divide *b* by *a* (*b/a*)
        Sample: sales = $200,000
        Cost of goods sold = $50,000
           50,000/200,000 = .25
    ☐ d. Total the variable expenses
        Sample: supplies = $1,200
        Credit card fees = $5,000
        Total $6,200
    ☐ e. Divide *d* by *a* (*d/a*)
        Sample: 6,200/200,000 = .031
    ☐ f. Add *c* plus *e* (*c* + *e*)
        Sample: .25 + .031 = .281
    ☐ g. Subtract: *f* from 1.0 (1.0 − *f*)
        Sample: 1.0 − .281 = .719

☐ 3. Determine your break-even point.
    ☐ a. Total fixed expenses
    ☐ b. Contribution margin
    ☐ c. Divide *a* by *b* (*a/b*)
        Sample: Fixed expenses for the first year = $70,000
        Contribution margin = .719
        Break-even point = $70,000/.719 = $97,357 in sales the first year

☐ 4. Determine the number of customers needed to reach the break-even point.
    ☐ a. Break-even point in dollars (3c) $_____
    ☐ b. Average amount of a customer's purchase $ _____
    ☐ c. Divide *a* by *b* (*a/b*) to get the number of customers for the first year _____
    ☐ d. Divide answer in *c* by the number of days the company is open each year to get the number of
        customers per day_____
        Sample: Break-even point = $97,357
        Average customer purchase = $10
        Number of customers per year = $97,357/$10 = 9,736
        If the business is open 360 days per year, the number of customers needed per day is 9,736/360 = 27

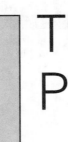

The Business Plan

THE LEGAL SECTION

LEARNING OBJECTIVES

$ To be aware of the many forms of organization available for small businesses.

$ To understand the tax consequences of each form of organization.

$ To realize that the entrepreneur's liability is a major factor in choosing a form of organization.

All entrepreneurs will encounter legal issues throughout the time they operate the business. When planning a business, the entrepreneur must select a form of organization; determine whether copyrights, patents, or trademarks will be needed; have contracts written and/or reviewed by a lawyer; and identify the type of taxes that will be due. See the Legal Section Checklist for a summary of these issues.

WHAT FORM OF ORGANIZATION WILL YOU CHOOSE?

The form of organization is one of the first legal decisions an entrepreneur must make. This may be decided after researching the alternatives, or it may be necessary to consult a lawyer. The following sections discuss some of the most important advantages and disadvantages of common alternatives.

Sole Proprietorship

The most common form of organization for a small business is the *sole proprietorship*. Sole proprietorships are unincorporated businesses owned by a single person. Of approximately 25 million nonfarm businesses in existence in 2000, 71.6 percent were sole proprietorships (see Figure B-19).[1]

> **Sole proprietorship** – unincorporated business owned by a single person.

Advantages This is the most common form of organization because it is easy to start; it requires fewer legal documents than other organizational forms. And because there is only one owner, that entrepreneur makes all of the decisions, takes credit for all of the success, and can determine how profits will be spent.

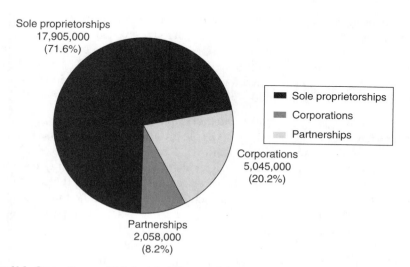

Sole proprietorships
17,905,000
(71.6%)

- Sole proprietorships
- Corporations
- Partnerships

Corporations
5,045,000
(20.2%)

Partnerships
2,058,000
(8.2%)

Source: U.S. Census Bureau, *2003 Statistical Abstract of the United States,* http://www.census.gov/prod/2004pubs/03Statab/business.pdf.

FIGURE B–19   Organizational forms of U.S. businesses.

CHECKLIST: LEGAL SECTION

☐ What organizational form will you choose?
☐ Why did you choose that form?
☐ What taxes will the company be required to pay?
☐ Does the company have any patents, copyrights, trademarks, or trade secrets?
☐ Does the company have any contracts or exclusive agreements with suppliers, customers, employees, and so on?

Disadvantages The biggest disadvantage of a sole proprietorship concerns liability because the business and the entrepreneur are considered the same legal entity. The entrepreneur, therefore, has *unlimited liability;* if someone sues the company, or if the company goes bankrupt, the entrepreneur may lose both personal and business assets. Adequate insurance may protect against lawsuits, but there is no insurance against the financial failure of the firm.

> **Unlimited liability –** the company owner may lose both business and personal assets.

The lack of other stockholders and partners also limits the company. The entrepreneur must bear the entire burden of responsibility, handle all functions of the business, and raise financing using only personal assets. For these reasons, the company may not grow as quickly as a company that has several owners.

Partnership

There are two common forms of partnerships—general and limited. In a *general partnership*, all partners have unlimited liability, just like sole proprietors. In a *limited partnership,* investors designated as limited partners cannot lose more than the amount invested.

> **General partnership –** all partners have unlimited liability.

Advantages of a general partnership General partnerships have two or more owners; thus, the burden of work may be shared by several people, each of whom may have expertise in a different area. Also, there are several people to invest money and more personal assets to help raise financing. General partnerships are not legally required to have a written partnership agreement, but if one is not developed, many problems are likely to result.

> **Limited partnership –** investors designated as limited partners cannot lose more than the amount invested.

Disadvantages of a general partnership As stated previously, the general partners have unlimited liability just as sole proprietors do. A lawsuit or financial failure of the company could result in the loss of personal assets. And, unless otherwise stated in the partnership agreement, each partner is fully responsible for debts. If a company is owned by three general partners and the company has a $100,000 loan, the bank may hold each partner liable for the full amount. The partners are also liable for the actions of other partners; if one partner signs an agreement for the company, the other partners may be held liable. A general partnership legally ends when a partner withdraws or dies.

Limited partnerships are different from general partnerships in several aspects. The advantages and disadvantages are discussed next.

Advantages of a limited partnership The limited partners have protection from full liability. They may lose the money they invest, but they are not liable for other company debts or if the company is involved in a lawsuit. Limited partners may not take an active role in the daily management of the company, however, so there must be at least one general partner who has full liability and who operates the business on a daily basis. Limited partners may sell their ownership in the company; the partnership does not end if a limited partner sells ownership or dies.

Disadvantages of a limited partnership A limited partner cannot take an active role in the daily management of the company. Therefore, a limited partner must be willing to invest money knowing that he or she will have limited control. Disagreements may develop between the general partner who manages the business and the limited partners who have invested money. A limited partnership will also need more legal documents than a general partnership. A certificate of limited partnership must be filed with the state; the partnership agreement may also be more complicated.

The following list of questions about partnerships highlights the issues entrepreneurs should be aware of when considering partnerships.

$ *Time.* How much time will each partner invest in the business?

$ *Decision-making authority.* What decisions need the agreement of all partners? What decisions can be made without the other partners' consent?

$ *Money.* How much money will each partner invest? If additional money must be invested, how will the additional money be raised? How will salaries and bonuses be determined?

$ *Buy/sell pricing.* If one partner wishes to sell his or her ownership, does the other partner have the first right of refusal? How will the value of the ownership interest be determined?

Corporation

Entrepreneurs may consider two types of corporations— a C corporation and an S corporation. A *corporation* is a legal entity separate from its owners. The owners, known as the *stockholders*, are issued stock certificates, which document their ownership. Some states require a corporation to have several owners; other states allow a single owner as long as there are at least three officers. The officers attend board meetings and vote on issues presented. The owners have control over most operating decisions. With a *C corporation*, the company net profit remains separate from the owner's personal income. The corporation profit is taxed at corporate rates; the owner records salary and dividends on the personal income tax return. With an *S corporation,* the corporation does not pay income taxes. The company profit is transferred to the owner's personal tax return, is added to salary and dividends, and is taxed at personal tax rates. The advantages and disadvantages of corporations follow.

Advantages One of the benefits of incorporating is that all the owners have *limited liability;* a lawsuit filed against the company cannot result in loss of personal assets. If the corporation goes bankrupt, personal assets cannot be taken by creditors to compensate for the loss. It must be stated, however, that many entrepreneurs are required to sign "personal guarantees" when borrowing funds from a bank. If a personal guarantee is given, the bank has the right to seize personal assets to pay for corporate debts. Thus, in this case, limited liability does not apply.

Corporation owners may sell their stock without affecting the legal existence of the company. Additional stock may be sold even after the company is operating

Corporation – a legal entity separate from its owners.

Stockholders – the owners of a corporation.

C corporation – business in which the net profit remains separate from the owner's personal tax return.

S corporation – business structure in which the profit is transferred to the owner's personal tax return.

Limited liability – a lawsuit filed against the company cannot result in loss of owner's personal assets.

in order to raise additional capital. Change in stock ownership or the death of a stockholder does not terminate the corporation.

Meeting minutes – a record of the discussion and votes that occur during a corporation's board meetings.

Disadvantages The biggest disadvantage of a corporation is the additional legal requirements. When corporations are formed, the owners must develop (usually with the help of a lawyer) articles of incorporation and corporate bylaws. Each corporation must have a board of directors and must hold annual meetings at which the *minutes* (discussions and votes) are recorded. Compared to proprietorships and partnerships, there may also be more paperwork required if a corporation wants to expand its business into other states.

S corporations are bound by even more restrictions than C corporations. S corporations can have only one type of stock (common, not preferred), and stockholders must be individuals, not other corporations. Because of these (and other) restrictions, many entrepreneurs find that the S corporation is not a good alternative. In recent years, the limited liability company has often been chosen in place of the S corporation.

Limited Liability Company

Limited liability company – corporate structure that provides limited liability to the company owner, but the company is taxed like a partnership.

A newer form of organization known as the *limited liability company* (*LLC*) is now available in all 50 states and the District of Columbia. An LLC provides the benefits of both a corporation and a partnership. The investors in an LLC are known as *members* (not stockholders or partners), but they have limited liability like stockholders of a corporation. However, the company is taxed like a partnership; the profits of the company are split among the investors and shown on their personal income tax returns.

When the company is first established, the members must file articles of organization and an operating agreement. This is similar to the articles of incorporation or the partnership agreement; it states the purpose of the business, the management structure, and the conditions under which the LLC would dissolve.[2]

Advantages LLCs are often recommended for family-owned businesses because the management and control of the company can be concentrated in the hands of a few members called *managers*, regardless of their financial stock in the company. Thus, family members who are involved in the company can be the managers while those who are inactive have no decision-making authority but still share in the profits.[3]

Disadvantages LLCs do have some potential disadvantages. Since the laws on this organizational form vary from state to state, any entrepreneur operating in more than one state needs to be familiar with each state's laws. Also LLC laws are new and many consultants believe there will be lawsuits testing the strength of the limited liability feature. It may also be costly. Good legal help is essential. There may be a state filing fee of several hundred dollars as well as the lawyer's charges to draw up the articles of organization and operating agreement.[4]

Joint Venture

Joint venture – a legal agreement between two parties to operate for a specific purpose and a limited period of time.

A *joint venture* is a legal agreement between two parties to operate for a specific purpose and for a limited period of time. For example, two companies may decide to form a joint venture to sell products during the hockey season. Once the Stanley Cup games are over, the joint venture no longer operates. Because of the time restriction, this is not a common form of organization for small businesses.

WHAT TAXES WILL BE DUE?

The following is a summary of the many taxes a company may owe. The taxes listed are the most common ones; however, depending on the industry and the state or city in which the business is located, additional taxes may be due. Every entrepreneur should call the Internal Revenue Service to determine which federal taxes are applicable. Calls should also be made to the state and city departments of revenue to identify all local taxes.

Federal Taxes

Income tax Federal income taxes must be paid on the net profit of a company, although the rates vary depending on the organizational form. The effect of organization form on taxes is discussed at the end of this section.

Excise tax For certain businesses, an excise tax is charged by the federal government. Businesses subject to excise tax include the beer, wine, and liquor industries; the firearms industry; and retailers of motor fuel. In order to determine whether a company must pay excise tax, the entrepreneur should call the Internal Revenue Service.

Social security tax In 1935, the federal government passed the Federal Insurance Contributions Act (FICA) to provide retirement and disability benefits to workers. Both the employer and the employee pay 7.65 percent of wages to the social security fund. The employee's portion is subtracted from each paycheck; the employer then contributes an equal amount. The money is held in a company bank account and paid to the federal government on a quarterly basis.

Self-employment tax Proprietors, partners, and workers who are considered "independent contractors" do not pay social security on their wages but instead pay self-employment tax. This is discussed in more detail later.

Federal unemployment tax The unemployment program was established to provide income to laid-off workers along with assistance in finding another job. The federal government charges an unemployment tax of 6.2 percent on the first $7,000 in wages. However, as explained later, the states also charge an unemployment tax. Therefore, the amount paid to the state unemployment fund is credited against the amount owed to the federal government.

Employee federal income tax withholding The federal government requires companies to withhold a portion of each employee's pay to cover income taxes the employee will owe. This is not an expense for the company, since it is withdrawn from the employees' checks; however, the company is responsible for all paperwork and for timely payment of the taxes. The amount withheld from each employee's check is determined after the employee completes a W-4 form.

State Taxes

This section contains a brief description of some of the state taxes a company may have to pay. Entrepreneurs should contact the state department of revenue to identify the taxes that will be due.

State income tax Most states charge businesses a state income tax that must be paid in addition to the federal income tax. Because each state sets its own rate, some states charge a set rate (for example, a flat rate of 6 percent) based on net profit, whereas others have rates that increase as net profit increases. A few states have no income tax for businesses.

State unemployment tax Each state establishes its own unemployment tax. Often the rate charged varies with the type of business and the employment record of the company. A rate is established when the company begins operations; however, the rate may increase if there are many claims from laid-off workers. Conversely, if the company operates for a long time without any claims, the rate may decrease.

Sales tax Many states also charge a sales tax on product. Although this is paid by the customers who purchase the product, the company collects the tax from the customer and pays it to the state. Some states require a deposit from new businesses based on the amount of sales tax that will be collected. Then, if the company does not remit the taxes owed, the deposit will be used to offset the debt.

Employee state income tax withholding As with the federal government, the states require companies to subtract a portion of each employee's check and remit it to the government. This amount is used to offset any state income taxes that the employee will owe at the end of the year.

In addition to federal and state taxes, companies may be liable for county and city taxes. The department of revenue in each county or city will be able to provide a list of taxes for that area.

ORGANIZATIONAL FORM AND INCOME TAX

Sole Proprietorships

> **Withdrawal** – the amount a sole proprietor takes from the business for personal expenses.

The sole proprietorship has an unusual taxing arrangement because the money that the owner takes for personal expenses (called a *withdrawal*) does not appear on the income statement and is not a tax-deductible expense for the company. For income tax purposes, the net profit or loss of the sole proprietorship is transferred to the personal tax return of the owner and is therefore taxed at the rate for individuals. The profit would be added to any other income of the proprietor; if the company loses money, the loss is subtracted from other personal income.

> **Self-employment tax** – a tax paid by proprietors in place of social security.

A sole proprietorship is also different because the proprietor does not pay social security taxes on the withdrawal but, instead, pays *self-employment* tax. This self-employment tax is currently 15.3 percent of net profit; it is not based on the amount of money the proprietor takes in withdrawals. Therefore, if the company is very profitable but the proprietor reinvests all of the profit back into the company, he or she will still pay self-employment tax on the net profit. (Refer to the sample income statement for a sole proprietorship in the financial section of the business plan.)

Partnerships

In a partnership, the profit or loss is split among the partners according to their percentage ownership. Each partner's portion of the profit or loss is then recorded on a personal tax return, just as a proprietor does.

> **Guaranteed payment** – a specified amount of money paid to a partner and taxed as a regular salary.

One difference between a partnership and a sole proprietorship concerns guaranteed payments. Often, if a partner works full time in the business, that partner takes a specified amount of money every week or month as a salary. In a partnership, this is known as a *guaranteed payment* and is an expense for the partnership. For the partner who receives the payment, it is taxed as a regular salary.

Corporations

Corporations are separate legal entities from the stockholders. If corporation owners take a salary, this is a deductible expense for the company. For the stockholders, this salary is taxed as any salary from a company.

One of the biggest disadvantages of a C corporation, though, is that the net profit may actually be taxed twice. The corporation first pays taxes on the net profit of the company. The rates are based on a graduated scale. Then, part or all of the corporation's profit may be given to the stockholders in the form of dividends. These dividends are payments based on the amount of stock that each owner has. If dividends are paid to stockholders, the stockholders must report the dividends on their personal tax return and pay income taxes. Because the corporation pays taxes on the profit and the stockholders pay taxes on dividends that come from profits, this is *double taxation,* which is considered one of the disadvantages of a corporation.

If the corporation incurs a loss, it is not subtracted from the stockholders' personal taxes. It can, however, be subtracted from profits of the corporation in future years.

S corporations are taxed in a manner similar to that of proprietorships or partnerships. Although the S corporation is a separate legal entity, it does not pay its own income taxes. The profit or loss of an S corporation is split among the owners and their portion of the profit or loss is recorded on the personal tax return.

> **Double taxation** – refers to the fact that a corporation pays taxes on net profit and stockholders pay taxes on dividends that come from profits.

WHAT OTHER LEGAL ISSUES NEED TO BE ADDRESSED?

The legal section of the business plan should also contain any information about contracts or legal arrangements with suppliers, customers, or employees. If the company has an agreement to service a specific geographic territory, or if there are contracts for jobs to be completed, this information should be included. Information concerning the company's patents, trademarks, and copyrights should also be provided. (See Chapter 9.) See Table B-11 for a summary of the

TABLE B–11   Summary of advantages and disadvantages of organizational forms

Sole Proprietorship
Advantages
  Fewer legal documents when starting business
  Simple financial reporting
  Owner makes all decisions unilaterally.
  Owner has complete control of profits and takes full responsibility for success.
Disadvantages
  Unlimited liability
  Growth may be limited due to limited financial and management resources.
General Partnership
Advantages
  Expertise of more than one person in ownership
  Shared responsibility
  Personal assets of several owners may help obtain financing.

(continued)

TABLE B–11   (*continued*)

Disadvantages
   Unlimited liability
   Each partner is responsible for 100 percent of company debts unless otherwise stated.
   Each partner may be held liable for actions of other partners.

Limited Partnership

Advantages
   Limited partners cannot lose more than the amount invested.
   Limited partners are not liable for company debts or claims from lawsuits.

Disadvantages
   Limited partners cannot be active in daily management.
   More legal documents than general partnership

C Corporation

Advantages
   Limited liability for stockholders
   Business continues if there is change in stockholders.

Disadvantages
   More paperwork when starting than for a sole proprietorship or general partnership
   Required annual meetings
   More paperwork if expanding into other states
   Taxed on both profits and dividends

S Corporation

Advantages
   Same as C corporation
   Profit or loss is transferred to personal tax return (no double taxation on profits and dividends).

Disadvantages
   Greater legal requirements than for a sole proprietorship or general partnership
   Need for annual board meetings
   More paperwork than proprietorship or partnership if expanding into other states
   Restrictions on the number of owners, type of stock, and who can be a stockholder

Limited Liability Company

Advantages
Members have limited liability.
Taxes as proprietorship or partnership
Fewer legal requirements than corporation

Disadvantages
Need for legal advice
More legal requirements than for a sole proprietorship or general partnership when starting

advantages and disadvantages of the various organizational forms discussed in this section.

Discussion Questions

1. When considering what organizational form to choose, what factors would be part of the consideration?

2. Suppose an entrepreneur is starting a restaurant and needs additional investors. From the entrepreneur's standpoint, what would be the advantage of

having a limited partner? What would be the disadvantages of having a limited partner?

3. What is the difference between an S corporation and a C corporation?

4. If sole proprietorships have unlimited liability, why are most businesses in the United States established as sole proprietorships?

Endnotes

1. U.S. Census Bureau, *2003 Statistical Abstract of the Unites States,* http://www.census.gov/prod/2004pubs/03statab/business.pdf.

2. Mark R. Hochberg, "Members Only: Need Estate-Planning Help with Your Business? Consider a Limited Liability Company," *Financial World,* July 1997, 114.

3. Ibid.

4. Patricia M. Carey, "A New Business Structure," *Home Office Computing,* February 1996, 90–92.

The Business Plan

INSURANCE

LEARNING OBJECTIVES

$ To be aware that companies are required by law to carry some type of insurance.

$ To understand the general categories of insurance.

$ To be aware of the many risks a company faces and the types of insurance available to minimize financial losses.

WHAT INSURANCE WILL YOU NEED?

Starting and operating a business involve risks of many kinds. Some risks are insurable while others are not. For example, a restaurant may be damaged by a fire; another one may be burglarized; still another may have a van damaged in an auto accident. These risks can be insured and are therefore considered *controllable*, not because they can be prevented but because the financial impact can be minimized by purchasing insurance. This section lists the most common types of insurance a small business may need. (The risks that are not insurable will be covered in another section.) The Insurance Checklist summarizes important insurance considerations.

> **Controllable risk** – a risk that is insurable.

Although a business may purchase many types of insurance, several types are required by law. Social security and unemployment are types of insurance; however, we usually think of them as taxes, and they have been discussed in the legal section of the business plan. Workers' compensation, however, is required by law, and entrepreneurs must make sure that the company is adequately covered.

Workers' Compensation Insurance

Workers' compensation provides income and payments for medical expenses to workers who are injured in job-related accidents. Because state laws govern workers' compensation, the laws and benefits vary greatly. In some states, workers' compensation is not required until the company has a certain number of employees or a minimum payroll amount.

The amount a company must pay for workers' compensation insurance depends primarily on the risk level of the job. For example, insurance for a construction worker would be substantially higher than for a clerical worker because the chance of injury is greater. Costs are also determined by the level of payroll (more workers and a higher payroll result in higher insurance costs) and the safety record of the company. If many injuries are reported, insurance costs will increase.

Companies may find that they are unable to obtain workers' compensation insurance from private insurance firms if they are very small, if they have a high accident rate, or if they are in a high-risk industry. In these instances, they are often assigned to a state-funded insurance plan designed to cover these special cases.[1]

In addition to workers' compensation insurance, there are four general categories of insurance that businesses may need. These categories include property, liability, earnings, and health/disability/life insurance. These are outlined next.

CHECKLIST: INSURANCE

- ☐ Research the laws covering workers' compensation in your state to determine if the insurance will be required by law.
- ☐ Identify the greatest insurable risks that your business will face.
- ☐ Identify other risks that you would like to insure.
- ☐ Determine how much you can afford to spend on insurance.
- ☐ Have you checked with an agent to determine the cost?

Property Insurance

Property insurance reimburses the company if the assets are damaged or destroyed. The most common types of property insurance are listed as follows:

Property Insurance	Losses Covered
Comprehensive vehicle insurance	Damages to the insured vehicle caused by fire, theft, falling objects, storms
Liability vehicle insurance	Damage to other vehicles and property: bodily injuries caused to others by traffic accidents involving the insured vehicle
Collision vehicle insurance	Damage to the insured vehicle caused by traffic accidents
Uninsured-motorist insurance	Damage to the insured vehicle or insured driver if an accident is caused by an uninsured driver
Fire insurance	Damage to company assets caused by fire and smoke; may cover damage from riots
Flood insurance	Damage to property caused by floods
Earthquake insurance	Damage to property caused by earthquakes
Theft insurance	Financial loss resulting from any illegal taking of property
Burglary insurance	Financial loss caused from theft of forcible entry
Robbery insurance	Financial loss from theft of property involving bodily harm or threat of bodily harm
Fidelity bonds	Financial loss caused by employee theft
Ocean marine insurance	Financial loss if assets are damaged, destroyed, or lost while being transported by ship
Inland marine insurance	Financial loss if assets are damaged, destroyed, or lost while on a truck, plane, or train

Liability Insurance

Liability insurance protects against financial loss caused by injury to customers or employees. The most common types of liability insurance are listed as follows:

Liability Insurance	Losses Covered
Employee liability	Claims resulting from employee lawsuits charging discrimination or sexual harassment
Workers' compensation	Provides medical payment and an income to workers who are injured on the job
Officers and directors	Personal financial loss of officers and directors of corporations if sued for negligent decision making
Surety bonds	Financial loss that occurs if job contracts are not completed correctly and/or on time
Completed-operations	Damage to others' property caused while completing a job

(continued)

(continued)

Liability Insurance	Losses Covered
Premises and operations	Financial loss resulting from claims by customers, suppliers, or others who are injured while on company property
Professional liability	Financial loss resulting from malpractice claims
Product liability	Financial loss resulting from claims by customers because of injury caused by the company product

Earnings Insurance

Although property insurance covers the loss of assets from fires, storms, and accidents, the loss of profits is not covered. Earnings insurance covers the loss of income and profits and includes the two types of insurance shown in the following table:

Earnings Insurance	Losses Covered
Bad-debt	Financial loss resulting from a customer not paying for goods or services rendered
Business-interruption	Financial loss resulting from the temporary closure of the business

Health, Disability, and Life Insurance

Health insurance for entrepreneurs and their employees has become very expensive, and many small firms cannot afford to cover their employees. Costs may be reduced by purchasing through associations that provide group rates. The following table lists the common types of insurance included in this category.

Insurance	Losses Covered
Health	Medical costs incurred due to sickness or accidents
Disability	Lost income due to illness or accidents
Key executive	Life insurance that compensates the company for lost income or services if the owner or a vital employee dies

Discussion Questions

1. What is the difference between comprehensive, liability, and collision insurance for a vehicle?
2. What is the difference between theft, burglary, and robbery insurance?
3. Why may insurance companies not want to provide workers' compensation to very small companies?

4. Choose a specific type of business and state the type of insurable risk that is most likely to occur. Then state the type of risk that is not as likely but would be the most costly if it did occur.

Endnote

1. Robert Steyer, "State Makes Offer on Workers Comp," *The St. Louis Post-Dispatch*, December 29, 1993, C1.

The Business Plan

SUPPLIERS

LEARNING OBJECTIVES

$ To be aware of the different types of suppliers.

$ To know what factors to consider when choosing suppliers.

$ To be able to identify sources for finding suppliers.

WHO WILL BE YOUR SUPPLIERS?

It is important to identify the suppliers of the business to obtain information concerning the products and services you will need. Suppliers generally can be categorized as follows:[1]

$ *Producers.* Producers include manufacturers, miners, farmers, and processors of natural products. Many producers, though, sell only large quantities to wholesalers and do not transact business with small firms.

$ *Wholesalers or merchant intermediaries.* Wholesalers buy from producers and take title for the goods. Wholesalers are a major source of supplies for small businesses. An excellent working relationship with the wholesaler is often essential for the small business to operate properly.

$ *Functional (agent) intermediaries.* Some intermediaries operate as wholesalers but do not take title to the goods. They represent the manufacturer, take orders, and provide service to the customers. This group of suppliers includes manufacturers' representatives, who sell products for many manufacturers within a geographic area. They usually have an ongoing relationship with the producers.

  Merchandise brokers are another type of agent intermediary and represent manufacturers by bringing buyer and seller together. They are usually located in large manufacturing areas.

  Resident buying officers are the third type of agent intermediary. They represent a group of retailers and offer a variety of services, including buying merchandise for those stores and furnishing market information and forecasts. Resident buying officers are paid by the retailers.[2]

After identifying possible suppliers, you will need to obtain the costs for their items as well as delivery schedules, their credit terms, and any minimum order quantities. It is common for suppliers to require new entrepreneurs to pay cash on delivery for several months until a track record of purchases and payments is established. Credit may then be extended for 30 days or longer. These credit terms are reflected in the cash flow projection by showing when payment for inventory would be made.

Some suppliers require a minimum order, since they do not want to bother with very small purchases. For this reason, it is important to check the minimum order amounts of suppliers to ensure that their required order amounts are not too large for your business.

Finding suppliers may be easy or difficult, depending on the types of goods and services needed. Possible sources for finding suppliers are as follows:

$ *The Internet.* The Internet is an excellent source for finding suppliers of many items. Just by typing a category such as "restaurant equipment" in a search engine, an entrepreneur can identify many potential suppliers.

$ *Yellow Pages.* An easy way to find local suppliers is to check the Yellow Pages for your area. For some industries in major cities, all goods and services will be available locally. For example, a restaurant owner needing a local supplier of food may find companies listed under the category of "Food Brokers" or under the specific type of food such as "Fish and Seafood—Wholesale."

$ *Encyclopedia of Associations.* The *Encyclopedia of Associations* lists organizations in many industries and is an excellent source for suppliers. For example, if a manufacturing firm in a small town needs to buy electronic components, the *Encyclopedia of Associations* lists several organizations that would be helpful.

$ *Thomas Register.* The *Thomas Register* lists manufacturers of products and service-related companies throughout the United States. This resource is available in many libraries and has listings for many items. For example, when one entrepreneur needed to find a manufacturer of kazoos, she had no idea of how to find them. She was surprised to find a kazoo manufacturer listed in the *Thomas Register*, and a telephone call to the manufacturer provided her with the product information she needed.

The Suppliers Checklist summarizes the issues discussed in this section.

Discussion Questions

1. What are the three different types of agent intermediaries?
2. If a supplier has a large minimum order quantity, what effect would this have on the supplier's customers?
3. In addition to the Internet, the Yellow Pages, the *Encyclopedia of Associations*, and the *Thomas Register*, what are other ways to identify possible suppliers?

Endnotes

1. Clifford M. Baumback, *How to Organize and Operate a Small Business* (Englewood Cliffs, NJ: Prentice-Hall, 1988), 263.
2. Ibid.

CHECKLIST: SUPPLIERS

- [ ] Identify your most important suppliers.
- [ ] What are their credit terms?
- [ ] How often do they deliver?
- [ ] What are the minimum order quantities?
- [ ] Are inventory shortages a problem in this industry?
- [ ] Are there many suppliers for your business, or do you have to choose from only a few?

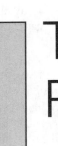

The Business Plan

RISKS, ASSUMPTIONS, AND CONCLUSION

WHAT ARE YOUR UNCONTROLLABLE RISKS?

Every business faces two types of risks—controllable and uncontrollable. Controllable risks cannot necessarily be prevented, but the financial loss can be minimized by purchasing insurance. Therefore, the risks of fire, vandalism, damage from storms, and so forth are considered controllable because insurance is available to pay for the financial loss.

Uncontrollable risks, however, are those that would have a detrimental financial impact but cannot be covered by insurance. Uncontrollable risks that are common to many businesses include the following:

> **Uncontrollable risks –** events that would have a detrimental financial impact but cannot be covered by insurance.

- $ A new competitor locating nearby
- $ A recessionary economy
- $ New technology
- $ Changes in consumer tastes
- $ A price war by competitors

Each business faces risks that are unique to that business. You should consider these carefully and briefly describe what steps would be taken if the uncontrollable risk actually develops. For example, if an entrepreneur believes that competitors would engage in a price war, the new entrepreneur may plan to differentiate the new business by offering products and services that the competition does not offer. If the risk of a recession would severely affect the company, the entrepreneur may consider what products or services could be offered that would not be as sensitive to a recessionary economy. See the Uncontrollable Risks Checklist.

WHAT ARE YOUR ASSUMPTIONS AND CONCLUSIONS?

The final section of the business plan will vary depending on whether the plan is for a new business or for an existing business.

If the plan was prepared to determine the viability of a proposed business, the conclusion answers the question, "Is this business feasible?" Keep in mind

---

CHECKLIST: UNCONTROLLABLE RISKS

☐ What uncontrollable risks will affect your business?
    ☐ The economy
    ☐ The weather
    ☐ New technology
    ☐ Price wars
    ☐ Changes in consumer tastes
    ☐ New competitors
    ☐ Other (specify)
☐ For each risk you have identified, explain what you will do to minimize the financial impact if the risk materializes.

that the conclusion was reached only by making assumptions throughout the report. The following assumptions are common:

$ A specific site

$ A certain dollar amount for start-up costs

$ The ability to obtain financing

$ No new competitors opening

Just as each business has unique risks, however, each depends on assumptions that are unique to that particular business. Therefore, you should identify the most important assumptions you have made while completing the business plan. It is especially important to identify those assumptions that are critical to the conclusion of the report. For example, suppose an entrepreneur plans to open an ice cream parlor near a school. The parlor will have 10 tables, with four chairs at each table. Two assumptions are as follows:

$ The seating capacity of the ice cream parlor is 40 people.

$ The school will remain in operation with a steady or increasing enrollment.

If the seating capacity is sharply reduced for any reason, if the school enrollment decreases, or if the school closes, the proposed business may not be feasible.

If the plan was written for an existing business, assumptions were also necessary and should be started in this section. The conclusion will then state the future of the business based on the information in the plan. See the Conclusion Checklist.

Discussion Questions

1. Suppose a video game arcade is opened near a school. The outlet has video game machines, pinball machines, and pool tables. What are some of the most important uncontrollable risks?

2. Consider a franchised fast-food business such as Taco Bell or McDonald's. What are some of the major uncontrollable risks for these businesses?

3. For the uncontrollable risks you identified in questions 1 and 2, state what steps could be taken to minimize the financial impact if those risks occurred.

4. Identify three uncontrollable risks for a jewelry store (do not use the ones listed in the text).

5. Identify two uncontrollable risks for a manufacturer of auto parts.

6. Identify two common assumptions that would be made while completing a business plan for a car wash (do not use those listed in the text).

7. Identify two common assumptions that would be made while completing a business plan for a health club and/or gym.

CHECKLIST: CONCLUSION

☐ Is this business feasible or not feasible?
☐ What assumptions did you make while completing the report?
☐ What assumptions must hold true for your conclusion to hold true?

Case Studies

CASE 1: ONLINE AUTO SALES

During the 1980s, Pete Ellis was an extremely successful car dealer, owning 16 auto dealerships and related businesses in California and Arizona. By 1988, he operated the largest Jeep, Eagle, and Chrysler dealership in the United States. However, most of his businesses were located in California and when that state's economy dropped sharply in 1990, car sales plummeted. Ellis was forced to close outlets or sell them to cover debts and eventually declared bankruptcy. He lost two houses and $15 million.[1]

Being a true entrepreneur, however, Ellis did not give up. During all of the time he was in business, he disliked the antagonism between auto buyers and sellers and believed that the industry's sales and distribution systems were very inefficient.[2] This led him to create Autobytel, an Internet auto-buying service that gives bargain hunters the information they need to negotiate a great price and delivers a no-hassle, no-haggle transaction.[3] Through Autobytel, a car buyer indicates the car he or she wants to buy, including the options. The nearest participating car dealer e-mails back an offer. There is no charge to the customer and no obligation to accept the offer. Autobytel makes money by charging a fee to the dealer.[4] Autobytel was launched in 1996 and by December 1997, it had processed one million online requests resulting in 600,000 purchases.[5] In 1997, Autobytel became the first Internet business to buy advertising time during the Super Bowl.[6] By 2000, the company was grossing $66.5 million.[7]

As could be expected, Autobytel's success resulted in many other companies entering the online market. National sites such as Microsoft's Carpoint, Cars.com, and CarsDirect.com were created, along with local sites such as Capital Car in Albany, New York. While some sites actually duplicate services like those offered by Autobytel, some of the local sites (such as Capital Car) offer information on cars but still require the buyer to go to the dealership to negotiate a price.[8]

The major car manufacturers then entered the market. Chrysler introduced its "Get a Quote" online program and GM announced its "Buy Power" model. Both programs required participating dealers to respond to requests within 24 hours and adhere to a no-haggle policy. Although it may seem that the Internet would allow car manufacturers to sell directly to the consumer, automakers in the United States are prohibited from selling direct because state laws require a dealership to be the intermediary. The car manufacturers also considered buying a minority partnership share in dealerships, which would allow them to be both the manufacturer and the retailer.[9]

When online auto sites were first established, many people questioned the viability of those dot-com businesses. One executive of a market research firm stated, "I think they're goners."[10] However, Autobytel has survived and by 2003, the company had sales of $88.9 million and a net income of $7.4 million.

The auto dot-com industry is experiencing a consolidation, just as many new industries have when competition increases. In an effort to increase sales and profits, Autobytel has purchased several other auto dot-com sites, including Autoweb.com and CarSmart.com. The future of these virtual car lots is still uncertain, but many auto dealers now find that many car sales start with an Internet lead. Thus, online services may continue to play a crucial role in the auto sales industry.[11]

Discussion Questions

1. What is the current role of an auto dealership?
2. Why did online auto sites survive even though some experts predicted they would be "goners"?
3. If car manufacturers had partnership shares in many of their dealerships, what changes would be likely to occur?
4. If the state laws that prohibit direct factory sales from the manufacturer to the consumer were abolished:
   a. Could dealerships be eliminated?
   b. What would be a disadvantage of shipping cars directly to consumers instead of shipping them all to the dealerships?
5. How could companies like Autobytel diversify to add value to their services?
6. In the long run, how will Internet sites affect newspapers?

Endnotes

1. Edward O. Welles, "Burning Down the House," *Inc.,* August 1997, 66–73.
2. Deborah Radcliff, "The Web Meets Auto World—Will It Kill the Flimflam Man?" *Software Magazine,* December 1997, 81–85.
3. Karen Bankston, "No Haggle, No Hassle," *Credit Union Management,* December 1997, 26–28.

(continued)

CASE 1 *(continued)*

4. David Pogue, "The Cheapskate's Guide to the Web," *Macworld,* April 1998, 178.

5. Radcliff, 81–85.

6. Sharon Machlis, "Web Businesses Spend Big on Ads," *Computerworld,* February 9, 1998, 2.

7. Norm Mayersohn, "Wheel Dealer," *Chief Executive,* April 2001, 20–21.

8. Ken Liebeskind, "Albany, N.Y. Dealer Advertises on Local, National Sites," *Editor & Publisher,* March 7, 1998, 20.

9. Radcliff, 81–85.

10. Nick Lico, "Can Cars Sell Via the Web?" *Advertising Age,* April 9, 2001, S20.

11. Ralph Kisiel, "Top Dot.coms Mine Data for Dealers," *Automotive News,* May 10, 2004, 32.

CASE 2: CHASING DREAMS THAT CAN BECOME REALITY

Lance Hamon grew up in a low-income neighborhood in California. Although he had a loving mother, she was the only good role model in his life. There was no reason to believe that Hamon would succeed. His friends ended up "dead, on drugs, in jail, or with low-income jobs trying to support a family."

Hamon never planned to go to college. He took a flight to the Midwest United States "to get out of town." After working in physically demanding jobs for low pay through a temporary employment agency and realizing that these jobs might be the best he could get, he flew back home. Hamon then went to a local community college and obtained two associate degrees—one in arts and anthropology and one in political science.

At that point, Hamon's life seemed to turn toward a more traditional path. He was hired by a Fortune 500 company and worked there for six years. However, he quickly found that he did not fit the typical mold of the corporate employee. He describes himself as a "free thinker," and the corporate culture did not reward creativity and free thinking. The company valued conformity and Hamon was not one to conform. Although he was making good money, when the company was downsizing its workforce, Hamon states, "I gave the company a reason to get rid of me."

He realized that he does not like to be required to "clock in." On one of his jobs, Hamon had to clock in twice each day and each time it "took a little piece of me." He decided to go into real estate because he could be his own boss and it would give him the freedom he needed. Hamon eventually hooked up with another real estate agent and formed a partnership. Both he and his partner are likely to have a six-figure income even though this is their first year in business.

Hamon admits that "I am the worst boss I ever had." He thought that being his own boss would mean he would give himself a lot of time off and many benefits. He now works at least 55 hours per week and often on weekends as well. But Hamon enjoys what he is doing to the point of being "passionate" about it.

Hamon's drive to succeed does not come from the desire for a lot of money. He knows he needs a good income to live comfortably, but his drive to succeed is because he has something to prove to himself. Hamon wants to prove to himself that he can be what he wants to be. He says he does not "want to be on the same plane as those my same age." He wants to be established in business like those who are 20 years older than he, so he must push himself to achieve this goal.

Hamon sees many ways to make money and many opportunities. He believes that when you have an opportunity, you have to take advantage of it. Because he is young and single, he has nothing to limit the time spent on his two passions—his business and traveling. By the end of 2005, Hamon had traveled to all 50 states and taken his second tour of Europe. When traveling, he looks for business ideas that work in other places that might be transplanted to new areas. Hamon describes himself as a "flight risk" because he has no real ties and loves to travel. If this business continues to go well, he will stay, but he knows that in 10 years he may easily be starting another type of business in another location.

Hamon's goal is just to be happy. He is "chasing dreams that can become reality; not chasing fantasy." His philosophy is that all entrepreneurs must be willing to risk and be willing to fail. He believes you must "know yourself and know who you are. Then you can know others. You can't build bridges without it."

In addition to building his real estate business, Hamon achieved another personal goal. In December 2004, he graduated with his bachelor's degree in business administration.

Discussion Questions

1. What personality characteristics does Hamon seem to have that are typical of many entrepreneurs?
2. Consider the "Big Five" personality characteristics. What has Hamon done that indicates he would score high on "openness"?
3. What circumstances in society helped to push Hamon toward entrepreneurship?

Based on a interview with Lance Hamon, January 2005. Reprinted with permission.

CASE 3: THE BODY SHOP

Anita Roddick's international empire, The Body Shop, began on her kitchen table in Brighton, England, in 1976. Her cosmetics and lotion company sold inexpensive cosmetics that were environmentally friendly and were not tested on animals.[1] Roddick's concept of the purpose of a business is radically different. She believes that business "can and must be a force for positive social change. It must not only avoid hideous evil—it must actively do good."[2] Because of this philosophy, the company is involved in many social causes, such as establishing "trade, not aid" with poor countries and helping nonprofit organizations such as Greenpeace, Amnesty International, rain forest activists, Survival International, and Friends of the Earth.[3]

Because of a lack of capital when the company began, Roddick emphasized the recyclability of the cosmetics containers and used plain packaging. This, along with the "no animal testing" emphasis and the theme of social responsibility, caught the 1980s wave of growing awareness of ecology, and the company grew at a phenomenal rate. The company expanded through franchising and by opening corporate-owned stores; by March 1997, there were more than 1,480 outlets in 46 countries, and a new shop opened somewhere in the world every two and a half days.[4]

This rapid growth, though, has not come without problems. Roddick decided to sell the company's stock publicly because she believed this would give the company more credibility when it was negotiating for retail sites. This has been a constant source of friction, however, because the company's emphasis on doing good instead of making a profit does not satisfy stockholders or financial analysts.[5] Roddick considered an attempt to take the company private again but realized the company would have to borrow an enormous amount of money, which could stifle growth.[6]

The Body Shop's enormous growth also attracted the attention of other companies. Because of The Body Shop's success, many other competitors have entered the marketplace and copied the "natural products" theme. These competitors now include Bath & Body Works, Garden Botanika, and Bare Essentials, as well as other companies that have started to offer similar lines such as Avon, Victoria's Secret, and Crabtree and Evelyn.[7] A new competitor, Virgin Retail, opened approximately 100 cosmetics stores featuring natural ingredients.[8] By 1996, experts stated that there was a "glut" in the soaps and scents business.[9] The Body Shop, which has always operated without high-pressure product advertising,

relying instead on publicity and word of mouth, now finds itself under attack from all of the competitors and is considering a change in promotional strategy.[10]

The company was also hurt by bad publicity. In 1992, a television documentary charged that The Body Shop made false claims about animal testing. Roddick sued for libel and won, but the company image was still tarnished. In 1994, an American journalist writing for *Business Ethics* challenged The Body Shop's claims concerning the environment, charitable contributions, and efforts to buy materials from the third world.[11]

Amid all of the other problems, personnel issues have surfaced. In 1992, the company's international general manager resigned,[12] and in May 1996 The Body Shop lost the husband-and-wife team of Mark and Liz Warom, the team responsible for building the Colourings line of cosmetics.[13] Colourings was one of The Body Shop's most successful lines and was voted the "best cosmetic product" by *Vogue* magazine.[14] Thoughts of leaving the company are even entertained by the founder. Anita Roddick talks at times about "packing it in," but then asks, "What, fire myself? No one else would employ me." But she states that for an entrepreneur to be in a company so large and bureaucratic is like death.[15]

All of the increased competition, bad publicity, and personnel problems had a devastating effect on the stock price, which dropped from a high of $6.55 in 1992 to around $2.29 by April 1996. The most common criticism of the company is that it lacked a plan for the future. The lack of a plan was one of the major reasons for the loss of the international general manager,[16] and a 1996 survey showed that one in three shareholders felt the company lacked a clear long-term business strategy.[17] An article in *Marketing Week* stated that the company had the appearance of a company without a clear sense of direction in its marketing.[18] Some analysts believe that Roddick's endless campaigning for environmental causes was no longer in tune with the mood of the public. They believed that the company needed to innovate radically and adopt new and adventurous directions to take it into the next century.[19]

By the end of the decade, the company was dramatically restructured, new products were introduced, much of its manufacturing was divested, and Anita Roddick took a backseat as a new CEO was brought in to turn the company around.[20]

(continued)

However, in 2000 and 2001, total sales continued to remain flat and many people believed the store format needed updating. A more contemporary image for the stores was being planned and 300 redesigned stores were expected to open in 2004.[21]

Company management also needed to consider sales by geographic region because sales were not consistent throughout the world. The Body Shop was experiencing increasing sales outside of the United States, but American sales had not improved and in some years even declined.

Discussion Questions

1. In what ways is The Body Shop experiencing problems similar to those of many rapidly growing companies?
2. If you were hired as a consultant, which problem would you consider most critical?
3. In what ways could the company "innovate radically"? Identify some "adventurous directions" the company might consider.
4. Why are sales in the United States not increasing when sales in other countries are improving?
5. What should the Body Shop do in the United States?

Endnotes

1. Julian Lee and Patrick Barrett, "Body in Need of Reshaping," *Marketing,* April 4, 1996, 10.
2. Andrew Davidson, "The Davidson Interview: Anita Roddick," *Management Today,* March 1996, 42–46.
3. Charles P. Wallace, "Can the Body Shop Shape Up" *Fortune,* April 15, 1996, 118–120.
4. David Lennon, "London: Roddick Isn't Finished Yet," *Europe,* March 1997, 39–40.
5. Davidson, 42–46.
6. Wallace, 118–120.
7. "A Global Case Study," *Planning Review,* November/December 1996, 22–24.
8. Nicholas Kochan, "Anita Roddick: Soap and Social Action," *Worldbusiness,* January/February 1997, 46–47.
9. Donald Davis, "Glut Indeed," *Drug and Cosmetic Industry,* November 1996, 22.
10. Kochan, 46–47.
11. Wallace, 118–120.
12. Ibid.
13. Helen Jones, "Virgin Eyes Up the Beauty Sector," *Marketing Week,* August 9, 1996, 8.
14. Body Shop Duo Exits," *Marketing,* May 16, 1996, 2.
15. Davidson, 42–46.
16. Wallace, 118–120.
17. Jennifer Conlin, "Battle for the Soul of The Body Shop," *Working Woman,* April 1996, 11–12.
18. Pippa Considine, "Growing Pains at The Body Shop?" *Marketing Week,* July 7, 1995, 19–20.
19. Lee and Barrett, 10.
20. Harriet Marsh, "Has The Body Shop Lost Its Direction for Good?" *Marketing,* May 10, 2001, 19.
21. "Time to Shape up at the Body Shop," *Design Week,* July 8, 2004, 9.

CASE 4: BOSTON CHICKEN/BOSTON MARKET

The original Boston Chicken store was started by two young entrepreneurs in Newton, Massachusetts. The concept was very different from anything offered by any other fast-food chicken franchises—it offered marinated rotisserie chicken, freshly made vegetables, and baked goods. The average customer check was more than $13, unusually high for a chicken outlet.[1]

George Naddaff had 20 years of franchising experience when he first visited Boston Chicken in 1987. In fact, he had owned 19 Kentucky Fried Chicken franchises with a partner since 1967. He had also started two other franchises—Living and Learning Centres, Inc., and VR Business Brokers, Inc.[2] Naddaff saw tremendous potential in the little Boston Chicken restaurant, and in 1988 he purchased the outlet from the two founders. Naddaff then led the company through a tremendous growth period. In 1989, the company began offering franchises; by the end of 1991, the company had 43 company-owned stores and 100 franchised outlets.[3]

In 1992, Naddaff became a multimillionaire by selling controlling interest in the company to a group of former Blockbuster Entertainment Corp. executives, who then named the company Boston Market.[4] The corporation's new chairman and CEO, Scott Beck, decided to sell the company's stock publicly in 1993 with plans to eventually open 3,000 stores.[5] It was a successful initial public offering, with shares gaining more than 140 percent over the initial price in one day.[6]

By 1997, though, the stock price had plunged more than 50 percent in three months and the company was in serious financial trouble. The company did not go from large profits to losses overnight, however. Many stockholders believe that the reported profits were misleading because losses were recorded on the books of the franchise's "area developers" but not on the corporation's statements. One stock analyst from Schroder Wertheim stated that the company's financial structure "is designed to decouple reported earnings from economic reality."[7] The corporation reported earnings soaring from $1.6 million in 1993 to more than $34 million in 1995; however, franchise area developers' average annual operating losses had increased from $54,750 to $180,400. The corporation said it had no obligation to report the operating losses at independent area developers.[8]

In 1996, Scott Beck argued that the individual stores were making money and the area developers' losses were just start-up costs of rapid expansion that would end in a few years.[9] However, by the end of 1997, the company had decided to change its entire strategy. It planned to scrap its franchisee system completely and convert to a company-owned concept.[10] It also was testing a change in format to a "home-meal replacement" outlet. The new format in some stores featured the traditional Boston Market menu but also included a dessert and bakery case, prepackaged store products, a grill for preparing entrées and sandwiches, and a fresh-tossed salad station.[11] The new format was designed to take advantage of the "ease-the-cooking" or takeout movement, a trend to replace home cooking but still allow the food to be eaten at home. In 1998, the home-meal replacement industry was estimated to reach $100 billion; it has been estimated that by 2004 this market will reach $450 billion.[12]

By mid-1998, however, the company admitted that it could not pay all of its debts, and investors and analysts were saying that the company was headed toward a "restructuring" bankruptcy.[13] By the end of 1998, Boston Market declared bankruptcy and McDonald's Corp. bought the chain of stores. Originally, McDonald's purchased the company with the intention of converting the sites to McDonald's outlets or to other McDonald-owned concepts. However, by the time McDonald's closed the sale, they found that many of the sites were generating a positive cash flow and that many Americans liked the food that was served. Therefore, instead of closing and converting all of the stores, McDonald's decided to keep many of the stores operating, add new food items, and promote the catering services.[14]

As of 2004, Boston Markets were offering delivery services in 115 stores, and the company was planning to expand the concept to the majority of its outlets. The stores that were offering delivery were showing sales increases of 10 to 15 percent. Boston Market and McDonald's were also testing a co-branded franchise—one unit that served both McDonald's and Boston Market's products.[15]

Discussion Questions

1. Who were the direct and indirect competitors of Boston Market in its original format? Who are the competitors with the new home-meal replacement market?

(continued)

CASE 4 *(continued)*

2. Why did the company buy back the franchises at a time when it was in financial trouble, since this action only placed an additional drain on company cash?
3. How did Boston Market benefit from declaring bankruptcy and being purchased by McDonald's?
4. Do you believe the co-branding concept is a good strategy? Why or why not?

Endnotes

1. Len Lewis, "By George, He's Got It," *Progressive Grocer,* January 1997, 77–80.
2. Joshua Hyatt, "The Next Big Thing," *Inc.,* November 1995, 62–69.
3. Lewis, 77–80.
4. Hyatt, 62–69.
5. Meryl Davids, "Boston Chicken's Barnyard Blues," *Journal of Business Strategy,* September/October 1997, 34–35.
6. Linda Canina, "Boston Chicken's IPO," *Cornell Hotel & Restaurant Administration Quarterly,* October 1996, 22.
7. Nelson D. Schwartz, "The Boston Chicken Problem," *Fortune,* July 7, 1997, 114–116.
8. "The Squawk over Boston Chicken," http://www.businessweek.com/1996/43/b3498139.htm.
9. Ibid.
10. Richard L. Papiernik, "Boston Chicken Set to Scrap Franchises," *Nation's Restaurant News,* November 10, 1997, 1.
11. Richard Papiernik, "Boston Chicken Plans New Format Rollout Amid $$ Woes," *Nation's Restaurant News,* April 13, 1998, 4.
12. "First," *Nation's Restaurant News,* March 16, 1998, S6–S9.
13. "Morning Briefing," *The St. Louis Post-Dispatch,* July 21, 1998, B1.
14. Kelly Pate, "A Golden Egg for Those Golden Arches," *The Denver Post,* June 3, 2001, K01.
15. Paul Frumkin, "Chicken Lenders Peck at Gains Despite Poultry Inflation," *Nation's Restaurant News,* June 28, 2004, 108.

CASE 5: A FAMILY AFFAIR

From the time Deanna could remember, she had helped her mother in The Pantry, a small but successful bakery and restaurant that was known for unique desserts and pastries. When she was young, she helped clean tables in the small customer seating area. As she grew older, she helped take phone orders and worked at the bakery counter.

Although succession plans were never discussed, Deanna always planned to work full time in the business after college and eventually take over the company management when her mother retired. Deanna's mother and father had divorced when Deanna was very young, and since Deanna was an only child, there were no other children to assume control of the company. If Deanna did not assume ownership, the business would have to be closed or sold to an outsider.

In 1999, Deanna went away to college to study restaurant management. She enjoyed being away from home more than she had anticipated and did very well in her courses. She also became aware of other career opportunities in the food industry that she had never before considered. She realized that she would gain valuable experience by working for other companies before she returned to her mother's business.

At about the same time, however, Deanna's mother remarried. Her new spouse had two daughters of his own, ages 16 and 17. Since employee turnover at The Pantry was always a concern, Deanna's mother was more than happy to have his daughters work in the business part time while they were in high school.

To Deanna, though, this was a cause for concern. Now that she had stepsisters, the ownership of The Pantry was not necessarily hers when her mother retired. She was concerned that if she accepted a position with another company after college, her mother might interpret that as a lack of interest in The Pantry. Once, when she was home during a spring break, she tried to initiate a conversation about the future of the business. Her mother's only response was, "I'm only 45 years old and I'm not going to retire for a long time. So don't worry about it."

Deanna also realized that, in the future, if her mother and stepfather gave equal ownership to all three daughters, this would result in her owning 33 percent, while the two stepsisters combined would own 66 percent. If the relationship did not work well, she would always be outvoted by the two stepsisters. She would not have control of the business, and, even under the best of circumstances, this was not appealing.

Discussion Questions

1. If you were in Deanna's position, what would you do?
2. Identify options that Deanna's mother and stepfather could consider rather than splitting the business ownership equally among the children.

CASE 6: ED'S AUTO PARTS

Ed Hernandez worked in auto parts stores for most of his life. He began working as a stock clerk in a neighborhood store when he was still in high school, and after graduating from college, he accepted a management position with a national chain of auto parts stores. After working with the large corporation for more than 10 years, he decided to open his own business to serve both the auto repair shops and the general public. Because of his experience in the industry, he was well known by many of the owners of auto repair shops and residents of his community, and they were happy to hear that he was opening his own store. In the first year of business, the company grossed $290,000 and had a net profit before tax of $8,000.

Although the customers from the general public paid with cash or credit card, Ed offered the auto repair shops 30 days' credit. This was necessary in order to be competitive with other parts stores in the area. The increasing level of accounts receivable, though, placed a great strain on the company cash flow and, because of the lack of cash, Ed found it difficult to replace the inventory as quickly as it was sold. When the business first opened, the inventory level was $65,000 and accounts receivable

were zero; however, by the end of the first year, accounts receivable were $25,000 and the inventory had dropped to $50,000. Ed's Auto Parts did not have a problem with bad debts; in fact, almost all customers paid within 30 days and only a few took 45 to 60 days to pay. However, the normal 30-day credit was enough of a delay to cause cash problems.

Ed was concerned that the drop in inventory could result in lost sales if the customers could not get the parts they needed. He might also start to lose the repair shops as customers if inventory shortages occurred frequently. Ed therefore decided to ask his bank for a loan of $25,000. He planned to use $15,000 to restock inventory to its original level; the remaining $10,000 would be used for working capital. Ed was willing to pledge his home as collateral if necessary; it had a market value of $100,000 and he still owed $40,000 on his mortgage. His personal credit record and that of the business were excellent. Since the economy was strong, Ed felt confident that sales would continue to increase in the coming years.

He took the financial statements shown below to his banker to ask for the loan.

Ed's Auto Parts, Inc.
Income Statement 1/1/00 to 12/31/00

Sales	$290,000
Cost of goods sold	170,000
Gross margin	$120,000
Expenses	
Employee wages	$50,000
Owner salary	20,000
Rent	15,000
Employee taxes	8,000
Advertising	5,000
Insurance	4,000
Utilities	6,000
Office supplies	1,000
Accounting/legal	3,000
Total expenses	$112,000
Net profit before tax	$8,000

Ed's Auto Parts, Inc.
Balance Sheet 12/31/00

Current Assets		Current Liabilities	
Cash	$5,000	Accounts payable	$25,000
Accounts receivable	25,000	Current portion of long-term debt	8,000
Inventory	50,000	Accrued expenses	2,000
Supplies	2,000	Total current liabilities	$35,000
Prepaid expenses	3,000		
Total current assets	$85,000		
Fixed Assets		**Long-Term Liabilities**	
Fixtures	$20,000	Note Payable	$80,000
Equipment	15,000	Less: current	(8,000)
Leasehold Imp.	25,000	Total long-term liabilities	$72,000
Total fixed assets	$60,000	Total liabilities	$107,000
Total assets	$145,000	Equity	38,000
		Total liabilities & equity	$145,000

(continued)

CASE 6 *(continued)*

Discussion Questions

1. In addition to the bank loan, what could Ed do to try to collect his receivables faster?
2. Consider Ed's request for $25,000. Is this enough? If you were Ed's banker, what financial information would be helpful in determining the appropriate amount of working capital?
3. Does the cash flow problem indicate that Ed is a poor manager?

CASE 7: ENTREPRENEURS IN THE BEVERAGE INDUSTRY

Entrepreneurs have been a driving force in the beverage industry for more than a century. In 1886, John Pemberton began marketing Coca-Cola as an over-the-counter medicine, and in 1929 Charles Grigg developed Bib-Label Lithiated Lemon-Lime Soda, today known as 7UP. The beverage industry has always provided opportunities for entrepreneurs, but in the current market, the cost of purchasing new ingredients and technologies and the intense competition make the odds of a successful new product introduction less likely than in the past.[1]

New beverages are developed every year. In some years, more than 3,000 new beverage products are brought to the market, but many do not succeed. Entrepreneurs who attempt to succeed in this industry must be aware of the changing consumer tastes and industry trends.[2]

Caffeinated Products: Coffee, Soft Drinks, and Water

Specialty coffee outlets in the United States experienced explosive growth during the 1990s, growing from only 200 in 1989 to approximately 10,000 by 2000.[3]

The most well-known name in the gourmet coffee industry is Starbucks, but few people realize the company began in 1971. The company was started by three entrepreneurs in Seattle's Pike Place Market. The focus was on coffee and equipment, including filters, grinders, and pots—no scones, no cappuccinos. By 1987, there were only six Starbucks outlets, but another entrepreneur, Howard Schultz, saw the potential of Starbucks after traveling to Italy and seeing the many coffee bars there. Schultz raised $3.8 million and bought the company. The company went public in 1992 at $17 per share and within five months the stock price had doubled.[4] By 2001, Starbucks had expanded to 3,500 stores in North America and 800 stores overseas.[5] By 2004, it had 7,569 stores worldwide.[6] Starbucks is also equipping its stores for high-speed wireless Internet access, so customers can surf the Net on their laptops or Palm Pilot. The longer people linger at the stores, the more likely they are to order another latte.[7]

Many entrepreneurs are not willing to let Starbucks own the coffee market, though. Caribou Coffee Company was started by entrepreneurs after they had climbed mountains in Alaska in 1990 and saw a herd of caribou in the valley below. By 2004, the company was the nation's second largest specialty coffee company, employing more than 3,000 people. The Caribou Coffee outlets look like Alaskan lodges with fireplaces and wooden cabinetry.[8]

A recent trend toward caffeinated soft drinks began with Jolt. Jolt was introduced in 1985 by C. J. Rapp, president of Global Beverages. Jolt became a moderate success and a fixture in the marketplace at a time when most other companies were taking caffeine out of their products. Although similar products entered the market after Jolt, there were few other successes.[9] However, by the late 1990s, caffeinated soft drinks were common and other companies were introducing similar products.[10]

By the mid-1990s, an entrepreneur had developed another successful idea. A college student, David Marcheschi, who used to pull all-nighters cramming for tests, developed the idea for caffeinated water. Although other students drank coffee or soda to stay awake, Marcheschi did not like the taste of either. He wondered why someone couldn't caffeinate plain water. A few years later, he mentioned his idea to a friend whose father owned a beverage company and within a few weeks, the formula for Water Joe was developed. In 1995, Marcheschi formed a partnership with Nicolet Forest Bottling and the product was launched.[11] A small article appeared in a local paper, and then the *Milwaukee Sentinel* ran a front-page story that was picked up by the Associated Press. Articles about Water Joe spread rapidly across the United States.[12] By the end of 1996, Water Joe was shipping 400,000 bottles each week and annual sales were about $12 million.[13] By the year 2000, Water Joe had become a subsidiary of Artesian Investments, a 16-year-old company in Green Bay, Wisconsin. The national account manager for Artesian Investments states, "What we're giving people is a healthier alternative."[14] As of 2003, Water Joe had expanded into Germany and was being introduced in the United Kingdom.[15]

Other creative entrepreneurs decided to sell similar products over the Internet. The founders of Thinkgeek. Com sell a "Case O' Buzz Water." Each bottle of water has the same amount of caffeine as two extra large cups of coffee.[16]

Herbal Drinks and Green Teas

Herbal drinks first become popular in 1970 when Morris J. Siegel founded Celestial Seasonings, Inc., which

(continued)

markets herbal teas.[17] Siegel has been described as a hippie with a penchant for herbs, and this persona has had a positive effect on the company. The culture of nonconformity led to a great deal of creativity, and by the mid-1990s, Celestial Seasonings was the leading specialty tea maker in the United States.[18] By 1998, Celestial Seasonings had jumped into the fastest growing segment in the tea industry—the green tea category. The market for green tea increased 53 percent in 1997 and showed no signs of slowing. Much of the growth in sales was attributed to research reports indicating that green tea may lower the risk of certain types of cancer and balance cholesterol.[19] By the end of the decade, Celestial Seasonings had teamed up with the company that introduced Arizona Iced Tea and launched a line of ready-to-drink teas in a smart retro bottle that looks like the melding of a glass bottle and a tin can.[20]

In 2000, Celestial Seasonings merged with the Hain Food Group. As of 2004, Celestial Seasonings was selling 1.2 billion cups of tea per year. Morris (Mo) Siegel retired to climb the last section of the Colorado mountains he had not yet climbed.[21]

John Bello, cofounder of SoBe Beverage Co., says his company is "taking the concept of herbal remedies to the mass market." SoBe's products include a variety of teas containing plant extracts that improve alertness. One of the company's "energy tonics" allows drinkers "to perform all day and all night." Other teas include echinacea, selenium, or bee pollen for additional therapeutic purposes.[22] A new marketing approach was implemented for some of its products in 2000. Six of its products—Energy, Lizard Fuel, Lizard Lightning, Elixir, Green Tea, and Lemon Tea—were marketed in paper cans. Each octagonal paper can was adorned with the radical SoBe lizard. The colorful labels come in pink, orange, tan and bright yellow.[23] As of 2004, SoBe beverages were available internationally. The company was selling its product in Canada, Mexico, the Bahamas, the United Kingdom, Barbados, and Guam.[24]

Richard Keer, president of The Natural Group, an importer of all-natural nonalcoholic beverages, has recently begun to market a product called Ame, a drink made with fruit juices, eastern herbs, and spring water. It is available in red, white, and rose and is packaged in 250-ml and 750-ml bottles. The company also sells Norfolk Punch, a nonalcoholic beverage based on an ancient monastic recipe of 35 different herbal extracts like fennel, rosemary, and peppermint.[25]

Juice Bars and Smoothies

Proponents of smoothies contend that the beverage is one of the most promising new beverage items since specialty coffees. The term *smoothie* is a generic term for a blender-made concoction typically made from fresh fruit, fruit juices, ice, and sherbet or yogurt. Optional add-ons include calcium, protein powder, bee pollen, or the herb gingko biloba. Smoothies are often sold at juice bars and are marketed as a lowfat, high-nutrition meal in a cup.[26]

One company, Smoothie King, has been in existence for 24 years, since long before the great demand for the product developed. Richard Leveille, vice president of franchise development, calls Smoothie King's products the first and best available. Its product is not yogurt- or sherbert-based, but primarily fruit-based. Smoothie King makes daily deliveries to the Dallas Cowboys camp, and during spring training it delivers 200 to 300 smoothies a day to the New York Yankees in Tampa.[27] By 2004, Smoothie King had 340 units in 34 states and also had three international units.[28]

Another company, Jamba Juice Co., was establishing itself as a leader in the juice bar segment. Founder, Kirk Perron, established his first juice bar when he was 26 years old. Perron states that his company did not "invent smoothies or squeeze-to-order juices," but his company was the first to "unlock the code and create a sensory experience in those products." Jamba Juice sells its products in an atmosphere of hot pinks, purples, greens, oranges, and natural woods.[29] By December 2004, the company had 430 units, with locations in airports and on college campuses.[30]

Discussion Questions

Refer to the methods of market segmentation discussed in the marketing section of the business plan to answer the following questions.

1. Using demographic segmentation, segment the market for
   a. Water Joe
   b. Celestial Seasonings tea
   c. Smoothies
   d. the green tea industry
2. Using benefit segmentation, segment the market for
   a. Water Joe
   b. Koppla
   c. Smoothies
   d. the green tea industry

(continued)

3. The rapid growth of Water Joe fueled the creation of the caffeinated water industry in 1996. How long do you expect the rapid growth of this industry to continue?
4. Identify potential market segments for Ame and the energy tonic, the products of SoBe Beverage Co.
5. What impact do entrepreneurs have on the beverage industry?
6. What national trend would be beneficial for Celestial Seasonings but detrimental for Water Joe?

Endnotes

1. Joan Holleran, "Lessons Learned: Diary of a New Product's Development," *Beverage Industry,* February 1998, 10–13.
2. Tom Vierhile, "New Products Fared Well in '97," *Beverage Industry,* March 1998, 44–46.
3. Carol Casper, "Caffeine Rush," *Restaurant Business,* January 1, 1996, 92–109.
4. Jennifer Reese, "Starbucks: Inside the Coffee Cult," *Fortune,* December 9, 1996, 190–200.
5. Suzanne Koudsi, "Remedies for an Economic Hangover," *Fortune,* June 25, 2001, 130.
6. Starbucks Coffee, "Starbucks Timeline & History," http://www.starbucks.com/aboutus/timeline.asp.
7. Koudsi, 130.
8. Caribou Coffee, http://www.cariboucoffee.com/aboutus/corporateprofile.asp.
9. Ian Murphy, "Beverages Don't Mean a Thing If They Ain't Got That Zing," *Marketing News,* April 14, 1997, 1.
10. "New Products: Growth or Cannibalization," *Beverage Industry,* 1999, 40.
11. Gianna Jacobson, "A Jolt of Inspiration," *Success,* February 1997, 21.
12. Greg W. Prince, "On the Joe," *Beverage World,* June 30, 1996, 3.
13. Jacobson, 21.
14. Carol L. Bowers, "Bottled Water Business Takes Off," *Utility Business,* March 2000, 36–37.
15. "Water Joe Energy Drink Prepares for UK Launch," *Marketing Week,* June 19, 2003, 11.
16. http://www.thinkgeek.com.
17. Sandra D. Atchison, "Putting the Red Zinger Back into Celestial," *Business Week,* November 4, 1991, 74–78.
18. Tim Triplett, "When Tracy Speaks, Celestial Listens," *Marketing News,* October 24, 1994, 14.
19. Stephanie Thompson, "Lipton, Celestial, Bieglow, See Green," *Brandweek,* February 9, 1998, 4.
20. Kent Steinriede, "The Year's Best Packaging," *Beverage Industry,* December 2000, 34–38.
21. Celestial Seasonings, "Our History," http://www.celestialseasonings.com/whoweare/corporatehistory/history.php.
22. Murphy, 1.
23. Steinriede, 34–38.
24. SoBe, "About Us FAQs," http://www.sobebev.com/about/faq.shtml.
25. Beth G. Fogarty, "California Marketer's Line Is All-Natural and All-Inclusive," *Beverage World,* June 30, 1996, 3.
26. James Scarpa, "Pulp Mixin'," *Restaurant Business,* May 1, 1998, 109–110.
27. Bonnie Brewer, "Smoothies: The Breakfast Substitute of Champions," *Nation's Restaurant News,* October 20, 1997, 43.
28. Smoothie King, http://www.smoothieking.com.
29. Ron Ruggless, "Jamba Juice, Smoothies Sail Full Steam Ahead," *Nation's Restaurant News,* May 11, 1998, 96–100.
30. Jamba Juice, "Background," http://www.jambajuice.com/mediacenter/background.html.

CASE 8: ENTREPRENEURS IN SPACE

In the spirit of entrepreneurship that has fueled innovation in the United States, a group of entrepreneurs has succeeded in launching a privately funded spaceship and creating the beginning of the space tourism industry.

In 1996, the X Prize Foundation, started by Peter Diamandis, announced a competition that would award $10 million as its prize. To claim the prize, a private company must fly a manned rocket into space and return safely. The rocket would have to be capable of carrying two people and it would have to complete two trips within two weeks. In May 2002, two entrepreneurs, Anousheh Ansari and Amir Ansari, became major donors of the prize money, and the contest was renamed the Ansari X Prize.[1]

Although many teams competed for the prize, a space plane called SpaceShipOne is the rocket that succeeded first. In November 2004, it won the $10 million prize. SpaceShipOne was designed by Burt Rutan, who owned a company that sold build-it-yourself airplanes. It was funded by Paul Allen, cofounder of Microsoft. When the space plane reaches it highest point, the wings flip up so the plane floats to earth like a badminton shuttlecock.[2]

The long-term goal of the X Prize participants is to create an afforadable space tourism industry. The hope is that trips into space will be available to everyone, not just to astronauts on government-funded missions. The entrepreneurs also envision new sources of energy, water, and minerals once space travel becomes a reality and trips to other planets become common.[3]

Peter Diamandis already offers zero-gravity flights to people using a Boeing 727-200 that has been altered by his ZeroGravity Corp. The ticket price for a ride is $3,000. The flight allows people to experience zero gravity but does not go into space.[4]

Richard Branson, owner of Virgin Galactic Airways, has ordered five space planes from Burt Rutan's company, Scaled Composites. Branson plans to offer space travel to the general public by 2007 at a cost of $190,000 per trip. The Virgin Gallactic Web site allows people to place their names on the waiting list for flights. More than 7,000 people have signed up.[5]

Considering the success of these entrepreneurs, the U.S. government has now discussed the possibility of government-sponsored aerospace prizes. The idea is that this will encourage entrepreneurs to take risks that the government would not be willing to take. NASA requested $20 million for this prize for fiscal year 2005.[6]

Discussion Questions

1. Identify some of the risks a privately funded space tourism company would face.
2. Should the U.S. government fund aerospace prizes? Give arguments for and against this idea.
3. Assume space tourism becomes a successful industry by 2050. What trends would you expect to see in this industry that also occurred in the dot-com industry?
4. Do you believe space tourism will be a successful industry? Why or why not?
5. Based on the information in this case, identify the different roles entrepreneurs have played in the space tourism industry so far.

Endnotes

1. Maureen Byko, "SpaceShipOne, the Ansari X Prize, and the Materials of the Civilian Space Race," *The Journal of the Minerals, Metals, and Materials Society*, November 2004, 24.
2. Chris Taylor, "The Sky's the Limit," *Time*, November 29, 2004, 64.
3. Byko, 24.
4. James M. Clash, "Fly Me to the Moon," *Forbes*, November 15, 2004, 218.
5. Taylor, 64.
6. Jafferson Morris, "House Witnesses Endorse Aerospace Prizes, with Cautions," *Aerospace Daily and Defense Report*, July 16, 2004, 4.

CASE 9: OPPORTUNITIES AND THREATS

The uncontrollable factors that affect entrepreneurs range from changing consumer tastes and technological advances to economic conditions, societal trends, and even changes in the weather. These changes often create opportunities for some entrepreneurs by creating a demand for new products and services. At the same time, other entrepreneurs find that their businesses may not survive because the new products and services will make their businesses obsolete. Here are some examples of recent trends and the impact on entrepreneurship.

The Low-Carb Diet

One of the recent trends that has a huge impact on the food industry is the low-carbohydrate diet. When the low-carb diet first become popular, most of the products were supplied by small business owners because the market was considered a niche market. Some entrepreneurs developed specialty products that were sold to small food stores. Other entrepreneurs opened low-carb restaurants or food stores.

The trend also had an impact on those who supply the food industry. Ranchers who sell beef saw demand for their products increase dramatically after years of low sales. But for farmers who grew potatoes and wheat, sales dropped substantially.

As the demand for low-carb products skyrocketed, many large businesses entered the market, and this had a detrimental impact on some independent entrepreneurs. Large corporations such as Kellogg's began selling low-carb cereal, and a wide variety of low-carb products began to appear in grocery stores. This took sales away from the independent entrepreneurs who were the first to supply products to the consumers, and many entrepreneurs closed their low-carb businesses.

Experts disagree as to the future of the low-carb industry. Many say that the trend has peaked and demand for products will decrease. Others believe the trend is here to stay.

Digital Trash

Digital trash has created problems for some and opportunities for others. Digital trash includes obsolete computers, TVs, cell phones, and other electronic devices. In a typical year, more than 1.5 billion pounds of electronics are now recycled. This trend was already creating entrepreneurial opportunities in the mid-1990s. In 1996, Stampp Corbin was a technology consultant who sold 200 computers to Cincinnati Bell. The corporation told him that as part of the deal he would have to take their old machines. Corbin therefore started his company, called RetroBox, to resell used computers.[1]

Legislation has also fueled the demand for companies like RetroBox. Recent legislation makes companies liable if customer information (such as financial information or medical information) is made available to unauthorized personnel. Retrobox has created customized software that completely erases the data.[2] Many state and local governments have legislation that makes it illegal to throw electronics into a landfill.[3] This creates great opportunities for entrepreneurs who can recycle the electronics.

As with the low-carb trend, though, large corporations have started to enter the industry. Both Dell and Gateway have recycling programs. Dell has also partnered with the Cristina Foundation to provide recycled technology to disabled and economically disadvantaged people.[4]

Discussion Questions

1. In what way is the low-carb trend and the digital trash trend similar to the dot-com trend?
2. What uncontrollable factors present a threat to entrepreneurs like Stampp Corbin? What could cause his recycling company to experience problems?
3. What is the competitive advantage of RetroBox?
4. In what ways can businesses protect themselves from the effects of changes in consumer tastes and legislation?

Endnotes

1. Chana R. Schoenberger, "One Man's Trash," *Forbes,* August 16, 2004, 106.
2. Tamara Holmes, "When Good PCs Go Bad," *Black Enterprise,* April 2004, 49.
3. Schoenberger, 106.
4. Dell Computers, http://www.dell.com.

CASE 10: BUSINESS PLAN FOR ONE HAND CLAPPING RECORDS

Executive Summary

One Hand Clapping Records will be formed as an independent record label that will work in association with the Mike Seaver Complex Recording Studio. The studio is also owned by One Hand Clapping Records. The company's founders Joseph Gierer and Christopher Schaller are musicians who have worked in the music industry. One founder has worked in the recording industry and the other has worked in the industry in a marketing and management capacity. With their combined talents, One Hand Clapping Records should become a major player in the record label industry.

The objectives of the company are to sign three to five musical acts and sell 900 to 1,000 CDs per act. The founders expect a gross margin of 30 percent or higher on CDs and a net income of 25 to 30 percent. A net income of 15 percent is expected on live performances. Projected sales, gross margin, and net profit for the first three years is shown below.

The music industry has experienced many changes in recent years. Illegal downloading of music from the Internet has had a detrimental impact on CD sales, which has reduced the income of bands and retail outlets. However, other technological changes, such as Apple's iPod, have been beneficial, and many analysts believe it will revolutionize the music industry.

One Hand Clapping Records will be a Missouri Limited Liability Company (LLC), based in St. Louis. Start-up costs for the record company will total $7,000. This does not include the cost of equipment that is already owned. Almost all of the recording equipment is already owned and operated.

Mission Statement

One Hand Clapping Records in association with the Mike Seaver Complex will become the leading independent record label and recording studio to bands and individual musicians in the genres of Rock, Pop, Alternative, Hip-Hop, and Rap in the Missouri and Illinois areas.

Business Environment

The business environment for the music industry has been chaotic for the past several years. Changes in

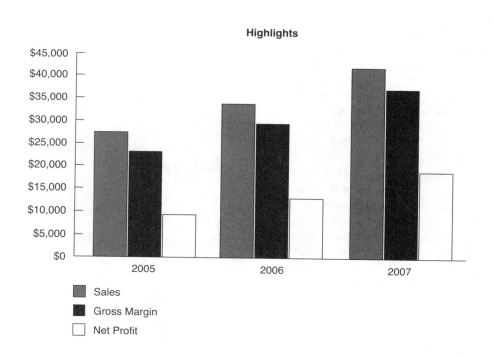

Highlights

Sales
Gross Margin
Net Profit

(continued)

technology have allowed music fans to illegally download music, resulting in lower revenue for retail stores and bands. However, new technology is also being developed to help the music industry. Items such as Apple's iPod have created new ways to download and listen to music.

There has also been an increase in the number of new bands, making it harder for fledgling groups to succeed. To rise above the competition, bands must be composed of excellent musicians and have excellent marketing strategies.

Consumer tastes change frequently. While pop music may be popular one year, the next year rap becomes the rage. Bands may see their market potential increase and decrease with these changes.

Product/Service Description

One Hand Clapping Records is a new independent record label for the St. Louis market that will provide musicians of all different backgrounds the opportunity to be heard in the music world. In association with the Mike Seaver Complex Recording Studio, which is owned by One Hand Clapping Records, the company will be able to record and promote local talent. The focus will be on the St. Louis market initially, but eventually the company will expand to the rest of the Missouri and Illinois areas. One Hand Clapping Records will record, produce, and mass market the music of bands or individual musicians and will focus on their success in the music industry. The bands and individuals will be promoted in live shows at different concert venues to create a fan base to help with their success. The process of mastering and duplication of the CD will be done by outsourcing. The company will also work with radio stations to get the music played on local radio stations. All artwork and CD case booklets will be designed in house. Miscellaneous items such as stickers, buttons, T-shirts, and posters will be outsourced; but all designs for these items will be done in house. Recording will be in the Mike Seaver Complex where all equipment will be provided for the recording process except for instruments that the musicians will bring. As the company grows, it will compete with other local recording labels and those that are regional and national.

Competition

Competitors include Four Seasons Recording Studios, Music Masters, and Liberation Music. Four Seasons and Music Masters offer quality recording at high prices but do not offer the management, promotions, and graphic designing that One Hand Clapping will provide. Liberation Music offers the management and promotion but does not offer the self-recording and customers must pay a high dollar amount for it. This requires a higher CD price to recoup the cost of the CD.

Pricing

Prices for recording studios vary depending on the size of the studio. Some major recording studios cost $75 to $150 per hour. Others price lower than that so they can gain a larger market share. Clients of the major studios pay higher prices for the professional work done because these studios spend thousands of dollars to buy big equipment and must recoup their costs. Because One Hand Clapping owns its own recording studio and all its equipment, the company can create high-quality digital recordings for a fraction of the cost of the major studios.

One Hand Clapping will offer recording, mixing, managing, promoting, and graphic designing at a lower cost than that offered by companies that do not have their own studio. Our musicians' CDs will sell for less than that of other bands, and this in turn will boost sales. Because of this, word-of-mouth advertising will result in the company signing more bands.

Credit Policy

Payment schedules will be negotiated with each band. One Hand Clapping will try to get payments up-front; however, some bands may pay a partial payment up-front with the remainder paid out of CD sales. If the full amount is not recovered from CD sales, the band will be billed directly.

One Hand Clapping will pay mastering and duplication costs upon completion and review of the final product.

Sales to the general public at live concerts will be paid by cash or credit cards.

Competitive Advantage

One Hand Clapping Records has a major competitive edge: there is no competitor that the company is aware

(continued)

of that has a record label with recording and mixing in house. One Hand Clapping Records offers the expertise of a certified recording engineer and uses state-of-the-art recording equipment to produce high-quality recordings. This competitive advantage is hard to match because if other companies did this, they would have to increase their prices.

One Hand Clapping Records will offer a "one-stop-shop" recording experience, offering full digital recordings, graphic designing, promotion, marketing, and management all under one roof. The company will have full control of the recording and promoting process.

Target Market

The target market will be segmented geographically and psychographically. The company will focus first on the St. Louis market and then expand into all of Missouri and Illinois. Efforts will be focused on the cities of St. Louis, Columbia, Springfield, Rolla, and Kansas City, Missouri, as well as Peoria, Chicago, and Springfield, Illinois. The focus will be on the genres of Rock/Alternative and Rap/Hip-Hop. A lot of work will be needed to get the Pop/Rock genre growth to be substantial in the area.

The company will promote and market music to increase growth in Rock/Alternative, Rap/Hip-Hop, and Pop/Rock genres. These three segments are the most commonly listened-to music in the Midwest. With the growth rate between 10 and 25 percent. The company will be able to take a substantial hold on the independent listeners' market. Each segment relies on its listeners to spread the word about the music to increase sales.

Location

This business will be run out of the owner's home until it becomes too large for the space. The recording studio is in a separate building on residential property and will remain there for the foreseeable future.

Promotion

Marketing in the independent record business depends on the recognition for expertise in recording, engineering, marketing/promotions, and management. It starts

with the certified recording engineer. The company will market the skills of the recording engineer and producer. It will also market the skills of the marketing and management experts.

The company will develop a database of customers by creating a mailing list of fans at live shows and concerts. This list will be used to send out advertisements and e-mails to inform people of future concerts. A newsletter will also be developed. However, going to shows and recruiting musical acts is the best way to get the company name known.

The One Hand Clapping Records Web site will be the virtual business card and portfolio for the company, as well as its online "home." It will showcase the background of the bands and musical acts that have been signed, as well as the portfolio of all the past and current acts of One Hand Clapping Records. We will also use the Web site as a means of selling CDs, T-shirts, and so on. The Web site, which will be designed in house, will be flashy and well designed.

The Web site http://www.onehandclappingrecords.com will be promoted at live shows. It will also be posted on the CDs, posters, advertisements, stickers, and other products that are sold. An online forum will be created so bands and fans can talk to each other.

All development of the main Web site will be created in house and the bands/musical acts' Web sites will be designed for a small fee. Fees would range from $100 to $500 depending on how elaborate the Web site is. One Hand Clapping Records would manage the Web sites for the musicians so they would have more time to prepare CDs or live shows.

Management

The initial management team will consist of the two founders of the company. Christopher (Topher) Schaller will be the recording engineer, executive producer, and manager. Joe Gierer will serve as management, marketing executive, and producer. As the company grows, it will do mastering and duplication in house instead of subcontracting it to outsides firms. A certified graphic designer would also be hired.

The following table summarizes the personnel expenditures for the first three years with compensation increases of 5 percent. Payroll will be 15 percent of total sales of CDs and recording time. The cost to make

(continued)

a 10-song CD in the studio will average $1,500. This is the salary cost for making the CD.

	2005	2006	2007
Joe Gierer	$4,500	$4,725	$4,961
Topher Schaller	$4,500	$4,725	$4,961
Total Employees	0	0	0
Total Payroll	$9,000	$9,450	$9,922

Financial Plan

(See financial plan at end of report.)

Legal Considerations

One Hand Clapping will be a Missouri Limited Liability Company (LLC). The LLC was chosen to provide tax advantages to the owners as well as limited liability.

Contracts with bands will be exclusive contracts; however, if another record label is interested in the band, a buy-out of the contract will be negotiated. The length of the contracts will be negotiated between the band and One Hand Clapping; a typical contract would be a renewable three-album contract. If the band does not perform well and does not produce a good fan base, One Hand Clapping reserves the right to terminate the contract.

One Hand Clapping and the band will file jointly for the copyrights. Because the band will write the songs and One Hand Clapping will add artistic flavor, both parties will have copyright protection.

Insurance

Property insurance will cover theft of equipment or loss due to fire, natural disaster, or so on. When the company first begins, no other insurance will be carried.

Suppliers

The mastering and duplication process will be outsourced. Outsourcing will not be to the cheapest company because it is essential to have a quality product. The choice of companies for these processes will have an impact on both quality and price.

Uncontrollable Risks

Many uncontrollable factors could have an impact on the success of this company. Some of the most important are as follows:

Risk: Changes in the music industry because of the Internet have already occurred. Future Internet developments could be beneficial or detrimental.

Strategy: In order to try to prevent negative impacts, the company owners will constantly monitor changes that are occurring and plan the company future accordingly.

Risk: Not all bands and musicians have the heart and drive to succeed. It is possible that One Hand Clapping Records could invest time and money in a band or individual musician that does not have the persistence needed to succeed.

Strategy: One Hand Clapping will screen potential clients and provide a realistic preview of the time and effort needed to succeed. This will help minimize the likelihood of this risk occurring.

Risk: Changes in technology could greatly affect recording, mixing, and mastering.

Strategy: One Hand Clapping Records will monitor all changes in technology and will use the best technological methods available.

Conclusion

This company is feasible if the following assumptions hold true:

1. The company can develop a strong fan base with the bands that will be signed.
2. The company will be able to adjust to any technological advances that impact recording, mixing, and mastering.
3. The company will carefully screen out any individual musicians and bands that will not be willing to invest the time and effort needed to succeed.
4. Both owners will have full-time jobs at other companies until One Hand Clapping is sufficiently profitable to pay them an adequate salary.

Case written by Joe Gierer. Reprinted with permission.

(continued)

CASE 10 *(continued)*

Start-up Costs

The start-up costs of One Hand Clapping Records will come to $6,600, which will cover legal expenses for customer contract formation, mastering and duplication of the first CD, and other miscellaneous expenses. These start-up costs are shown below:

Legal fees	$2,500
Miscellaneous	$ 500
Insurance	$ 750
Equipment	$ 750
Mastering	$1,100
Duplication	$1,000
Total	$6,600

These costs do not show the cost of the recording equipment that is already owned by the company. Start-up costs will be paid through investments by each owner. No debt is expected until the company grows to a larger size.

Sales Forecast

The following table gives a summary of forecasted sales. CD sales are expected to increase 25 percent per year. It is also assumed that there will not be any sales for the first few months due to the recording, mastering, and duplication process. The chart shows sales once these processes have been completed. The biggest growth is expected to come between the months of February and October. This is the prime time for CD sales from smaller, independent record companies because the majority of the major record company sales occur between October and February.

Projected Income Statement

The projected income statement is shown on the next page with sales increasing more than $26,000 in the first year and growing to over $41,000 by the third year. Profits will be less than $10,000 the first year but will quickly improve to approximately $20,000 by the third year.

Opening Day Balance Sheet

Current Assets	
Cash	$5,100
Prepaid Insurance	$ 750
Total Current Assets	$5,850
Fixed Assets	
Equipment	$ 750
Total Fixed Assets	$ 750
Total Assets	$6,600
Total Liabilities	
Current Liabilities	0
Long-term Liabilities	0
Total Liabilities	0
Total Equity	$6,600
Total Liabilities & Equity	$6,600

	2005	2006	2007
Compact Discs	$25,282	$31,602	$39,503
Live Shows	$1,283	$1,411	$1,552
Total Sales	$26,565	$33,013	$41,055

Direct Cost of Sales	2005	2006	2007
Recording	$1,592	$1,672	$1,755
Mastering	$875	$919	$965
Duplication/Paraphernalia	$1,751	$1,838	$1,930
Subtotal Direct Cost of Sales	$4,218	$4,429	$4,650

(continued)

CASE 10 *(continued)*

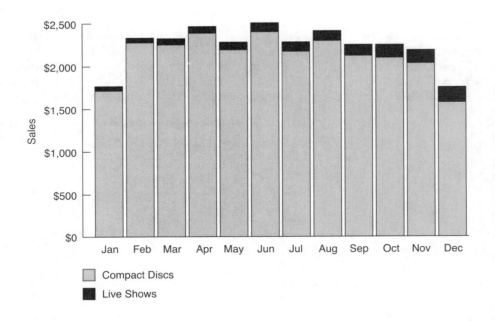

Pro Forma Profit and Loss

	2005	2006	2007
Sales	$26,565	$33,013	$41,055
Direct Cost of Sales	$4,218	$4,429	$4,650
Other Costs of Sales	$0	$0	$0
Total Cost of Sales	$4,218	$4,429	$4,650
Gross Margin	$22,347	$28,584	$36,405
Gross Margin %	84.12%	86.58%	88.67%
Expenses:			
Payroll	$9,000	$9,450	$9,922
Sales and Marketing and Other Expenses	$1,008	$1,008	$1,008
Depreciation	$504	$504	$504
Legal Fees	$1,500	$1,500	$1,500
Supplies	$600	$600	$600
Payroll Taxes	$1,350	$1,418	$1,488
Other	$0	$0	$0
Total Operating Expenses	$13,962	$14,480	$15,023
Profit Before Interest and Taxes	$8,385	$14,105	$21,382
Interest Expense	$0	$0	$0
Taxes Incurred	$1,258	$2,116	$3,207
Net Profit	$7,127	$11,989	$18,175
Net Profit/Sales	26.83%	36.32%	44.27%

(continued)

Profit Monthly

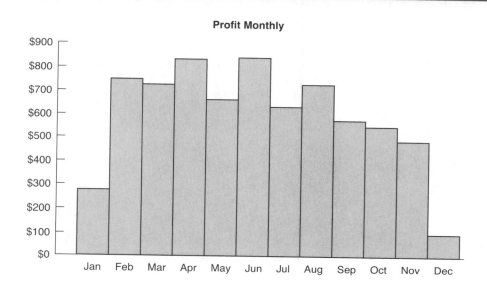

Profit Yearly

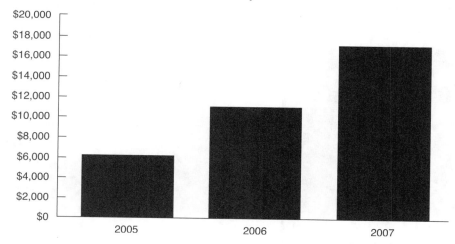

Break-even Analysis

Costs for the company are a minimum of $3,500 per CD created. This includes $1,500 for the studio and mixing, $500 for mastering, and $1,500 for duplication and packaging. The $1,500 for studio time and mixing is done in house and is not a "payment" made to an outside company. Payments to outside companies will total a minimum of $2,000 per CD created. This is shown as direct cost of sales. The gross margin percentage as shown in the projected income statement is 84.12 percent (.8412). All projections for the first few years assume that two CDs per year are created. CDs will be sold directly to the general public for $10 each. Fixed costs the first year will be

Payroll	$9,000
Sales/Marketing	$1,008
Legal Fees	$1,500
Supplies	$600
Payroll Taxes	$1,350
Depreciations	$504
Total	$13,962

(continued)

Cash Flow Projection	January	February	March	April	May	June	July	August	September	October	November	December
Cash Received	1,694	2,253	2,232	2,366	2,174	2,387	2,155	2,272	2,098	2,078	2,011	1,560
Cash Out												
Mastering	0	0	0	0	0	1,000	0	0	0	0	0	0
Duplication	0	0	0	0	0	1,100	0	0	0	0	0	0
Payroll	750	750	750	750	750	750	750	750	750	750	750	750
Sales/Marketing	84	84	84	84	84	84	84	84	84	84	84	84
Legal Fees	125	125	125	125	125	125	125	125	125	125	125	125
Supplies	600	600	600	600	600	600	600	600	600	600	600	600
Payroll Taxes	112	112	112	112	112	112	112	112	112	112	112	112
Total	1671	1671	1671	1671	1671	3771	1671	1671	1671	1671	1671	1671
Cash Balance	23	582	561	695	503	–1,384	484	601	427	407	340	–111

(continued)

CASE 10 *(continued)*

Gross Margin Monthly

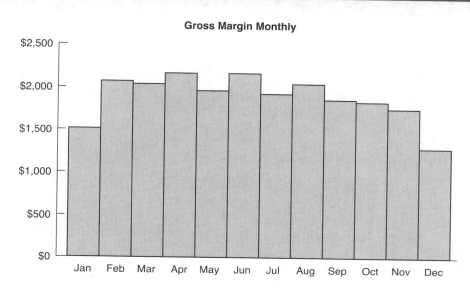

Break-even for the first year is therefore $13,962/ .8412 = $16,597.71

Since CDs are sold for $10 each, a total of 1,659.7 CDs (or 1,660.0) must be sold to reach the break-even point.

Discussion Questions

1. Assume you are a potential investor in this company. What information has not been included in the business plan that you would like to know?

2. What is the competitive advantages of One Hand Clapping? Is this important to bands? Why or why not?

3. The break-even analysis shows that if CDs are sold for $10 each, the company must sell 1,660 CDs the first year to break even. Do you believe this is realistic? Why or why not?

4. Do you believe this business is feasible? Why or why not?

CASE 11: BUSINESS PLAN FOR FASHION FOOTWEAR FASHION FOOTWEAR COMPANY

Executive Summary

Fashion Footwear Company will be a men's dress/dress casual shoe and accessory store located in Richmond Heights, Missouri. It will be a sole proprietorship owned by Patrick Imming. Fashion Footwear will carry a wide variety of styles, sizes, and widths. The target market will be professional men ages 25 to 60 in St. Louis County. Our primary market area will be a five-mile radius from the store.

Fashion Footwear will be located in The Boulevard Shopping Center, which is currently being constructed on Brentwood Boulevard directly across from the St. Louis Galleria. This area has recently become a retailing hot spot. It is within a 10-minute drive of 80 percent of St. Louis's office population.

There is minimal competition in the area. The shoe stores at the mall carry both men's and women's shoes, and therefore the selection is limited. The department stores have a men's shoe selection, but the service is often poor. Even the stores that have a good selection do not carry the brands and widths that Fashion Footwear will carry.

Projected sales for the first three years are approximately $530,000, $634,000, and $758,000, respectively. Profits are expected to be approximately $24,500, $67,700, and $114,835, respectively.

Patrick Imming, the proprietor, has four years' experience in the shoe retailing industry, and it is this experience that has convinced him that there is an unmet market for men's dress shoes and dress casual shoes.

Mission Statement

Fashion Footwear Company is an upscale men's shoe and accessory store that is dedicated to servicing our customer by providing only the highest quality, most comfortable dress shoes and dress casual shoes on the market along with outstanding customer service. We keep a wide selection of brands, sizes, and widths to accommodate even the hardest-to-fit foot. Our sales staff will be very knowledgeable about our products, provide customers with advice, and create an overall positive environment, for we believe the customer is our most important asset. Our goal is to have every customer who leaves the store feeling 100 percent satisfied.

Business Environment

Every year, U.S. consumers spend more than $20 billion on footwear. Shoes are sold in a number of venues, including specialty stores, department and discount stores, and vendor-owned outlets. According to the Census Bureau's *Statistical Abstract of the United States* (2002), the number of shoe stores in the United States dropped to 29,700 (down from 37,200 in 1996). This is largely due to the economic recession that has occurred in the first years of the 21st century and low consumer confidence that has slowed spending. This has affected not only the shoe industry but also retail stores across most industries. Overall, the men's footwear market has recently been shaped by two forces—an increasing dominance of imported shoes and a shift to more dress casual shoes. This is because more casual work attire has been accepted in American offices. As a result, men's dress shoe sales have fallen, but the sales of men's dress casual shoes have soared. In the late 1990s, men's retail footwear sales in the United States outperformed women's, as men's shoes generated $17.4 billion in sales compared to women's $16.8 billion. Despite these figures, the retail shoe industry has slowed a bit overall. In order for a shoe store, especially a new store, to become and remain successful, it must do the following things:

Offer exceptional customer service

Offer competitive prices

Stay fresh by keeping new styles

Be able to adapt to changing conditions

Fashion Footwear will be able to succeed in this market because we will do these things. By doing this along with an aggressive marketing approach, we will be able to establish ourselves and increase sales over the first few years of operation.

Product/Service Description

Fashion Footwear will offer the highest-quality men's dress and dress casual shoes and accessories. The accessories will include belts, shoe laces, and shoe care products. The shoe care products will include water repellent spray, cream shoe polish, leather cleaner, leather conditioner, shoe brushes, and shine sponges. We will offer a wide variety of sizes and widths to fit almost everyone. Brands we carry include Cole Haan, Kenneth Cole New

(continued)

York, Kenneth Cole Reaction, Ecco, Josef Seibel, Rockport, Born, Timberland, Clarks, and Bacco Bucci. Most of these shoes will be available in different widths such as narrow, medium, and wide.

When purchasing footwear, customers care about such things as looks, price, quality, and value. People will pay more for a nicer pair of shoes if they feel they are getting more value. That is something that must be expressed to the customer. The perceived benefits of the pair of shoes must outweigh the price. Well-known, reliable brand names are also important when it comes to customers' buying decisions. People will pay more if they know they are getting a pair of shoes from a reliable company whose products have a good reputation for quality and comfort.

When buying dress and dress casual shoes, customers need a knowledgeable salesperson who can measure their feet to ensure proper sizes and width. A shoe must fit properly in order to be comfortable. The salesperson must also answer any technical or general questions about the products offered.

Competitors

The men's shoe retail industry is made up of several types of companies. These include shoe-only stores that sell only shoes. These stores will primarily sell both men's and women's shoes or strictly dress shoes for either sex. There are also large department stores that sell everything, including shoes. Finally, there are men's retail stores that primarily sell clothes. They may have a small selection of shoes but not as many as an actual shoe store.

The primary competition that Fashion Footwear will face is located within the five-mile target area. There are three department stores located in the nearby mall, the St. Louis Galleria, that sell men's shoes along with a discounted shoe warehouse and men's shoe and accessory store that is similar to Fashion Footwear. These competitors are as follows:

Department Stores: These include Famous-Barr, Lord and Taylor, and Dillard's and are located within the St. Louis Galleria. These stores sell everything from shoes to appliances. Although these stores are large and have lots of purchasing power, their men's shoe selection isn't that impressive. Famous-Barr does not have a large selection of men's shoes, and Lord and Taylor and Dillard's carry all shoes from athletic to dress, which leads

to a reduced selection of both. These stores do not carry top-of-the-line brands, and the customer service is not that good.

DSW Shoe Warehouse: This is a large discount shoe store located on Eager Road (not in the Galleria Mall). The store carries a large selection of shoes; however, most of them are women's. There is little customer service, and most of the dress shoes it carries are unknown brands. They are lower-quality imitations of names like Kenneth Cole and Cole Haan.

Johnston and Murphy: This will be Fashion Footwear's closest, most direct competitor. It is a new store located in the St. Louis Galleria Mall. The company sells Johnston and Murphy shoes, jackets, belts, shoe care products, and so on. Both dress and dress casual are sold. Most of the shoes are in the same price ranges as the brands that will be sold by Fashion Footwear, and they have a professional, well-trained sales staff. However, they only sell Johnston and Murphy products and not all customers like this brand.

Competitive Advantage

Our main competitive advantage comes from our selection of styles and sizes, especially widths. This is important because most shoe stores that sell men's shoes don't carry different widths or they have a very limited number of styles that come in different widths. Fashion Footwear will advertise that it has different widths because that will bring in many customers who have had trouble finding shoes.

Another advantage will come from the selection of styles. Fashion Footwear will carry some of the basic styles that other stores carry, but we will also have the harder-to-find styles. If we do not have a particular style, we will try to order it.

Location will also play an important role in the competitive advantage. Fashion Footwear will be located close to downtown Clayton, Missouri, which has a large percentage of the office population of metropolitan St. Louis. Also, Fashion Footwear will be in a shopping center that is not as big as the Galleria Mall so it will be easier for customers to stop and make a purchase on their way home from work.

Our final competitive advantage will be the level of customer service and product knowledge of the staff.

(continued)

Target Market

The target market will be professional men between the ages of 25 and 60 with disposable income. Our customer base will primarily come from within a five-mile radius of the store. There are more than 245,000 men between the ages of 25 and 60 in St. Louis County. We are also planning to draw customers from St. Louis City, where many younger professionals have moved in recent years. Customers from Illinois will also come to shop.

There are about 302,851 residents living within a five-mile radius of the store. Almost half of these residents (47 percent) are men. Of this percentage, roughly 88,251 are men between the ages of 25 and 60. The median age for this area is 36.2 years old, which fits right into the target market. Overall, this is one of the more wealthy areas of St. Louis County with an average household income of $82,395 within a three-mile radius.

Fashion Footwear will focus on men with white-collar jobs. Within the five-mile radius, more than 73 percent of the workers hold white-collar jobs. Approximately 80 percent of the St. Louis area's office population is located within a 10-minute drive. The store is very close to Clayton, Missouri, which is St. Louis County's largest business district with more than 1,200 businesses and an annual combined payroll of $500 million.

The customers will fall into two major groups—men looking for dress/work shoes and men looking for dress/casual everyday shoes. These groups are more completely defined as follows:

Men looking for dress shoes: These are professional men, probably working in the business world who are looking for high-quality, comfortable dress shoes to wear to work or anywhere else they need to wear a suit. They want shoes that look dressy but not flashy. The shoes must be appropriate for the business world. These customers have a household income of $50,000 or greater, and they can afford to pay more for higher-quality shoes. The average price for a pair of dress shoes will be around $160 to $180.

Men looking for dress casual/everyday shoes: These men are looking for a good quality, comfortable shoe they could wear to work with more casual attire or wear every day. These will also be professional men with disposable income in jobs that don't require a suit and tie every day. This segment has been growing significantly in the past years, due to many companies allowing more casual dress at work. The average price for a pair of dress casual shoes will be around $100 to $120.

Target Market Projections	2004	2005	2006
Men Purchasing Dress Shoes	322,500	334,755	347,476
Men Purchasing Dress/Casual	645,000	690,150	738,461

Location

Fashion Footwear will be located in the Boulevard Shopping Center that is currently being constructed on Brentwood Boulevard across from the St. Louis Galleria Mall. This area has recently become a retailing hot spot in St. Louis County. Along with the Galleria Mall, customers come from all across the area to shop at nearby locations, including the Brentwood Square, The Promenade, and The Meridian. Many unique shops are located within this area, including Crate and Barrel, REI, Orvis, and Mark Shale. The Boulevard Shopping Center will contain retail stores, restaurants, condominiums, and offices. This is similar to the "urban village" concept that is new to St. Louis.

Promotion

Marketing efforts will be focused on professional men between the ages 25 and 60 who are looking for quality, comfort dress and dress casual shoes. Fashion Footwear will put free advertising to work whenever possible. The first is the visibility of the location. When the shopping center opens, it will be swarmed with new customers because it is a new shopping center. An attractive storefront with good merchandise display will help get recognition. Once customers enter the store, they will be exposed to a positive, friendly atmosphere. Another form of free advertising is word of mouth. Fashion Footwear plans to impress customers so much with selection and service that they will tell family members, friends, and coworkers about our store.

The marketing strategy will also use paid forms of advertising. There will be an ad in the phone book. It will not be large but it will be well placed to attract attention. Ads will be placed in the local, community newspapers where potential customers live. These papers will include but not be limited to *The Clayton World, The Ladue News, The West-End Word,* and the *Webster-Kirkwood Times.* Ads

(continued)

will also be placed in *The St. Louis Business Journal.* Many potential customers read these publications. The metropolitan paper, *The St. Louis Post-Dispatch,* will also be used but not as frequently as the local, community newspapers.

Radio ads will be placed a few times during the year. These ads will be focused on AM Talk Radio stations and FM stations that are played at the workplace.

Once a customer base has been established, mailings will be sent to inform customers of any sales or special offerings.

Management and Personnel

Fashion Footwear will be owned by Patrick Imming. Patrick has a bachelor of science degree in business administration and four years' experience working at Overland Trading Company, a men's and women's casual shoe store. Patrick gained much of his knowledge of the retail shoe business while working at this store. This is also where he began to see there was an unmet need for men's dress and dress casual shoes in different widths in the area. Patrick is confident that his knowledge of the business will allow him to create a store that will serve professional men looking for a large selection of styles and sizes of shoes. Patrick will manage the day-to-day operations of the store, including selling, until the store is successfully up and running. There will also be a full-time assistant manager, another full-time employee, and two part-time employees. Once the store has become successful, a full-time manager will be hired to run day-to-day operations and Patrick will concentrate on long-term strategy for the store. This full-time manager will not be hired in the first three years.

Salaries for personnel are shown below:

	2005	2006	2007
Patrick Imming	$35,000	$38,000	$45,000
Assistant store manager	$24,000	$24,500	$25,000
Full-time employee	$20,000	$20,300	$20,600
Part-time employee	$5,184	$5,400	$5,616
Part-time employee	$4,320	$4,500	$4,680
Total Payroll	$88,504	$92,700	$100,896

Legal

Fashion Footwear will be established as a proprietorship in order to give Patrick Imming full control over the company's management decisions. Adequate insurance will be purchased to minimize the impact of unlimited liability.

Insurance

Insurance will include property insurance to cover typical risks such as fire and theft. Liability insurance will also be purchased and will include workers' compensation, premises and operations, and employee liability.

Suppliers

Inventory will be purchased from a wholesaler/distributor that purchases shoes directly from the manufacturer. Fashion Footwear will use the wholesaler because it will not incur the expense of a warehouse to store large quantities of inventory. Also, Fashion Footwear is not large enough to obtain quantity discounts from the manufacturer. Inventory will be tracked using the point-of-sales system, which will have software that indicates what items have been sold each day, when they are sold, which items sell quickly, and which items don't. Fashion Footwear will continually update the selection of styles based on which ones sell well. It will be important to keep the selection of styles new and fresh so customers keep coming back.

Uncontrollable Risks

Risk: A competitor locates in the same shopping center. Because the shopping center is still being built and some of the spaces have not been leased, it is possible that a company (even an indirect competitor) could locate in the same shopping center.

Strategy: Although another competitor may draw customers away from Fashion Footwear, it may also help to draw the target market to the shopping center. If another competitor locates nearby, Fashion Footwear would use advertising and window displays to stress its large number of styles and sizes. This would help bring customers into the store.

Risk: The new shopping center may not be as successful as expected, and pedestrian traffic at the center would be low. There are many shopping centers being built in the

(continued)

CASE 11 *(continued)*

metropolitan area, and some have not been as successful as expected. For some, pedestrian traffic is far below projected levels.

Strategy: Although Fashion Footwear may benefit from some impulse purchases, it is more likely that this will be a "special trip" purchase for our target market. Therefore, if pedestrian traffic is low, advertising will be increased to encourage men to stop at the store.

Assumptions and Conclusion

This business is feasible if the following assumptions hold true:

1. Some stores in the new shopping center (such as Crate and Barrel) will have the first and only location in the St. Louis area. This will bring more business to the center because this will be the only place customers can shop at these stores.
2. A friend who is a carpenter will do much of the renovation work. This will result in lower start-up costs than if a construction company were hired.
3. The shopping center is open and fully completed by the fourth quarter of 2005. This will allow

Fashion Footwear to be open for most of the 2005 holiday season.

Discussion Questions

1. The business environment section states that the number of shoe stores has decreased largely due to the economic recession. What other reasons could account for the decrease in retail shoe stores?
2. If the need exists for a larger variety of sizes and widths, why do the large department stores not carry these items? Is this really a good competitive advantage for Fashion Footwear?

Start-up Costs

Working Capital	$57,000
Supplies	1,000
Inventory	163,020
Prepaid Expenses	13,767
Furniture and Fixtures	50,000
Leasehold Improvements	102,900
Total Start-up Costs	$387,687
Investment:	
Patrick Imming	100,000
Loan Amount	287,687

Opening Day Balance Sheet

Assets	
Current Assets	
Cash	$57,000
Supplies	1,000
Inventory	163,020
Prepaid Expenses	13,767
Total Current Assets	234,787
Fixed Assets	
Furniture and Fixtures	50,000
Leasehold Improvements	102,900
Total Fixed Assets	152,900
Total Assets	387,687
Liabilities	
Current Liabilities	
Accounts Payable	2,000
Current Maturity of	
Long-term Debt	32,242
Total Current Liabilities	34,242
Long-term Liabilities	55,445
Total Liabilities	289,687
Total Equity	98,000
Total Liabilities and Equity	387,687

(continued)

CASE 11 *(continued)*

Total Profit and Loss

	2005	2006	2007
Sales	$530,878	$634,168	$757,939
Direct Costs of Goods	$273,920	$314,069	$360,183
Other Costs of Goods	$0	$0	$0
Costs of Goods Sold	$273,920	$314,069	$360,183
Gross Margin	$256,958	$320,099	$397,575
Gross Margin %	48.40%	50.48%	52.48%
Expenses:			
Payroll	$88,504	$92,700	$100,896
Supplies-Sales and Marketing Expenses	$2,940	$1,750	$1,750
Depreciation	$0	$0	$0
Rent	$56,004	$56,004	$56,004
Utilities	$4,800	$4,800	$4,800
Insurance	$5,880	$4,800	$4,800
Payroll Taxes	$13,276	$13,905	$15,134
Advertising	$15,924	$18,000	$22,000
Professional Fees (Legal/Accounting)	$1,008	$1,010	$1,010
Maintenance	$840	$840	$840
Credit Card/Check Processing Fee	$7,164	$8,498	$10,156
Other	$0	$0	$0
Total Operating Expenses	$196,339	$202,307	$217,390
Profit Before Interest and Taxes	$60,619	$117,792	$180,366
Interest Expense	$25,601	$21,057	$16,316
Taxes Incurred	$10,505	$29,021	$49,215
Net Profit	$24,513	$67,715	$114,835

3. If you were going to rename this store, what would you call it?

4. Evaluate Patrick's education and work experience as if you were an investor or loan officer.

5. What other uncontrollable risks should be considered?

6. The start-up costs show $57,000 in working capital. If the projected numbers in the financial section are correct, how much working capital is really needed? Explain your answer.

(continued)

	December	January	February	March	April	May	June	July	August	September	October	November
Beginning Cash	57,000	96,014	83,149	78,075	76,272	79,689	85,957	91,999	99,111	72,985	80,378	42,159
Cash In	67,185	28,428	30,229	33,807	39,642	43,434	43,784	44,900	46,194	45,520	46,918	60,837
Cash Available	124,185	124,442	113,378	111,882	115,914	123,123	129,741	136,899	145,305	118,505	127,296	102,996
Cash Out												
Payroll	7,376	7,376	7,376	7,376	7,376	7,376	7,376	7,376	7,376	7,376	7,376	7,376
Supplies	140	140	140	140	140	140	140	140	140	140	140	140
Rent	4,667	4,667	4,667	4,667	4,667	4,667	4,667	4,667	4,667	4,667	4,667	4,667
Utilities	400	400	400	400	400	400	400	400	400	400	400	400
Insurance	490	490	490	490	490	490	490	490	490	490	490	490
Payroll Taxes	1,106	1,106	1,106	1,106	1,106	1,106	1,106	1,106	1,106	1,106	1,106	1,106
Advertising	1,327	1,327	1,327	1,327	1,327	1,327	1,327	1,327	1,327	1,327	1,327	1,327
Professional Fees	84	84	84	84	84	84	84	84	84	84	84	84
Maintenance	70	70	70	70	70	70	70	70	70	70	70	70
Credit Card Fees	907	384	408	456	535	586	591	606	623	614	633	821
Interest	2,314	2,282	2,249	2,216	2,183	2,150	2,117	2,084	2,051	2,018	1,985	1,952
Principal	2,290	2,322	2,355	2,388	2,421	2,454	2,487	2,520	2,553	2,586	2,619	2,652
Inventory	7,000	20,645	14,631	14,890	15,426	16,316	16,887	16,918	51,433	17,249	64,240	17,316
Total Cash Out	28,171	41,293	35,303	35,610	36,225	37,166	37,742	37,788	72,320	38,127	85,137	38,401
Cash Balance	96,014	83,149	78,075	76,272	79,689	85,957	91,999	99,111	72,985	80,378	42,159	64,595

Executive Summary

The Noiz Vodka Bar is a bar, a music venue, and a specialty liquor lounge all in one. It will serve more than 100 types of vodka and imported beer in a nightclub setting. Live music will be offered every night and will include local and national bands.

The Noiz will cater to young professionals, college students, and the local music scene enthusiasts. Allison Miller will be president of the company. She has her own record label and has an exceptional knowledge of the local music scene. Delores Diaz DeLeon is currently employed by Enterprise Rent-A-Car, where she is a computer technician. She will be the main investor for The Noiz and will have a minimal role in the management of the company. Francisco Martinez has owned two previous businesses—Liberation Music, a record label, and a financial advising company. His experience in the local music scene has provided him with the knowledge to start and run a successful business. Francisco will be Vice President of Finance.

The Noiz will be located on Washington Street in downtown St. Louis, which is currently undergoing a revitalization.

Start-up costs, including working capital, total $112,500. Projected sales and profits for the first year are $459,000 and $88,000, respectively.

Mission Statement

The Noiz Vodka Bar is not only a bar but a music venue and specialty liquor lounge all in one. The company caters to young professionals, college students, and local music scene fanatics, bringing them the best cocktail drinks and live music St. Louis can offer. The company strives to support the local music scene but also brings in national touring acts of all types of music, from hip-hop to punk rock. The Noiz Vodka Bar serves as a bar for the metropolitan downtown area and as a music venue for the entire St. Louis area.

Business Environment

Many trends are favorable for businesses like The Noiz Bar. First, there are many young professionals and college students in the St. Louis metropolitan area. The demographics show a large number of young people due to the "baby boom echo"—the children of baby boomers. These people are the target market for The Noiz Bar.

Trends in the liquor industry also show an upward trend in sales of expensive, luxury brands. This is despite the fact that sales of many other types of liquor are static or declining. The Noiz Bar will cater to those who appreciate specialty liquors.

Finally, the downtown St. Louis area is undergoing a revitalization, and many young professionals are moving into nearby lofts and condos.

Product/Service Description

The Noiz Vodka Bar provides products and services as follows:

Specialty bar—Over 100 types of vodka, imported beer, and domestic beer will be stocked.

Nightclub—The Noiz is an alternative to dance clubs. It will feature live music in a nightclub setting.

Music venue—Live music will be offered every night and will feature local and national bands.

The Noiz Bar will have an exciting and posh environment and will offer more than the average bar or music venue.

Competition

Competition for The Noiz Bar includes the following companies:

Mississippi Nights—Located on Laclede's Landing in downtown St. Louis, this is one of the top venues for concerts of local and national bands.

The Pageant—The Pageant is the largest music venue in the St. Louis area. Its two levels usually host nationally touring bands. It includes the Halo Bar, a small bar that caters to the concert goers.

Pop's—Located in Illinois, Pop's is a larger venue that books both local and national touring bands.

Creepy Crawl—The Creepy Crawl is a small music venue that books mostly local artists.

High Pointe—The High Pointe books mostly local bands.

(continued)

Sub-Zero—The only existing vodka bar in the area, this company provides a lounge-type atmosphere. It serves sushi and more than 100 types of vodka. It does not host music events.

Pricing Strategy

The pricing strategy of The Noiz Vodka Bar is not to be the lowest price venue. The company will use a differentiation strategy by offering more variety and better quality. For this reason, an upscale pricing approach will be used.

Special promotions will be offered, however, to help develop relationships with customers and bring them back on particular nights. For this reason, special discounted drink nights will be established.

Credit Policy

The Noiz Vodka Bar will accept cash and credit cards. No personal checks will be accepted.

Competitive Advantage

The Noiz Bar's competitive advantage will be the unique atmosphere that combines three different places in one—a nightclub, a music venue, and a bar. This will attract a wider audience than the normal bar. It will be the only place in St. Louis that offers both premium liquor and great live bands.

Our competitive advantage will be strengthened by the following strategies:

Emphasizing atmosphere—The Noiz Vodka Bar will be differentiated from the everyday bar. It will be established as a clear and viable alternative for the target market.

Building a relationship-oriented business—The Noiz will build long-term relationships with clients, not single transaction deals. The Noiz Vodka Bar will strive to be the customer's favorite bar and concert hall.

Focus on target markets—The Noiz will focus on its target market of those ages 21 to 30 years.

Fulfill the promise—The Noiz will not just be marketed as a unique bar; it will fulfill its promise.

Target Market

The target markets are young professionals (ages 21 to 30) working full time, college students, and local music scene enthusiasts. It is estimated that 40 percent of the target market will be college students, 40 percent will be young professionals, and 20 percent will be local music scene enthusiasts.

Target Market Projections Table

	2005	2006	2007
Young professionals	16,680	19,427	20,204
College students	28,020	29,141	30,307
Music enthusiasts	9,340	9,714	10,103

The target markets selected were based on trends with the local specialty bar/music venue scene in the area. When visiting a martini bar, the customers are usually young professionals. When visiting a music venue, the customers are known as emo (emotional rock), indie (independent, local rock), hardcore rock, and punk-rock kids. Regular bars attract college students. Since Noiz Vodka Bar will provide all three of these features, the company expects to draw from each of the groups.

The Noiz Bar expects to attract 20 to 30 people on weekdays and 150 on Friday and Saturday nights. An average customer is expected to spend $20.

Promotional Plan

Marketing and promotion will include radio advertising on a local pop station and a local rock station. Print advertising will be used in *Playback*, a publication for local music scene enthusiasts, and in the *Riverfront Times*, a local newspaper, to reach many people in each of the target groups. To reach college students, the company will pass out flyers on all major campuses in the area.

Special promotions will include drink specials, happy hours, and drink menus at every table. The bartender/waiters will inform each customer of the nightly specials and will make recommendations.

Web advertising will be done in several ways. First a banner will be placed on a local music scene enthusiast's Web page and possibly on the local newspaper Web page to reach young professionals.

The company will also have its own Web page that will be interactive and easy to navigate. It will include flash, which will appeal to the younger generation. The Web site will also have a page dedicated to information about the company, which will explain the inspiration

(continued)

for the business and will give the owners' backgrounds. There will also be a staff page, featuring the staff, their favorite drinks, and favorite bands. In addition, a concert calendar will list all upcoming shows at The Noiz Vodka Bar. The Web site will also feature a drinks menu page showing all brands and flavors of vodka and the cocktails that can be mixed.

Location

The Noiz Vodka Bar will be located on Washington Avenue in downtown St. Louis. It will require 5,000 square feet and will hold up to 175 people. There will be tables for individual seating in addition to the bar. The location was chosen based on St. Louis City's plan to renovate Washington Avenue and the surrounding loft district.

Management and Personnel

When the bar opens, employees will include two bartenders, four cocktail waitresses, and two bar backs to assist the bartenders.

Door fees for bands vary but are expected to range from $5 to $10 per person. This door fee is split between the band, the sound technician, and the bouncer/door person. For this reason, the cost for these people is not shown as an expense, and the door fee is not included in the sales figure.

Wages for each of the other employees are shown below.

	2005	2006	2007
Bartenders	$15,000	$15,750	$16,537
Cocktail waitresses	$13,500	$14,175	$14,883
Bar backs	$13,200	$13,860	$14,553

The management/ownership of The Noiz Bar includes Allison Miller, Delores Diaz De Leon, and Francisco Martinez. Allison has her own record label and has an exceptional knowledge of the local music scene as well as experience in small business. Her knowledge and contacts will be beneficial in planning the music and generating customers through word of mouth.

The management philosophy is based on responsibility and mutual respect. People who work at The Noiz Bar want to work at The Noiz because we have an environment that encourages creativity and achievement.

The team will include eight employees initially and two of the three owners will work as managers. The third owner will be an investor but will not work in the company.

Legal

The Noiz Vodka Bar will be a limited liability company. The LLC form of organization was chosen because of tax issues and the provision of limited liability to the owners.

Insurance

Full insurance coverage will be necessary, including property insurance on furnishings and inventory, theft, and liability in case of injury to a customer. Workers' compensation insurance will be carried on the employees.

Suppliers

The liquor will be purchased from two distributors—Glazer's and Missouri Beverage Company. Supply problems are not expected in this industry. We expect to pay cash for supplies for the first few deliveries and then to obtain credit from the vendors for future purchases.

Uncontrollable Risks

Many uncontrollable risks could affect this business.

Risk: The first is a change in consumer tastes of young adults away from this type of music/specialty lounge. Although this does not seem likely, new forms of entertainment could draw customers away from this type of venue.

Strategy: In order to plan for this possibility, The Noiz Bar owners will continually monitor trends in consumer tastes and adjust the product/service offering accordingly.

Risk: Local legislation could limit the number of liquor licenses granted in the area and prevent The Noiz Bar from obtaining the location it prefers.

Strategy: If this occurs, the owners will continue to look for an alternative site.

(continued)

CASE 12 *(continued)*

Start-up Costs

Prepaid Expenses

Legal	500
Advertising	4,000
Insurance	500
Working Capital	51,000
Inventory	10,000
Equipment	45,000
Liquor License	1,400
Supplies	100
Total	**112,500**

Opening Day Balance Sheet

Current Assets		
	Cash	51,000
	Inventory	10,000
	Prepaid Expenses	5,000
	Supplies	100
Total Current Assets		66,100
Fixed Assets		
	Equipment	45,000
Other Assets		
	Liquor License	1,400
Total Assets		112,500
Liabilities		
Current Liabilities		
	Current Maturity of Long-term Debt	9,526
Long-term Liabilities		
	Long-term Debt	75,474
Total Liabilities		85,000
Equity		27,500
Total Liabilities and Equity		112,500

Risk: Efforts by the city to encourage people to visit downtown may be both helpful and detrimental. If city-sponsored events bring more people to the area, this will help increase the visibility of The Noiz Bar and increase business. However, other city-sponsored events, such as outdoor concerts on the Riverfront, may actually draw customers away from The Noiz Bar.

Strategy: The owners will monitor the scheduled events and use marketing techniques to capitalize on as many events as possible.

Assumptions and Conclusion

This project is feasible if the following assumptions hold true:

There is a slow-growth economy without a major recession.

The owners are able to raise adequate debt and equity funding to maintain the financial plan as it is shown.

No major change in consumer tastes or legislation occurs that might have an effect on the project.

Disscision Questions

1. Assume you are a potential investor for The Noiz Bar. What information is not included in the business plan that you would like to know?
2. Critique the "Business Environment" Section. Do you think the information provided is adequate? Why or why not?
3. What is the competitive advantage of The Noiz Bar? Do you believe this is a good competitive advantage? Why or why not?
4. Review the start-up costs. What cost is not shown that could be a substantial cost?
5. Review the sales projection. Does the projected sales volume of $459,500 for the first year seem achievable? Why or why not?

(continued)

Adapted from *The Naiz Bar*. Written by Allison Miller. Reprinted with permissions.

Appendix Table: Profit and Loss

Pro Forma Profit and Loss		Jan	Feb	Mar	Apr	May	Jun	Jul	Aug	Sep	Oct	Nov	Dec
Sales		$38,296	$38,296	$38,296	$38,296	$38,296	$38,296	$38,296	$38,296	$38,296	$38,296	$38,296	$38,296
Direct Costs of Goods		$7,270	$7,270	$7,270	$7,270	$7,270	$7,270	$7,270	$7,270	$7,270	$7,270	$7,270	$7,270
Other Costs of Goods		$0	$0	$0	$0	$0	$0	$0	$0	$0	$0	$0	$0
Cost of Goods Sold		$7,270	$7,270	$7,270	$7,270	$7,270	$7,270	$7,270	$7,270	$7,270	$7,270	$7,270	$7,270
Gross Margin		$31,026	$31,026	$31,026	$31,026	$31,026	$31,026	$31,026	$31,026	$31,026	$31,026	$31,026	$31,026
Gross Margin %		81.02%	81.02%	81.02%	81.02%	81.02%	81.02%	81.02%	81.02%	81.02%	81.02%	81.02%	81.02%
Expenses:													
Payroll		$9,200	$9,200	$9,200	$9,200	$9,200	$9,200	$9,200	$9,200	$9,200	$9,200	$9,200	$9,200
Sales and Marketing and Other Expenses		$1,000	$1,000	$1,000	$1,000	$1,000	$1,000	$1,000	$1,000	$1,000	$1,000	$1,000	$1,000
Depreciation		$0	$0	$0	$0	$0	$0	$0	$0	$0	$0	$0	$0
Rent		$6,250	$6,250	$6,250	$6,250	$6,250	$6,250	$6,250	$6,250	$6,250	$6,250	$6,250	$6,250
Utilities		$1,000	$1,000	$1,000	$1,000	$1,000	$1,000	$1,000	$1,000	$1,000	$1,000	$1,000	$1,000
Insurance		$1,000	$1,000	$1,000	$1,000	$1,000	$1,000	$1,000	$1,000	$1,000	$1,000	$1,000	$1,000
Payroll Taxes	15%	$1,380	$1,380	$1,380	$1,380	$1,380	$1,380	$1,380	$1,380	$1,380	$1,380	$1,380	$1,380
Other		$0	$0	$0	$0	$0	$0	$0	$0	$0	$0	$0	$0
Total Operating Expenses		$19,830	$19,830	$19,830	$19,830	$19,830	$19,830	$19,830	$19,830	$19,830	$19,830	$19,830	$19,830
Profit Before Interest and Taxes		$11,196	$11,196	$11,196	$11,196	$11,196	$11,196	$11,196	$11,196	$11,196	$11,196	$11,196	$11,196
Interest Expense		$708	$708	$708	$708	$708	$708	$708	$708	$708	$708	$708	$708
Taxes Incurred		$3,146	$3,146	$3,146	$3,146	$3,146	$3,146	$3,146	$3,146	$3,146	$3,146	$3,146	$3,146
Net Profit		$7,341	$7,341	$7,341	$7,341	$7,341	$7,341	$7,341	$7,341	$7,341	$7,341	$7,341	$7,341
Net Profit/Sales		19.17%	19.17%	19.17%	19.17%	19.17%	19.17%	19.17%	19.17%	19.17%	19.17%	19.17%	19.17%

Projected Income Statements for the First Three Years

Sales	459,552	491,721	526,141
Cost of Goods Sold	87,240	93,347	99,881
Gross Margin	372,312	398,374	426,260
Expenses			
Payroll	110,400	118,128	126,397
Sales & Marketing	12,000	12,840	13,739
Rent	75,000	80,250	85,868
Utilities	12,000	12,840	13,739
Insurance	12,000	12,840	13,739
Payroll Taxes	16,560	17,719	18,960
Total Expenses	237,960	254,617	272,440
Net Profit	134,352	143,757	153,820
Interest	8,496	9,091	9,727
Taxes	37,752	40,395	43,222
Net Profit	88,104	94,271	100,870

Appendix
Summary of Business
Plan Checklists

USING THE CHECKLISTS

On the following pages, the business plan checklists are repeated to provide you with a step-by-step method for completing a business plan. Answer all of the questions that are applicable to your business, emphasizing any topics that are critical in your industry. When you have finished, you will have a business plan that is helpful in managing the business or in obtaining financing.

THE EXECUTIVE SUMMARY

The following topics should be summarized in two pages or less:

A brief description of the proposed business and the product and/or service it will provide

The most important trends in the industry

The type of advertising and promotion that will be implemented

Sales and profits from the past three years (if the company is an existing business)

Projected sales and profits for the next three years

The education and work experience of the owners and key personnel

Important legal considerations such as exclusive agreements, customer contract and patents

Any other information that is critical in understanding how your business operates

THE MISSION STATEMENT

State the purpose of your business.

Identify the products and services to be offered.

Describe your management philosophy.

ANALYZE THE BUSINESS ENVIRONMENT

Describe national trends that will affect your business.

Consider demographic changes, legislative actions, technological changes, economic trends, and so forth. (Possible sources of information include the *Census of the Population,* the *Census of Businesses,* and the *Business Conditions Digest.*)

Provide current industry information. Answer the following questions:

Is this industry dominated by large or small firms?

What is the failure rate of the industry?

Is this a new industry or one that is well established?

What is the typical profitability in this industry?

What are the positive and negative trends occurring in the industry?

Consult sources of information such as *The Encyclopedia of Associations, Annual Statement Studies,* Dun and Bradstreet's *Key Business Ratios, U.S. Industrial Outlook,* and *Standard and Poor's Industry Surveys.*

Include information about the community. Answer the following:

Is the population of the community increasing or decreasing?

What is the attitude of the community toward your business? Is it positive, negative, or neutral?

Will the community help provide financing for your business or help in getting it started?

Is the local economy strong or in a recession?

(Possible sources of information include the local chamber of commerce, the local economic development office, city hall, and other government agencies.)

DESCRIBE YOUR PRODUCT OR SERVICE

Include information concerning any applicable data, such as size, shape, ingredients or materials, colors, weight, speed, packaging, and texture.

Include information concerning services, such as personalized attention, guaranteed response time, custom ordering, trial offers, and money-back guarantee.

ANALYZE THE COMPETITION

Identify three of your main competitors by name.

State the distance between you and each of the competitors.

Describe their trading areas in comparison to yours.

Identify the strengths and weaknesses of your competitors by using the following checklist. Complete one checklist for each of the three competitors and then summarize the information in a paragraph. (Note: Not all information will be available on all competitors.)

How is your competitor's . . . ?

Product selection	Large	Average	Small
Market share	100%	50%	0%
Product quality	Good	Average	Poor
Quality of service	Good	Average	Poor
Amount of advertising and promotion	Heavy	Average	Very little
Pricing	Higher than most	Average	Lower than most
Workforce turnover	Very stable	Average	High
Workforce knowledge	Good	Average	Poor
Financial condition	Very profitable	Average profits	Incurs losses
Level of debt	Low	Average	High
Equipment	New (state of the art)	Average	Obsolete
Production capacity	Operating at full capacity		Has excess capacity

DESCRIBE YOUR PRICING STRATEGIES

State your pricing objective, the goal to be achieved through pricing. (Possible objectives may include a certain level of profit, a specific market share, or to reach a certain sales volume.)

If you are a retailer or wholesaler, state your average markup on cost and markup on selling price.

If you are a service firm, state your labor and materials costs per hour. Then give your per hour.

If you are a manufacturer, identify your total direct costs and total fixed costs. State how many units you plan to produce each of the first three years.

If you are a wholesaler, state whether you will use average cost, first-in/first-out, or last-in/first-out.

Describe the typical markup in this industry and how your prices compare.

Identify your pricing policies and general pricing guidelines. For example, will you run seasonal sales? Will you try to match competitors' prices? Will you use coupons? Will you give employees discounts on merchandise purchased?

Describe any special pricing strategies, such as the following:

Introductory prices: Low prices used to gain entry into the market.

Skimming: Setting a high initial price and then gradually lowering it.

Price-lining: Grouping inventory into categories and then setting the same price for all items in each category.

Odd-ending: Prices set at odd numbers such as $1.99, $3.95, etc.

Loss-leader: Selling one or a few items below cost in order to attract customers.

All-one-price: Setting every item equal to the same price.

Bundling: Grouping items together and selling them for less than if each item were purchased separately.

Determine the shipping costs for the goods you will order. What are the terms—F.O.B. Seller, F.O.B. buyer, or something else? Be sure to include the shipping costs when you establish your sales price. If you ship goods to your customers, state who pays the shipping costs.

DESCRIBE YOUR CREDIT POLICY

Describe your credit terms to customers.

Compare your credit terms to those of your competitors.

State whether you will accept checks, credit cards, or other forms of payment.

If you will use a check verification system or a credit reporting agency, give the agency's name and the costs for those services.

DESCRIBE YOUR COMPETITIVE ADVANTAGE

Describe your competitive advantage in as much detail as possible. This may include quality, price, location, selection, service, and/or fast turnaround.

Explain how you will achieve your competitive advantage. For example, how will you have better quality? What will make your service better? Why is your location better? Try to combine several advantages, if possible.

DESCRIBE THE MARKET SEGMENTATION METHOD YOU WILL USE

This may include the following:

Geographically: The geographic area you will serve

Demographically: The age, sex, race, and/or income of your target market

By benefit: The benefits customers are buying, such as status, security/safety, convenience, romance, sociability, entertainment, comfort, self-indulgence, and durability

By usage rate: The percentage of your customers that account for the largest portion of your sales

Psychographically: The values and lifestyle of your customers, such as outgoing, introverted, scholarly, party-loving, athletic, and family-oriented

DESCRIBE YOUR LOCATION

If Your Business Is Retail or Service

Give the business address.

State whether the property is correctly zoned or if rezoning is necessary.

Describe your trading area.

Provide the demographic data for your trading area giving age, sex, race, income, occupation, and so on.

Give the average traffic count in front of the outlet.

Describe anything hindering accessibility, such as medians, one-way streets, congested traffic, or a difficult entrance. Identify any factors helping accessibility, such as multiple entrances or a location near major highways.

Identify the businesses adjacent to your site. State whether these businesses serve the same customers as your business and whether these businesses have similar operating hours. Discuss any adjacent or nearby businesses that attract a large number of customers.

Provide information concerning the visibility of the site by stating whether it is visible from 400 feet, 200 feet, 100 feet, or less. Do any signs, trees, buildings, or other objects hinder visibility?

Research and describe the community's sign laws. Describe any restrictions that would affect the sales of the business.

Research and describe the parking ordinances. State the minimum number of parking spaces you need for the size of your store. Is there a parking lot or street parking? How many parking spaces are available?

If Your Business Is a Manufacturing Plant

State the business address.

State whether the property is correctly zoned or if it needs to be rezoned.

Describe the labor climate and the level of union activity. Identify average wage rates and describe the work ethic of the residents. If possible, determine absentee rates and turnover rates in neighboring businesses.

State whether your company needs to be near raw materials or customers.

Describe utility access and rates.

Identify tax rates and state how they compare to other sites you considered.

Describe the quality of the transportation facilities—air, water, rail, highway, and so on.

Describe any environmental regulations that will apply.

Describe the quality of life in the area.

If Your Business Is a Wholesale Firm

State the business address. Is this within city limits or an outlying area? Why did you choose this site?

State whether the property is correctly zoned or if rezoning is necessary.

Describe the quality of the transportation facilities that will be needed—air, water, highway, rail, and so on.

Provide information concerning the financial condition of the community. Are the retail stores financially strong? Do other wholesalers serve your industry? Will you locate your business in the city or in an outlying area?

DESCRIBE YOUR PROMOTIONAL PLAN

List the types of promotion you will use: sales and direct marketing, advertising, publicity and public relations, and sales promotion.

State your promotional goals. These may include a specific sales volume, a percentage increase in sales, or an increase in awareness. Or you may seek to inform customers of a sale or to eliminate seasonal merchandise.

Provide information on your inside and/or outside sales force. State whether you will hire only experienced salespeople or will hire inexperienced personnel and train them.

Describe the compensation packages for the sales force (salary only, salary plus commission, and so on).

Describe how customer accounts are divided among the sales force—geographically, by industry, by company size, and so on.

If you will use telemarketing, state whether you have your own telemarketing staff or if an outside telemarketing firm is used.

Describe any direct mail, catalogs, or direct-response ads that will be used.

Identify any trade-oriented or consumer-oriented sales promotions that will be implemented. State the objective of the promotions and the total annual cost.

Describe how you will evaluate the promotional plan.

How many people in the target market will see or hear the ad?

How many times will they see or hear it?

Where will the potential customers be when they see or hear the ad?

Will they be distracted?

How much advertising will be wasted on people who are not potential customers?

How much will the advertising cost?

State whether you will sponsor a youth sports team. If so, identify which one.

If you participate in local business organizations such as the chamber of commerce, identify those organizations.

___(Month)____Advertising Plan
(Medium)____
Size of ad____
Number of ads this month____
Message of the ads____
Cost for each ad____
Total number in target market reached____
Total ad costs for this medium____

(Medium)____
Size of ad____
Number of ads this month____
Message of the ads____
Cost for each ad____
Total number in target market reached____

Total ad costs for this medium____

(Medium)____
Size of ad____
Number of ads this month____
Message of the ads____
Cost for each ad____
Total number in target market reached____
Total ad costs for this medium____

Total advertising costs this month $____

If you donate time or funds to charitable organizations, identify them.

Identify company activities that can be used for publicity. Will you write an article for the local newspaper concerning the grand opening, expansion plans, new products that are developed, employee promotions, employee anniversaries (10 years with the company), and so on? Are any company activities interesting enough to be featured on local radio or television stations?

For each month, complete the above chart to help determine your total advertising budget.

IDENTIFY YOUR MANAGEMENT AND PERSONNEL

Include a paragraph describing the education and work experience of the owner(s) and all key personnel. Emphasize any management experience and any experience in the industry of the proposed business. Include complete resumes if they are available.

Explain in paragraph form the type of employee positions that will be filled and the pay and benefits that will be provided. Then complete the following chart to show all personnel needed:

Job Title	Number Needed	PT/FT (Part/Full Time)	Salary or Hourly Pay	Benefits

Identify paid holidays the company observes. Which employees are entitled to holiday pay?

State how vacation time is accrued and which employees will have paid vacations. (Full time and part time, or only full time?)

What is your policy concerning sick days? Are paid sick days available to full-time and part-time, or only full-time, employees?

What is your policy concerning funeral leave? How many days are granted? For which relatives?

How many employees do you have? Are hiring and firing policies legally governed by:

> Title VII of the Civil Rights Act?
>
> Age Discrimination in Employment Act?
>
> Americans with Disabilities Act?
>
> Family and Medical Leave Act?

Complete an organizational chart.

Complete a work schedule for a typical work week.

COMPLETE THE FINANCIAL SECTION

Start-up Costs and Financing

Complete the following checklist for furniture, fixtures, machinery, and equipment.

Furniture and Fixtures

Item	Quantity Needed	Price Each	Total Price
Sample:			
Desk	3	$150	$ 450
Shelving	7	$100	$ 700
___	___	___	___
___	___	___	___
___	___	___	___
___	___	___	___
___	Total for Furniture and Fixtures		$___

Machinery and Equipment

Item	Quantity Needed	Price Each	Total Price
Sample:			
PC and software	1	$1,200	$1,200
Telephone/fax combination	1	600	600
___	___	___	___
___	___	___	___
___	___	___	___
___	___	___	___
___	___	___	___
___	Total for Machinery and Equipment		$___

Start-up Costs

Inventory

Furniture and fixtures _____

Machinery and equipment _____

Prepaid expenses _____

    Insurance _____

    Grand opening advertising _____

    Legal fees _____

    Accounting fees _____

    Employee wages _____

    Other (specify) _____

Total prepaid expenses _____

Deposits

    Lease _____

    Utility _____

    Tax _____

    Other (specify) _____

Total deposits _____

Building and renovation

    If purchased

        Sales price _____

        Construction/renovation _____

    If leased

        Leasehold improvements _____

Total location costs _____

Working capital

	Cost per month
Owner's salary	____ $\times 3 =$ ____
Employees' salary	____ $\times 3 =$ ____
Employee taxes	____ $\times 3 =$ ____

    (approximately 11 percent of owner and employee wages)

Rent	____ $\times 3 =$ ____
Advertising	____ $\times 3 =$ ____
Utilities	____ $\times 3 =$ ____
Supplies	____ $\times 3 =$ ____
Telephone	____ $\times 3 =$ ____
Legal/accounting fees	____ $\times 3 =$ ____
Loan payment	____ $\times 3 =$ ____
Repairs/maintenance	____ $\times 3 =$ ____
Auto/travel expenses	____ $\times 3 =$ ____
Inventory	____ $\times 3 =$ ____

    (If customers do not pay cash for purchases, this amount will be needed to replace inventory until payment is received.)

Miscellaneous	____ $\times 3 =$ ____
Other (specify)	____ $\times 3 =$ ____

Total working capital _____

Total start-up costs _____

Financing

1. What are your total start-up costs? $____
2. How much will you invest from personal funds? $____
3. How much will you obtain in other equity? $____
   Family and friends
   $____ invested for ____percent ownership
   Dividends paid? Yes ____ No ____
   ____percent of profit
      paid quarterly____ annually ____
   Private investors
   $____ invested for ____percent ownership
   Dividends paid? Yes ____ No ____
   ____percent of profit
      paid quarterly ____ annually ____
   Venture capital
   $____ invested for ____percent ownership
   Dividends paid? Yes ____ No ____
   ____percent of profit
      paid quarterly ____ annually ____
   Silent partners
   $____ invested for ____percent ownership
   Dividends paid? Yes ____ No ____
   ____percent of profit
      paid quarterly ____ annually ____
   Other investors (specify) $_____
   $____ invested for ____percent ownership
   Dividends paid? Yes ____ No ____
   ____percent of profit
      paid quarterly ____ annually ____
4. How much will you borrow? $____
   Friends and family $_____
   Borrowed for ____ years at ____percent interest
   Monthly payments of $____
Bank loans $_____
   Borrowed for ____ years at ____percent interest
   Monthly payments of $____
Finance companies $_____
   Borrowed for ____ years at ____percent interest
   Monthly payments of $____
Other (specify) $_____
   Borrowed for ____ years at ____percent interest
   Monthly payments of $____
(Note: #1 = #2 + #3 + #4)

Opening-Day Balance Sheet

Assets

Current assets:

   Cash (working capital)   ____

   Supplies   ____

   Prepaid expenses   ____

   Inventory   ____

Total current assets   ____

Fixed assets: ____

   Furniture/fixtures   ____

   Machinery/equipment   ____

   Renovations   ____

Total fixed assets   ____

Total assets   ____

Liabilities

Current liabilities:

   Current portion of

     long-term debt   ____

Total current liabilities   ____

Long-term liabilities:

   Note payable   ____

   Less: Current portion   ____

Total long-term liabilities   ____

Total liabilities   ____

Equity   ____

Total liabilities and equity   ____

(Note: Categories may need to be added or deleted depending on the type of business.)

Income Statement

Complete the following income statement if your business is a corporation.

Sales	$ ____
Cost of goods sold	
Beginning inventory	____
+ Purchases	____
+ Freight	____
− Ending inventory	____
= Cost of goods sold	____
Gross margin	____
Expenses:	
Officer's salary	____
Employee wages	____
Accounting/legal	____
Advertising	____
Rent	____
Depreciation	____
Supplies	____
Utilities	____
Telephone	____
Interest	____
Repairs	____
Taxes	____
Insurance	____
Miscellaneous	____
Credit card fees	____
Dues/subscriptions	____
Total expenses	____
Net profit	____
Less: Income taxes	____
Net profit after taxes	____

For planning purposes, compute the following:

Net profit	____
Less: Income taxes	____
Less: Loan principal	____
Net cash	____

(Note: Categories may need to be added or deleted depending on the type of business.)

Projected Income Statement

Complete the following income statement if your business is a proprietorship or partnership.

Sales	$____
Cost of goods sold	
Beginning inventory	____
+ Purchases	____
+ Freight	____
− Ending inventory	____
= Cost of goods sold	____
Gross margin	____
Expenses:	
Employee wages	____
Accounting/legal	____
Advertising	____
Rent	____
Depreciation	____
Supplies	____
Utilities	____
Telephone	____
Interest	____
Repairs	____
Taxes	____
Insurance	____
Miscellaneous	____
Credit card fees	____
Dues/subscriptions	____
Total expenses	____
Net profit	____
Less: Income taxes	____
Less: Self-employment tax	____
Net profit after taxes	____

Note that the owner's wages have not been subtracted anywhere on the income statement. However, the money must come out of the business. Therefore, the following format is recommended for planning purposes.

Net profit	____
Less: Income taxes	____
Less: Self-employment tax	____
Less: Owner's wages	____
Less: Loan principal	____
Net cash	____

(Note: Categories may need to be added or deleted depending on the type of business.)

Cash Flow

Complete a monthly cash flow projection for the first year using the following as a guide.

	Jan.	Feb.	. . .	Nov.	Dec.
Beginning cash					
Cash in					
Cash available					
Cash out:					
Rent					
Telephone					
Advertising					
Insurance					
Equipment leases					
Office supplies					
Car phone lease					
Owner's salary					
Employee wages					
Employee taxes					
Accounting/legal					
Repairs/maintenance					
Auto expense					
Loan payment (P&I)					
Inventory purchases					
Income taxes					
Other (itemize)					
Total cash out					
Cash balance					

(Note: Categories may need to be added or deleted depending on the type of business.)

Break-even Point

Complete the following to determine your break-even point.
1. Categorize all of your operating expenses as "fixed" and "variable."
Sample:

EXPENSE	FIXED	VARIABLE
Rent	$3,000/yr	
Office supplies		$1,200/yr
_____	_____	_____
_____	_____	_____
_____	_____	_____
_____	_____	_____
_____		
Total	_____	_____

2. Determine your contribution margin.
   a. Projected sales for the first year
   b. Projected cost of goods sold for the first year
   c. Divide b by a (b/a)
        Sample: Sales = $200,000
        Cost of goods sold = $50,000
               50,000/200,000 = .25
   d. Total the variable expenses
        Sample: supplies   = $1,200
                  credit card fees = $5,000
                  total $6,200
   e. Divide d by a (d/a)
        Sample: 6,200/200,000 = .031
   f. Add c plus e (c + e)
        Sample: .25 + .031 = .281
   g. Subtract f from 1.0 (1.0 – f)
        Sample: 1.0 – .281 = .719

3. Determine your break-even point.
         a. Total fixed expenses
         b. Contribution margin
         c. Divide a by b (a/b)
              Sample: Fixed expenses for the first year = $70,000
                        Contribution margin = .719
                        Break-even point = $70,000/.719 = $97,357 in sales the first year
4. Determine the number of customers needed to reach the break-even point.
         a. Break-even point in dollars (3c) $ _____
         b. Average amount of a customer's purchase $ _____
         c. Divide a by b (a/b) to get the number of customers for the first year _____
         d. Divide answer in c by the number of days the company is open each year to get
         the number of customers per day _____
         Sample: Break-even point = $97,357
                  Average customer purchase = $10
                  Number of customers per year = $97,357/$10 = $9,736
                  If the business is open 360 days per year, the number of
                  customers needed per day is 9,736/360 = 27

DISCUSS LEGAL CONSIDERATIONS

State the organizational form you choose and the reason for your decision.

Identify which taxes the company will be required to pay.

Describe any patents, copyrights, trademarks, or trade secrets owned by the company.

Describe any contracts or exclusive agreements with suppliers, customers, employees, and others.

IDENTIFY INSURANCE REQUIREMENTS

Research the laws covering workers' compensation in your state to determine if the insurance will be required by law.

Identify the greatest insurable risks your business will face.

Identify other risks you would like to insure.

Determine how much you can afford to spend on insurance.

Check with an agent to determine actual costs and list the costs.

IDENTIFY SUPPLIERS

Identify your most important suppliers.

State their credit terms, delivery schedules, and minimum order quantities.

State whether inventory shortages are a problem in this industry.

Describe the availability of suppliers—are there many to choose from or only a few?

LIST YOUR UNCONTROLLABLE RISKS

Identify uncontrollable risks that affect your business. Consider the economy, the weather, new technology, price wars, changes in consumer tastes, new competitors, and other factors.

For each risk you have identified, explain what could be done to minimize the financial impact if the risk occurs.

STATE YOUR CONCLUSION

State whether the business is feasible or not feasible.

List the assumptions you made while completing the report.

State which assumptions must hold true in order for your conclusion to hold true.

If the business is an existing business, describe the future of the business and the assumptions that must hold true for that future to be realized.

Index